A NEW MAORI MIGRATION

LONDON SCHOOL OF ECONOMICS
MONOGRAPHS ON SOCIAL ANTHROPOLOGY
Managing Editor : Dr Paul Stirling

The Monographs on Social Anthropology were established in 1940 and aim to publish results of modern anthropological research of primary interest to specialists.

The continuation of the series has been made possible by a grant in aid from the Wenner-Gren Foundation for Anthropological Research, and by grants from the Governors of the London School of Economics and Political Science. Income from sales is returned to a revolving fund to assist further publications.

The Monographs are under the direction of an Editorial Board associated with the Department of Anthropology of the London School of Economics and Political Science.

This volume has been published with the aid of a grant from the Maori Purposes Fund Board in New Zealand, to whom the Editorial Committee are grateful.

Urban employment: working for the Council

LONDON SCHOOL OF ECONOMICS
MONOGRAPHS ON SOCIAL ANTHROPOLOGY
No. 27

A New Maori Migration

Rural and Urban Relations in

Northern New Zealand

by

JOAN METGE

UNIVERSITY OF LONDON
THE ATHLONE PRESS
1964

First published by
THE ATHLONE PRESS
UNIVERSITY OF LONDON
at 2 Gower Street, London WC1
Distributed by Constable & Co Ltd
12 Orange Street, London WC2

Printed in Great Britain by
ROBERT CUNNINGHAM AND SONS LTD
ALVA

Preface

THIS book is a revised version of a thesis presented for the degree of Doctor of Philosophy in the University of London in November 1957. It is based on field research carried out in New Zealand, in the city of Auckland, for two years in 1953 and 1954 with occasional short visits during 1955, and in a rural community (to which I have given the pseudonym of Kōtare) in Northland for a total of five months during the first seven of 1955.

Acknowledgment of financial assistance is gratefully made to the University of New Zealand for a Science Research Fellowship, which financed my two years' fieldwork in Auckland; and to the Carnegie Social Science Research Committee (University of New Zealand) for a grant which enabled me to spend another six months in the field (mainly in Kōtare) in 1955, and for a research fellowship, awarded for a two-year term beginning in June 1958, during which I revisited Kōtare to check material and hypotheses presented in the thesis and completed the revision of the thesis for publication (as well as carrying out new research). I am most grateful to the Maori Purposes Fund Board for a grant towards the cost of travel to London and another towards the cost of this book, including illustrations; to the Emslie Horniman Anthropological Fund for the award of a Horniman Anthropological Studentship for the academic year 1955-6 and for a grant towards the cost of maps and tables in this book; to the New Zealand Federation of University Women, who awarded me their 1956-7 Fellowship; and to the International Federation of University Women for a Winifred Cullis Grant (1957).

I owe a deep debt of gratitude to my teachers and colleagues over the years. Messrs V. F. Fisher and R. A. Scobie and Dr G. Archey of the Auckland War Memorial Museum first fostered my interest in Anthropology. To Professor R. Piddington of Auckland University I owe my early theoretical training and kindly and helpful supervision during my period in the field. I am deeply grateful to my tutor at the London School of Economics, Professor Raymond Firth, for his wise and stimulating guidance and his unfailing encouragement. I am also indebted to Professor Schapera and to my postgraduate colleagues at the School for their constructive criticism during seminars.

The number of those in New Zealand who assisted and encouraged me in my work is too great for individual acknowledgment, but I should like to record my appreciation of the co-operation received from the Department of Maori Affairs, consistently and over many years, in Auckland,

Wellington and Kaitaia; from the Department of Census and Statistics in Wellington; from the Waitemata Tribal Executive and the City Branch of the Maori Women's Welfare League; from the Maori Missioners of the Anglican, Methodist, Presbyterian and Roman Catholic Churches in Auckland, and from the Wardens of the United Maori Mission Hostels. I also thank Mr John Waititi for advice on the spelling of Maori words.

I owe more than I can say to my parents for the many ways in which they have given me their support in my work. I should also like to thank Miss D. Wyatt, who gave me a home in London, and Dr Alice Dewey, Miss Gladys Rice, Miss Myrtle Pulham, and Mr Stephen Rumsey for their assistance with the reproduction, assembling and checking of the thesis and its revised copy.

Lastly, in the place of honour, according to their own custom, I try to find words to pay my debt of gratitude to the Maoris with whom I worked in Auckland and in Kōtare. Knowing that they would prefer to preserve their anonymity, I shall refrain from mentioning them by name. Instead, I thank them collectively for their patience and forbearance, for their warm hospitality, and above all for the priceless gift of their friendship. I hope that the affection and respect which they inspired in me will shine through the cold print of the following pages.

A. J. M.

Auckland
1960

Contents

Plates

Figures

I

Maori Urbanisation:
The Problem and its Background

OF all the changes taking place among the New Zealand Maori to-day, urbanisation is the most obvious and the most discussed. It began dramatically in the early years of the Second World War. Maoris[1] from all over the country were directed by the Department of Labour and Employment to work in essential industries in the city. Many more migrated of their own accord, to help with the war effort and to take advantage of a favourable labour market and wages that were high by rural standards. The Maori urban population[2] increased from 10,342 in 1936 (13 per cent of the total Maori population) to 20,071 in 1945 (20 per cent). It is estimated that the number of urban Maoris was even higher at peak periods during the war. After 1945, the rate of urban increase remained high, though it fell below that of the war years. By 1951, there were 27,346 Maoris living in towns and cities (23 per cent of the total Maori population). This percentage was low compared with the non-Maori figure (66 per cent), but it represented an important change from the pre-war situation. Most of the Maori urban movement was and is directed mainly to the chief regional and industrial centres of the North Island, and especially to the city of Auckland.

From the beginning, the Maori urban trend attracted a great deal of attention, partly because it attained significant proportions so quickly, and partly because the Maori are a highly distinctive element in New Zealand society. With their brown skins and Polynesian features, they have a high visibility in a population that is predominantly of European stock. In the towns and cities, this visibility was accentuated (particularly in the early years of Maori urban migration) by patterns of dress and public behaviour which singled them out not only as country folk but also as Maoris, cultur-

[1] 'Maoris' as a plural form is common usage in New Zealand, particularly when referring to a relatively small number of individuals or a specific section of the Maori population, e.g. in the title *Some Modern Maoris*. I have, however, also used 'the Maori' in the plural when referring to the Maori people as a whole (cf. *The Coming of the Maori*).

[2] The population of Cities and Boroughs, the entirely urban counties of Eden and Heathcote, Town Districts, and certain parts of counties included in Urban Areas as defined by the Census and Statistics Department; *New Zealand, Population Census 1951*, vol. i, pp. 14, 29–33. See also Table 1.

ally as well as ethnically 'different' from the Pakeha (New Zealanders of European stock).[1]

For some years after the war, the influx of Maoris to the cities was almost universally deplored. It was popularly referred to as a 'problem'. Common use of the phrase 'drift to the cities' implied something undesirable and badly organised. Maori elders in the country scolded emigrants for their defection from the rural way of life which, they preached, was natural and right for Maoris and the cultivation of Maori virtues. Urban and national leaders, Maoris as well as Pakehas, expressed open concern about bad living conditions, 'footlooseness', absenteeism in employment, thriftlessness, marital instability, crime and delinquency among Maoris living in the city. Means of stemming the tide were debated in the Press and at conferences of many kinds. By the turn of the decade it was generally accepted as impossible. Most of the immigrants came from areas where employment and housing were already inadequate, while increases in the general level of Maori education were reflected in increased economic aspirations. The focus of interest switched to the problems of adjustment.

Discussion about Maori urbanisation tended to be couched in the most general or the most particular terms. Most of the protagonists argued from *a priori* convictions about urbanisation and the Maori way of life, or from specialised knowledge of one particular section of the Maori population: members of a religious denomination, workers in an occupational group, those with housing problems, bad health, or delinquent records. Little of this detailed knowledge was published and it had not been correlated. The experts did not always agree. Between about 1948 and 1953, when the first volume of the 1951 Census was published, specialist estimates of the number of Maoris in Auckland ranged from 8,000 to 15,000. As always, the noisiest and most unsatisfactory members of the Maori group attracted the most attention, and few stopped to ask whether they were in fact typical. There was need for detailed information about a representative cross-section of Maoris living under urban conditions.

As a problem in the scientific as well as the popular sense, Maori urbanisation greatly interested me. Awarded a research fellowship for 1953–4, I decided to work among Maoris living in Auckland.[2] I set out to discover who was involved in immigration into Auckland and why, what problems they had encountered, how they handled them, whether a Maori community of any sort was being formed in Auckland, and what sort of relations existed between Maoris in Auckland and the rest of Maori society. This project involved many technical problems, in particular how to choose representative informants from a large and

---

[1] I have decided to use the Maori word *Pakeha* to describe New Zealanders of European stock as it is the most satisfactory term available and the most commonly used by New Zealanders, especially in the context of Maori–Pakeha relations. 'European' is too ambiguous.   [2] See Preface, p. v.

scattered group about which so little was precisely known. My greatest difficulty, however, was the conceptual one.

Three local studies of Maori life already existed: *The Changing Maori*, Keesing, 1928 (the East Coast area); *The Maori: A Study in Acculturation*, Hawthorn, 1944 (an isolated community in the Far North in the 1930's); and *Some Modern Maoris*, Beaglehole and Beaglehole, 1946 (a west-coast community forty-six miles from Wellington, in 1940). These studies were all of rural areas. Even the most recent dealt with a community in which the urban movement had hardly begun. I was aware from my own previous research that there were significant regional variations in the socio-economic background of rural Maoris (Metge, 1951, 1952). But in general I accepted the popular conceptualisation both of Maori rural society and of the process of urbanisation. As my work in Auckland progressed, I found this more and more inadequate. Finally, I decided to make a complementary study of a rural community in the Far North, one of the major areas of Maori settlement, and one which had been seriously affected by urban immigration. This book examines both situations.

When I began fieldwork in Auckland, Maori and Pakeha alike saw the problems attendant on Maori urbanisation as the result of transplanting a traditionally rural and communally oriented people to the competitive and individualistic life of a western industrial city. The life of urban Maoris was contrasted to its disadvantage with an idealised stereotype of Maori rural life. According to this stereotype, country Maoris lived in small settlements where community life was highly developed and Pakeha influence at a minimum. Kinship was the most important principle of social organisation in such communities, though the precise nature of the kinship structure was not specified. The people relied on employment in primary production for their livelihood, and their level of technological achievement was low in comparison with that of the Pakeha. They disregarded the rational control of economic resources and cash income in favour of the observance of community and kinship obligations. Community life was centred on the *marae* (originally the village plaza),[1] where all members of the community gathered frequently. Co-operation was the keynote of personal and public activity, and leadership and social control were provided by elders, who commanded respect and obedience by right of age and descent.

Given this stereotype, it was easy to infer that country Maoris were not adequately equipped to deal with urban life. Most people, moreover, assumed that the city was synonymous with a Pakeha way of life. Instability in employment, residence and marriage among urban Maoris was interpreted as a symptom of maladjustment not only to urban conditions but also to the dominant Pakeha culture. It was expected to disappear in individual cases as immigrants became 'urbanised', and eventually for the group also. Thus both Pakeha and Maori regarded the cultural assimi-

[1] Buck, 1949, pp. 374-5.

lation of Maoris in the city as necessary and inevitable, advocating or deploring every course which would hasten it, according to their point of view. They also postulated a fundamental cleavage between the new urban Maori group and the traditional rural society.

The view that urbanisation produced a breakdown in traditional values and virtues in the migrant group and a break with their rural origins is supported in the writings of many anthropologists and sociologists. Because anthropologists first studied its effects upon primitive community and emigrant group, they saw urbanisation as a deviation from the traditional way of life, and described it in terms of disorganisation and detribalisation.[1] Sociologists, occupied with analysing the urban situation, came to similar conclusions.[2] They saw urbanism as a "way of life", characterised by social and economic heterogeneity, segmentalised, superficial human relations, highly developed specialisation, a high degree of social and economic mobility, and the acceptance of instability and insecurity in the world at large as normal. Various caveats have been entered against the false equation of urbanism and industrialism,[3] but the hypothesis that the urban "way of life" differs significantly from that of nonurban societies has not been seriously challenged. In this view, the rural-urban dichotomy is one so basic that it cross-cuts cultural differences and modifies cultural homogeneity within the one society.

My original conceptual framework entailed thinking about Maori urban society as a separate entity, a social and cultural world not only different but severed from Maori rural society. To my surprise, I found that length of residence in the city was by no means consistently correlated with the weakening of bonds of kinship and decline in attachment to "Maori ways".[4] Personal temperament, the specific rural community from which he derived, previous experience of migration, the strength of links with the home community: all had a bearing upon the immigrant's adjustment to life in the city. I was reminded that Maori urbanisation takes place within a more general situation of acculturation, and that, while the rural Maoris retain many value orientations and patterns of behaviour which are peculiarly their own, they are at the same time an integral part of New Zealand society. I further discovered that urban Maoris maintained close contact with rural kin and their communities of origin after as much as twenty-five to thirty years in the city, and into the second generation. In short, I became aware that there were many variable factors in the situation for which I had made no allowance. I began to re-examine my premises.

I queried, first of all, the assumption that the process of urbanisation was entirely responsible for restlessness in employment, marital instability and similar "problems" in the city. Were they lacking or unimportant in rural society? This led me to question the popular stereotype

[1] Redfield, 1946–7; Schapera, 1947; Wilson, 1941.   [2] e.g. Wirth, 1928.
[3] e.g. Beals, 1951; Miner, 1952.   [4] See p. 94.

of Maori rural communities, and to ask whether they were in fact as well-integrated, homogeneous and conservative as was generally believed.

Secondly, were the urban immigrants a representative cross-section of Maori rural society, or were their responses to urban conditions affected by the fact that they were drawn from certain restricted sections of the rural population?

Thirdly, was adjustment to urban conditions necessarily identical with assimilation to a completely Pakeha way of life: were immigrants of long standing and those born or bred in the city alienated further from Maori rural society than those recently settled in the city?

Fourthly, was there in fact any social hiatus or fundamental opposition between Maori urban society and Maori rural society?

In the following chapters I have attempted to answer these questions for Auckland and the Far North on the basis of my own research, carried out with small groups in those areas in 1953–4 and the first half of 1955. Inevitably I have not been able to cover all aspects of so wide a subject, even within these territorial limits. Certain lines of inquiry (notably those relating to incomes and spending patterns, *tapu* practices, and delinquency) proved particularly difficult to pursue with informants who were literate, and sensitive to publicity. My fieldwork material also reflected limitations in my own research experience. As a result, I have been forced to omit any discussion of socio-economic differentiation or of crime and delinquency, and to deal with many topics in less detail than they deserve. However, I feel that it was necessary to attempt a general survey of this kind, in order to identify the problems that require intensive study and to provide a general frame of reference.

This book was originally written as a doctoral thesis and presented in the University of London in November 1957. I have since revised it for publication. As a result of a further five months' fieldwork in Kōtare (the Maori community described in Chapters 2 to 5) in 1958, I have made some corrections and modifications in the original text of the Kōtare section, taking care, however, to add nothing that was not true for 1955. Revision of the rest of the book was concerned mainly with making it as clear and concise as possible and has not substantially altered either content or conclusions.

I could not have written this book without the co-operation of many informants. Since they, and those among whom they live, will be able to buy and read it, I have left out many personal illustrations which I could have quoted in support of my generalisations. In those which I have retained I have endeavoured to protect the anonymity of the original actors or informants by changing all names and eliminating irrelevant detail. I have also used pseudonyms for Kōtare and for the adjacent township (Raumati). (For a note on the pronunciation of Maori words, see Glossary, p. 287.)

Because the Maori are changing so rapidly, I have used the past tense in reporting my research. Finally, I have used double inverted commas for verbatim quotations from informants and for words and phrases in common use by the Maori group concerned, reserving single inverted commas for terms used in a technical sense, after they have been defined in the text.

THE FIELD

Auckland, situated on the Tamaki isthmus between the rich farming areas of Northland and the Waikato, is the largest commercial and industrial centre in New Zealand. The Far North, an area covering roughly the four northernmost counties of New Zealand (Mangonui, Whangaroa, Hokianga and Bay of Islands), is distinguished from the rest of Northland by its large Maori population and exceptionally high rate of Maori emigration. (Maoris living in the Far North in 1951 accounted for 48 per cent of the total and 52 per cent of the rural population in the area; of the four counties, the Bay of Islands was the only one whose Maori population showed any increase between 1945 and 1951.) Maori communities in the Far North vary widely in accessibility and size. Kōtare is eleven miles from the nearest country town. In 1955, it was one of the largest in the area. However, its division into several sub-districts was a typical feature of Maori communities in the Far North, and not merely a function of its size. It was unequivocally recognised as a single community by its residents and its neighbours.

During a total of five months spent in Kōtare, I lived in six houses in different parts of the district and visited all but six of the others. Housewives predominated among my informants. It was difficult to obtain interviews with the workers, since most worked for wages or on contract and many spent their free time working on the land. However, several full-time farmers were most co-operative, and I was able to meet all the workers at family and community gatherings.

In Auckland, I was faced first of all with the problem of how to select informants from a large, unevenly scattered urban population. A random sample, while statistically rewarding, would have been difficult to isolate because of lack of precise information about distribution. I decided to take several sets of domestic units defined on a territorial basis, using as informants as many members of each as practicable, and to complement this study by observation at public gatherings and at the Maori Community Centre in the central city.

Originally, I planned to work with (1) a central city group consisting of all the Maoris living in several arbitrarily delimited residential blocks; (2) the only all-Maori settlement in the urban area; and (3) one or possibly two neighbourhood groups in the outer suburbs. This part of the project was never wholly achieved. Introductions were not easy to arrange. Tribal Committee members and Maori Welfare Officers (Department of Maori Affairs) knew only a fraction of the Maoris in Auckland personally, and

FIG. 1. Geographic Regions and Major Towns, North Island, New Zealand

their recommendation was in any event not always acceptable. In the case of the central city, this problem was largely overcome when I obtained official permission to help Maori Welfare Officers with a survey of Maori housing in the city late in 1952. However, I still had to win acceptance as a research worker from those met in this way. There were other difficulties, too: there was a considerable "floating population" in the area, which was continually changing in composition; some families seemed to come home only to sleep; and many Maoris were moved out of the area in the course of slum clearance. I got to know only about 75 per cent of the Maoris in my chosen area really well. In the all-Maori settlement, I secured the co-operation of only six families and abandoned the study after nine months. I established working relations with a number of households in the outer suburbs, in many cases meeting them in the central city before they moved into State houses. But they were scattered widely and in no instance comprised all the Maoris in their particular neighbourhood.

Ultimately, I had three 'sets' of domestic units which I visited regularly over periods ranging in individual cases from one to two and a half years (see Table 2). Set A consisted of fifty-four domestic units, occupying twenty-four houses in three streets in the central city and comprising 80 per cent of the houses with Maori occupants in those streets; Set B of nineteen units, occupying ten houses within a radius of half a mile of the area of Set A; Set C of eleven households widely scattered in the suburbs of Tāmaki, Te Papapa, Mt. Albert, New Lynn and Avondale (see Fig. 7, p. 112). These 'sets', which had a total of 369 members, have provided the raw material for the analysis of derivation, occupations, tribal membership, housing conditions, marriage and migration patterns in Tables 18 to 26.

Housing conditions made it impossible for me to live with any of the families in the 'sets'. I had to rely mainly upon more or less formal interviews. I had at least one informant in each household in the 'sets'. Again, the majority were housewives and I met the workers more rarely in the evenings and at public gatherings. I found the middle-aged the most co-operative, because they were interested in trying to view the situation objectively. It was difficult to hold the attention of the young people, who had many interests and disliked sitting still for any length of time.

I visited the Maori Community Centre as planned, more particularly during the second year, when I spent four to five hours every weekend there and one or two evenings during the week. I also attended church services, dances, club meetings, weddings and other public gatherings. On these occasions and at the Centre I met and talked with many other urban Maoris. These casual contacts provided me with valuable checks and supplementary material.

In spite of the unavoidably haphazard methods of selection of informants in the city, the families with whom I had intensive contact proved reasonably representative in those things which could be checked against published statistics—age, sex and marital status (see Tables 2 and 25).

THE STRUCTURE OF TRADITIONAL MAORI SOCIETY[1]

At the end of the eighteenth century, Maori society was divided into a large number of politically autonomous tribes (iwi), each of which possessed an extensive territory by right of conquest and continued occupation.

The members of each tribe shared descent from a founding ancestor associated with one of the great voyaging canoes (waka) from Eastern Polynesia which, according to tribal traditions, arrived during the fourteenth century. Certain tribes acted frequently, but not invariably, in alliance, linked by the fact that their ancestors were reputed to have travelled in the same waka.

With few exceptions, the members of each tribe lived on the tribal territory. They did not, however, comprise the whole population, which included spouses, taken from other tribes, slaves, and sometimes members of a defeated tribe living in a state of vassalage. Each tribe was divided into a number of hapū or sub-tribes, which were also descent-groups and stemmed from progenitors linked to each other by descent from the tribal ancestor. Each hapū occupied an allotted part of the tribal territory where it had one or more pā (hill fort) or kāinga (unfortified village), beside various temporary encampments near fishing and hunting grounds. Though closely linked, hapū and village community did not coincide completely. In each generation some members of the hapū left the village to join spouses or other kinsfolk in another, while others brought in spouses from outside. Most communities also included slaves. The hapū was in turn made up by a number of whānau, bilateral descent-groups under the authority of patriarchs descended from the progenitor of the hapū. Whānau members cooked, ate and slept together, and possessed rights of usufruct over defined stretches of the hapū territory.

The production of food was the most important activity of the village community and required the application of the entire labour force for the greater part of the year. The tribes of the Northland peninsula, the Waikato river basin and the northern littorals of the North Island were devoted to settled agriculture, their staple crop being the sweet potato. Other tribes had cultivations where possible but relied mainly upon the resources of forest, river, swamp, lake and coastal shallows, the emphasis varying between hunting, fishing and gathering according to the physical environment.

Affiliation to descent-groups of every order—iwi, hapū and whānau—was ambilateral, that is, it could be traced through either parent.[2] When both parents belonged to the same group emphasis was placed on derivation from the parent of higher rank. When they belonged to different groups,

[1] Best, 1924, vol. i; Buck, 1949, pp, 331–432; Firth, 1959, pp. 90–141.
[2] Firth, 1957, p. 5.

residence was the determining factor. Patrilateral affiliation was preferred, and since marriage was usually (but not invariably) virilocal most persons became active members of their father's *whānau* and *hapū*. Choice of residence and active descent-group membership was not, however, irrevocable. Rights of membership in other groups were never wholly abandoned in a person's lifetime. They were passed on to his heirs, who could revive them by going to live with the group concerned. It was common practice for a woman to send home a child or grandchild to 'keep warm' her land inheritance and her group membership.

Within the tribe, primogeniture was the ruling principle of social precedence, with the male line of succession taking precedence over the female. Those descended from the senior heirs of the tribal and sub-tribal ancestors, especially through a line of senior males, were recognised as of high rank—*rangatira* or aristocrats. Leadership devolved upon the senior male in each descent-group.[1] The chief of the tribe, the *ariki*, could ideally trace his descent through the eldest son of the eldest son right back to the gods of heaven and earth. His authority was paramount in the tribe as a whole, as well as in the *whānau* and *hapū* of which he was head. The senior male of the senior *whānau* in each *hapū*, the *rangatira*, supervised the government of the village. The *whānau* patriarchs or *kaumatua* looked after family and domestic matters. They also supported and advised the *rangatira*, speaking and acting on behalf of their *whānau*. Matters of community importance were discussed publicly in assemblies at which all free members of the *hapū* had the right to speak, although precedence and attention were accorded on the basis of age and rank. Ceremonial usages and *tapu* regulations guaranteed respect for the persons of *ariki* and *rangatira*, but to be truly powerful and effective they had to win support by force of personality and lavish hospitality. The wealth necessary to maintain their position was provided by large polygamous households including many slaves, and by gifts from their followers.

The social control exercised by the chief and elders was strongly reinforced by magico-religious sanctions and public opinion. The most important of the former was *tapu*. Anything which was possessed or infected by the power of supernatural beings was *tapu* (sacred, prohibited or defiled according to context), and therefore to be avoided, for this mysterious and dangerous quality was imparted to everything with which it came in contact. Infringement of *tapu* brought immediate and automatic punishment, usually in the form of sickness. The communal nature of Maori life made public opinion an important check on individual behaviour. Security, both physical and emotional, was to be gained only by following patterns of behaviour valued and approved by the community as a whole. Nevertheless, the ambilateral character of the descent-group structure made it possible for offenders to seek a new life in another community as an alternative to loss of status in their own. Finally, the

_____
[1] Winiata, 1956, p. 212.

smaller descent-groups themselves took punitive action in the case of certain socially disruptive crimes, such as homicide, adultery and theft. The injured group carried out a raid for compensation upon the delinquent and upon his descent-group, the whole *whānau* or *hapū* being involved according to the magnitude of the offence and the status of the offender.

Thus in classical Maori society, control over natural resources, the production and distribution of goods, patterns of social intercourse, leadership, and social control were all linked inextricably with a particular type of social structure, that of ambilateral, segmentary, and locally-based descent-groups.

POST-EUROPEAN CHANGES

The history of Maori social and economic development since Captain Cook discovered New Zealand has been divided into four phases: the phase of initial impact, the enthusiastic adoption of European culture forms, the mood of reaction, and the acceptance of European standards.[1] A fifth period might also be identified, beginning with the Second World War; it has been distinguished by urbanisation and rapidly rising standards of living and occupational status.

The period of initial contact—first with whalers and sealers, later with missionaries and traders—effected comparatively little change in the social and economic structure of Maori society, for contact was largely localised and superficial.[2] But the seeds of change were sown. The production of foodstuffs, kauri spars and flax, to be bartered for certain specific types of goods which the Maori coveted, required some adjustment in the distribution of labour, while mission stations introduced literacy and various agricultural and industrial skills.

The second phase was initiated in 1840 by the Treaty of Waitangi, by which the Maori chiefs ceded sovereignty of the country to the British Crown in return for the protection of Maori rights as full citizens. Organised European colonisation spread rapidly while the Maoris enthusiastically adopted much of European culture. They produced large surpluses of agricultural produce for sale in the young towns and invested heavily in mills, agricultural implements and sailing vessels. Land and fixed capital of this nature was owned by the group, and most productive effort, the distribution of the proceeds, and occasions of social importance were still organised on a communal basis, directed by the chief of tribe or *hapū*. But tendencies towards individual employment and control over expenditure became apparent. Conversion to Christianity was almost universal, leading to a modification of *tapu* observances and the abandonment of polygamy and slavery, which had been the main sources of the chiefs' wealth. As a result the authority of the chief was weakened and distinctions of rank began to be broken down.

[1] Firth, 1959, pp. 433–91. For general historical background, see Sinclair, 1959.
[2] Wright, 1959.

This period of expansion and enthusiasm came to an abrupt and tragic end when war broke out between the Pakeha settlers and certain Maori tribes of the western and central parts of the North Island, chiefly as a result of Maori resentment over the continuing alienation of their land. The Maori Wars involved most of the major tribes of the North Island on one side or the other, except those of Northland. After the war the general mood among the Maori was one of profound despondency and apathy, even among those who had been "friendly" to the Government. Vast areas of land had been confiscated, even—by an incredible blunder—from non-combatant and "friendly" tribes. Cultivations and capital goods had suffered badly; and the people themselves, drastically depleted by war and disease, continued to decrease. Economic and moral resources were at a low ebb. There was a marked reaction against the Pakeha and their ways, some tribes (notably those of the King Country)[1] withdrawing entirely from all intercourse with them. A number of nativistic and religious sects emerged during the wars and the following period.

But at the end of the nineteenth century the decline in numbers was arrested. After falling as low as 42,113 in 1896, the Maori population began to increase, slowly at first but after 1920 at an exceptional rate. In 1928 the Maori rate of natural increase (the excess of births over deaths per 1000 of mean population) rose above that of the non-Maori population, in spite of a much higher death-rate. By 1953 the death-rate had been reduced to a little above the non-Maori rate, and the rate of natural increase for that year was 33·70 per 1000 (compared with 16·39 for the non-Maori population).

Hand in hand with the increases in population went a renewed vitality and hope in the future. Active and thoughtful leadership began to emerge again. The Young Maori Party, of whom Sir Peter Buck and Sir Apirana Ngata are the best known members, played a major part in improving standards of health and hygiene and raising Maori aspirations. Maoris in increasing numbers took paid employment, most of it of a temporary and seasonal nature at first, connected with pioneer activities directed by Pakehas: bush-work, road-making, breaking in farm land, and digging for kauri-gum.[2] Some attempted commercial farming, but they had great difficulty obtaining financial assistance because of lack of clear title to the land.

The Maori Land Court, set up by the Government in 1865 and for many years viewed with the deepest suspicion by the Maoris, was able to push on more quickly with its task of determining titles to Maori land and authorising their transmission, not only from Maori to Pakeha but from one Maori generation to the next. (The term 'Maori land' was and is

[1] The King Country is that part of South Auckland for which Te Kuiti is the regional centre; it was the cradle of the King Movement and is associated with Ngāti Maniapoto (see Figs. 1 (p. 7) and 9 (p. 125)). See Gorst, 1864.

[2] The solidified resin of the *kauri*, *agathis australis*. See Firth, 1924.

used in law in a specialised sense, referring primarily to land which has never been alienated from Maori ownership.)[1] The transmission of Maori land was governed by special legislation (Native Land Acts 1862, 1865, 1909 and 1931) which provided for individualisation at the request of the owners and established the principle of bilateral succession, i.e. the division of the inheritance between male and female heirs on an equal basis. First the Court established the identity of the rightful owners to each block after hearing evidence from all claimants, and thereafter, as each owner died, the Court divided his share equally among his children, on their application for a *succession* order. (If any of the latter had pre-deceased him, their shares were divided among their children.) At any point, co-owners could apply to the Court for *partition*, that is, the division of the land area itself, on the basis of a land survey, into two or more new blocks, which might have one or several owners. As the generations passed, the number of owners in each block increased while the value of the shares decreased proportionately; individuals inherited shares or "interests" in many different blocks, and might even have several different shares in the same block, acquired from different forebears; and the blocks themselves were often reduced to uneconomic proportions. Fragmentation and multiple ownership became serious obstacles to the development of Maori farming.[2]

In an attempt to overcome this problem, the Department of Maori Affairs introduced the system of *incorporation*, which was pioneered on the East Coast as early as 1908. Under incorporation, the shareholders of a block of Maori land form themselves into an incorporated body for the purpose of utilising the land as a farming unit. It is usually placed in the hands of a manager, supervised by a management committee elected from among the shareholders. Wages are paid to the workers employed (preference being given to shareholders) and dividends in proportion to the value of shares. In 1953, there were some 300 incorporations, most located on the East Coast and in the Rotorua area where they were concerned with sheep and cattle farming. They were less suited to intensive dairy farming.

A second solution, *consolidation* (of titles), was developed on the East Coast but first applied on a large scale in the Far North in 1928. Consolidation collected the scattered interests of each individual into one block by a complicated system of exchange and conversion. It was a lengthy and complex task, and the consolidated shares were still subject to re-division on the death of the holder.[3]

The most important step forward in the establishment of Maori farming was taken in 1929, when the Native Land Development Act provided for the application of State funds to the development of Maori land.[4] In addition to granting loans to Maoris already struggling to farm their land,

---

[1] See below, p. 16.   [2] Sutherland, 1940, pp. 130–6, 139, 200.
[3] *Ibid*, pp. 140–2, 201–5.
[4] Ngata, 'Native Land Development' in Sutherland, *op. cit.*, pp. 140–54.

the Department of Maori Affairs undertook to bring in large areas of unutilised or partly utilised Maori land. Adjacent holdings were grouped together in 'land development schemes', cleared, sown in pasture, ditched and fenced by gangs of Maori labourers (where possible, shareholders in the land) and then run as 'stations' under a manager until ready for intensive farming. Most were then subdivided into one-man dairy farms, and a few into sheep farms; the poorer blocks continued as sheep and cattle stations. The Department built houses and other farm buildings where necessary and stocked the farms from its own 'base farms'. In the case of dairy farms, the Department short-circuited the problem of title by the *nomination of occupiers*, preferably from among the co-owners. In the early days, when it was important to settle families on the land as quickly as possible, the officers of the Department chose occupiers without waiting to consult all the owners or to conclude formal agreements, but later it became standard practice for owners to be called together to decide questions of occupancy, and for the occupier to lease the shares of the other owners. Under the terms of the lease, the occupier assumed responsibility for all debts and expenses on the land, while the others waived their claims to income from the land and improvements upon it in return for freedom from liability and proportionate shares of the lease-money. Each occupier remained under the supervision of the Department of Maori Affairs as an "assisted unit" until he had paid off the mortgage incurred in development and the Department was satisfied he could manage it competently.

By 1936, the number of Maori farm families had increased by nearly 2,000, waste land was turned into producing farms, and the dispersal of Maori rural settlement became general in farming areas. At the same time, Maori land development softened the effects of the economic depression of the thirties, which hit the Maoris very hard. Many were forced to revert to subsistence agriculture eked out with "relief work" (State unemployment relief), while the women tramped the countryside selling wild and garden crops.

The Second World War absorbed most of the young men into the Armed Forces. Many went overseas, all as volunteers.[1] At home, large numbers migrated to work in essential industries, especially in the cities. As the result of an acute demand for labour, Maoris were able to enter many types of employment (both rural and urban) of which they had little or no previous experience. After the war, urbanisation continued, at a slightly more sober rate, and inter-regional migration increased with improvements in transport and communications. The general level of Maori education rose steadily; between 1948 and 1953 the percentage of

---

[1] Under the National Service Emergency Regulations 1940 (amendment no. 13) Maoris were not required to serve overseas unless they volunteered. Under this system the Maori Battalion was maintained at strength, while many Maori volunteers served in other units.

Maori school-children who went on from primary to secondary school rose from 63·6 per cent to 76 per cent.[1] The proportion of skilled, clerical and professional workers also increased, partly as a result of rehabilitation training for returned servicemen.

In the post-war period, two laws which distinguished between Maori and non-Maori were eliminated, and two important Acts were passed relating to Maori welfare and land. The Licensing Amendment Act 1948 lifted the restrictions on the sale of liquor to Maori women on licensed premises and permitted Maori men to buy liquor for consumption off the premises. The Marriage Act 1951 repealed earlier provision for the recognition of customary marriages and required Maoris to conform to the same regulations as Europeans with regard to registration.[2] The Maori Social and Economic Advancement Act 1945 provided for the extension of Maori welfare services and the establishment of Maori Tribal Committees. The Maori Affairs Act 1953 gave the Department of Maori Affairs wider powers with regard to the conversion of Maori land titles. This last Act enables the Department to simplify the list of owners in any given block by amalgamating all the interests of each part-owner; it also authorises the Maori Trustee to buy uneconomic interests (under £25 in value) for sale or lease to other Maoris. The Department's present policy is to encourage occupiers to buy out the other owners, assisting them with a loan if necessary. However, even when a farmer has secured sole title to his holding, the land remains Maori land and must be divided among his heirs at his death. In order to prevent a return to multiple ownership, the Department advises farmers to make a will leaving the farm to a single heir, on condition that he pays his siblings for their shares. Maori land held by one owner *may* be declared European land by the Maori Appellate Court, but neither the owners nor the Department favour this course, as it facilitates alienation from Maori ownership.

In 1953, the Maori as a group were fully incorporated into the New Zealand economic system, but they still differed from the Pakeha pattern in many particulars. In the first place, according to the 1951 Census, 77 per cent were still rural dwellers, and 35 per cent of Maori workers were engaged in primary production, compared with 19 per cent of the non-Maori group. Of those engaged in manufacturing (36 per cent), nearly half were employed in construction. Maoris were not as well represented as non-Maoris in service occupations (15 per cent compared with 20 per cent), especially in the professions, and the proportion engaged in commerce was exceptionally low (3 per cent compared with 17 per cent).[3] Maori standards of living and housing were generally below

---

[1] Information supplied by Department of Education.
[2] Metge, 1957, pp. 166–7; *New Zealand Yearbook, 1951-2*, p. 69.
[3] The remaining Maori workers were employed in transport, storage and communications (8 per cent) or not specified (3 per cent). *New Zealand Census 1951* vol. vi (Maori Census), p. 10; cf. vol. iv, p. 6.

those of the Pakeha: 12 per cent of the Maori population occupied simple dwellings classified as "huts, whares and baches", as against 2 per cent of the rest of the population.[1] Proportionately more Maoris were employed on a casual and seasonal basis; and only 2·8 per cent of those in gainful employment earned more than £700 a year. (The comparative non-Maori figure was 15 per cent.[2])

In 1953–5, the period covered by this work, Maoris were legally differentiated from non-Maoris in three spheres, in each case, it might be argued, to their advantage. Firstly: Maori land was protected from alienation and bankruptcy by special legislation summed up in the Maori Affairs Act of 1953. Maori land, as defined by this Act, was primarily land which had never been alienated from Maori ownership. But it also included Crown land granted to Maoris under conditions which made it inalienable, customary land vested in the Crown for the benefit of Maoris, and land which had become Maori land by certain legal processes, principally exchange. Freehold land bought by Maoris from non-Maoris, including the Crown, was not Maori land in the technical sense; it could, however, be declared Maori land by the Maori Appellate Court at the request of the owner(s). With the exception of certain lands vested in the Maori Trustee and land sold to the Crown under certain circumstances, transactions relating to Maori land had to pass through the Maori Land Court.[3] Interests in Maori land were protected from being taken in execution for debts or as assets in bankruptcy, except in relation to mortgages, rates, and taxes on the land. They were not computed as part of the owner's dutiable estate at his death, but a succession fee of 2 per cent of the total value had to be paid to the Maori Land Court on each share or holding over £1000 in value.

Secondly: under the Electoral Act 1927 (which embodied the Maori Representation Act 1867), Maoris were represented in the New Zealand House of Representatives by four Maori Members of Parliament elected from four Maori electorates. Those who were more than half Maori were qualified to vote only in the Maori electorates but 'half-castes' might register on either the Maori or non-Maori roll. Provision for a secret ballot for Maori electors was first made by the Electoral Amendment Act 1937.

Thirdly: in areas of dense Maori settlement, there were special 'Maori schools', which were controlled directly by the Department of Education, instead of being administered by regional Education Boards as were other State schools. In these Maori schools special emphasis was laid on practical education, Maori arts and crafts, and health; the children cleaned the schools and received free stationery and textbooks. However, 60 per cent of the Maori children at primary school in 1953 attended Board schools

---

[1] *New Zealand Census 1951*, vol. vi, p. 12; cf. vol. vii, p. 6. For *"bach"* and *"whare"*, see Glossary.

[2] *Ibid*, vol. vi, pp. 38–9; cf. vol. iv, p. 110.

[3] Smith, 1960; Sutherland, *op. cit.*, pp. 96–154.

while Pakeha children accounted for 10 per cent of the enrolments in Maori schools (see Plate 8a, facing p. 103).[1]

Legal definition of a Maori was by no means standardised. In the Maori Social and Economic Advancement Act 1945, a Maori "means a person belonging to the aboriginal race of New Zealand, and includes any person descended from a Maori". The Maori Affairs Act 1953 classified only persons of pure descent, 'half-castes' and persons intermediate between the two as Maoris, but allowed any descendant of a Maori so defined to succeed to interests in Maori land, to be nominated as occupier of a Maori land holding, or to be eligible for a Maori Affairs Housing loan. The Electoral Act made separate provisions for 'half-castes' and persons with less or more than half Maori blood. But a Maori could have himself declared a European by Order in Council under the Native Land Amendment Act 1912. Very few had availed themselves of this opportunity. Under the Maori Births and Deaths Registration Regulations 1935, separate rolls were kept for the registration of births and deaths of persons who were half Maori or more, and the degree of Maori blood of the parents was recorded on the certificates in both cases. (The certificates of those with less than half Maori blood bore no reference to their Maori ancestry.) The Census and Statistics Department numbered full Maoris, half Maoris and those with intermediate degrees with the Maori population, and those with less than half Maori blood with the European population.

MAORI DISTRIBUTION[2]

At the time of the 1951 Census, the Maori population was 115,676 or 5·9 per cent of the total New Zealand population. The overwhelming majority of Maoris were located in the northern half of the North Island, 72 per cent in the Auckland Provincial District, where there were 12·7 Maoris to 100 non-Maoris (compared with 6·3: 100 for New Zealand as a whole). Maoris actually outnumbered non-Maoris in certain rural areas (see Fig. 2).

The Maori population was predominantly rural, only 19·3 per cent residing in Cities and Boroughs, with 4·3 per cent in the semi-urban category (Town Districts and parts of Counties included in Urban Areas by the Census Department). In comparison, 66·2 per cent of the non-Maori population was urban (including 1·7 per cent in semi-urban areas) (see Table 1).

The Maori rural population was far more unevenly distributed than the non-Maori. There were three major areas where Maoris were numerous in relation both to the developed land and the non-Maori population: (1) the Far North, (2) the East Coast and Wairoa, and (3) the Bay of Plenty. There were nearly 15,000 Maoris in each of the first two in 1951

[1] Holst, 1958. Figures for 1953 supplied by Department of Education.
[2] Metge, 1952, p. 104; *Report of the Board of Maori Affairs for Year ended 31 March 1958*, pp. 7-17.

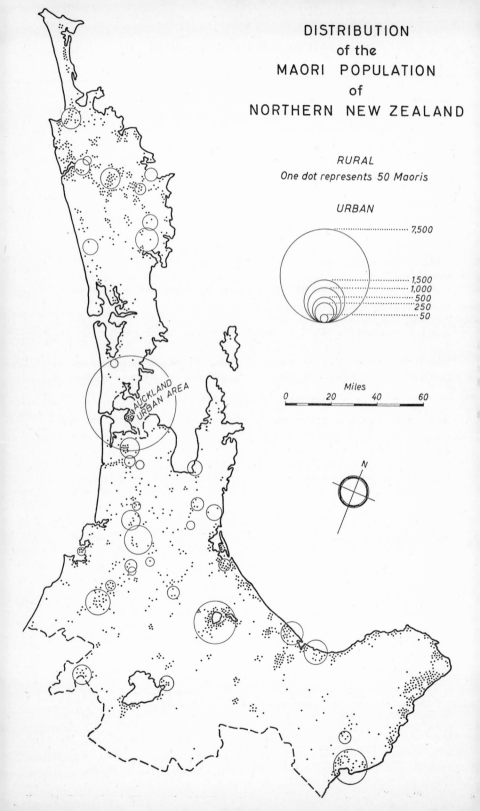

DISTRIBUTION
of the
MAORI POPULATION
of
NORTHERN NEW ZEALAND

RURAL
One dot represents 50 Maoris

URBAN

7,500

1,500
1,000
500
250
50

AUCKLAND
URBAN AREA

Miles

0   20   40   60

N

and just over 12,000 in the third. However, Maoris were relatively few in number and restricted to a few localities, in the rich and closely settled farming districts of the Near North, Manukau-Franklin and the Hauraki Plains. The Maori population of the South Island was negligible, amounting to less than 2 per cent of the total.

The Far North was a reservoir area which consistently lost large numbers of Maoris by emigration. Since 1945, the Bay of Islands was the only county in that area whose Maori population showed any increase, and that was confined to the Kaikohe, Moerewa and Kawakawa districts. The proportion of Maoris to non-Maoris had decreased in each of the Far Northern Counties. The East Coast and the Bay of Plenty were both divided into two parts with divergent population trends. On the northern East Coast and in Wairoa, Maoris were still increasing in number, but at a rate below the average for the Maori population as a whole (which was identical with the rate of natural increase, since the Maori population recruited no members by immigration from outside New Zealand). In the Bay of Plenty, Maoris had practically ceased to increase in the eastern sector (Ōpōtiki county) where Maoris predominated. In contrast, the southern East Coast had an exceptionally high rate of Maori increase, and that of the western Bay of Plenty was slightly above average, though in neither case was it enough to offset the losses from the other part of the region. The rate of Maori increase was well below average in the Waikato and the King Country, but well above in the Central Plateau area, Hawkes Bay, the Near North and Manukau-Franklin. In particular, Maoris from all over the country were attracted to the timber camps and mills of Rotorua, Kāingaroa and Tokoroa, and to Mangakino, public works base for the hydro-electric schemes on the upper Waikato River. The other parts of the North Island failed to maintain even an average rate of increase. The South Island had gained slightly by immigration of Maoris from the North.

The Maori urban population was concentrated in a limited number of industrial regional centres in northern and central New Zealand. In 1951, 55 per cent of the urban Maoris were distributed between eight centres: Auckland (7621), Wellington and Hutt (2404), Rotorua (1441), Gisborne (1112), Wanganui (923), Hastings (730), Hamilton (692) and Napier (608). All except Rotorua were classified by the Census Department as Urban Areas and situated in areas of predominantly non-Maori population. Increasing urbanisation had little effect on the number of Maoris living in small regional centres; many outside the main areas of Maori settlement had actually lost Maori population since 1945. Maoris were always a small minority in urban areas. The only town of any size where they formed over 10 per cent of the population was Rotorua (13·5 per cent).

FIG. 2 (*opposite*). Distribution of the Maori Population of Northern New Zealand, 1951

PART ONE

The Country

2

The People and the Land

THE rural area which I have called Kōtare lies in the western sector of the Far North, which is distinguished from the rest of Northland by the exceptionally high proportion of Maoris in its rural population (nearly 50 per cent in 1951, according to the Census). Within the Far North, the distribution of the Maori population differs from that of the Pakeha, so that some districts have an even higher percentage of Maoris and others only a minority. Kōtare has always been a predominantly Maori community. At the end of June 1955, the 537 Maoris resident in the district made up 78 per cent of the population.

The local residents defined Kōtare's limits fairly precisely, by reference to natural features—watersheds, the coast, and several streams—which the Maori elders identified as the traditional Maori boundaries. The Education and Post and Telegraph Departments accepted these limits for their school and postal districts, and the Census Department also adopted them in 1951. The name of the district was itself a legacy from pre-European times.

In 1955, the bulk of Kōtare land, including most of the fertile lowland, was Maori land,[1] a fact which was closely associated with the predominance of Maoris in the district. However, Pakehas owned a number of farms around the periphery of the district and numerous house sections along the seafront. A certain amount of land was held by Maoris on ordinary freehold title and by the Crown.

Like Northland in general, Kōtare was characterised by the beauty and variety of its landscape and by the large proportion of its area which had defied attempts at development and occupation. The heart of the district was a fertile, gently rolling plain. This was mainly in permanent pasture, sub-divided by barbed-wire fences, with occasional patches of *mānuka* (tea-tree scrub) and gorse, a scatter of native evergreens, and shelter belts of pine and macrocarpa. Along its northern margin, which tended to be swampy, drainage ditches and fences were marked by lines of pampas grass. Fed by many tributaries, two main streams wound across this lowland between high banks, joining forces in the northwest corner to break through the sand-hills to the sea. Bordering the lowland, heavily dissected hill-country occupied the eastern margin of the district and the

[1] See p. 16.

whole of its southern reaches. The foot-hills, once cleared and sown in pasture, had been invaded by gorse and *mānuka*, but the inner ranges were still clothed for the most part in native sub-tropical rain-forest (the New Zealand "bush"), except for pasture in two wide valleys opening on the lowland. The western part of Kōtare was typical Northland 'gum-land',[1] a steep-sided, relatively flat-topped, inhospitable upland. In the heyday of the kauri-gum industry (from the 1880's to 1914), it had been the chief site of settlement in the district, attracting diggers from all over Northland and beyond. But the diggers' methods had destroyed the natural cover and the structure of the soil, leaving it sour and waterlogged. In 1955, the gum-land was deserted, supporting only stunted scrub, gorse, wild grasses and swamp plants, a meagre cover eroding away along its northern edge, where it ended in great cliffs overlooking the open sea, into vast drifts of yellow sand. On its fourth and northern side, the Kōtare lowland was bounded by peaty swamps and a wide belt of sand-hills stabilised by gorse and marram grass, beyond which lay the sea.

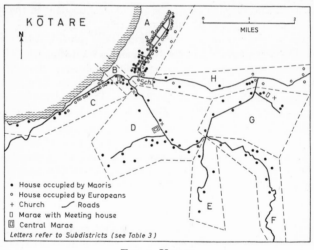

FIG. 3. Kōtare

In all, well over half the land area of Kōtare was unoccupied and virtually unutilised, providing only good shooting in season and occasional loads of firewood. But these wastelands gave many of the inhabitants the pride and the intangible advantages of owning Maori land, if no material ones; and the rugged, desolate hills made an impressive backdrop for life on the lowland and along the seashore.

Settlement was entirely confined to the more hospitable parts of the district (see Fig. 3 and Table 3). Houses were scattered along the roads traversing the lowland and its tributary valleys, rather more closely than

[1] Land that has been dug over by gum-diggers.

is typical of purely farm settlement in New Zealand, but without nuclea-
tion. A stream divided the lowland into two sub-districts: Karaka (the
eastern one) had a "family *marae*" and a church, Pūriri (the western) two
churches and the main *marae*.[1] Adjoining the plain in the northwest lay
the sub-district of Hākea, where six houses clustered round a "family
marae" between the gum-land and the sea. Westward from Hākea,
twenty-nine houses and 'baches' (simple cottages) were strung out along
the coast; the most remote, in a cove nine miles away, were occupied by
four Maori families, who were accounted part of the Kōtare community
in spite of their isolation. Settlement of yet another type was found in
Te Kāinga ("the Village"). Situated on the inner edge of the sand-hills,
Te Kāinga consisted of sixty-three houses on quarter- or half-acre sections
fronting on a central, no-exit road about half a mile long or on one of its
several side roads. Not a traditional village site, Te Kāinga had grown
rapidly in the last ten years. Most of its land had been alienated from
Maori title and thirty-eight of the houses were owned and occupied by
Pakehas. Nevertheless, Te Kāinga was an important part of the Maori
community, accommodating, besides a quarter of the Maoris in Kōtare,
the only two stores in the district, the Post Office, two church buildings, a
cinema of corrugated iron which showed films twice a week, two petrol
pumps, the bus company's garage, a Maori Primary School[2] and a Sports
Domain.

In relation to the outside world, Kōtare was reasonably accessible in
1955, at least by Northland standards. A main highway ran through the
district, connecting it with rural settlements to the south and east, and
with Raumati, a small country town eleven miles away. A bus company,
owned and managed by a local resident, had its terminus in Kōtare and
ran three return services a day to the town for the workers, the secondary
school children and "the shoppers", with "picture buses" on Friday and
Saturday night. Approximately half the Maori households and most of
the Pakehas had cars or trucks, and there were a number of motor-cycles.
Transport presented problems to those without vehicles of their own, for
bus timetables were not always convenient, and many houses were well
off the bus route. Taxis, available on call from the town, were expensive,
but could be used in emergencies. Most homes had a telephone, the local
and many town stores delivered goods at least once a week, and newspapers
were delivered on an afternoon bus run. There was a local Post Office but
no mail delivery. The township, Raumati, was linked by road, bus and
air with other Northland towns, with Auckland and through Auckland
with the rest of New Zealand. Indeed, it was often easier and less expensive to travel to places outside the Far North than to other country

---

[1] To-day, the term *marae* is applied firstly, to an area of land, not usually above
five acres, which has not been individualised, and secondly, to the combination of
such an area and a 'meeting-house'. Most recognised *marae* are legally registered
as Maori Reserves. [2] See pp. 16–17.

districts within that area, even those for which Raumati was the regional centre, because they were not well served by buses or connections were poor. As a result, co-operation in the use of cars and taxis was the rule, and for special occasions it was common for the community or one of its sub-groups to charter a bus.

MAORI AND PAKEHA IN KŌTARE

Pakehas as well as Maoris lived in Kōtare. In their relations with the Maoris, the Pakehas fell into three main categories: those married to Maoris, farming families whose forebears had been connected with Kōtare for several generations, and the non-farming residents in Te Kāinga and along the foreshore.

There were ten Pakehas who were or had been married to Maoris, all but two with part-Maori children living in the district. Accepted into the Maori community to a large extent, they did not play an active part in it, keeping mainly to their own family circle. Only one played a sustained role as mediator between the Maori community and what the Maoris thought of as "the Pakeha world".

The nine farming families had had a long association with the local Maoris, with whom they were on friendly but not intimate terms. In several cases they were linked through marriage in an earlier generation to Maori families, who sometimes bore the same surname. But they were separated from their Maori neighbours by their cultural background, their relative wealth and their way of life. Their holdings were larger than the Maori farms and much more developed, with larger herds and more capital equipment; and their farm methods were more closely geared to a competitive commercial economy. They were all full-time farmers. Most employed casual and seasonal workers and two hired permanent hands, for whom they provided accommodation. In this way they were known to many local Maoris as employers and landlords as well as neighbours. The farmers sent their children to the local Maori Primary School, attended weddings and funerals involving the Maoris they knew best and took an interest in local sports clubs and the School Committee, the main groups with mixed Maori and Pakeha membership. One of them, a County Councillor, was accepted by the Maoris as spokesman for the district in public affairs.

The third group had much less contact with the Maoris in Kōtare, except for a few interested in local sport. Most had come to the district since the war and their house sections were so distributed that few had Maori neighbours. Some were elderly, retired persons who led a quiet, self-contained existence. Most of the rest had their own cars and spent their working and much of their social life outside Kōtare; some indeed occupied their cottages only for weekends and holidays. In many cases, however, they worked with or employed Kōtare Maoris in Raumati.

Maoris and Pakehas living in Kōtare came into frequent contact as neighbours, in school, at work, in business and in sport. They worked together for the benefit of the district, organising field days, fairs, dances and, on one occasion, a Queen carnival, to raise money for projects such as extra electrical equipment for the school, dressing sheds for the sports domain, and a strip of tar-sealing in front of the school. Most of the Maoris had Pakeha friends, as well as numerous acquaintances. At the same time, however, the Kōtare Maoris formed a distinct community-within-a-community. Distinguished from the Pakeha residents in physical appearance and in certain aspects of culture and living standards, they also maintained certain separate forms of social organisation. This Maori community had its centre in the Pūriri *marae*.

THE MAORI COMMUNITY

At the end of June 1955, there were 537 Maoris in Kōtare, living in ninety-eight households. There was a slight preponderance of females. The most striking characteristic of the group was its youthfulness: 51 per cent under fifteen years of age, 28 per cent between fifteen and thirty-four. In comparison, the proportion of elders was small: 5 per cent over fifty-five years (see Table 3).

The Maori community was divided into many social groups of various kinds, but to the people themselves the most fundamental distinction was that between the *tāngata whenua*[1] or "native inhabitants" (literally, "people of the land") and the *tāngata haere mai* (people who have come in) who were most often referred to as "immigrants". The *tāngata whenua* were described as "really belonging to Kōtare", whereas, from the Maori point of view, 'immigrants' "belonged" elsewhere, even when born in the district. *Tāngata whenua* were well in the majority in Kōtare in 1955, numbering 384, or 72 per cent, of the Maori population. Spouses and foster children[2] derived from other communities accounted for 12 per cent and 14 per cent had settled in Kōtare independently of close ties with the land or the *tāngata whenua* (see Table 4).

The title of *tangata whenua* was accorded to all those who could trace a lineal association with Kōtare back through at least three generations of forebears who had lived there or been recognised as local landowners by the Maori Land Court. It was accepted that these ancestors derived their rights from a line of earlier landowners. According to the local experts in genealogies and traditional history, some of those recognised by the Maori Land Court as landowners at its first sittings had in fact come as adults from other districts, close kinsmen brought in by the "chiefs" of

[1] The plural form of *tangata* (man, human being) is distinguished from the singular by a lengthening of the first vowel.

[2] Adoption was common among Kōtare Maoris, but was often not legally registered. A child who had been legally adopted had the status and rights of own offspring, legally and in the eyes of the people, inheriting land, tribal and *hapū* membership from the adoptive parents. But a foster child was in an equivocal position, lacking legal rights.

local *hapū* to counter losses by death and emigration. However, according to Maori custom, they had every right to the title of *tangata whenua* secured to them by the Maori Land Court, for land and the rights associated with it were traditionally transferred by adoption and by chiefly gift as well as by lineal succession.

The *tāngata whenua* were divided into a number of "families", each consisting of the descendants of a given landowner. These "families" were social groups of considerable importance and solidarity. When asked who "really belonged" to Kōtare, local informants always gave a list, not of individuals, but of "families".

"Belonging" was closely associated with land ownership, or more precisely, with the ownership of Maori land (including potential rights in the holdings of a parent still alive). The people felt that a *tangata whenua* without rights in the land of his forebears was a contradiction in terms. Most of those descended from earlier landowners did have at least shares in Maori land in the district, but a few had none. In practice, however, these few were always numbered with the *tāngata whenua*, the fact that they could clearly establish membership in one of the *tangata whenua* "families" outweighing their landless estate.

The term 'immigrant' was applied to all who lacked ancestral association with Kōtare, a minor distinction being made between those who had married or been fostered by *tāngata whenua* and those who settled in Kōtare independently. Most of the latter were fairly recent settlers, and their offspring born in Kōtare were still mostly under fifteen years of age. By definition, 'immigrants' owned only freehold land in Kōtare. A minor anomaly was created by two who had shares in blocks of Maori land, apparently acquired by deed of gift from kin; they could not, however, claim membership in any of the *tangata whenua* "families". Another 'immigrant' claimed to be *tangata whenua* on the basis of descent from a Kōtare landowner eight generations back, but his claim was rejected because the intervening ancestors had not lived in Kōtare and had disposed of their land interests there. Many 'immigrants' were related to the *tāngata whenua*, but only through kin "belonging" to other areas.

The distinction between *tāngata whenua* and 'immigrants' was correlated with differences in access to land resources, in rights in the *marae* and in precedence in community life in general.

ACCESS TO LAND

The *tāngata whenua* owned all the Maori land in Kōtare with the exception of two small holdings. This amounted to roughly three-quarters of the total area but well under half the developed area, as several large holdings of Maori land lay on the gum-fields and in the southern hills. Several had also acquired freehold land by purchase or inheritance: a few house lots, two small blocks of farm land and a farm inherited from a Pakeha father. But although the *tāngata whenua* as a group owned most of the land in

Maori hands in Kōtare, the only individual who owned enough to support his family was the young man who had inherited the freehold farm. None of the rest had sole title to a block suitable for farming, and very few to blocks larger than a house lot. Most had shares in blocks held in common by descendants of a former owner (many of whom were not living in Kōtare) or the prospect of succeeding to such shares at the death of a parent. Land held by several owners in this way was often called "family land". Consolidation[1] of shares in Maori land had been started in Kōtare but never completed. Many had shares in several different blocks. The blocks themselves were often small. Excluding holdings in the hills and on the gum-land, there were seventy blocks, of which twenty-six were under ten acres, only fifteen over fifty and none exceeded a hundred acres. With the help of the Department of Maori Affairs, the owners had overcome the problem to a certain extent by leasing some blocks and by nominating occupiers to work the most suitable as farm units. Even so, only nine occupiers depended on farming for their livelihood. The only other *tangata whenua* who made a living from the land cut and sold firewood from "family land" on no firmer basis than the goodwill of the other owners.

The rest of the *tāngata whenua* looked to their land for a supplementary income, not for a full livelihood. Thirteen were part-time farmers. Five families lived on farms, sharing the farm-house with the farmer's family or occupying an adjacent cottage; ten lived on holdings of less than an acre, to which one of the parents had sole title; and eighteen lived on blocks under twenty acres, three of which accommodated more than one household. A considerable number of *tāngata whenua*, however, did not live on their land because it lay on the gum-land, which was difficult of access and expensive to develop. Eight of those in this position had bought sections at Te Kāinga and built homes there; the other sixteen rented houses from both Maori and Pakeha owners. From their holdings of Maori land they obtained only firewood, flax, and fruit from abandoned orchards.

In comparison with the *tāngata whenua*, 'immigrants' owned a very small proportion of Kōtare land. The majority of 'immigrant' settlers (twelve households out of twenty) owned and occupied quarter- or half-acre house lots on freehold title, mostly in Te Kāinga. Six families lived in rented cottages, owning no land at all in Kōtare. Two 'immigrants', however, occupied, without owning, farms on Maori land. One was the wife of a Pakeha leasing a farm from his first wife's family. The other had been nominated as occupier before the death of his first wife, who had shares in the land, and had managed it so successfully that the Department of Maori Affairs and the shareholders had agreed to his staying on, even though he had married again. (At his retirement, the farm would revert to the owners, probably to one of his sons by his first marriage.)

[1] See p. 13.

While their land resources varied greatly, *tāngata whenua* and 'immigrants' had equal access to the resources of the sea and seashore, which were also open to Pakehas and visitors from outside the district. Both made good use of them, a few making a living from the sea and all gathering seafoods. In the shooting season, those with guns and licences shot over the hills and unfenced gum-land for fowl and wild pig, mostly without reference to ownership.

The dichotomy between *tangata whenua* and 'immigrant' was not then clearly translated into economic terms. Most of the *tāngata whenua* depended primarily on cash income from other sources than the land, and many derived no more from it in material terms than did the 'immigrants'. Nor were the two groups separated territorially. Although Te Kāinga was known locally as "Immigrants' Row", *tāngata whenua* were well represented there, some occupying land still held on Maori title and others freehold sections, while 'immigrants' rented seven houses in the lowland farming area and its tributary valleys.

MARAE RIGHTS

The *marae*[1] (places of public assembly) were both the physical and the emotional foci for Maori social life in Kōtare. There were three of them: the main *marae* in Pūriri and two "family" *marae* in Karaka and Hākea respectively. The Pūriri *marae* consisted of five acres legally registered as a Maori Reserve and was distinguished by a traditional name. Apart from two tennis courts occupying one corner, the area was in rough pasture, kept cropped by horses owned by neighbouring farmers, with a dilapidated forty-year-old "meeting-house", a separate dining-hall-and-cookhouse, and a single earth closet to the rear. The meeting-house was a rectangular wooden building with a hip roof of corrugated iron, one sash window in the rear wall and one either side of the front door. Like most Northland meeting-houses, it was completely undecorated by carving, *tukutuku* (reed panels) or painted rafter patterns; it was furnished only with benches along the walls, a table, a few wooden chairs and a pile of flax mats which were stored in the rafters. The two "family" *marae* were not officially recognised: each was a half-acre site set aside for their common use by a group of kinsmen who held it in common by inheritance from a common ancestor. Each had a hall built by voluntary labour with funds collected by "family" members and subsidised by the Government. The Hākea hall was the larger and better equipped, and it had a separate corrugated-iron cook-house.

Rights in a *marae* were limited to those who had rights in the Maori land with which it was associated—in Maori land anywhere in Kōtare in the case of the Pūriri *marae* and in "family" land in that of the "family" *marae*. Those who had rights in a particular *marae* were known as *tāngata marae* in relation to that *marae*. (All but the landless *tāngata whenua* were

1 There is no difference between the singular and plural forms of *marae*.

automatically *tāngata marae* on the Pūriri *marae*, but only members of the Samuels and Hohaia "families" respectively were *tāngata marae* on the Hākea and Karaka *marae*.) My informants all agreed that, properly speaking, only *tāngata marae* had the right to speak publicly on the *marae*, to participate in its management, to use it whenever they liked free of charge, and to invite others there. In practice, the *tāngata marae* allowed those without rights to share their privileges "out of courtesy". But the *tāngata marae* always took precedence. If anyone without rights pushed himself forward unduly, they did not hesitate to put him in his place.

The *tāngata marae* allowed other local Maoris to speak in formal discussions on the *marae*, not only at club meetings and purely local gatherings, but also when there were visitors present. Usually, however, they reserved the right to make the speeches of welcome. Some members of other "families" always spoke at gatherings on the "family" *marae*. On all three *marae*, 'immigrants' married to *tāngata marae* spoke more often than 'immigrant' settlers, none of whom were experienced in public speaking. Those who were without rights in the *marae* at which a *hui* (gathering) was held usually waited until the *tāngata marae* had all spoken before rising to speak.

The "family" *marae* were both managed by *komiti marae* (*marae* committees), which in each case included not only "family" members but also their spouses, and in one case a couple of complete "outsiders". The Pūriri *marae* was managed by the Kōtare branch of the Maori Women's Welfare League, which had taken it over from a *komiti marae* four years before. This was a break with tradition. The League included several 'immigrants'.

No-one living in Kōtare was debarred from using any of the three *marae*, but *tāngata marae* as well as those lacking rights had to reserve it beforehand with the *marae* committee. The League made no charge for the use of the Pūriri *marae* for *hui*, whether sponsored by *tangata marae* or 'immigrant', but charged a small sum to cover electricity costs when it was used by clubs or for money-making activities. But when anyone outside the "family" used the Hākea or Karaka *marae* they paid a hiring fee. This the *komiti marae* invariably refunded in the case of *tangi*.[1]

When questioned, the adults carefully explained that only the *tāngata whenua* really had rights in the Pūriri *marae*, but in casual conversation they often referred to it as "the Kōtare *marae*" or "the community *marae*", implying that it was the centre for the *whole* community, including 'immigrants'. And so in practice it was. Arapera Smith, one of the leading *kuia* (elderly women), put it this way: "The Hohaias can't welcome people

---

[1] The proper word for the three-day wake associated with modern Maori burial is *tangihanga*, a noun formed from the verb *tangi*, to weep or mourn. Maoris in Kōtare (and also in Auckland) dropped the suffix in ordinary speech. The noun *tangi* properly means a lamentation, mourning or a dirge. See also Beaglehole, 1945, and Phillipps, 1954.

on the Hākea *marae* or the Samuelses on the Karaka one. But Pūriri is a public *marae*, it is everybody's. Any of the Kōtare *hapū* can speak there— at least, not just anyone, but their appointed speakers. It's not out of place if you stand up, no-one says anything. There is no need to wait for others, it's a public hall, all donate to it. And if you don't want to speak it doesn't matter."

UTILISATION OF NATURAL RESOURCES

Kōtare was by reputation and appearance a farming community. The lowland and valley areas were given over to fenced fields of pasture and hay, to cowsheds and pig-styes, with occasional gardens growing *kūmara* (sweet potato), maize, potatoes, pumpkins and marrows in quantity. Close investigation, however, revealed that the natural resources of the district fully supported only a little over one-seventh of the Maori inhabitants.

Farming

The land was the most important of Kōtare's natural resources—but out of a Maori population of 537 only 64 (ten families) depended upon it for their living. At least 12 per cent of the total and rather more of the developed area was owned by Pakehas.

The Maori-owned land was in general under-developed. Almost half was hill country or gum-land which could be developed only at a cost beyond the reach of the owners. Of the 1,500 odd acres enclosed within the limits of producing Maori farms, roughly one-third was undeveloped or rough grazing used only as "run-off" when the better pasture was too wet or needed resting. Even on the lowland and in the valleys, there were ten holdings between five and sixty acres which grew only gorse and scrub, except for a few acres round shareholders' houses, while another twelve, let out on short-term leases, were in poor condition, with fences awry and pasture infested with weeds and gorse, because the lessees had neither the incentive nor the means to improve them or even to arrest deterioration.

Dairy farming was the dominant form of land utilisation. There were twenty-two Maori farms in Kōtare, all concentrating on the production of cream, which was collected daily by lorries from a butter factory fifteen miles away. Most farmers also kept a few pigs and put down between half and one acre in gardens, using the products from both activities in the home or in fulfilling obligations to kin, club or community. Only three farmers regularly cultivated more than one acre, often in two or three lots; the total acreage, like the site, varied from year to year but did not usually exceed three acres. Their major crop was always *kumara* (sweet potatoes) and in good seasons they sold part of it in the township, after retaining enough for their own family and social needs (see Plate 1, facing p. 38).

Only nine farmers devoted themselves full-time to farming and their farms were not large nor productive enough to support a second full-time male worker. The best had less than sixty acres in pasture and four farmers managed with barely forty acres, supplemented by "run-off" in the hills. The largest dairy herd was one of forty-five cows. Annual production varied from 2,000 to 5,000 pounds of butterfat, an average of 100 to 150 pounds per cow (compared with the Northland average of 200 to 300 pounds). With the exception of a sixteen-year-old daughter, who was helping her mother to run the farm during her father's prolonged illness, the employable members of the farmers' families all worked off the farm, though some of the young men put in a few days, weeks or, occasionally, a month or two on the farm between jobs. Two or three of the farmers themselves periodically supplemented their cream cheque by casual labouring and one was regularly engaged as a drover in the twice yearly movement of beef cattle from the Mangonui area to the freezing works at Moerewa.

Thirteen part-time dairy farmers derived their basic livelihood from full-time employment in other occupations. Five were hoping to improve their financial situation enough to start farming full-time in the next year or two, but the rest were likely to continue in other employment, either because their farm was unable to support even one elementary family or because they preferred it. Much of the routine work on these farms was done by the farmer's wife and children, while in three cases a teenage member of the farmer's household (a brother and two daughters) worked on the farm for their keep and pocket-money.

Only one of the farmers had exclusive title to his farm: the rest worked holdings of Maori land, in which with one exception they held shares. All the full-time and seven part-time farmers were nominated occupiers,[1] their tenure and exclusive right to income from the farm secured by legal contract (arranged by the Department of Maori Affairs), while they paid running expenses and instalments off the debt on the land. The nominated occupiers had all begun farming under the Maori Land Development Scheme as State-assisted "units". One had succeeded in paying off his development loan and was independent of control, but the others were still under supervision by the Department of Maori Affairs. Four of the full-time farmers had each occupied his farm from its establishment, but the other farms had changed hands at least once. Two had had a succession of more than six occupiers, to their detriment. Four of the present holders (only one a full-time farmer) had taken over directly from their fathers, but in most cases the earlier occupiers had quit in favour of other employment. Three farmers were in the process of bringing their farms back into production after they had lain idle for several seasons.

The general level of Maori farming in Kōtare was not efficient nor even moderately productive by New Zealand standards. But Maori farmers had to contend with many problems that did not confront others. Maori

[1] See p. 14.

farming in Northland had an extremely short history, amounting to little more than twenty years. A few farmers were struggling to make a living in the 1920's, but they were severely handicapped by lack of clear title and the consequent difficulty of borrowing capital. The State established a Maori Land Development Scheme in Kōtare in 1932–3, absorbing existing farms and developing the land on a group basis with the labour of the landowners, but it was not until 1935 that the land was subdivided and the first farm units established. Again, the farmers as a group lacked training and experience. Most of them were first-generation farmers, sons of bush-workers, gum-diggers and labourers, and all but four had themselves spent long periods in other occupations. They were still paying off mortgages incurred in development and stocking. At the existing level of production, they were left with an income that was at best barely adequate to support a family, so that in order to pay for the machines and fertiliser essential to increased production, the farmer had to maintain or increase the debt. Then there was the problem of multiple ownership. Occupiers of holdings with several owners could not raise capital from the usual sources; their only hope of assistance was through the Department of Maori Affairs. Their occupancy, upon which depended their security of income and residence, lasted only for the span of their working life. Maori farmers in Kōtare thus lacked strong incentives to improve production. Though they struggled through most of their occupancy on a reduced income to pay off the debt on the land, it remained only partly theirs and they had no guarantee that the fruit of their labours would pass to their sons rather than to another shareholder. As a result, it often needed only a poor season or a quarrel with other part-owners to decide an occupier to walk off the farm. Efficient land use was further reduced by fragmentation: seven farms consisted of two or more blocks some distance apart. Lastly, low farm incomes tended to perpetuate themselves, since the farmer felt compelled by the shortage of ready cash to take casual or permanent employment, and so had less time to spend on the farm.

It has often been suggested that the Maori farmer's output is reduced and the farm schedule disrupted by the fulfilment of obligations towards kinsmen which is an important part of the Maori cultural pattern. In Kōtare, kinship responsibilities certainly did at times call the farmers away from the farm or require the donation of produce, but rarely to an extent that threatened the farm economy. The farmers contributed generously in labour and in kind to local weddings, funerals and "unveilings" (the ceremonial unveiling of gravestones) when they involved their kinsfolk, especially those of the same "family", but such occasions did not usually affect any given individual more than two or three times a year. Though a farmer put in a lot of work at the *marae* at these gatherings, the farm did not usually suffer, for they lasted at most three days, and most tasks on a dairy farm could be safely suspended for so short a time, except for milking and the feeding of calves and pigs, which either brought the farmer home for short periods or could be delegated to other members of his family. If his presence on the farm were essential, Maori custom allowed his wife or children to represent him on the *marae*. The contributions the farmer made in kind were mostly goods not intended for sale: garden produce, firewood, and hay. Occasionally, in honour of a very close kinsman, he would give a can of cream or a pig, a cow or a steer for killing. Part of the value of gifts as substantial as these was often refunded after the accounts of the *hui* (gathering) had been made up, but they could represent real sacrifice to the farmer, especially at certain times of the year. In general, however, contributions to *hui*, both labour and goods, were a loss or drain on the farmer's resources only on a short-term view. He was recompensed, not for each specific gift but in a general way, when a wedding or a death occurred in his own immediate family, for then he received from kinsfolk (not necessarily those to whom he had given or in the same measure) contributions which in the aggregate covered all or the greater part of the expenses of staging the necessary *hui*. The Kōtare farmers also gave frequent gifts of meat, milk, fruit, and vegetables to kinsmen who lacked them, but these also were usually returned indirectly, in the form of labour or gifts of goods not produced on the farm, such as seafoods.

Other Forms of Land Use

Those landowners who did not produce for sale made restricted use of their land for gardens, for keeping pigs and sometimes a house cow, and as a source of firewood and flax for making floor mats and baskets in the traditional style. The people said that gardens were much smaller than they had been before the Second World War, when jobs and money were scarcer. However, many whose gardens were limited to a quarter- or half-acre house lot, both *tāngata whenua* and 'immigrants', increased their store of produce by working on the big farm gardens, planting, weeding and harvesting in return for a share of the crop. Most labour of this kind was done by the women and pensioners, but the workers helped at weekends and after work, the children when out of school. A farmer sometimes allotted a specific section of his gardens to his siblings, especially if they had an interest in the land, ploughing and harrowing it along with the rest in return for labour when he needed it on his own crops. But in spite of these practices, it was doubtful if many families were able to keep themselves in potatoes and sweet potatoes all the year round.

Apart from the farmers, a firewood contractor was the only Maori in Kōtare who made a living from the land. The kauri-gum industry was virtually at a standstill, but two Pakehas, who had been diggers most of their life, still won enough from concessions on the gum-land to support their Maori wives and children.

Utilisation of Sea Resources

Several workers, however, derived the whole or greater part of their cash income from the sea. Two of the older men were commercial fishermen, owning power-driven launches and refrigerated vans in which they hawked their catch round the surrounding countryside. But fishing on this unsheltered coast was a hazardous occupation, virtually impossible in winter and halted by spells of bad weather even in summer. One of the fishermen, who had a large family to support, also took on contract work of various kinds, assisted in both enterprises by two adult sons. The sea yielded yet another and richer harvest in the form of commercial varieties of seaweed which wind and current drove into remote rock-bound coves. Four couples, two with children, lived all the year round in one of these bays in rented cottages, swimming out into the surf to "pick" the seaweed in summer, when they made enough to support them during the rest of the year, and gathering it from the beach in winter. (Only one man and two women figure as full-time seaweed-pickers on Table 5; two of the men were Pakehas, the third a pensioner, and the other two women had children to care for.) In summer some eight other families camped there for several months, a few of the wage-earners relinquishing their jobs for the season but most picking seaweed only as an enjoyable way of increasing their regular income.

Seafoods figured prominently in the diet of every Maori family in Kōtare, for they were relished greatly. The children made frequent excursions to the beach to dig in the sand for bivalve shellfish, and on Saturday and Sunday, whenever tide and weather permitted, a large proportion of the community trekked 'round the rocks' on foot, horse, truck or tractor, in search of mussels and other shellfish, sea-eggs and crayfish. Those who could take advantage of favourable tides during the week or had adolescent children to send gave part of their harvest to kin or neighbours, in return for other favours. But with regard to fish, Kōtare households bought most of their needs from the commercial fishermen, for the coast was not suitable for small boats and shore fishing was uncertain and often dangerous.

OTHER EMPLOYMENT

In Kōtare

For those who could not make a living by direct utilisation of resources of land or sea, there were few opportunities for earning a cash income in Kōtare itself. In June 1955 a young Maori was working temporarily for a Pakeha farmer. The bus company (which had its depot in Kōtare) employed two men, a driver and a motor mechanic. The only other Maoris employed locally were the five teachers at the Kōtare Primary School: a married couple with considerable experience, a Junior (uncertificated) Assistant and two Probationary Assistants, who were all three young and unmarried and boarded with local families. In 1955 all five teachers were 'immigrants'.

Outside Kōtare

Of the 130 Kōtare Maoris who were "gainfully employed" (as the Census puts it), 101—the large majority—earned their living by work *outside* Kōtare (see Table 5). Most commuted daily. About half those involved worked in Raumati and nine in a quarry located on the road into town. They travelled to and from work five days a week by two "workers' buses" and several private cars and trucks, the latter usually filled to capacity by the owners' kin and neighbours. The others ranged over much of the Far North, working for employers, or building houses or bridges on contract. When possible, they travelled to work each day by their own vehicles or by transport provided by their employers, but sometimes they camped on the job for a week or more at a time.

Among the men who worked outside Kōtare, there was considerable differentiation of occupation. Just over half (56 per cent) were employed as labourers, three out of four in permanent jobs which were, however, subject to retrenchment in bad years. Most of these labourers were engaged in road and drainage maintenance for the Raumati Borough Council, the County Council or the Public Works Department, but eight were quarrymen, two worked at the timber mill and one at a dairy factory. Four others with labouring experience had "risen from the ranks", two to become foremen of labouring gangs and two contractors driving a bulldozer and cleaning farm ditches respectively. The proportion of tradesmen was surprisingly high (16 per cent). There were nine carpenters (five trained at the Returned Services Rehabilitation Training School at Kaikohe after the war), a plasterer, an apprentice painter and a boilerman with a second-class engineer's ticket employed at the Raumati Hospital. Six, all carpenters, were in business on their own account. The only worker in the professional-and-clerical category, on the other hand, was a lad teaching in a neighbouring district as a Junior Assistant. The rest (22 per cent) were employed in jobs requiring intermediate skills and training, mainly as linesmen, drivers, and storemen (see Plate 2, facing p. 39).

Women played a much smaller part in the daily exodus of workers. Only twenty-three were involved, all employed in Raumati. Eight held jobs requiring certain educational qualifications, as typists, shop assistants, civil servant and head waitress at a hotel; they were all comparatively young and most unmarried. The other fifteen women were generally older and married, four supporting children without a husband's help, and eight working to increase family resources for such cherished projects as keeping their children at secondary school or building a new house. They were all employed in laundry and domestic work, either at the hospital or hotel on wages, or by the half-day at business premises and private homes.

OTHER MEANS OF SUPPORT

Excluding those over fifteen who were still at school or assisting relatives without regular payment, there were sixteen men and nineteen women in Kōtare who were not "gainfully employed" at the end of June 1955. Of the men, nine were drawing old age pensions and five invalid pensions from the State, while two, both able-bodied, were unemployed. Some twelve others who were in employment at that date, were sometimes out of work, especially in the winter months. They seemed able to survive short periods of unemployment, putting in the time on their own farm or gardens, or working on a kinsman's in return for produce. But those who did not find another job within a matter of weeks usually left the district.

The women who did not work full-time either for employers or for relatives were all housewives. Sixty-eight were supported by husbands in gainful employment or (in seven cases) on pensions, two drawing old age pensions themselves. There were also twelve widows living on widows' pensions, either in their own homes or staying with grown-up children, and twelve unmarried women living with their parents or (in one case) a sibling. Two of the latter were invalids on pensions, two kept house for widowed fathers, and the others, who were mostly under twenty, helped their mothers in house and garden, sometimes because they were really needed but often because they had not been able to find or hold jobs.

Most of the women engaged in home duties contributed largely to their family's invisible income by work in the gardens and collecting shellfish, while a dozen by their labour really earned part of the income produced by their husbands' farms. A few also earned small sums of money, working for local Pakeha housewives for two or three hours a week, making flax mats for sale (to order and in small quantities), dressmaking for kin and neighbours, and occasionally helping out during periods of emergency as nurses and domestics at the Raumati hospital. Some of the menfolk also worked part-time, but in every case in addition to full-time employment. Besides the part-time farmers, one worked part-time as barman at a Raumati hotel, while five formed a "Polynesian Orchestra" (consisting of guitars and drums) which played (for fees) for dances and social gatherings over much of the western sector of the Far North.

PATTERNS OF PRODUCTION AND CONSUMPTION

The majority of Kōtare workers in "gainful employment" worked as individuals, earning either wages or a cash income from the investment mainly of their own labour, and controlling its spending themselves or (if married) in conjunction with their spouses. In those few cases where two or more adults were involved in the same cash-earning enterprise (i.e. partnerships and enterprises in which relatives assisted without wages), the net income was divided between them at some stage, so that either all or part of it was consumed separately.

PLATE I. (*a*) A Maori dairy farm in Northland; and (*b*) a typical farm family. See pp. 32–5.

PLATE 2. Rural employment: (*a*) carpenters building a house for the Department of Maori Affairs, and (*b*) driving a road-grader. See p. 37.

Business partnerships had been formed by seven carpenters, who built houses on a contract basis. Sometimes they employed labourers, usually from Kōtare, because they were hard-pressed or to oblige a kinsman or friend out of work. One partnership consisting of three married brothers could also be regarded as a family enterprise. A second, however, was made up of two brothers and an unrelated 'immigrant', while another 'immigrant' was partnered by an affine living in another community. These partnerships governed only the process of production. The net profits were divided on receipt by the partners, who administered their shares independently and in every case maintained separate households.

Most farmers received a good deal of unpaid assistance from wives and children. Four farmers and a fisherman were assisted by sons, daughters, and a brother, who received in lieu of wages full lodging and clothing or, in the case of one who was married, a rent-free cottage, together with occasional sums of money. Such arrangements usually lasted only a few years.

Wage-earners, while employed and paid individually, worked as part of a team or under the direction of foremen or employers. Those working on their own account often worked alone, but few did not spend at least some of their working hours with others—trade partners, wives, children and other young relatives, or other farmers or seaweed pickers. The farmers had established several informal work-rings in which three or four (kinsmen, neighbours and friends) worked together from time to time, butchering, harrowing, hay-making, sowing manure and clearing gorse for each in turn. In this way, those who did not have tractors, harrows or farm horses of their own secured their use not for cash but for labour. The membership of these rings changed fairly often, as members quarrelled over the division of labour or for personal reasons, emigrated or took other employment.

LEVELS OF INCOME

I was unable to make a comprehensive survey of individual and family incomes in Kōtare in 1955. In general terms, wages for a forty-hour week began at £3 for males under sixteen and £2. 10s od for females and rose to between £9. 10s od and £12 for men over twenty-one and between £6. 10s od and £8 for women (e.g. £9. 10s od for storemen, £10. 10s od for labourers and £11. 10s od for truck and grader drivers, £6. 13s 4d for female shop assistants, £7. 9s 9d for domestics at the hospital and £8. 16s od for typists, subject to adjustment according to qualifications and service). Overtime was not generally available but in certain limited types of employment (notably for hospital and construction workers) it could amount to as much as £100 a year. However, a restricted bus timetable prevented most Kōtare commuters from taking overtime even if available. The full-time farmers earned less in cash than many wage-earners. Their annual cream-cheques were between £400 and £600; the sale of calves brought in a little extra, and two or three made not more than £50 a year from pigs and kūmara. But out of this cash income they had to pay farm expenses and between £100 and £150 in loan repayments. However, they reaped a really large invisible income from the farm in the form of meat, milk, vegetables and firewood. By far the highest incomes were those of the contracting carpenters, who made between £800 and £1,000 after clearing their expenses. At least one in each set of partners owned a light truck or old car, so that they could work till daylight failed and if necessary camp on the job. In 1955 they rarely had a gap between jobs, securing contracts in the open field (including some from the Department of Maori Affairs) for houses in Raumati and Mangonui County generally. On the other hand, four families were chronically on the verge of poverty because their heads could not hold a job. Of the others who were periodically out of work, six were young men without dependents who were "carried" by their parents between jobs in return for various services, and two had working wives.[1]

Most Kōtare families depended on a single breadwinner. Only eleven married women were in full-time employment. Unmarried workers living at home (twenty men and eight women) contributed to household expenses no more than it cost to keep them, except in the case of five whose parents were pensioners.

The amount of cash coming into a household was not in itself a very reliable guide to the economic position of the occupants. Various factors tended to reduce its real value, either generally or in particular cases. In the first place, prices of many goods were higher than in Auckland because of freight and delivery charges. Secondly, it cost many up to sixteen shillings a week to travel to work. Thirdly, large families were fairly common: twenty-five householders were supporting between four and six children and seven between seven and nine. Popular jokes notwithstanding, the Child Benefit of ten shillings a week paid by the State lightened but did not meet the cost of keeping each child. Many parents were also assisting older offspring earning low wages, refusing or taking only a token payment for their keep, and sending periodic remittances to those who had left home. Fourthly, thrift and careful budgeting were unfamiliar concepts to the Maoris of Kōtare, either as practices or ideals. (As shoppers, they tended to spend a disproportionate amount on luxury goods and to buy for appearance and cheapness without regard to quality.) But there was also a strong cultural bias against carefulness in the handling of money. Generosity was regarded as a cardinal virtue, "stinginess" as un-Maori. They liked to boast that when giving to kin, friends, church, or community they "never counted the cost". This attitude was easily carried over into the management of personal and household finances. They could and did

[1] Information supplied by Raumati businessmen, Mangonui County Council, Secretary, Hospital Board, Department of Maori Affairs and Kōtare carpenters.

save, however, for objects that were socially approved and could be attained within the foreseeable future, such as a house, a car or a grave-stone for a deceased relative, usually through the medium of Maori Affairs housing loans or hire purchase. Fifthly, in the handling of property other than land, little stress was laid on conservation and repair. Lack of attention shortened the useful life of most purchased goods and accounted in part for general shabbiness of dress, furnishing and vehicles and for the dilapidation of private houses and *marae* buildings.

On the other hand, most families were able to add to their cash income an important non-cash increment as a result of cultivating gardens, keeping pigs, horses, or a house-cow, trapping eels, cutting *mānuka* for firewood, and collecting wild vegetables, fruits and seafoods, or by exchanging the products with kin or neighbours. Most paid no rent because they owned the land they lived on, though the advantages were mixed for the many who were only part-owners. The importance of this invisible income varied according to the size of the family, the amount of land owned, proximity to the beach and the possession of special skills, but there was no household in which it was insignificant.

HOUSING AND HOUSEHOLD ORGANISATION

Among Kōtare Maoris in 1955, the range in housing standards was con-siderably greater than that in income (even on a *per capita* basis), ranging from definitely sub-standard to brand-new and spacious. Nor was income always adequately reflected in housing, some households living in poor conditions having some of the largest incomes, in terms both of individual and aggregate earnings. This was partly because higher incomes were often matched by high spending rates, partly because there was a time lag between improvement in economic conditions and improvement in hous-ing. The latter was retarded by the multiple ownership of so much land in Kōtare. Those who were only part-owners of the house and land they occupied naturally hesitated to spend much of their own money on them, while cutting a house section out of a block with many owners cost so much and took so long that many part-owners had bought and built on freehold sections in Te Kāinga instead.

Owners and part-owners (who were almost equal in number) together made up 75 per cent of the Maori householders in Kōtare. Thirteen lived in houses on Maori land to which they had exclusive title, twenty-five on freehold sections, and thirty-seven in "family houses", whose ownership they shared (along with the land on which they stood) with kinsfolk descended from a common parent, grandparent or great-grandparent. Those occupying "family houses" paid no rent to the other shareholders, but shouldered the burden of loan repayments, rates and maintenance. They also recognised an obligation to accommodate other shareholders at any time. Two other "family houses" were occupied by householders without interests in the land, one as nominated occupier, the other (a

Pakeha with a Maori family) as lessee, of the attached farms. One school teacher boarded with Pakeha relatives. The remaining twenty households rented houses, mostly from Maori owners.

The houses themselves were nearly all built of wood, with weatherboard walls and corrugated iron roofs. A few shacks were built entirely of corrugated iron; and there was one rough-cast bungalow a few years old. Just over half (53) had been built privately, prior to 1945. Of these, six were fairly well preserved, but the rest showed signs of deterioration: peeling paint, rotting boards and spoutings, uneven foundations, the result of age, hard wear and often poor materials, aggravated by the local rough, salt-laden winds. A few were the spacious villas of thirty to forty years before, with sash windows and long verandahs, but most were plain, square cottages with the minimum of conveniences (no bathroom, only one or two inside taps if any, and outside earth closets). Some had been added to over the years, but thirty were one- or two-room shacks. Another important group, making up a quarter of the total, were "land development houses" built by the Department of Maori Affairs in the nineteen-thirties and early forties, first for farm units and later for wage-earners, on Maori land. Built to a few simple designs to cut costs and rarely exceeding 900 square feet of floor space, they had four to six rooms, the largest combining the functions of kitchen and living room, the smallest those of bathroom and laundry. In 1955, these houses were in reasonable repair, though in need of repainting. They were, however, almost invariably too small by modern standards, especially for the large households most accommodated. Since the war, another fourteen houses had been built with the help of housing loans from the Department of Maori Affairs. These, too, were distinctive in style, though their designs and colour schemes were much more varied. Ranging from 900 to 1200 square feet, they had up to four bedrooms, living room, kitchen, bathroom and laundry, and often a water closet under the same roof. Finally, there were five houses built privately since 1945, most smaller and plainer than the Maori Affairs houses and one, half finished, being built on periodic visits home by a cargo-worker in Auckland out of current savings (see Plate 3, facing p. 54).

Water was a problem to all Kōtare householders. Most relied on rainwater tanks of corrugated iron, but water had to be carefully conserved during the long, hot summer. The children regularly bathed in the creeks except in winter, and ten housewives did their washing on their banks in tin baths and old 'coppers' (boilers) left there for the purpose. A few households on the edge of the hills used natural springs, and water could be bought from a touring tanker in emergencies. Electricity, on the other hand, was laid on to all but the isolated cottages of the seaweed pickers and a few shacks on the fringe of the lowland. Apart from these, every house had electric lighting and eight out of ten a party-line telephone. Houses built since the war all had electric stoves and water-heaters, and these had also been installed in many of the older houses, alongside the old wood-burning ranges. A dozen homes had refrigerators, and a similar number washing machines. Radio sets were found everywhere, powered by batteries where necessary.

The housing situation in Kōtare was not static. Renovations and improvements were gradually being made in many of the older places. Many families were merely putting up with their present condition while saving for a new home. Ten had arranged housing loans with the Department of Maori Affairs and hoped to have their houses built within the next two years. Four wage-earners had bought sections and planned to build homes out of current income and savings, with their own labour.

Although there were some fairly large and complex households in Kōtare, the most common household consisted of a single elementary family (see Table 6). In June 1955, sixty-nine out of the ninety-eight Maori households in the district included only parents and their unmarried offspring (including foster children), while another thirteen consisted of elementary families with the addition of one or two "boarders". The latter were often but not always collateral kin, and they rarely stayed more than a year or two. In comparison, there were only six households consisting of three generations (parents, children and their spouses, and children's children). These, however, were among the largest in the district and accounted for 12 per cent of the Maori population. The only other households which followed a pattern were three consisting of two or more siblings and their spouses and children. The largest of these was on the point of division, for one of the families involved was building a house of its own. The others would probably also split up within a year or two; such households had not lasted long in Kōtare in the past.

The Maori households in Kōtare were large by Pakeha standards. Thirty-two had seven or more members, accommodating 54 per cent of the population. But small households were also common: forty-three had less than five members. In general, the number of persons per room was fairly high, and even the smaller households usually had little space to spare. In many homes, three or four children slept in the same bedroom and children commonly shared beds.

In matters of domestic organisation—payment of expenses, allocation of chores, cooking and eating—the members of Kōtare households always formed a single unit, even when two or even three elementary families were involved. But with regard to income, control over property, and personal behaviour, not only each elementary family but each earning adult claimed and largely exercised independence. Unmarried workers living with their parents normally retained control over their wages and the distribution of their time. They sometimes paid "board", usually less than that paid by boarders from outside the family, but often parents "felt sorry for them" and refused or returned most of it. As they said, "it isn't the Maori way to be hard on young people and they aren't earning much". However, as has already been observed, young adults usually contributed a good deal by work in the gardens or on the farm and by collecting wild foodstuffs; they also frequently bought clothes for younger siblings and took them to the cinema, to sports matches and even on visits to the city, paying all expenses. Married couples sharing a house with parents, siblings or other kin were similarly independent, often owning furniture, stock and motor vehicles of their own. Many things that were individually owned were, however, used in common for the sake of convenience and the Maori ideal that "you shouldn't have to ask a relative for anything". Sharing was encouraged as a Maori virtue from an early age and in most homes clothes and play-things were virtually common to the children of pre-school and school age. Adults who had bought their clothes and other property out of earnings rarely refused to lend them, provided they were asked for their use beforehand.

CONCLUSION

In economic terms, the relationship between the Maoris and the land in Kōtare was not nearly as close as it appeared or as could fairly be expected for a rural district. Primary production based on the natural resources of the district provided full-time employment for 17 per cent of the Maori workers and supported 15 per cent of the Maori population. Land utilisation could have been more intensive and more productive. Improvements in that direction would probably increase the numbers making a living from the land but not dramatically, as much of the increase would be absorbed in raising the standard of living of those already on the land. Kōtare was clearly overpopulated in relation to its local resources.

At the same time, a remarkably high proportion of the Kōtare Maoris were dependent on the availability of employment within commuting distance of their homes, and to a lesser extent on the provision of public transport. Some of those who thus worked outside the district were engaged in primary production, but the majority were employed in manual labouring, trades, service industries, communications and transport. If outside employment and the means of reaching it had not been available, many Maoris living in Kōtare in 1955 would have had to migrate in search of work providing a cash income. Other things remaining equal, the standard of living in Kōtare would probably have fallen, since most of those engaged in farming and other forms of primary production relied on outside employment to bring in extra cash and in some cases to provide their basic cash income. As it was, any recession in employment or wages in Raumati or the surrounding area was quickly felt in Kōtare, as men were put off work and cash became short; if it lasted any length of time, the rate of emigration increased. But while outside employment increased Kōtare's economic dependence on the external economic situation, it did not create it. The incomes derived from primary production from local resources depended on the prices prevailing on an external market as well as on efficiency of production, and their real value on the cost of the many goods and services obtained from outside.

Why did so many continue to live in Kōtare when they could not make a living in the district? They could have saved time and money by moving to Raumati. But other considerations than the purely economic were involved in their relationship with the land in Kōtare. A few stayed because they had rights in houses or had been offered a tenancy there: there was an acute housing shortage in Raumati. Others had built homes in Kōtare because they had sections of Maori land there or, more commonly, because they had been able to buy freehold sections there more cheaply than in Raumati. The seashore was an important attraction, for its seafoods rather than the view. More important still, Kōtare had a large Maori population which formed a community in the fullest sense of the word, with a *marae* as the physical and emotional focus of community life on the *Maori* pattern. Raumati, on the other hand, had only a small percentage of Maoris and no *marae*. But for most of those concerned, the strongest reason of all was attachment to Kōtare as the land and community of their ancestors, reinforced by childhood and sometimes lifelong associations. There, by virtue of descent and land ownership, they enjoyed the rights (particularly with regard to the *marae*) reserved by Maori custom for *tāngata whenua*, rights which they could claim in few other places. They chose to live in Kōtare, because they "belonged" there.

3

Kinship and Descent

NO- ONE living in Kōtare could avoid the conclusion that kinship played a large and important part in the lives of the Maori inhabitants. They themselves continually stressed *whanaungatanga* (kinship) as a fundamental characteristic of the Maori way of life, not only to the enquiring anthropologist but in their everyday conversation, particularly to the children and adolescents. The Pakeha, they alleged, "lives only for his own (elementary-) family", but "Maoris never turn a relative down". The rights and duties of kinsfolk in relation to each other were clearly formulated in their minds and speech, and their observance carried the weight of a moral obligation. On certain social occasions, notably *tangi* (funeral wakes) and weddings, kinship was acknowledged as the primary principle of organisation, determining who took active part and in what role, and overriding other social divisions. And for better or worse, kin loyalties and hostilities were carried over to some extent into groups organised on other bases.

The Kōtare Maoris did not confine their interest to known and demonstrable kin and to living generations, but were also extremely interested in kinship based on descent. They valued *whakapapa* (genealogies) as a means of placing themselves both in relation to their ancestral past and to other Maoris, especially to those not normally reckoned as kinsmen. They recognised the existence and social validity of several orders of descent-groups, and senior descent was generally regarded as one of the major qualifications for leadership, both in descent-groups and in the Maori community at large.

THE KINDRED

The Maoris of Kōtare prided themselves on knowing and maintaining relations with a large number of kinsfolk related to them through both parents and by marriage, including many living outside Kōtare. The personal *kindred*[1]—the circle of kin recognised by each individual or *Ego*— naturally varied in size and range according to each person's kinship knowledge and the number of kinsmen available to him, but in general

[1] Firth, 1956, p. 16. Rivers applied the term to a bilateral descent-group of restricted depth (*Social Organisation*, 1924). I have preferred to use it, as most anthropologists do, for an *Ego*-oriented group of kin.

both were extensive by Pakeha standards. Most adults were able to identify kinsmen up to the fourth and sometimes sixth degree on both parents' sides, and they also accepted as kin many with whom they were unable to trace their relationship in full, because they were identified (or descended from persons identified) as kin by parents or elders, or because they were able to demonstrate relationship to other known kin. Most Kōtare Maoris also maintained effective relations with a large proportion of their known kin; effective kindreds[1] of over an hundred persons were common. They lost touch only with distant relatives living outside Kōtare, especially those who lived really far away and had not visited Kōtare for a long time.

Within each kindred, kin were arranged concentrically, as it were, in relation to *Ego*, the inner circle consisting of those members of the same elementary-family or grand-family who were part of the same domestic unit. (A few, boarding with more remote kin, lacked this inner circle.) In general, frequency of contact, personal intimacy and the observance of the rights and duties regarded as appropriate to the relationship diminished as the genealogical relationship became more distant, but in any given case this rule was modified by accessibility and by personal likes and dislikes. Most reckoned the descendants of the same great-grandparent as "close" kin and those further out than fourth cousins as "Maori cousins", at least in ordinary conversation. No general distinction was made between father's kin and mother's, though in individual cases one side was often more numerous or socially more important to *Ego* than the other. Ties with affines were normally weaker than those with consanguineous kinsmen. Interest in kinship duties and to a lesser extent in kinsfolk in general also varied considerably with age. Those in their teens and twenties carried their kin responsibilities fairly lightly, while older residents, more particularly the retired, gave a lot of time to kinsfolk and their affairs (health permitting).

Everyone had some kin outside the community, not only in neighbouring districts but in more distant parts of the Far North and beyond. In the case of very close kin—those within the secondary degrees of relationship —frequency of contact and the performance of certain duties might be greatly diminished for long periods, but they usually corresponded at least occasionally, knew how to contact each other urgently if necessary, and came together in cases of death and marriage. And whenever and wherever they met again, the relationship was resumed in all its former warmth. But when more distant kin were involved, the relationship usually became more or less permanently attenuated and sometimes lapsed altogether; at any event, it was much less important to *Ego* than that with kin of the same degree who lived in Kōtare or adjacent settlements. At the same time, there were several cases of close kin living in Kōtare who did not get on together, and others of distant kin who were

[1] *Ibid*, p. 45.

close friends. But even if the former rarely visited each other, they usually set aside their differences to co-operate during *hui* (gatherings on the *marae*), when a display of kinship solidarity was regarded as desirable. The point at which effective relations ceased—separating the effective kindred from the rest of the known kindred—was not fixed; it varied with the individual, according to the range of kin available, where they were living, the extent of his interest, and his personal reactions to particular kin.

Both known and effective kindreds inevitably changed over time as a result of birth, death and marriage. The effective kindred was also affected by migration. Some kin were lost when they moved to distant or inaccessible places, while effective relations were resumed with others when they came to live in Kōtare or nearby.

RIGHTS AND DUTIES OF KINSFOLK

Most of the rights and duties of kinsfolk outside the primary and secondary degrees of relationship were framed in general terms as mutual obligations of friendship and helpfulness. It was generally agreed that kinsfolk ought to keep in touch and take a personal interest in one another's fortunes. Their homes should be open to each other at all times: they were entitled to enter without knocking and in the absence of the occupants. They should freely share such possessions as another fancied or lacked. Kinsfolk should help each other in time of trouble with their presence, sympathy and labour. They should also give or lend money when requested, though it was admitted that circumstances sometimes justified a refusal (if, for instance the giver's family was in straitened circumstances or if the borrower had already borrowed heavily without repayment). Kinsfolk should support each other in particular on those occasions of social crisis normally celebrated by a *hui*: *tangi*, "unveilings" of gravestones, weddings, and twenty-first birthday parties. The obligation to attend a *tangi* was the most binding; if possible, kin should "pay their respects" on the first day that the *tūpāpaku* (corpse) lay on the *marae*. At *hui* of these kinds, kin helped with the work involved and contributed to the expenses by donations (*awhina* or "*marae* money") in cash and in kind. Finally, kinsfolk should be loyal and defend each other against attack, even (many felt) when in the wrong.

Certain specific duties were allotted on a kinship basis, mainly in connection with the *hui* just mentioned. At such gatherings, the roles of *kai-whakahaere-o-te-hui* (general director or "master of ceremonies") and *kai-awhina rangatira* (chief helpers) were assigned to men and in the latter case women with the required skills as closely related to the person (or persons) honoured as possible.[1] At a *tangi*, the women most closely related to the deceased acted as "chief mourners", led by the closest or oldest among them, while the closest male kinsmen (except the elderly)

---

[1] The prefix *kai-* attached to a verb means "one who . . .".

dug the grave. The pall-bearers were sometimes close kin, but at some *tangi* places were allotted to more distant kin, such as third or fourth cousins, to representatives of the various *hapū* of the deceased's tribe, personal friends, or important local or visiting personalities. At weddings, the important roles of bridesmaids, groomsmen, flowergirls, waiters and waitresses were distributed among the effective kin of bride and groom on the basis of one to each family or "family line", their own siblings providing only one or two and sometimes foregoing the honour entirely in favour of more distant kin. At unveilings, the ties attaching the cover to the gravestone were loosed and the cover removed by someone genealogically close to and beloved by the deceased.

Apart from these specialised roles, kin of varying degrees differed from each other not so much in what they did for each other as in the amount of time, money, and energy they expended in doing it. Those who were close—in personal as well as genealogical terms—dropped in and out of each other's houses and performed small services for each other all the time, while more remote kin helped each other mainly on special occasions. The last obligation to be abrogated (usually long after those involved had ceased visiting each other) was that of attending and contributing towards a *tangi*.

Subject to variation according to the closeness of the relationship, the Maoris of Kōtare largely succeeded in carrying out their ideals of how kin ought to behave to each other, particularly in relation to those living in Kōtare and adjoining districts. It was their boast that they could always provide a meal or a bed for kinsmen who "dropped in" without notice; children and adolescents in particular frequently ate and slept in the homes of kinsfolk, and housewives always cooked more than their family needed "in case of visitors". Whenever anyone went to the beach to gather shellfish, dug his sweet potato crop or hauled a load of firewood down from the hills, he distributed part of the harvest to one or more kinsmen, and sacks of sweet potatoes and corn were sent off by bus to others in the city. Most local Maoris put in an appearance at *hui* sponsored by kin, helping with the work and contributing to the expenses in such numbers that only the closest kin were really burdened by either. At the same time, they did not hesitate to ask kin for labour, transport, produce, or company when they had need of them. Kinsfolk could be expected to spring to each other's defence, even in situations in which kinship was ostensibly unimportant. Kin who were close friends and perhaps also neighbours sometimes formed cliques within non-kin clubs.

My informants in Kōtare often grumbled about the demands made on them by "relations" (*whanaunga*), both in general and in particular. They complained that family photographs, bottles of jam and pickles, and other small treasures disappeared without trace if they did not hide them; that they were "expected to drop everything and neglect our families to work flat out at the *marae*"; and that everyone always knew their private business. But they readily admitted that these were small considerations compared with the benefits received from kin. They were never at a loss for kinsmen to turn to for help. In particular, they were grateful for the assurance that, on important occasions in *their* life, their kin would rally round in large numbers, sharing not only the work and expense, but also their joy or grief. This was especially important at a time of death. As Maoris, they felt that a poor attendance at a *tangi* in the family was a very great misfortune.

The fulfilment of kinship obligations was thus strongly sanctioned by the threat of withdrawal of support. This threat was usually made explicit only by parents impressing the proper behaviour upon their children. I was, however, told of one man who was forced into parting with two good milking cows for a *tangi* by first cousins who threatened to boycott the next *tangi* in his immediate family. The sanction was not usually carried to this extreme of social blackmail. Most people realised themselves that they had to give help if they were to receive it when they needed it. Besides, their own conscience endorsed the "right" behaviour in this regard. They felt guilty when they failed to act as Maoris should, even when prevented by circumstances beyond their control, such as illness. And they were afraid of being accused of having "lost their Maori *aroha* (love)".

Even when the deceased or his family had alienated the sympathy of their kin or the community at large, Maoris in Kōtare did not in fact stay away from *tangi*. Their sense of duty was too strong, and death (they felt) absolved a man's faults. Besides, when it came to the point, disapproval was usually outweighed by other considerations: curiosity, the lure of "a feed of Maori *kai*" (food), interest in oratory in the traditional Maori style, and frank enjoyment of large gatherings.

KINSHIP TERMINOLOGY

Most of the Maoris in Kōtare were familiar with and themselves often used the traditional Maori kinship terminology.[1] Even those who spoke little Maori knew most of the terms and their application. For they understood more of the language than they could speak, and they also heard them used by the elders, who interlarded their English speech with Maori words, especially those for which there was no precise equivalent.

The most striking feature of Maori kinship terminology was the lateral extension of classificatory terms in each generation (defined on a genealogical and not an age basis). Thus each *Ego* extended the terms *matua* (father) and *whaea* (mother), according to sex, to kin of the same generation as his parents, *tupuna* (grandparent of either sex) to those of his grandparents' generation, *tamaiti* (child), *tama* (son) and *tamahine* (daughter) to the children of kin of his own generation, and *mokopuna* (grandchild) to *their* children. In his own generation, a man used the term *tuahine* for his sisters and his female cousins, a woman *tungāne* for her brothers and

[1] Buck, 1949, pp. 338–43.

male cousins. But with regard to siblings of the same sex, both men and women made a distinction between those older and younger than themselves, using the terms *tuakana* and *teina* respectively. These terms also were extended to cousins of the same sex and generation, but on the basis of seniority of descent not of absolute age: thus *tuakana* was used by a man for the sons and by a woman for the daughters of *matua* and *whaea* senior to their own parent, and *teina* for those whose parents were junior. Elders versed in genealogy often used the reciprocals *tuakana-teina* and *matua-tamaiti* (in the sense of uncle-nephew) in describing relationships not only between individuals but also between family groups and *hapū* (sub-tribes), where their founding ancestors stood in that relationship to one another.

Many of these terms were also used symbolically to describe role rather than exact relationship. Kinsfolk as a group regularly applied the term *matua* to certain older men among them, though in a strict sense they were *matua* only to some, belonging to the same generation as others or to that of their grandparents. The term was thus extended to those who were recognised as filling a fatherly role, protecting, guiding, and if necessary disciplining younger kinsmen. In this sense, *matua* was synonymous with *kaumātua* (elder), except that it emphasised the kinship link. (In Kōtare in 1955 *kaumātua* was commonly used for elders in general, whether related to the speaker or not: those wishing to indicate kinship as well used *matua* or referred to "my (or our) *kaumātua*".) In the same way *whaea* was used interchangeably with *kuia* (elderly woman). (In the singular, *kaumātua* was reserved for men, and *kuia* used as its feminine equivalent; but *kaumātua* in the plural might include women.) Occasionally a very elderly and venerated person of either sex was called "our *tupuna*" by younger kinsmen (including own offspring). Conversely, older persons sometimes used *tamaiti* and its plural *tamariki* to refer to younger kin— "the young people"—as well as for their real and classificatory children.

Even in their use of English kinship terms, the Kōtare Maoris revealed the persistence of Maori concepts. They used many English terms in ways which differed from standard Pakeha practice, having acquired them in childhood from parents more at home in Maori. They commonly used *uncle* and *aunt* for those (other than parents) whom they called *matua* and *whaea* in Maori, thus including many who were properly cousins at various removes. They used *grandfather* and *grandmother* for all whom they called *tupuna*, *niece* and *nephew* for the children of cousins of their own generation as well as those of siblings, and *grandson* and *granddaughter* for the children of nieces and nephews as well as their own grandchildren. Thus it happened that a childless widow once spoke to me of her grandchildren, and an only child of his numerous nieces and nephews. They used *cousin* in two ways: in the Maori sense for cousins of the same generation (whom they occasionally referred to as *brother* or *sister*), and without qualification in what they understood to be the Pakeha usage, for all kinsmen other than those belonging to *Ego*'s elementary-family or grand-family. The expression "*Maori cousin*" was in great vogue. It was used in speaking to Pakehas to refer to kinsmen whom it was believed Pakehas would consider too remote to recognise, and in speaking to other Maoris for distant kin, especially those with whom they could not trace every step in the chain of relationship.

The lateral extension of kin terms, carried over as it was into English, made it easy for distant kin to be assimilated to the status and roles of close kin where the latter were lacking or personal attachment was strong. Terminological distinctions between generations were linked with a strong tendency towards age grading in the community at large, the use of the same terms for paternal and maternal kin with the absence of any patterned distinction between the two "sides" (as they were called in Kōtare). Finally, the way in which *tuakana* and *teina* were applied outside the elementary-family indicated an interest in descent, as distinct from other kinds of kin relationships, even within the kindred.

DESCENT-LINES
Whakapapa

To my informants in Kōtare, descent first of all meant *whakapapa*— literally, genealogy or descent-line, but also, generically, the study of genealogies. A *whakapapa* traced descent from a given ancestor to a living descendant, through a single link (male or female) in each generation. As one of the Kōtare *kaumātua* defined it for me, "a *whakapapa* is a single line going straight back—it is only how it affects you". Each individual had not one but an array of possible *whakapapa*, varying with the ancestor chosen as starting-point and the links chosen in each generation. Each *whakapapa* started with a person of distinction and of historic or legendary importance: the founder of a tribe or sub-tribe or a *rangatira* (aristocrat) living in Hawaiiki (the legendary Maori homeland). Thus a Maori's *whakapapa* linked him with famous figures and events in the ancient Maori past, giving depth to his social identity.

Whakapapa were vitally important in establishing rights in Maori land and in making claims for assistance from tribal funds to tribal Trust Boards. They were quoted during speeches on the *marae*, when welcoming visitors, or in order to demonstrate the high rank of the person (or persons) honoured, or the speaker's relationship to him.

In Kōtare in 1955, only six men were really expert in *whakapapa*. All in their sixties or older, they had been instructed or had inherited "*whaka-papa* books" from a *matua* or *tupuna*. Most adults confessed to knowing only a fraction of what they should. Those over thirty usually knew the salient facts of their own *whakapapa*, but few could recite even one in full without prompting. When necessary, they went to the experts for help.

In his *whakapapa* books, each expert kept records of his own *whakapapa* and those of other descendants of the previous owner (including some

A PAGE FROM A WHAKAPAPA BOOK

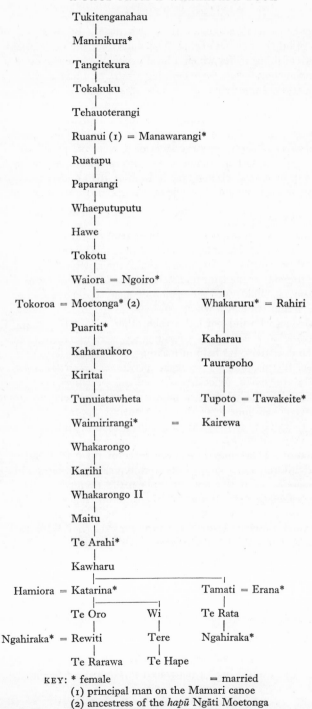

Tukitenganahau
|
Maninikura*
|
Tangitekura
|
Tokakuku
|
Tehauoterangi
|
Ruanui (1) = Manawarangi*
|
Ruatapu
|
Paparangi
|
Whaeputuputu
|
Hawe
|
Tokotu
|
Waiora = Ngoiro*
|_____|
Tokoroa = Moetonga* (2)   Whakaruru* = Rahiri
| |
Puariti*   Kaharau
|
Kaharaukoro   Taurapoho
| |
Kiritai   Tupoto = Tawakeite*
|
Tunuiatawheta
|
Waimirirangi*   =   Kairewa
|
Whakarongo
|
Karihi
|
Whakarongo II
|
Maitu
|
Te Arahi*
|
Kawharu
|_____|
Hamiora = Katarina*   Tamati = Erana*
|_____| |
Te Oro   Wi   Te Rata
| | |
Ngahiraka* = Rewiti   Tere   Ngahiraka*
| |
Te Rarawa   Te Hape

KEY: * female   = married
(1) principal man on the Mamari canoe
(2) ancestress of the *hapū* Ngāti Moetonga

FIG. 4. With the permission of Te Rarawa Pateriki Kerehoma of Te Rarawa
(*hapū* Ngati Moetonga)

relating them to ancestors outside their own tribe), the most important *whakapapa* of other branches of their *hapū* and tribe, and perhaps also the main "lines" of other tribes which a local expert ought to know. For the sake of convenience, *whakapapa* deriving from the same ancestor were grouped together. Important tribal *whakapapa* and those relating to the expert and his siblings were written out in full, often including the names of spouses and siblings of those chosen as links in particular generations. Other *whakapapa*, written in the margins or on subsequent pages, and often in abbreviated form, gave the anterior descent of spouses and lines stemming from siblings thus named. Sometimes, space permitting, lines were traced from several siblings, rarely in more than one or two generations at once and usually only over the four to six most recent generations. It was significant that female links figured largely on many of the *whakapapa* in these books (see Fig. 4).

Having mastered the *whakapapa* in their books (and often others) by memory, the experts were able, at short notice, to trace the descent of a wide range of persons, including many outside their own effective kindred, back to the founder of the tribe and to various other ancestors; to indicate which person or "line" was the senior in many specific situations and often in *hapū* and tribe as a whole; and also to demonstrate relationship between persons who did not know each other as kin, by tracing them back to a common ancestor. As a result, they were much in demand for advice on land matters, for help in making out claims for assistance from tribal Trust Boards, and as speakers on the *marae* when there were visitors to be welcomed, especially at *tangi* and weddings.

These custodians of *whakapapa* knowledge were reluctant to transmit it to younger generations who (they felt) did not appreciate it properly. The books themselves were regarded as *tapu* ("sacred", not to be handled without due ceremony), kept in some special place and rarely brought out for examination. There may have been more of them in Kōtare than I knew. The children and young adults were typically uninterested in such knowledge and evaded the few attempts made to instruct them. The middle-aged showed signs of a developing interest, but not to the extent of spending much time in study. Mostly they "picked it up" by listening to the experts during *hui*. At one stage during my stay in Kōtare, two of the experts decided to hold a "*whakapapa* school" on the *marae* on Sunday afternoons. They insisted on the observance of *tapu* to the extent of forbidding smoking, but allowed notes to be taken. The school met twice, attended by nine and eleven pupils respectively, including the experts' wives; all were over forty years of age. It was discontinued as a result of a misunderstanding between one of the experts and the *marae* committee.

Rank

In pre-European Maori society, rank depended on descent. Those who belonged to the senior "line" (that traced through the eldest male link in

PLATE 3. (a) A farm-house built in the course of State-sponsored land development; and (b) a new house and the 'bach' it replaces. See pp. 42, 43.

PLATE 4. (*a*) The *marae*: speech-making at a *hui*.
(*b*) Inside the meeting-house: a Tribal Committee meeting.
See pp. 74, 76, 86–8.

every generation) in *iwi* or *hapū* were of *rangatira* (aristocratic) rank. In any given situation involving kinsfolk, precedence and leadership were accorded those whose descent was senior to that of the rest. In Kōtare in 1955, rank did not seem to be very prominent either in kin-groups or in the community at large. Precedence was accorded certain elders whenever they were present, but it was not clear if it was on the basis of their descent or their personal ascendancy. No-one was prepared to rank these elders in any order of seniority. Many of the most effective leaders were not the most senior available. And in practice the older kinsman always took precedence over the younger, even if the latter belonged to a senior line.

DESCENT-GROUPS

The Kōtare Maoris accepted as axiomatic the fact that all Maoris belonged by birth and descent to one or more *iwi* (tribe) and *hapū* (sub-tribe). These groups they knew to consist of the descendants of a founding ancestor who had lived and died either in Hawaiiki or in New Zealand before the coming of the Pakeha. Both groups were frequently identified by the personal name of their ancestor after the prefix Ngāti- (descendants of), though Te Rarawa, the tribe to which most of the Maoris in Kōtare belonged, bore a name associated with a particular event in its history.[1]

My informants also used the term *whānau* to refer to certain groups of effective kin which were recognised within the community as having corporate identity and some corporate functions.[2] Careful study of the groups thus described established that they were in fact descent-groups, but of a much more extensive kind than the patriarchal extended-family to which the term was applied in pre-European times.[3] The self-same groups were as often described as *hapū*, though they were much smaller in depth and extent than the "sub-tribe" to which that term was usually applied. In English they were always referred to as "families". In view of the confusion over the Maori terms, I propose to adopt this latter usage, especially as the groups concerned differed in many respects from their pre-European prototypes. (From now on, when using "family" in this special technical sense, I shall place it in single inverted commas.)

As descent-groups, *iwi*, *hapū* and 'family' all cross-cut the kindred. Each individual had some effective kin outside each descent-group to which he belonged. By definition, every Maori was linked to the founder of his tribe and *hapū* by an unbroken line of forebears. In Kōtare in 1955, few adults knew by heart the *whakapapa* that validated their claim to membership in particular *iwi* and *hapū*: the majority simply inherited or "followed" the tribal and sub-tribal membership of their parents. But they could always obtain the details from their family books or from the experts.

Theoretically, a tribe contained several *hapū*, whose ancestors were

---

[1] Buck, p. 335.
[2] Kindreds cannot act as corporate groups because they differ for every individual.
[3] See p. 9.

descended from the tribal ancestor, and each *hapū* contained several 'families' whose progenitors were descended from the *hapū* ancestor. Apart from the experts, the people of Kōtare were extremely hazy about the structural relations between the three groups. Because of the practice of deriving membership directly from parents and because of the variety of factors which could influence each individual's choice among several possibilities, it was not uncommon for first and second cousins who were active members of the same 'family' to claim to belong to different *hapū*.

When they talked about "belonging" to any of these descent-groups, the Maoris of Kōtare could mean one of three things: (1) that a person had the right to claim membership in the group because he was descended from its founder, whether he knew or acknowledged it or not; (2) that he himself publicly claimed to belong to it; and (3) that he acted as an effective member whenever or on most occasions that the opportunity occurred. However, the larger the group, the fewer opportunities existed for backing up verbal claims to membership with action.

Iwi, hapū and 'family' were not exclusive units. If a person's parents belonged to different groups at any level, it was not considered necessary to make a choice between them: one could belong to two or even more at once. In theory a person could claim membership in any descent-group to which one of his forebears belonged; but in practice only the experts did so for forebears further back than grandparents. Even so, because their parents had inherited double membership from their grandparents, many could claim to belong to three or four groups at any level. Most claimed membership in fewer groups than they could. When asked to name their *iwi, hapū* or 'family', they gave only a single name or at most two, specifying e.g. "Ngati A on my father's side and Ngati P on my mother's". These were the groups in which they acted most consistently as members. But in addition they recalled membership in one or two others for short periods on special occasions and for special purposes, when it was to their social or economic advantage—when trying to establish friendly relations with a stranger who belonged to one of them, when applying for financial assistance from group funds, or when special marks of honour were accorded their members, as in the flower ceremony at weddings or the choosing of pall-bearers at a *tangi*.

The reasons why a Kōtare Maori chose to acknowledge membership in any given descent-group, either for general purposes or on a specific occasion, were numerous and varied. They differed in combination and relative weight from one person to another, so that even in the same family one or two siblings often made a different choice from the rest. There was a slight bias in favour of patrilateral affiliation (preferred in the traditional system), but affiliation through females was so common as to cause no comment. The most consistently important consideration was the comparative advantages offered by the groups concerned, not only in economic terms (i.e. access to land and financial assistance) but also in terms of the prestige or precedence conferred on their members in given situations. But the decision was also affected by the accessibility of the group, the nature and degree of past association with other members, accidents of kinship knowledge (and ignorance), and personal likes and dislikes.

Descent-group affiliation in Kōtare is not easy to classify because it does not fit any of the standard categories. It could be described as largely bilateral for any given person in the most recent one or two generations— largely and not wholly, because membership in some of those theoretically available was often forgotten, and because there was a tendency to rank in an order of preference the groups in which it was acknowledged. When a person died, his heirs usually professed membership in the group to which he gave first preference and forgot the others, so that a continual weeding out took place. In earlier generations, affiliation *appeared* to be ambilateral, that is, through one parent in each generation if they belonged to different groups. In pre-European times, a Maori whose parents belonged to different groups at any level had to choose which he would validate by continued residence and participation in group activities.[1] He depended on the *whānau*, *hapū* and *iwi* he chose for his right to land, his livelihood, and his social status, for companionship, protection from enemy attack, and revenge if wronged. But reversal of choice was possible and probably more common than is usually recognised, and a man's children or grandchildren could and did revive his rights in the groups he did not choose. In short, affiliation could be described as ambilateral in *effect* rather than in fact.

Under modern conditions, a Maori does not need to make any choice among the descent-groups open to him, except for the sake of convenience and brevity. Much less depends upon any choice he does make, or any preference he bestows than in pre-European times. In Kōtare in 1955, every adult obtained from other sources most of what his forebears obtained from the descent-group. The aims and functions of descent-groups were limited in scope and largely "occasional", i.e. associated with special occasions. A host of new factors had come in to affect what general choices were made, to enable many individuals to act as members of two or more groups at once, and to prevent some from belonging effectively to any descent-groups at all.

Te Iwi

Every Maori in Kōtare belonged to an *iwi*, and many to more than one. Membership in a tribe was regarded as axiomatic. Individuals derived their tribal membership in the first place from their parents, but they knew that their descent could be traced right back to the tribal ancestor, by the experts if they could not do it themselves. No legal procedure was required (or existed) to establish tribal affiliation.

The *tāngata whenua* of Kōtare belonged by definition to Te Rarawa,

[1] Firth, 1959, p. 114.

since Kōtare lay in the territory which that tribe occupied (by right of conquest) when its chiefs signed the Treaty of Waitangi in 1840. Many spouses married to *tāngata whenua* and many 'immigrant' settlers were also Rarawa. But 13 per cent of the Maoris in Kōtare (fifty-one adults and twenty-one children) gave their primary allegiance to other tribes: there were twelve Aupouri, nine Ngāti Kahu, twenty-eight Ngāpuhi and fourteen Ngāti Whātua from the Northland tribes; five from the Waikato and two from Taranaki tribes; an Arawa and a Ngāti Awa (see Fig. 9). Some of those from other tribes could lay claim to a Rarawa forebear, but he was usually too remote to affect their loyalty to the tribe to which most of their forebears belonged or to assure them of acceptance by Te Rarawa should they wish it. Of those normally reckoned as Rarawa roughly half also belonged to other tribes. They emphasised their membership when travelling in the territory of the tribe or tribes concerned, when meeting others belonging to them, and at gatherings (even in Kōtare) when their representatives were specially honoured. As one *kaumātua* explained: "I call myself Rarawa here in Kōtare among my mother's people, and when I go to Ngāti Kahu, my father's people, I call myself Ngāti Kahu."

For the Kōtare Maoris, the tribe was largely an abstract concept. Tribal membership carried few or no material advantages and no specific obligations. Such land as they held was inherited from their parents (through the Maori Land Court) or purchased on the open market. Most did not depend on Maori land for their livelihood anyway. Many tribes had tribal trust funds administered by a Trust Board of elected tribal members; these were built up by investment from money from the sale of non-individualised tribal land, compensation for land confiscated by the Crown or taken for roading and for reserves, and income from land legally vested in the Trust Board. Te Rarawa had no such fund in 1955. Some half dozen families in Kōtare with rights in other tribes had at some time applied for and received grants from tribal Trust Boards, mainly in connection with the advanced education of their children. Such payments were usually under £50 per year. In this twentieth century, under the rule of a national system of law and order, the tribe was not called upon to protect the persons or the property of its members. The latter for their part were never required to take up arms to defend its territory or its honour. They did not contribute directly to its wealth nor to the support of its leaders.

What then did tribal membership mean to Maoris living in Kōtare? It gave them, first, a connection with important and exciting figures and events in the classical Maori past and, secondly, a defined place in the modern Maori social world. Those who belonged to the "home tribe", Te Rarawa, derived a particular feeling of security from "being among their own (people)". They also had certain ceremonial duties and privileges. In Rarawa territory generally they stood in the same relation to members of other tribes as *tāngata whenua* to 'immigrants' in Kōtare.

They took ceremonial precedence and supplied the "proper" leaders at Maori gatherings and in Maori affairs in general in the tribal area, and also in formal relations with outside groups (Maori and Pakeha). Tribal loyalty sometimes led them to discriminate against local members of other tribes whom they classified as "outsiders". Traditional hostilities and grievances were revived when individuals fell out for any cause. But the lines of tribal division were blurred by ties of kinship and friendship. During *hui*, non-Rarawa were singled out for special honour as representatives of their respective tribes. In general, the Rarawa, being the hosts and in the majority, felt it neither necessary nor becoming to be aggressive towards members of other tribes living in Kōtare.

An interesting light was cast on tribal loyalty (and on the importance of football in modern Maori life) by the fact that the local Rugby football club had adopted the tribal name of Te Rarawa, in spite of protests from the elders. The club had become in some measure a focus for tribal sentiment in Kōtare, largely for want of any other. When playing outside Rarawa territory, club members tended to regard themselves as champions of the tribal honour. But this attitude could not be sustained inside the Rarawa area, because the club had several Pakeha and non-Rarawa players and, though it drew a few players from beyond Kōtare, many more Rarawa played for competing clubs.

The Rarawa tribe, to which most Kōtare Maoris belonged, held no corporate assets, lacked centralised leadership and never took concerted action. Much of the land it had owned in pre-European times was now in Pakeha hands and the rest was held individually or by groups of its members. It held no money or land in trust. Instead of a single chief, it recognised a number of leaders living in many different communities within the tribal territory. These tribal *kaumātua* (elders) were all men in their fifties or older, who had claims to superior descent in the tribe and were further qualified by an extensive knowledge of *whakapapa* and Maori tradition and by ability as orators. None was recognised as of higher rank than the others. One particular community *marae* was identified as "*the* Rarawa marae" on historical grounds, but it was neither large nor well equipped and received no financial support from outside its own community. It did not seem to be used more often than other fairly accessible Rarawa *marae* for discussions of tribal significance.

Only a fraction of the tribe assembled on any given occasion and members of other tribes and Pakehas were never excluded. Tribal gatherings were rarely called as such. The Department of Maori Affairs called occasional public meetings (on different *marae* or in a hired hall in Raumati) to sound tribal opinion or explain policy; these often included the neighbouring and related tribes of Aupouri and Ngāti Kahu and were attended mainly by the elders and those personally affected by the issue under discussion. Tribal matters were generally discussed during *hui* called for other purposes on *marae* throughout the tribal territory, especially at *tangi*. The tribal elders and those aspiring to tribal leadership made a point of attending most of the larger *hui* on Rarawa *marae*, and also represented Te Rarawa at major *hui* in the territory of adjoining tribes. Certain subjects cropped up at one *hui* after another, in particular the prevention of alienation of Maori land, advanced education for Maori children, and the preservation of traditional knowledge. These discussions were never brought to a decisive close, nor did they lead to concrete tribal action. But by this means members of the tribe kept in touch with each other's thinking and tribal opinion slowly crystallised.

Te Hapū

The *hapū* was also an abstract concept to the Kōtare Maoris. They appreciated that it was necessary to belong to one, but were rather hazy as to its definition, except that it was smaller than and contained within the tribe. They knew that certain *hapū* were Rarawa *hapū*, certain others Ngāpuhi *hapū*, and so on. Most informants said that they "followed" the *hapū* membership of their parents. Where their mother and father belonged to different *hapū*, they claimed membership in both if pressed, but stressed one most of the time.

None of the *hapū* to which Kōtare Maoris belonged acted at any time as a recognisable social group. There were no clubs or committees formed on a *hapū* basis, no gatherings sponsored by *hapū*. Even their names were not often mentioned in conversation except among experts. In a public context, they seemed to be important only in the "flower ceremony" at weddings. In this ceremony, the Master of Ceremonies "called" one by one the names of the tribes and *hapū* represented among the guests and presented a slice of cake wrapped in a paper napkin and ornamented with a favour (properly a flower) from the cake to a representative of each group. Once, I was told, claimants for a "flower" had to prove their right to represent their group by reciting their *whakapapa*, and challenges from others claiming superior descent made the ceremony exciting and instructive. But in Kōtare in 1955 the ceremony was little more than an entertainment for the children. Many guests did not bother even to watch; favours were sometimes called without being claimed; and instead of giving their *whakapapa*, claimants "sang for their flower", usually in the modern, popular style. There was no standard list of *hapū*, even for the Rarawa tribe. The lists used on specific occasions were tailored to fit the guests and usually included some of the larger and most active local 'families'.

The *hapū* was divorced to a far greater extent than either the tribe or the 'family' from its former territorial base. No tract of land in Kōtare was identified with a particular *hapū*, nor were any of the *marae*. Even the oldest inhabitants, detailing to me who "belonged" to Kōtare, gave me a list of 'families' and not *hapū*.

The 'Family'

Before I went there, several Auckland informants who came from Kōtare told me that the Maori community there consisted of "a dozen or so families—the Tīmotis, the Browns, the Samuels, the Hohaias" and some six to ten others identified, in the same way, by a surname. In Kōtare itself, I heard constant references in the same terms to thirteen distinct 'families', though no-one had ever reckoned up just how many there were. All these 'families' were basically of *tangata whenua* stock, though some 'immigrants' were associated with each by marriage or fostering. The 'immigrant' settlers had not been living in Kōtare long enough to have formed any of their own.

One of the most prominent of the Kōtare 'families' was that known as "the Samuels family" (see Fig. 5). I soon learnt that most of those said to belong to this 'family' bore the surname of Matthews! Inquiry revealed that the name Samuels was derived from Hamiora Waimangu, who had been dead some fifty years; the 'family' was known collectively by an anglicised version of his given (i.e. first) name because his sons had used it (in accordance with old Maori custom) as their surname. (Hamiora's second name was *his* father's given name.) I also found that the people made a distinction between the "real" members of the 'family' and those whom they had married or fostered. The "real" members all proved to be descended from Hamiora, through both male and female links. The 'family' was occasionally referred to in Maori as "*te uri o Hamiora*" (the descendants of Hamiora). The offspring of Hamiora's daughters and granddaughters seemed to predominate in the 'family', especially those of his daughter Rongopai, who had married Nika Matthews. Hence the paradox of a "Samuels family" composed largely of Matthews's!

The other 'families' in Kōtare followed the same general pattern, though the predominance of female links was not usually so marked. Excluding spouses and foster children, the members of each could be traced back bilaterally to one progenitor, usually a parent, grandparent, or at most great-grandparent of the oldest, who remembered him personally. None of the Kōtare 'families' was more than approximately seven generations in depth or included more than three generations of deceased persons.

The progenitor had in every case lived in Kōtare and was believed to have handed on rights in Maori land there. According to the experts, three had really been 'immigrants' and the land held by their descendants derived from their wives, but in the popular mind these facts had been obscured by the passage of time. Hamiora himself had been an 'immigrant', but in this case his descendants had kept the knowledge alive. They explained that his wife's mother's brother Aperahama, who "was a big chief here in those days", had adopted him as his heir. The Samuels 'family' inherited their land from Aperahama through Hamiora, the succession having been legalised through the Maori Land Court.

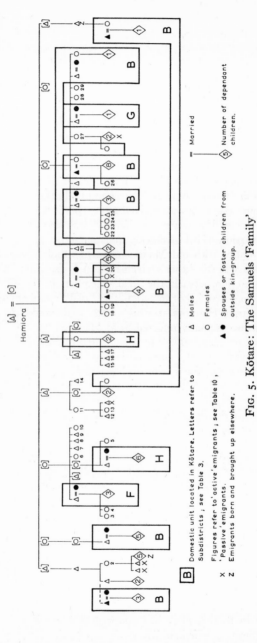

FIG. 5. Kōtare: The Samuels 'Family'

The Samuels 'family' alone of all the Kōtare 'families' sometimes identified itself by what its members described as "a *hapū* name", Ngāti T——. It was the name of the *hapū* to which Aperahama had belonged. The ancestor whose name it bore was a remote one, more than six generations before Aperahama. The *hapū* name itself was used now only by this group, who had inherited it from Aperahama through his niece, Hamiora's wife.

Within each 'family', there were a number of "branches", each stemming from a living elder or one only recently deceased, a son, daughter or grandchild of the 'family' progenitor. In those 'families' in which the progenitor was most remote from the living, these branches were usually large and sometimes acted independently of each other. In each case, it seemed certain that, with the death of those who had known the progenitor, the branches would establish complete independence, becoming new 'families' in their own right. Such segmentation had clearly occurred in Kōtare in the past, for several 'families' stemmed from progenitors who were siblings or closely related. The Samuels 'family', for instance, was connected with the Aranga and Iraia 'families', which stemmed from Hamiora's wife's brothers. 'Families' related in this way felt a special bond and turned to each other first for help in situations which they could not handle alone—for instance, when short-handed at a *hui*.

The Kōtare Maoris were emphatic that all descendants of a 'family' progenitor belonged to the 'family' of right, whether they lived in Kōtare or elsewhere. Only legal adoption by someone outside the 'family' cancelled out membership.

But only a proportion of those who "really belonged" to a 'family' in theory were active as members at any given time. In the first place, participation in 'family' affairs was entirely voluntary. A few living in Kōtare held aloof from 'family' doings, on account of ill health, age or temperament. In most cases, their role and obligations were filled by a spouse or offspring. Secondly, those who in every generation left Kōtare to settle elsewhere were cut off from continuous participation. Most kept in touch by letters and visits, coming home specially for 'family' *hui*, when they took part as if they had never been away. Their offspring were immediately accepted when they visited or settled in Kōtare. But emigrants who failed to maintain their interest in the 'family' and in Kōtare were eventually forgotten.

At the same time, spouses and foster children, who never became 'real' members of the 'family', took full part in its activities, especially when living in Kōtare. They contributed to 'family' burial funds, served as officers in 'family' clubs and shared fully in 'family' discussions and in the work involved in 'family' *hui*. They could be described as *attached* members. The only role closed to them, in all but exceptional circumstances, was that of spokesman for the 'family' in public.

Thus while the 'family' could be defined in *structural* terms as a bilateral descent-group of shallow depth which segmented every one or two generations, in terms of *organisation* and *action* it consisted of all those descendants of its progenitor present in the community at any given time, together with their accompanying or widowed spouses and foster children, in so far as any chose to take part.

Because 'family' membership was bilateral, every Maori in Kōtare belonged at least potentially to more than one 'family', including some associated with other districts. 'Families' over-lapped each other both in structure and in organisation. Most Kōtare Maoris fulfilled at least some of the obligations attached to 'family' membership for each parent's 'family' (or 'families') and also for the 'family' into which they married. But usually they attached themselves most closely to one. Some indeed— by no means all women—gave most in terms of labour, time and money to the 'family' into which they had married, to the comparative neglect of those into which they had been born. The choice made between different 'families' was neither final, exclusive nor irreversible. Rather it constituted a ranging of possibilities in an order of preference which could be altered, temporarily or permanently, by circumstances and by personal decision.

In choosing which of the 'families' open to him should command the greatest share of his loyalty, money and energy, an adult in Kōtare was influenced by many considerations: where he lived in Kōtare in relation to the other members, how long and how well he knew them, whether his parents were still alive and which 'family' they favoured, how strongly his wife was attached to her parents, and, most important of all, the relative solidarity of the 'families' concerned. 'Families' which co-operated frequently and successfully, especially those which ran 'family clubs' or 'family *marae*', not only held their real members but also attracted most spouses and foster children into active participation.

Two illustrations from the Samuels 'family', one of the most unified in the district, should prove helpful here. The Matthews siblings, children of Nika Matthews and his wife Rongopai (Hamiora's daughter), were very strongly attached to their mother's 'family'; they nearly all lived in Hākea on land inherited from Hamiora, and were the backbone of the *komiti* which ran the Samuels 'family' *marae*, where they held their *tangi* and other *hui*. But one of the brothers occupied a farm in Karaka inherited through his father, all stressed their Matthews descent at weddings and *tangi* sponsored by the Matthews's, and when the youngest brother married in 1955 one bridesmaid and one groomsman were chosen from the Matthews 'family'. At the same time, two of the hardest workers at any gathering sponsored by the Samuels 'family' were two brothers. Tama and Pita Timoti, neither of whom were "real" members. Tama had been brought up in the 'family' by Mita Samuels and his wife, who was Tama's father's sister; while Pita had married one of Rongopai's daughters. Both lived on Samuels land close to other Samuels households and were subscribing members of the Samuels *komiti marae*. Yet both gave occasional service to their father and their father's 'family' in another part of Kōtare.

The Kōtare 'family' held little or no land in common, its members did not co-operate in economic production, nor did they all live together or even near each other. The land associated with any given 'family' and derived from its progenitor was divided into several holdings legally registered through the Maori Land Court in the names of certain of his descendants, most of whom were elderly or deceased. It had, in short, been individualised at various times in the past, though the process had not been brought up to date and most of the present blocks were held by several co-owners. Though sometimes more than one occupied the land, only one (if any) farmed it, the rest taking individual employment. 'Family' members living in Kōtare were divided among a number of autonomous households—ten in the case of the Samuels 'family'. These households were scattered, sometimes widely, over the whole of Kōtare, for they did not all occupy 'family' land. Certain 'families', it is true, were identified in common speech with certain sub-districts: the Samuels 'family', for instance, with Hākea. But the correspondence between descent-group and locality was incomplete. One-third of the members of the Samuels 'family' living in Kōtare did not live in Hākea, and the other 'families' were even more scattered.

The 'family' acted as a group for certain restricted purposes and occasions, mainly in connection with the social crises of marriage, death and (to a lesser extent) coming of age. The 'family' of the person (or persons) honoured sponsored, organised and underwrote the cost of *tangi*, "unveilings", weddings, and twenty-first birthday parties. (In the case of weddings, the bride's 'family' and the groom's acted as joint sponsors, sharing expenses and work, while often several 'families' arranged a joint unveiling.) Some 'families' formed 'family clubs', with the aim of building up a 'family' fund as insurance against the cost of a *tangi*. Two owned and managed 'family *marae*'. The 'family' as a group was *not* concerned with the succour of individual members in need; in such cases, assistance was given individually and informally. 'Family' activities were "occasional" in both senses of the word and periodic, so that a person could take part in those of more than one 'family' without difficulty. No-one, however, belonged to more than one 'family' club: it was too expensive.

While all kinsmen of the person(s) honoured were expected to attend and assist at *hui*, those who belonged to the sponsoring 'family' were always much more deeply involved, both in the preparations beforehand and during the *hui* itself. The assistance given by other kin was generally less directed and less sustained. 'Family' clubs and *marae* committees occasionally included kin who did not belong to the 'family', but it was recognised by all parties that their inclusion was by courtesy and not by right.

It is significant that the 'family' did not handle the observance of all social crises, but only those which, according to Maori ideals, should be celebrated ceremonially on the *marae*. The *tomo* (the formal call paid by a young man and his kin to "ask for" a girl in marriage[1]) was attended by the close kin of the couple concerned, not by their 'families' in force. Religious *rites de passage*, such as baptism and confirmation, were recognised only informally. On the other hand, the *hui* usually sponsored by the 'family' were not all of traditional origin. Twenty-first birthday parties, "unveilings" and even weddings were based on ideas borrowed from the Pakeha. In every case, however, the ceremonial connected with them had been so adapted that it had a distinctive Maori flavour.

'Family' sponsored *hui* were not family gatherings in the usual sense, confined to 'family' members: they were on a large scale and open to the public, being held on the *marae* and not in the home. Formal invitations were considered unnecessary, though they were usually issued to Pakehas who could not accustom themselves to the Maori attitude on this point. Those who attended were provided with all meals during *tangi* (which usually lasted three days) and unveilings (one and a half to two days), and with one major meal at weddings and twenty-first birthday parties. Guests from a distance were given sleeping-places in the meeting house for one or two nights at most *hui* and for up to three at a *tangi*. The bereaved family were also accommodated at the latter, and many local people stayed for the discussions, which lasted into the early hours of the morning. There were at least three hundred guests at the weddings I attended and over five hundred at *tangi*.

Accounts paid in connection with such *hui* ranged from £10 to £30, but the real costs were much higher, because 'family' members made generous contributions in kind: live beasts for killing, sacks of vegetables, cans of cream, bottles of preserves and pickles, loads of firewood and hay, the use of trucks and tractors. They also lent table linen and tea towels, mattresses and pillows, and crockery and cutlery to supplement that supplied by the *marae* committee. Cash expenses were offset, however, by smaller donations in cash and kind from kin outside the 'family', by "*marae* money" from other guests, and by auctioning the surplus food after the last meal. (Cooked food from steam-ovens of Maori style always commanded a good price in Kōtare. Not even stores were carried over; in the case of a *tangi* it was traditionally believed that to do so was to invite another death.) 'Families' with 'family' funds drew heavily on them for *tangi* but only for small sums, if at all, for other *hui*. Any deficit was covered by special donations from 'family' members, those closest to the person honoured giving most as a matter of pride.

There was never any shortage of workers at *hui* in Kōtare. The organising and most of the labour was done by 'family' members, supported by other kin and friends. Only the closest kin and those directing operations

---

[1] *Tomo* is the Northern usage; south of Auckland the terms *tono* and *taumau* are both in use, the latter more specifically with reference to infant betrothal, which is practically unknown to-day; cf. Best, 1924, vol. i, pp. 454–60.

were on the scene all the time: the other workers came and went largely at their own convenience. Somewhere between fifty and a hundred were involved, especially at *tangi*. There were in fact far more workers than were really needed. They got in each other's way, duplicating some tasks and overlooking others. The people themselves recognised that there were 'always too many bosses'. Individuals were usually appointed to take charge of certain aspects of operations (the oven, the puddings, the serving, the washing of dishes), but their authority depended largely on personality. Last minute crises were almost invariable. A smaller band working to a carefully co-ordinated plan under centralised leadership would have completed what had to be done much more quickly. But getting the work done as quickly and efficiently as possible was *not* the workers' aim. They enjoyed working together in happy comradeship, and were not averse to spinning the pleasure out. Besides, they disliked plans that were "cut and dried" on principle, and they were proud of their ability to cope with emergencies as they arose. What did it matter if they were largely of their own making?

Most of the Kōtare 'families' organised their *hui* on an *ad hoc* basis. Members of some 'families' claimed that they were so used to working together that they did what had to be done without any formal planning or direction, the most experienced automatically assuming control of the catering, the ovens, the ceremonial, and so on. Other 'families' formed a *komiti* (committee) to meet the occasion, disbanding it afterwards. The only *komiti* of this kind which I actually saw in action was restricted to the older 'family' members closest to the deceased (see account of *tangi* on pp. 75-7).

Five 'families', however, had established *komiti* on a permanent basis, two in association with 'family' *marae* (*komiti marae*). These *komiti* comprised respectively 7, 15, 16, 26 and 31 subscribing members, including nine living in adjacent districts. Subscribers were mostly married and nearly all 'family' members, real or attached, though two *komiti* had accepted a couple of 'immigrant' kinsmen, who had asked if they might join. Only a few of the younger unmarried adults belonged to their 'family' *komiti*, but they worked at the gatherings it organised, along with 'family' emigrants home on a visit. The latter made occasional donations to *komiti* funds, sometimes a year's subscription in one payment. The subscribers elected a Chairman, Secretary and Treasurer, who kept minute and account books and acted as an executive committee in emergencies. Subscriptions were paid formally at meetings held, in theory, once a month. In practice, meetings were held over sometimes for several months if there was no other business. Subscriptions were usually 1s a head per month, but they were sometimes raised temporarily or special levies were imposed in order to build up a depleted fund. The money itself was deposited in a Post Office Savings Bank account. Discussion and individual speeches at meetings conformed to Maori rules of oratory and etiquette and were mostly in Maori (as were the minutes). The ordinary *komiti* (usually described as a 'family club') was formed primarily to handle *tangi* (the ceremonies associated with funerals), but it also organised 'family' *hui* in general. The *komiti marae* performed the same functions and also managed the 'family' *marae*, caring for buildings and grounds and arranging dates and terms of hire. Income from letting the *marae* was paid into the 'family' savings account, along with profits from dances run by the *komiti*, donations, and an occasional net gain from a *hui*, but an attempt was made to keep the *marae* fund separate from the 'family' fund proper in the account books. In all these permanent *komiti*, the 'family' fund was reserved as much as possible for the financing of 'family' funerals, though they made small payments not exceeding £5 from it as a donation to funerals involving kin outside the 'family' and to other 'family' *hui*. Otherwise these latter were financed at the time by special contributions from 'family' members.

It should be noted briefly that *komiti marae* were also commonly known as *komiti wāhine* (women's committee), though their membership was not confined to women. (The latter term was also used in referring to the committee, composed of *tāngata whenua* of several different 'families', which had formerly managed the central *marae*; originally composed entirely of women, it had included men in its latter days.) The men explained half-seriously that "the women do the work, that is why it is called a women's committee. They speak out only when they disagree with what we say." The women rarely raised their voices in *komiti* discussions; they preferred to let their menfolk speak for them, after briefing them at home. But they did speak when necessary, and they held most and sometimes all of the executive positions. The chief burden of preparing for a gathering fell on them because they were at home on weekdays.

None of the Kōtare 'families' was dominated by a single leader. Most, it is true, acknowledged one *kaumātua* (elder) as "head of the family", but whether he was accorded more than ceremonial precedence depended on the strength of his personality. It was generally agreed that the rightful head was the most senior male of the senior branch of the 'family', or at least the most senior available in Kōtare, but in practice primogeniture and seniority of descent were set aside in favour of superior command of the Maori language and traditions. Women were not usually recognised as head of a 'family' unless there was no male candidate. (After her brothers had all died, and in the absence of her eldest brother's son, Rongopai Matthews dominated the Samuels 'family' for some fifteen years prior to her death.) In Kōtare in 1955, several of those identified as heads of their respective 'families' failed to carry out even the ceremonial duties expected of them. Still respected for their past leadership, they were now handicapped by ill health or advanced age. Many others lacked confidence and ability. Only three provided their 'families' with really effective leadership and even their authority was far from absolute or unchallenged.

Significantly, the term *kaumātua*, which was reserved in classical Maori society for the heads of *whānau*, was now extended to all those members of the 'family' who were elders in age (not less than about fifty-five and preferably grandparents). The 'family' looked not only to the nominal head but to its elders in general for guidance and advice and for the performance of the appropriate ceremonial both in private and in public. They were expected to act as spokesmen for the 'family' in relation to other groups, and to do most of the speech-making at 'family' discussions. They were "the talkers" (*ngā kai-kōrero*), as distinct from "the workers" (*ngā kai-mahi*). But while they were always listened to with respect, the 'family' did not automatically accept their decisions or direction: 'family' matters were ultimately decided after full discussion by consensus of opinion among adult members. Attempts to establish control over the private lives of other members were firmly resisted. What influence the *kaumātua* were able to exert depended on the affection and respect which they could command and was naturally greatest where their own descendants were concerned.

The executive functions of leadership were mostly carried out by those in the middle generations. In 'family' *komiti*, a *kaumātua* was generally elected as Chairman, while the Secretary and Treasurer were workingmen or housewives in their forties. At 'family' *hui*, while the *kaumātua* spent their time listening to and making speeches, those of the parental generation directed and worked with the younger people in the preparation and serving of meals.

The occasion often modified the order of precedence and the allocation of roles in the 'family'. Kin closest to the person honoured were expected to play a prominent part as organisers and speakers, especially at *tangi*. In some cases the closest male relative, even when normally among the less important members, actually took precedence over *kaumātua* from other branches of the 'family'. It was usually at 'family' *hui* that young men (and women) made their maiden speech under the stress of strong emotion, and that older men made the transition from occasional speaker to *kaumātua*.

Although Kōtare 'families' conformed to a general pattern in their composition and functions, they varied considerably in size, in the frequency and effectiveness with which they acted as a group, and in the strength of their "family feeling". Some seemed to lack cohesion entirely until death brought their members together to organise the *tangi*. Several consisted of branches which sometimes took independent action and were only loosely linked together; these were clearly moving towards segmentation. But there were five in which 'family' solidarity was particularly strong, expressed in 'family' clubs or focused on 'family' *marae* inherited from earlier generations.

To sum up, the typical Kōtare 'family' was neither strongly unified nor centrally controlled. It was a cluster of autonomous elementary-families and individuals deriving from a common progenitor, according precedence and not power to one or more senior members, and held together largely by sentiment and by common action at the major social crises in the lives of its members. Membership in a 'family' provided the individual with a feeling of security and social identity. It made demands upon his money, time and labour, but it also assured him of large-scale assistance at the most important crises in his life and those of his dependents. Above all, it relieved him of anxiety over his responsibility as a Maori to honour his dead with a large and costly *tangi*.

'Family', whānau and hapū

As already noted (see page 55), the Kōtare Maoris used the Maori terms *whānau* and *hapū* interchangeably for the 'family'. It resembled the pre-European *whānau* in that it was a bilateral descent-group which periodically segmented; but it was characteristically larger and of greater genealogical depth, including two or three generations of deceased persons, and it was not the basic unit of daily living in terms either of domestic organisation or of economic production. On the other hand, the 'family' was not as large nor as deep as the sub-tribe with which the term *hapū* is usually associated and which formerly constituted the village community.

At this point, I would suggest that the standard practice of translating *hapū* as sub-tribe needs re-examination. It implies that all groups so called are major divisions within the tribe and of comparable importance. But in the accounts of traditional history preserved in Maori Land Court records and in other publications, Maori speakers and writers use *hapū* to describe descent-groups which vary widely in depth. Frequently the term is applied in the same sentence or paragraph to one group stemming from an ancestor (for example) ten generations back and to another stemming from an ancestor six generations back, who is himself a direct descendant of the first.[1] This means that the second *hapū* is contained within the first, since its members are all automatically members of the latter by descent. Thus instead of the standard threefold division into *iwi*, *hapū* and *whānau*, we should properly recognise a four-, five- or sixfold division involving several grades of *hapū*. The reality of such a division has been indicated in most authoritative works on pre-European Maori society, but how often or for what purposes *hapū* of minor order took corporate action has not been explored.[2] Some grew to be as large and powerful as groups of greater genealogical depth and established themselves as separate communities. Those which remained merely sub-groups within the village seem to have acted independently in respect of marriage arrangements and for compensation claims when they involved

[1] See *Minutes of the Investigation of the Title of Mokoia Island*, Book 2, 1916, pp. 9, 71–2; Best, 1925, vol. i, pp. 214–5.
[2] Firth, *op. cit.*, p. 113; Buck, *op. cit.*, p. 335.

other village members or those of lower rank. Perhaps also the larger *hapū* divided into smaller ones when it was necessary to set up temporary encampments at fishing and hunting grounds at a distance from the village.

The Kōtare 'family' was closest in structure and functions to a pre-European *hapū* of minor order. It had ceased to be a land-holding unit and its constituent households were scattered instead of grouped together, but in other respects it acted as a group in much the same way: that is, for certain restricted purposes and occasions only, notably those associated with marriage and death. If a Maori term must be found to describe the modern 'family', perhaps we could coin a phrase and call it *hapū-iti* (small *hapū*).

TWO KŌTARE HUI

In order to illustrate how kinship and descent provided the basis for the organisation of certain kinds of *hui* in Kōtare, I propose to end this chapter with accounts of a wedding and a funeral which I attended during my stay there. Each followed the general pattern of such gatherings, with minor variations due to the peculiar circumstances of the kin-groups involved.

The Matthews–Tātana Wedding

A Maori wedding in Kōtare had its real beginning in the *tomo*. When Mavis Tātana accepted Rob Matthews's proposal of marriage, Rob (whose parents were both dead) asked his eldest brother Manu to arrange a meeting with Mavis's 'family'. The time and date were fixed by letter and the *tomo* took place at the Tātana's home one Wednesday evening. It was attended by the closest kin on both sides, a total of twenty persons: on the girl's side, Mavis, her parents, her two sisters and their husbands (who lived outside Kōtare), and her father's sister's eldest son, Daniel Johnson, who was being groomed to take over the leadership of the Tātana 'family' from Mavis's father Pera; on the boy's side, Rob, four of his brothers, four sisters, one brother-in-law and two sisters-in-law, and a classificatory nephew (mother's sister's daughter's son). After formal greetings Manu Matthews "asked for" Mavis as a wife for Rob, her kin gave their consent, and the young couple were formally asked if they agreed. The date of the wedding was decided, and in which of the local churches the ceremony would take place. It was agreed that the *hui* should be held on the *marae* of the Samuels 'family', to which Rob and his siblings belonged.

Six more meetings were held between the *tomo* and the wedding; these were organised by the Samuels *komiti marae* and attended by an average of fifteen subscribing members, and by Pera Tātana and Dan Johnson representing the bride's side. Promises of contributions in cash and kind were recorded, grocery lists drawn up, *marae* equipment checked, and important aspects of the preparations (such as the placing and collecting of orders at the shops, the selection and slaughter of beasts for the oven, and the erection of tables in the hall) were entrusted to the various individuals present. The bridal attendants were chosen at an early meeting. Three bridesmaids, three groomsmen and a flower-girl were allotted to each side, which distributed them in a way that would "remember" the main lines in each of the 'families' to which bride or groom belonged. On the eve of the wedding, however, Pera's sister, arrived that day from her home three hundred miles away, publicly declared that she and her children would boycott the wedding unless her son was included among the groomsmen. After a battle royal, one of those already chosen was

OFFICIAL FAMILY WORKERS AT A KŌTARE WEDDING

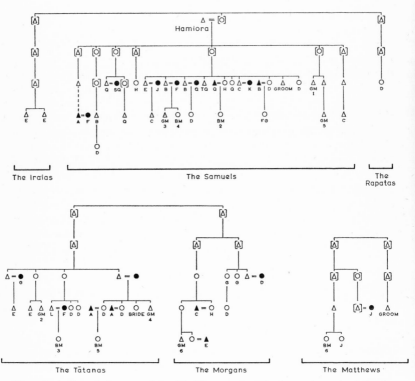

The principal symbols are explained in Fig. 5, p. 62. The letters have the following meanings: BM 1, 2, 3 *etc.*, bridesmaid; GM, groomsman; FG, flowergirl; A, tenders of *hangi*; B, carvers of meat; C, hot water carriers; D, waitresses; E, waiters; F, supervisors of children's table; G, canteen assistants; H, dish-washers; J, pudding servers; K, bread cutters; L, Tribal Committee Warden; Q, important members of *komiti marae* omitted from official list of workers for various reasons (see p. 73); S, Secretary, Samuels *komiti marae*; T, Treasurer, Samuels *komiti marae*. See Table 7, p. 274.

FIG. 6.

dropped in his favour. The Maori view construed her insistence as a compliment to the bride and as proper family feeling. The final choices are indicated in Fig. 6.

The Samuels 'family' assumed most of the initiative in arranging the wedding, being much larger and better organised than the Tātana 'family'. A high proportion of the latter's members had emigrated; there had been a breach between branches over a religious issue; and it had no permanent *komiti*. As a matter of pride, its members endeavoured to match the groom's side in contributions in cash and kind. They provided the three-tier wedding cake. On the wedding day and for the previous day of intensive preparations, their strength was augmented by the arrival of Pera's sister and her grown-up family and by workers drawn from a 'family' derived from a progenitor who was brother to their own.

On the eve of the wedding, many people turned up at the *marae* to help prepare the food and decorate the hall and the tables (see Plate 5, facing p. 86). Rather more than half belonged to either the Tātana or Samuels 'families' and another third were other kinsmen. A meeting of the *komiti marae* was held in the hall in the midst of the bustle. After three hours' heated discussion, in which everyone took part, the *komiti* produced an official "List of Workers", which included the bridal attendants. (This was pinned to the door of the hall, where it remained during the wedding in full view of the guests, see Fig. 6.) Out of the sixty-eight persons named on this list, twenty-four were drawn from the bride's paternal and maternal 'families' and from a 'family' closely related to the former, while thirty-one came from the groom's paternal and maternal 'families' and from two related to the latter. (The bride's mother came from a community several hundred miles away; the only member of her 'family' who attended was a niece, who was appointed chief bridesmaid as a mark of respect to her 'family'.) The remaining thirteen workers were remote or affinal kin or personal friends (see Table 7). By no means all these official workers lived in Kōtare: over a third did not. The list was followed fairly closely on the wedding day, but there were many additional workers. However, the ratio remained approximately the same between members of the Samuels and Tātana 'families', members of their related 'families', other kinsmen and non-kin.

Not all the members of the *komiti marae* figured on the list. Some were forgotten in the heat of the moment, and others omitted in order that some related line might be recognised. Two important *komiti* members (the groom's mother's sister's son and his wife) were omitted because they were in mourning for the wife's mother, and the groom's nephew (who was at the *tomo*) because he was playing in an important football match that afternoon.

On the wedding day itself, the *marae* was busy from an early hour. The oven fires, laid the day before, were lit at six and busloads of visitors (some of whom had been travelling all night) began to arrive. Each party was "called" on to the *marae* by one of Rob's older sisters (the *karanga* or "bidding") and welcomed by a reception line hastily formed by the workers. Towards ten the guests moved to the church some two hundred yards away, where they waited in the sun—the custom before any church service in Kōtare—until Mavis arrived on her father's arm, followed by six bridesmaids and five groomsmen. Mavis's mother and sisters attended the ceremony but all of Rob's siblings remained at the *marae* preparing the bridal feast.

After the marriage ceremony, the guests returned to the *marae*, the bridal party arriving last. Their entrance was ceremonially challenged (the *taki*) by one of Rob's brothers, brandishing a wooden staff in lieu of a *taiaha*. He threw down a small stick between the gate-posts—a humorous touch: a challenge stick should be carved and at least a foot long. It was retrieved by a member of the bridal party, who then pursued the challenger on to the *marae*. Few of those present were able to explain the symbolism of the *taki*: it was regarded primarily as entertainment. One informant suggested that as the marriage ceremony had made "new people" out of Rob and Mavis they had to be challenged as strangers. They picked up the stick as a sign that they came in peace. The way having been opened, the pastor led the bridal party on to the *marae*, to the accompaniment of *haka* (posture dances) of welcome performed by those members of the Samuels and Tātana 'families' who could be spared temporarily from the work going on behind the scenes. The guests rushed forward to greet bride and groom with *hongi* (touching noses) and kiss.

Then followed a number of speeches (*mihimihi*), expressing the pleasure of the community at the forging of a new link between "two old Kōtare families", stressing the duties of married life, and wishing the young couple well (see Plate 4a, facing p. 55). Neither the Samuels nor the Tātana 'family' was notable for its orators and Rob's brothers were pre-occupied with the ovens at this stage, so that the speeches were all made by *kaumātua* from outside the 'families' chiefly concerned. Manu Matthews appeared in time to invite the company into the hall for the feast, "calling" the most important guests (*kaumātua*, clergy, teachers, and Pakehas) by name. The latter were seated at the bridal table (see Plate 6a, facing p. 87). They alone remained in their places; guests at other tables made way, as soon as they had finished, for those waiting outside. When justice had been done to the feast, the workers cleared away some of the tables so that everyone could return to the hall for the toasts, which were conducted by one of the local Pakehas. These were something of an innovation at a Maori wedding in Kōtare; they were few in number and the speeches were mostly in English. The wedding cake was then cut, followed by the ceremonial unwrapping of the presents under Manu's direction, the accompanying cards being read aloud by the bridesmaids. Everyone now returned to the open *marae*, for the weather was hot and sunny, and Manu conducted the flower ceremony on the steps of the hall, assisted by one of his brothers-in-law.

The flower ceremony used half of the bottom tier of the cake. The rest of that tier was distributed to the guests by the bridesmaids, the second was divided equally between the two sides for distribution to absent kin, and the small top tier, together with the notes and silver placed upon it by guests, was given to the bride and groom. Though entitled to retain the money, Rob passed it on to the *komiti marae* to help defray expenses.

For the rest of the afternoon there was a lull in the activities. Most of the guests vanished to the football ground, the hotel in Raumati or to private homes; a few were left sitting around catching up on Kōtare and other news. The hosts cleared the debris and prepared the hall for the wedding dance in the evening. Cups of tea and a snack were provided for those still at the *marae*. The dance was open to the public, the only charge made being for supper. The highlight of the evening was the Grand March by the bridal party, their kinsfolk and the workers, whose contribution to the success of the day was now publicly acknowledged.

After the wedding, the Samuels *komiti marae* met the bride's father and cousin once more to balance the accounts. A small deficit was met by voluntary contributions from both sides. And there the association ended.

The Tangi (Funeral Ceremonies) for Ātawhai Brown

Ātawhai Brown died in her early seventies in the home of her sister, who had been nursing her. She was childless and married to a Pakeha, so that the whole burden of arranging the *tangi* fell upon her own 'family'. Most of her siblings and kinsmen who were not away at work were at the house when she died; the rest were notified by telephone. The neighbours came to pay their respects as soon as they heard the shrill keening raised by the older women. When the first expression of grief had subsided, neighbours and friends departed, leaving the close kin to make their preparations.

Ātawhai belonged to the large and amorphous Hohaia 'family', within which her siblings and their descendants formed one branch. This branch undertook the organisation of the *tangi*, but drew heavily on the other branches for workers. As soon as they were alone, Ātawhai's three siblings and their spouses conferred with her husband and then formed a temporary *komiti* to direct operations. The eldest sister, Mairehau, was elected Chairman, Hepa Hohaia, the younger brother (a man in his late forties) Secretary-Treasurer. Each member of the *komiti* undertook certain duties and promised contributions of food and services from his (or her) family. Then they dispersed to their various tasks: to purchase the coffin, notify the minister, bespeak the central *marae* and prepare the meeting-house, order food and firewood, light the cooking fires, and begin the preparation of meals.

In the late afternoon, the corpse was moved (in the coffin) to the Pūriri *marae* on a neighbour's truck. It was laid in the middle of the far end of the meeting-house, with feet pointing toward the door. Photographs of the deceased and 'family' forebears were hung on the wall above the coffin. Ātawhai's sisters and nieces, the chief mourners, took their places on either side of the coffin, reclining on mattresses brought from home. They were joined from time to time by their menfolk, but the latter were mostly engaged in the dining hall and cookhouse. (Her husband, a Pakeha of retiring disposition, sat with friends in the body of the hall.) The women remained by the coffin with only the shortest of necessary breaks until the burial. Hay spread thickly on the floor and covered with flax mats provided comfortable accommodation for the visitors, with an aisle left free from the door to the foot of the coffin.

On the first evening most of the local people and kinsmen from neighbouring settlements came to pay their respects. On the second day, mourners began to arrive from further afield, including nieces and nephews from southern Northland. The funeral took place on the third day, which was jokingly referred to as "the Pakeha day", when Pakehas who had known the deceased or members of her 'family' attended.

The mourners arrived mostly in parties of from five to twenty. They were called on to the *marae* by a *kuia* (elderly woman) who, though not related to the Hohaia 'family', had been asked to act as *kai-karanga* ("caller") because she was the best in Kōtare. The chief mourners began to keen as soon as they heard the *karanga*, and the wailing was taken up by the women among the new arrivals. Preceded by the *kai-karanga*, the party entered the *marae*, pausing every ten paces or so as the wailing reached a crescendo, until they were within ten or fifteen feet of the coffin. Once within the door of the meeting-house, their leader (usually a *kaumātua*) began to address the dead, his voice rising above the keening of the women as he bade her go to join her ancestors, scolded her for leaving her friends and relations bereft, recounted her virtues and her weaknesses, and recalled the main features of her life. (In some parties, more than one person spoke to the dead in this way.) After some ten to fifteen minutes spent thus in mourning, the leader moved forward to look on the dead woman's face, then turned to wail and *hongi* with the chief mourners, and finally moved round the hall, shaking hands with those already present. The rest of his party followed him. Then greetings were exchanged between hosts and visitors (*mihimihi*) until Hepa called from the dining hall "*Haere mai ki te kai!*" (come and eat).

In the intervals between arrivals and all through the night, the speech-making went on, touching not only on the funeral arrangements but on many unrelated topics. Some of the local people went home; the rest slept in the meeting-house, rolled in blankets and rugs they had brought with them (see Plate 6b, facing p. 87). The question of where Ātawhai was to be buried was argued intermittently for two nights. There were three possibilities: the cemetery belonging to the Ratana Church, of which Ātawhai had been a member, another church cemetery, where her husband would be buried, or a 'family' burial ground on a 'family' farm. A final decision was made in favour of the latter about four a.m. on the second night, after Ātawhai's siblings (who according to Maori custom had taken little part in the discussion till the last) had cast their vote for it. Then Ātawhai's closest relatives paid their last tribute to their *whaea* (mother) in formal speeches.

Throughout the *tangi*, the members of the *komiti* were assisted in cookhouse and dining-hall by their adult children, by the able-bodied members of other branches of the Hohaia 'family', and by a scattering of other kin. The deceased's brothers and nephews dug the grave on the morning of the funeral, at first light. Pall-bearers were not specially chosen on this occasion. Those who carried the coffin from the *marae* after the funeral service were all close kinsmen (including her husband), but as the way lay uphill over open fields for half a mile, frequent changes of bearers were necessary. At the graveside, the chief mourners and their husbands stood at the foot of the grave, the minister at the head and other close kin along the sides. The men who dug the grave filled it in, and the children and teenagers who had carried the flowers from the *marae* laid them over the mound.

After the funeral, everyone returned to the *marae*. While they waited for the call to the dining hall, a few speeches were made, specifically designed to lighten people's spirits and begin the task of leading the bereaved back to normal life. The funeral feast which followed was the most elaborate meal of the *tangi*. After it the mourners began to disperse, and the workers set about cleaning the *marae*. The 'family' then adjourned to the house where Ātawhai died, where they "lifted the *tapu*" and relieved the strain of sustained mourning and hard work with liquor and singing. (No liquor was consumed on the *marae*.)

Finally, the next evening, after those not at work had finished cleaning the *marae*, the *komiti* met and went through the accounts, balancing expenses against the sum of money left for the purpose by the deceased, the proceeds from auctioning the surplus food, and the "*marae* money" given by mourners outside the 'family'. The Secretary was authorised to pay all the bills and the *komiti* was disbanded.

4

Community Divisions, Leadership and Solidarity

WHILE still important, kinship and descent were far from being the only bases of social organisation in Kōtare. Members of the community also grouped themselves together in different ways for different purposes according to local distribution, sex, age, religion and recreational interests, both informally and in formal associations. Always there was the fundamental distinction between *tāngata whenua* and 'immigrants'. Internally, the community was differentiated and divided on many issues. But in relation to the outside world, both Pakeha and Maori, it strove for and achieved an important degree of solidarity.

NON-KIN GROUPINGS

Local Distribution

The local people distinguished five major and four minor sub-districts or neighbourhoods, giving each a separate name (see Fig. 3, Table 3). Each neighbourhood had a distinctive character. Te Kāinga, for instance, was "new": it had a high proportion of 'immigrants' and purchased land holdings, was divided mainly into small house lots, and none of its householders made his living by primary production. Pūriri, the western lowland area where lay the main *marae*, was owned on Maori title except for two small blocks, had a predominance of *tāngata whenua* (members of five different 'families') and was mainly farmland, though only seven of its twenty-one households were directly concerned with farming. Hākea in contrast was a very small area, entirely owned and occupied by members of a single 'family', who used the land only for small gardens and grazing horses; its 'family' *marae* had the best hall in Kōtare.

While certain neighbourhoods were associated in the minds of the people with certain 'families', Hākea was the only one which did not accommodate several other households, and no 'family' was entirely confined to one neighbourhood. Local distribution modified the solidarity of 'family' groups in Kōtare.

Residents in the same neighbourhood co-operated with each other in many small ways, especially when they were also kin. Farmers took it in turn to kill and share their meat and exchanged the use of machinery and labour. Neighbours helped each other with transport whenever possible.

But they never took action together as a group to the exclusion of others.

Although neighbourhoods were not social units, local distribution had a considerable influence on community life as a result of the difficulties of internal communication, especially after dark. If an evening function was held at the school, it was attended only by those living within easy walking distance (that is, from Te Kāinga) and those who had their own transport. If it was held at the Pūriri *marae*, those present were mainly "Pūriri folk". But on "big" occasions, usually held at the weekend, the sponsors often arranged for a truck or several cars to make a circuit of the district.

Divisions based on Sex and Age

Among the older generations in Kōtare, men and women tended to separate in social relations outside home and 'family'. This division was especially evident at out-door gatherings such as football matches, and at church services, when the men often sat on one side, the women and children on the other. It appeared in the formation of five women's groups (including a basketball club) and of a separate Women Supporters' Committee within the football club. Though women were not forbidden to speak in public on the *marae* in Te Rarawa, no woman had ever been elected to the Church of England Church Committees or to the Kōtare Tribal Committee. There was a popular tendency to pair these bodies with specific women's groups, the local branches of the Mothers' Union and the Maori Women's Welfare League respectively.

A marked cleavage also existed between the young and unmarried on the one hand and the older generation on the other. The former showed great interest in sport and other recreational activities but little or none in those of a "cultural"[1] or instructional nature. They preferred each other's company, both in and out of formal associations. They spent very little of their leisure time in the company of older people and were both *hoha* ("can't-be-bothered") and *whakamā* (shy, embarrassed) in their relations with *kaumātua*. This kind of behaviour was deplored by the older generations, but accepted as normal. They themselves were reluctant to give "the young ones" responsibility or authority: those elected to club, School and Tribal Committees were mostly over forty years of age. The young people evaded responsibility, even while they complained about the "bossiness' of their elders. The only youth group in Kōtare depended for its vitality upon two officers who were married and over thirty.

Voluntary Associations and Representative Bodies

Kōtare was characterised by a proliferation of formal voluntary associations. 'Family' clubs and *komiti marae* should be included under this heading. Outside the field of kinship, religion and sport were by far the

---

[1] i.e. associated with the more concrete aspects of culture, such as arts and crafts, literature and oratory.

most important bases of association. Four religious denominations had church buildings and congregations including or entirely composed of Maoris in Kōtare, each with administrative committees and branches of church movements. There were five sports clubs: football (men), basketball (women), softball (mixed), and two tennis clubs (also mixed), attached to the Pūriri and Karaka *maraes* respectively. Finally, there were local branches of the Maori Women's Welfare League and the Countrywomen's Institute (a Maori one). The football, basketball and softball clubs were divided into players, who were mostly under twenty-five, and management committees of older persons; the first also had a Women's Committee which "poured tea and raised funds". The other clubs were run by committees elected by and from club members.

Not quite half the Kōtare Maoris belonged to the Church of England, which had two churches in Kōtare, built by Maori labour on Maori land, and administered within the framework of a Maori pastorate by local Maori Church Committees; to each was attached a branch of the Mothers' Union. Next in size (a third of the Maori population) was the Ratana congregation, which had a small temple in Pūriri, a Church Committee and a Ratana Youth Club.[1] Eleven families attended the Roman Catholic Church and five the Brethren hall in Te Kāinga; in both cases the congregations and their administrative committees were composed of Maoris and Pakehas in roughly equal numbers. None of the denominations had a resident minister. A few families and individuals belonged to other religious groups: Mormon, Jehovah's Witness and Seventh Day Adventist.

Public relations between adherents of the different denominations were amicable on the whole. At public gatherings of any length, especially *tangi*, joint services were held, or else one denomination was made responsible for morning service, another for evening service. But, beneath the surface, divisions often went very deep. At *tangi* and *tomo*, a good deal of time was spent discussing which church and minister should perform the ritual, for even 'families' were often divided in their religious allegiance. In 1955 at least one *tomo* failed because the parents on each side refused to accept the match unless the couple were married in *their* church. At the same time, it was felt that religious differences should *not* be allowed to disrupt the unity of 'family' or community, on the grounds of kinship sentiment rather than religious belief in tolerance. Differences were usually resolved sooner or later: parents who withheld approval for a marriage, for instance, normally gave in when they realised that insistence might lose them their child and grandchildren.

In addition to the executive committees of Kōtare clubs, there were two committees which were representative at least in theory, the Primary

---

[1] The Ratana Church is a legally recognised religious body founded in the 1920's by Wiremu Ratana. Its headquarters are at Ratana Pa near Wanganui, where Ratana gathered his early followers about him for instruction and to revive Maori community life.

School Committee of the whole community (including Pakehas), and the Tribal Committee of the Maori community. The School Committee elected in 1955 included three Pakehas among its fourteen members, a representation roughly proportionate to their place in the total population. (The names of only seven were forwarded to the Education Department, which limited School Committees to that number; two of these were Pakehas.) Neither committee was truly representative of the Maori community, partly because in both cases only a third of the eligible Maori electors attended the election, partly because Maori tradition favoured the exclusion of women, young people and 'immigrants' from positions of community responsibility. The School Committee was much less affected by the latter than the Tribal Committee: it included men and women in equal numbers, the ages of its members ranged from thirty-two to fifty-five, and nine were 'immigrants' (three married to *tāngata whenua* and six 'immigrant' settlers). The proportion of the latter was exceptionally high because the annual general meeting, held in the school, was attended mainly by Te Kāinga residents. The Tribal Committee on the other hand was composed of men only (although women were eligible for election), seven out of the twelve[1] members were over fifty-five, though four were only in their thirties, and nine were *tāngata whenua*. The School Committee was the more active and successful. Its money-raising gatherings were well attended and supported with gifts of remarkable generosity. The Tribal Committee was dormant in 1955.

The difference in the personnel elected to these two committees and in the support and enthusiasm accorded them reflected differences in their purposes and activities as conceived by the Maori electors. The aim of the School Committee was "to work for the school", that is, to support Headmaster and staff in improving school grounds and equipment. Thus capability and interest in the school were accepted as the most important qualifications for election. Moreover, because there were Pakehas on the committee, it was assumed that things would be "done the Pakeha way" out of courtesy. The Tribal Committee, on the other hand, had been set up by Act of Parliament to represent the people to the Government and vice versa. There was a conflict between the conviction that the "proper" Maori leaders should be elected and a desire for younger and more active members who would "get things done".

All the formal associations in Kōtare, voluntary and representative, had ties with similar groups outside the community. Kōtare religious groups were all part of denominations with national status and organisation; the sports clubs were registered with regional associations in order to secure regular competition with other teams; the women's groups were affiliated to national movements; and the School and Tribal Committees were formed at the injunction of the Education and Maori Affairs Departments respectively. Interference or too many demands on local funds from higher

---

[1] Eleven elected members plus an appointed Maori Warden.

levels were resented. Emphasis was invariably placed on the local value and service of the group in preference—even in opposition—to its place in a regional or national network.

Membership of non-kin groups, particularly the women's groups, was affected to a limited degree by kinship loyalties, reinforced by transport problems. Jeannie Matthews who lived along the sea-shore told me that neither she nor her neighbours belonged to the Welfare League because of its attachment to the Pūriri *marae*. It was a long way to walk to meetings, especially at night, and most of its work and funds were applied to the Pūriri *marae*. The women from the shore felt a much livelier interest in the Hākea *marae*, which was much nearer, especially as many were members of the Samuels 'family'.

Membership in the various Kōtare clubs and committees overlapped a good deal. Competition between clubs was not highly developed. Money-raising activities—card-evenings, jumble-sales, basket-socials and dances—were arranged so that they did not clash, for the number of patrons and money available for such purposes in the district were both limited.

Most club or committee activities brought in non-members from all sectors of the community as patrons, spectators and even as workers. It was customary for subscribing members to bring along a teenage relative to assist with the work, as well as rallying the support of other kin. Behind the elected members of the School Committee stood some twenty faithful supporters who never failed to attend a committee function and gave as freely of their time and labour in its service as the official members. No committee deliberated in strict privacy. Even the Maori Church Committees held their meetings on the *marae*, before an interested audience of men, women and children. Spectators took a lively part in committee discussions, only voting being limited to official members.

The 'Immigrant' and the Community

The distinction between *tāngata whenua* and 'immigrants' was not expressed in any formal opposition of groups. The former were divided into numerous 'families', some of which were chronically or occasionally in opposition. The 'immigrants' did not see or organise themselves as a coherent group, nor had they formed any clubs like the local 'families'. Those who had married or been fostered by *tāngata whenua* took an active part in the activities of their spouses' and foster-parents' 'families', especially as workers. Twenty were subscribing members of 'family' clubs. The 'immigrant' settlers, on the other hand, had not aligned themselves with any of the local 'families', except for two elderly widows who had joined one of the 'family' *komiti* on the strength of a remote kinship link.

The *tāngata whenua* dominated community life in Kōtare of admitted right and because they were in the majority. Their priority was always observed in matters of ceremonial, especially in the order of speeches on the *marae*. They were perfectly willing, however, to accept 'immigrants' as participants in their social activities and even as leaders in positions for which they had the necessary qualifications. Some 'immigrants' were always present at any public gathering in Kōtare. Those who had not married *tāngata whenua* or joined 'family' clubs, attended 'family' *hui* on much the same footing as *tāngata whenua* from outside the 'family', helping with the work if kin or friends of the persons honoured, and making donations as guests. The few who stayed away from local *hui* and were on visiting terms with only one or two neighbours were "left to get on with it".

'Immigrants' were most prominent in community life as executive officers in non-kin associations, particularly in sports clubs, women's groups and on the School Committee. Nine of the fourteen members elected to the latter in 1955 were 'immigrants', including six 'immigrant' settlers. Three 'immigrants' were also elected to the Tribal Committee, one who was married to a *tangata whenua* as Chairman and an 'immigrant' settler as Treasurer. As a whole, the 'immigrants' were in the middle generations and younger, inexperienced in Maori lore and diffident as public speakers. Although the *tāngata whenua* allowed them to speak freely on the Pūriri *marae*, only two did so with any regularity, outside the meetings of sectional associations. Eru Richards, a man in his early sixties, had settled in Kōtare over thirty years ago when he married a *tangata whenua*. Respected for his *rangatira* descent, his command of *whakapapa* and his ability as an orator, he had early been accepted as *kaumātua* by her 'family' and then by the community as a whole. Two years before, however, he had resigned from the Tribal Committee and in 1955 he did not appear or speak in public as often as formerly. The other prominent 'immigrant', Tere Wepiha, was also married to a *tangata whenua* but had comparatively little to do with her 'family'. A much younger man—barely fifty—and regarded as somewhat of a "go-getter", his rise to community prominence had been a recent and stormy one. First elected Chairman of the Tribal Committee four years before, he had been dropped as too dictatorial, but was re-elected in 1955 after committee affairs had got into a tangle. He was also elected Chairman of the School Committe that year. It was generally conceded that he was improving as a speaker and becoming more co-operative in private as well as public life. His story was an interesting commentary on the difficulty of transition from the ranks of the *kai-mahi* to those of the *kai-kōrero* in Kōtare, accentuated in his case by his 'immigrant' status.

The people of Kōtare explained the ease with which 'immigrants' were accepted into community life as the result of kinship. In actual fact, few 'immigrants' had more than one or two demonstrable kinsmen in Kōtare and some none at all. Most came from other parts of the Far North and, since it was general knowledge that the four northern tribes (Aupouri, Rarawa, Ngāti Kahu and Ngāpuhi) stemmed from founders who were related, it was easy to recognise anyone from the Far North as a kinsman of sorts. But even members of tribes still regarded with hostility by "Northerners" were accepted without difficulty. (An 'immigrant' Waikato with a Pakeha wife, who had no links with any of the local Maoris, had worked for ten years in partnership with two *tāngata whenua*, was an elected official in two sports clubs and often acted as Master of Ceremonies at local dances.) Although such cases were explained on the grounds that "all Maoris are related if you go back far enough", kinship recognition was here extended beyond meaningful limits. The acceptance of 'immigrants' is more accurately interpreted as the product of the need for solidarity among the Maoris of Kōtare vis-à-vis the outside world. It rested on their willingness to identify themselves with the local Maori group, a kinship of the spirit rather than of blood.

LEADERSHIP

Leadership in the Kōtare Maori community was diffuse and largely informal, and the same was true of the social control exercised by the community outside matters handled by the State. The identity of the recognised leaders, the kind of leadership expected of them, and the extent of their authority varied with each kin-group, each set of friends or age-mates, and each formal association, and also with the occasion. The Tribal Committee, an official community council established by law,[1] was intended to provide leadership within the community and representation for it in relation to outside bodies (especially Government departments), but it was ineffective in both spheres in 1955.

The Leaders

Asked to name the community leaders, most Kōtare Maoris enumerated nine *kaumātua*, all men, whom they described as "the proper leaders", that is, according to Maori custom. These men were all over fifty-five years of age, married, and expert (to varying degrees) in the Maori tongue, traditions and ceremonial forms. They were also leading members in their respective 'families'. Now one of these men was Eru Richards, mentioned earlier as an 'immigrant' married to a *tangata whenua*. Accepted by her 'family' as its spokesmen because of his qualifications and in default of any other candidate, he had been prominent in Kōtare for so long that most people had to be reminded that he did not in fact "belong". In 1955 three of these "proper" leaders were too elderly to play an active role even within their own 'families', Eru's public appearances tended to be erratic, and two had relatively little to say in public except in relation to 'family' affairs. The remaining three, all in their late fifties, emerged as the major speakers at any gathering they attended in the district, and were introduced to me as "the big chiefs of Kōtare". They also spoke for the Kōtare community whenever they attended Maori gatherings in other places. None of these *kaumātua* were identified as senior to the others; a

[1] See below, p. 86.

great deal of intermarrying between their forebears had made it difficult to say exactly how their 'families' were related and which took precedence.

Rather as an afterthought, most people added a tenth name, that of Tere Wepiha, also mentioned above. Though an "outsider", his value was being increasingly (if reluctantly) admitted. In time perhaps he might even be accepted as a "proper" leader, as Eru had been, on the basis of his ability and knowledge of Maori tradition. It might be noted that these two were not complete aliens, but could claim descent from at least one ancestor who had lived in Kōtare many generations before, though they had inherited no land from them.

The part played by any one of these ten men had changed over time. Two now in their late seventies and virtually house-bound had been strong and respected leaders in their day. Eru Richards had "dropped everything" when he went to the city two years before, but was beginning to pick up the threads again. Two more, newly admitted to *kaumātua* status, were still acquiring assurance in their new role.

As long as a man who had been accepted as a spokesman and leader was alive, he was named as such in 'family' and community whenever any discussion about leadership arose. His successor may have taken over the whole or part of his duties, might even be recognised as *kaumātua* and not simply *kai-mahi* in the 'family', but he did not assume his mantle in the community at large until his death. It took a long time for the community (especially the older members) to accept the fact that the rising generation was ready and fitted for leadership. The people frequently complained that "there are no real *kaumātua* left: they are all dying and leaving us without leaders". I even heard this complaint voiced by one of the "big three"!

None of the recognised leaders won unqualified approval and support from all sections of the community. Some were criticised as poor speakers or as inadequately versed in the "proper" Maori ceremonial, others as too high-handed and inclined to "show off", several for heavy drinking. As within the 'family', they were listened to with respect when they spoke, but not necessarily followed. Their views were often challenged, and they themselves frequently clashed with each other over specific issues.

Besides these community elders, other individuals attained prominence in various limited spheres, and for occasions of limited duration, in 'family' and formal association. At 'family' gatherings, the senior representatives of the 'family' or the closest relatives of the person honoured took charge; at club affairs, the Chairman or Secretary. *Kaumātua* from outside the group might offer advice or try to scold them into a particular course, but the final decision was theirs. This arrangement baffled the local Pakehas, who expected those they knew as "chiefs" in the Maori community to take the lead in all situations. One unwittingly offended Maori feelings at a *tangi* by ignoring the chief mourner, addressing himself instead to a *kaumātua* who did not belong to the bereaved 'family'. Although the former was socially and personally insignificant at other times, on this occasion he took precedence.

There were sixteen men and sixteen women who consistently acted as secondary or executive leaders, the chief of the *kai-mahi* or workers as distinct from the *kai-kōrero* or talkers. All but two of each sex were in their thirties and forties. Besides directing various activities at *hui*, they served as officers in 'family' and other clubs and committees, half of them in two or more. Six of the men had been elected to the Tribal Committee; two in their fifties were as old as some of the *kaumātua* but classed with the younger generation because of inexperience and retiring personalities. A seventh was appointed Maori Warden for the district by the Tribal Committee.

Among the men, the most prominent were tradesmen. Two were being groomed for 'family' leadership; a third had had the opportunity and let it slip. In general, they lacked confidence and knowledge with regard to ceremonial and oratory. Work and family made heavy demands upon their time and limited their participation in community life, especially in the all-night speech-making sessions. The women were most active in their own groups, in 'family' affairs and on the School Committee. They rarely spoke in public or publicly expressed opinions on matters of policy, but addressed themselves to the work to be done. Their influence on community affairs was by no means negligible, but it was exercised mainly through their menfolk or through membership in women's groups.

The elderly women in the community played little part as leaders. Only four were generally recognised as *kuia*. They performed the *karanga* at *hui*, helped male speakers with the chants they sometimes used to close or illustrate a speech, and spoke themselves on rare occasions, when they felt that the men had omitted some courtesy to visitors.

The Kōtare Tribal Committee

As well as quite a large number of recognised and *ad hoc* leaders, the Kōtare Maori community had an official community council which was intended to be a source both of leadership and of social control in matters outside the scope of the State law. The Kōtare Tribal Committee was part of a national network of Tribal Committees set up under the provisions of the Maori Social and Economic Advancement Act of 1945.[1] This Act provided for Tribal Committee Areas to be delimited either by application from the Maori residents or, if necessary, by the Minister of Maori Affairs. Each Tribal Committee Area had its own Tribal Committee consisting of five to eleven persons elected as their representatives by the Maori residents at a biennial general meeting, together with a Welfare Officer appointed *ex officio* by the Minister. Once elected, the Committee

[1] *Maori Social and Economic Advancement Act 1945*, Government Printer, Wellington, 1946. For a history of officially authorised Maori local self-government, see 'Fifty Years of Maori Self-Government', *Te Ao Hou*, No. 1, 1952, p. 21.

PLATE 5. The *hui*: (*a*) preparing the vegetables, and (*b*) making a *hangi* (earth oven). See pp. 73, 74.

PLATE 6. The *hui*: (*a*) the *hakari* (feast), and (*b*) sleeping arrangements in the meeting-house. See pp. 74, 76.

could appoint one or two Wardens to whom it delegated certain tasks. Several Tribal Committee Areas were grouped together in a Tribal District which was controlled by a Tribal Executive, consisting of two representatives from each constituent Tribal Committee and a Welfare Officer appointed by the Minister (see Plate 4b, facing p. 55).

According to the Act, the Tribal Committees were "to promote, encourage, guide and assist members of the Maori Race" and to collaborate with and assist State departments, local bodies, associations, institutions, trustees of native reservations or any person or persons in "any matters pertaining to the well-being of the Maori Race". The Act specified the procedure, application of funds and so on proper to Tribal Committees.

The Kōtare district was registered as a Tribal Committee Area and its Tribal Committee established in 1945. In 1955, however, it played a negligible part in the organisation of community affairs. It held only one meeting in the year, its first for two years. In general its activities were limited to the attempts made by the Warden to control drinking on the *marae*, the endorsement (required by law) of claims for subsidies on public building projects and the granting of liquor licences for gatherings on the *marae*. No subsidies had been required in Kōtare for two years, and the signatures necessary for liquor licences were apparently obtained from office-holders without calling a meeting. It was no more effective in providing a channel of communication between the local community and the central Government and its departments. No reports on its activities or finances had been forwarded to the capital for two years. When several high-ranking officers in the Department of Maori Affairs and two Adult Education Officers (all Maoris) visited Kōtare in 1955, the Maori Welfare Officer in Raumati notified several of the local elders, some of whom were not on the Tribal Committee, of the date and time of their visits, and the latter telephoned other households in the community. There was no suggestion that they were calling the community together in their capacity as Tribal Committee members.

The Maoris of Kōtare were aware that the Tribal Committee was a failure. They themselves blamed organisational difficulties and alleged weaknesses in the system. Meetings were difficult to arrange because Committee members lived scattered over Kōtare, some up to three miles from the Pūriri *marae* (where meetings were held), no public transport was available in the evenings, most engaged in day-labour outside the community and some carried on part-time farming as well. Secondly, Tribal Committee members, especially the Warden, complained about their lack of power, by which they meant coercive authority. Actually, they had greater powers than they realised or used. The real problem was that they were uncertain of what they were supposed to do and how they could go about it. They found the Act difficult to understand; few had read it in full. They also complained that they were inhibited by the conventions of Pakeha committee government which the Act required them to adopt.

These procedures were widely used in clubs and committees in Kōtare, but they were imperfectly understood and used with a large degree of latitude.

Lack of support from the people of Kōtare was a serious handicap. They mistrusted the Tribal Committee, in the first place, as a threat to individual autonomy, but mainly because it was imposed upon them by the Government (in their view a Pakeha institution). The system was in fact worked out in the Department of Maori Affairs and approved by the highest ranking of its Maori officers. It did not conflict openly with the traditional form of community government, but was an enlightened attempt to recognise officially and standardise the procedure of the unofficial councils of elders which existed in most Maori communities at least into the 1930's. The Central Government reserved a certain minimum control over Tribal Committees by requiring that the boundaries of their Areas and the names of elected members be submitted to the Minister for approval, but left the election in the hands of the people in the belief that they would elect those they regarded as their leaders. In some areas, *kaumātua* of *rangatira* rank were reported to have refused to stand for election on the grounds that to submit their candidacy to the vote was an insult to their *mana* (inherent power and prestige). This had not happened in Kōtare, but several of the "proper" leaders had not stood for election because of age, ill-health or other commitments. Only four of those elected in 1955 were traditional leaders. Several of the others were inexperienced and commanded little respect from the community.

The Tribal Committee was further hampered by the fact that few people in Kōtare grasped the concept of a separation between public and private roles and spheres of influence. Its members were influenced in their decisions by personal relationships with those with whom they had to deal. Moreover, the lines of division in the community were reproduced on the Committee itself. Old men grumbled about "forward youngsters"; young men about "old fogies". Members of 'families' involved in feuding skirmished for position. Although no women served on the Committee, competition between the sexes also played its part, for the Tribal Committee blamed some of its difficulties on its loss of control over the Pūriri *marae*, which it had allowed the Maori Women's Welfare League to take over from the *komiti wāhine* which formerly managed it. The League branch was an exclusively women's group whereas the old *komiti wāhine* seems usually to have included men. The Tribal Committee (and indeed most men in Kōtare) felt that the League had usurped control of the *marae* to an extent neither intended nor desirable. This was undoubtedly true, but it had occurred in default of active interest in the *marae* on the part of the (male) Tribal Committee.

SOCIAL CONTROL

(1) *by External Authorities*

The Maoris of Kōtare were subject to the general law of New Zealand and to the complete range of State mechanisms of social control. The external judiciary rarely had to intervene in Kōtare. The police visited the district twice in the course of 1955, once to investigate thefts and attempted conversion of several vehicles, crimes which were traced to youths from outside, and once to arrest a Kōtare man who had been away for five years and returned with the police already on his trail. Members of the Kōtare community called in the police only in cases of serious loss by theft. If the suspect came from Kōtare itself, the accuser almost invariably regretted his action when his first anger was past, and refused to lay a charge. A threat to call in the police was often effective in securing private redress.

Kōtare Maoris were affected to varying degrees by State policy on Maori affairs. This policy was mediated through the Department of Maori Affairs, which had a regional office in Raumati, through the Department of Education which maintained a Maori primary school in the district, and through the Council for Adult Education (University of New Zealand), which arranged whatever classes the community wanted. The Department of Maori Affairs played an important role in the lives of many individual Maoris in Kōtare and indirectly in that of the community as a whole. All but one of the productive farms were bound to it as "assisted units"; most of the new houses were erected with the help of a Maori Affairs housing loan; it handled all Maori land transactions, and Maori welfare and employment problems; and it supervised the functioning of the Tribal Committee. Relations with the Department and its officers (many of whom were Maori) were on the whole amicable, though its connection with the Government was never forgotten. Its assistance was readily sought in relation to farm production, housing and employment, but need for outside help in social matters was less easily admitted.

Kōtare also fell within the jurisdiction of the County Council, which had its headquarters in Raumati and controlled matters such as housing standards, roving livestock, payment of rates and maintenance of roads and bridges. Though none of the Kōtare Maoris served on the Council they regarded a local Pakeha farmer elected to it as their spokesman. Occasionally there was some resentment over Council actions, such as the impounding of Kōtare horses grazing the "long paddock" (the road-side) or the claiming of land for road improvement, but misunderstandings were not serious or frequent. Many Maoris found employment with the Council both permanently and casually, even (in one case) as casual assistant to the poundkeeper.

The Department of Maori Affairs and the County Council relied upon economic sanctions and ultimately upon the police force and the law court. They had not had to call upon either in Kōtare for several years.

(2) *within the Community*

There were many aspects of social order which the law left untouched, especially in the field of Maori customary usage. The older Maoris in Kōtare recalled that within living memory the *kaumātua* used to call *kōrero* or public meetings to discuss matters of community significance, to censure offenders against community mores, and if necessary to impose penalties. They seem to have been concerned in particular with relations between the sexes, drunkenness, and breaches of *tapu* and religious observance. A boy and girl did not dare be seen alone together more than two or three times, I was told, or the elders haled them before a *kōrero*, insisting that they marry (if their kin agreed) or breaking up the romance if they were too closely related or of unequal rank. One *kōrero* was called about seventeen years before to protest against the choice of a highly valued ancestral name for the child of a couple living in adultery. These attempts at social control seem to have met with only variable success. The most recent were 'family' rather than community affairs and occurred before the end of the war.

As we have seen, the Tribal Committee did not function as the arbiter of social standards in Kōtare in 1955. It did not exercise disciplinary functions nor provide a framework for the taking of community decisions. Its influence was limited to a slight modification in the public consumption of liquor achieved by the Warden.

None of the other groups outside the elementary-family exercised any control over its members. The 'family' operated to support and protect its members, not to discipline them. The clubs presumably could fine or expel unruly members, but I heard of no cases in which they did so. Attempts by individuals even of senior age and status to assert authority outside their own 'family' were generally abortive.

Matters of community concern were not referred to any particular body: they were thrashed out unofficially, in private and in the all-night speech-making sessions at *hui*. Relations between persons of opposite sex were no longer discussed directly in public but public opinion was indicated obliquely by innuendo and joking. The problem of over-consumption of liquor was treated in the same way but also attacked directly by the elders in long exhortations.

Even these informal controls seemed to be weakly developed. Discussion did not lead to direct action. There was a considerable amount of petty theft and drunkenness, breaches of the avowed sexual code were varied and persistent, and the people themselves were continually finding fault with the way Maori ceremonial was performed in Kōtare. Although gossip was rife and often malicious, it did not seem to prevent people from doing what they knew would arouse it. In many cases, nothing at all appeared to be done. An offender went entirely unpenalised if his peccadilloes were not too grave, or if they had the saving grace of being funny or scoring off someone who was not popular.

However, consistent offenders did not "get away with it" indefinitely. A series of offences built up community disapproval against an individual or a family over a long period, until it eventually reached saturation point. Even then the community did not speak as a whole. Instead, some interested individual administered a powerful rebuke. The act that called forth the rebuke was usually quite trivial, and the rebuke phrased in terms of it; without the history of offences it would not have been administered at all. The role of the community was a passive, almost negative one: by doing nothing, it withheld sympathy and support from the offender and thus endorsed the action of the self-appointed disciplinarian. The situation was not, however, completely unstructured. The rebuke was given by someone of status in the community, in public, particularly during the long discussions at *hui*, or at club and committee meetings. The rebuke itself and the publicity of it constituted punishment, reinforced by varying degrees of ostracism, ridicule, and the withholding of sympathy by the rest of the community.

Once the rebuke had been delivered, the mechanisms of reintegration began to operate almost immediately. Kinsfolk and friends rallied to the defence of the delinquent. Excuses were found: "He isn't a bad boy, just wild"; "he was led astray by bad company from other settlements"; or "he's only young yet, he'll improve as he gets older". This was particularly pronounced in those cases where the State intervened. Vis-à-vis the State, the delinquent was still a member of the community, related by kinship to some or most of its members, known personally to all. The punishment inflicted by the State was not increased by punishment inflicted by the community: on the contrary, it was mitigated by its sympathy. Once punishment had been suffered, the delinquent was restored to grace and the incident apparently forgotten. Many years before, strong community disapproval had been focused on a local youth suspected of a series of daring thefts in Kōtare, from Maori and Pakeha alike; when he was caught red-handed by the police and sentenced to prison, the general verdict was that he had "got what was coming to him". But when he eventually returned to Kōtare, transformed into a law-abiding family man, he was readily and fully accepted into the community. Those who persisted in their ways, however, eventually alienated the sympathy even of kinsfolk, and either lived in a state of partial ostracism or left the community.

Here we have a system which was far from automatic in its operation. Informal controls existed but they functioned slowly with, as it were, a delayed action, in direct contrast to the judicial institutions of the Government, whose intervention after a crime was immediate and swift.

What were the reasons for the high degree of permissiveness and tolerance which characterised relations between members of the community? Why did the community fail to act decisively to control the social behaviour of its members? The explanation that very few people really cared about the standards of behaviour which they professed can, I think, be dismissed as too facile and not to be sustained in the face of intimate knowledge of the people themselves.

First, there were the technical considerations. In a community where households were dispersed and self-supporting, where workers typically engaged in a variety of different occupations, the majority of them spending their working life outside the community, the frequency and intensity of social contact was limited and it was relatively easy to keep to oneself and to ignore criticism. Secondly, so many avenues of escape were available to the offender (who could emigrate to Raumati, other rural areas, or the city, or withdraw from the community while continuing to reside in it) that the expression of disapproval was consciously softened lest it should "drive them away". Thirdly, disapproval was rarely general and unanimous in the community. Some sections of it always found their judgments modified in any given case by kinship, friendship, and knowledge of mitigating circumstances. Fourthly, other ideals argued against active expression of censure, notably the concept of "Maori *aroha*" (love) and a passionate belief in the rights of the individual. There was a general feeling that the only persons who had the right to curb and direct the behaviour of others were members of the same elementary or at most the same grand-family. Senior members of a 'family' were, in a sense, held responsible for the conduct of their juniors, but it was recognised that their authority depended on how far it was admitted by the latter. In the final analysis, the maintenance of happy and non-censorious relations was valued more highly than adherence to rules of conduct.

Lastly, because it could rely on an outside judicial body to deal with the most serious and disruptive offences the community did not need to be harsh with its own members. In a small, completely self-governing community, the local authorities have to judge and punish as well as to aid and protect members of the community. The transfer of coercive power and punitive rights from the community to an external authority permitted Kōtare the luxury of "feeling sorry" for delinquents and of emphasising affection rather than discipline. This tendency was strengthened by the position of the community as part of an ethnic and cultural minority within the State: the community identified itself more with the wrongdoer, whom it knew personally, than with the external judicial institution, which was alien and impersonal. Also, reluctance to betray a Maori to a non-Maori body arose in part from a justifiable fear that the disclosure of his offences would reflect dishonour on the community and indirectly on the whole Maori people. Because distrust of the judicial body was strong enough to cause the community to protect offenders and conceal offences, local control of those aspects of social behaviour not controlled by the State was inevitably impaired also.

KŌTARE AS A COMMUNITY

Kōtare lacked unified community organisation or leadership. It consisted of a number of sectional groupings of varied structure, aims and functions, with a number of leaders whose role and influence fluctuated with the occasion and other circumstances. Attempts at the establishment of bodies which would represent or exercise control over the community were generally unsuccessful.

Kōtare was not a self-sufficient, self-contained community in the social sphere any more than in the economic. Residents were linked with individuals and groups outside the community, not only in the Far North but further afield, by ties of kinship established as a result of marriage, fostering and emigration, and by the affiliation of its formal associations to regional and national movements. They were dependent upon an external judiciary for the punishment of crime and the maintenance of law and order, and subject to the legal rulings of Government departments and local bodies.

Nevertheless, community feeling was strong in Kōtare. It was built mainly on two things, pride in Kōtare and its reputation in the Far North, and shared *Maoritanga* ("Maoriness").

The territorial area of Kōtare was defined on a traditional Maori basis. Although it covered a very considerable area and was divided into neighbourhoods of some local significance, it was regarded as a unit by people living outside, and identified as such by a single name. Kōtare residents on their side presented a united front to the outside world. Differences between residents of local and non-local derivation, between members of different churches, and so on, were minimised, and their common residence stressed. Local clubs proudly bore the district name in their relations with the regional or national movements to which they were affiliated. In the Far North to-day, the query, "Where do you come from?", elicits the name of a place, not a descent-group. All Kōtare residents were proud of Kōtare's name and reputation, particularly in the field of sport. No-one from Kōtare had achieved prominence in local politics or in "cultural" circles in the Far North; only three had achieved notable success in the field of education, and *they* had settled in the city. But the district had produced some fine sportsmen, especially in Rugby football, and its many sports teams had had considerable success in the past. Interest in sport, especially football, was in fact a strong unifying force in the community, extending even to the Pakehas. Everyone but the aged, the very young and the invalid turned out for Saturday matches played on the home grounds in the winter, and parties of twenty to sixty—one or two busloads—accompanied the team for "away" matches. The association of the football club with the tribal name served to emphasise its role as a focus for community co-operation and support.

The Maoris of Kōtare were also highly conscious of themselves as Maoris, and as a Maori community. They had in common not only the same ethnic characteristics, especially dusky skins, but almost without exception they placed high value on *Maoritanga*. *Maoritanga* is a difficult concept to define. Sir Apirana Ngata described it as "an emphasis on the continuing individuality of the Maori people, the maintenance of such Maori characteristics and such features of Maori culture as present day circumstances will permit, the inculcation of pride in Maori history and traditions, the retention so far as possible of old-time ceremonial, the continuous attempt to interpret the Maori point of view to the Pakeha in power".[1] In my experience in Auckland and in the Far North, Maoris gave *Maoritanga* two distinct but related meanings. They used it, first, to denote "things Maori"—Maori culture or "Maori ways"; and secondly, for pride in things Maori or what they often referred to as "Maori heart". The Maoris of Kōtare were not in the habit of defining these "Maori ways" in any detail, but the kinds of behaviour and the ideal values which I heard constantly praised as characteristic of and proper to Maoris can be summarised as follows:

(a) loyalty to other Maoris;

(b) attachment to the land and community of one's ancestors;

(c) the recognition and observance of obligations towards kinsfolk;

(d) generosity, sociability and co-operativeness, especially towards other Maoris and if necessary at the cost of personal economic gain (i.e. the practice of "Maori *aroha*");

(e) enjoyment of group activity;

(f) faithful attendance at gatherings on the *marae*;

(g) adherence to Maori ceremonial forms, especially at *hui*;

(h) interest in *whakapapa* and Maori history;

(i) the use of the Maori language, at least ceremonially;

(j) a deliberately happy-go-lucky attitude to time and money;

(k) refusal to worry over the future or plan too far ahead; and

(l) a taste for "Maori *kai*", foods gathered from sea, forest and wilderness and/or cooked in a *hangi* (earth oven).

The actual practice of Maori ways was by no means uniform within the community. There were considerable variations in the knowledge of Maori lore and language and in the recognition and observance of Maori obligations. These were correlated to a marked extent—but not wholly— with age. Young people knew comparatively little about genealogies, Maori ceremonial forms and the like; they were rather perfunctory in their performance of Maori obligations, tending to limit the number of *hui* attended and the range of kinsfolk assisted; they spoke English most of the time, and the Maori they understood best and occasionally spoke was highly colloquial. Parental generations were not, in general, particularly knowledgeable in these matters, for they confessed that they too had failed "to listen to the old folk and pay attention at *hui*" in their youth,

[1] Sutherland, 1940, pp. 176–7, 411 f., 421 f.

and their command over the Maori tongue was in most cases only a fumbling one, because they had gone to school at a time when educational policy punished its use. But they were keen to learn; they sought the company of the elderly and took active and faithful part in *hui*, especially those connected with death. The elderly were accepted as the experts in things Maori; they spoke Maori almost exclusively, except to children and young people. But even the elders sometimes failed to fulfil all their obligations, absenting themselves even from *tangi* when other commitments, personal grudges or illness intervened. And only a handful were really expert in *whakapapa* and Maori history, or skilled orators.

Lack of knowledge of and occasional lapses from the ideal pattern of Maori behaviour did not constitute rejection of *Maoritanga* as a whole. Those who were indifferent, even at times critical of (but never militantly hostile to) certain Maori ways, invariably placed a positive value on certain others. Young people—and some older ones—might be relatively uninterested in the ceremonial aspects of *Maoritanga*, but they thoroughly enjoyed the social ones. There was a high proportion of children and young people at every gathering on the *marae*, many of them involved as workers: they congregated outside the meeting-house, on the open *marae*, "yarning" and flirting, while the "real business" (the ceremonial) took place inside. They were no more careful in their management of time than any of the older residents, and they were quite as strongly attached to "Maori *kai*", spending an important part of their leisure in gathering it. They liked to hear Maori spoken, even if they had only a hazy idea of its meaning. But above all, their loyalty to their ethnic group and their consciousness of themselves as different from the Pakeha were in no way less than those of their elders. They retained the "Maori heart".

Maori community sentiment in Kōtare was emphasised and internal differences minimised in relation to the outside world. Kōtare Maoris worked together most successfully when staging gatherings which they knew would attract outsiders, because they wanted to show other Maori communities that Kōtare could "turn on a good Maori show" and to vindicate the Maori way of doing things before Pakehas. To the Pakeha in particular, they almost invariably presented a united front, partly out of defensiveness and pride, partly because they were jealous of their reputation for getting on well together, and partly because contact with Pakehas threw into relief their common interests and values. In Kōtare itself, friction between Maoris was notably reduced in situations in which they were involved with Pakehas, as on the School Committee and in sports clubs.

5

Migration

THE Maori population of Kōtare was far from static. Quite apart from the changes brought about by the natural processes of birth and death, the community was continually losing some members by emigration and gaining others from outside.

Someone left Kōtare every month during my stay there in 1955. Most local residents had relatives living elsewhere who had once lived in the district. Most of the emigrants still remembered in Kōtare were *tāngata whenua* there, but some 'immigrants' were also involved.

In deciding who ranked as a 'Kōtare emigrant', I was confronted with two difficulties. First, some of those who had once lived in Kōtare had (it was reported) stayed only a year or less and regarded another community as "home". Secondly, some who had been 'immigrants' in Kōtare had left no kin there and had lost touch with the community. I have excluded both groups from the following discussion because of lack of information about them. I have defined as a 'Kōtare emigrant' any Maori living elsewhere in 1955 who was born or had lived in Kōtare for at least two years above the age of three and who belonged either to a *tangata whenua* 'family' or to an 'immigrant' family still represented there. Those who were less than fifteen when they left Kōtare I shall call 'passive' emigrants. Fifteen years is a convenient dividing line between those who played a passive and an active part in the decision to migrate, because it is the age at which children can leave school and take employment. (Maori parents in Kōtare regarded a child as an independent adult as soon as he could support himself.) Sixteen, the age at which he may legally leave his parents' home, would be as good a choice, but in Kōtare Maori youngsters of fifteen did sometimes migrate alone, with their parents' consent. The number of those who emigrated between their fifteenth and sixteenth birthdays was very small, so that a change in definition would not make any appreciable difference in the proportion of 'passive' to 'active' emigrants.

Children were involved in emigration from Kōtare far less than adults. At least eighteen had left with parents, twelve when under ten years of age. (There may have been a few more: my informants could not always remember how many children a kinsman had when he left.) Another six had been sent to boarding schools for advanced education, mostly in the city; all six would probably remain away to find the jobs for which their education was preparing them. Another six had left Kōtare for foster homes in other rural communities, four adopted by kinsfolk after the death or separation of their parents and two placed in foster homes by the Child Welfare Department.

With the help of those left in Kōtare, I was able to trace 247 Maoris deriving from Kōtare who had emigrated as adults and were living else-where at the end of June 1955—approximately as many as the adults resident in Kōtare at the time. The majority of these 'active' emigrants were *tāngata whenua*, but ten men and eight women had been 'immigrants' in Kōtare. The sexes were equally represented in the group as a whole, but there was a predominance of young adults: two-thirds were still under thirty-five in 1955, though many had migrated some years before. Barely a tenth were married before their departure, but another tenth left Kōtare as a direct result of marriage. One-third were living in other rural areas. Just over half were to be found in the cities, nine out of ten in Auckland. Towns had attracted only a small proportion. It is worthy of note that emigrants living in the cities were on the average younger than those in other places, and a higher proportion were unmarried (see Tables 8 and 9).

Emigration to Rural Areas

Emigration from Kōtare to other rural areas was not confined to adjacent settlements, the Rarawa tribal area or the same geographic region. Only slightly more than half the Kōtare emigrants living in other rural areas in 1955 were to be found in the Far North (48 out of 84). Moreover, they were widely scattered over the whole region (which included Aupouri, Ngāti Kahu and Ngāpuhi as well as Rarawa territory), without any con-centration in the districts nearest to Kōtare. The majority of those outside the Far North (24 out of 36) had by-passed both adjacent regions and the city of Auckland and settled in regions to the south of Auckland, in spite of the traditional hostility of the tribes of those parts to "Northerners". They were living mainly in the Waikato and on the Hauraki Plains, where they engaged in farming and mining, and in the King Country and on the Central Plateau (Rotorua-Taupo), where bush-workers were in demand.

Women predominated among Kōtare emigrants living in the Far North (30 out of 48), but male emigrants outnumbered women by 18 to 6 in regions south of Auckland. Men and women were equally represented among those in the southern parts of Northland. Thus male emigrants tended to range much further afield than the women, who settled mainly in the Far North.

Emigrants to other rural areas were in general older than those found in urban areas, only 24 per cent being under twenty-five years, and ex-ceptionally few under twenty. Also a remarkably high proportion were married in 1955: 78 per cent of the men and nearly 90 per cent of the women. In recent years most of the young and unmarried leaving Kōtare had been diverted to the city. Nevertheless, over two-thirds of the Kōtare emigrants living in other rural areas had settled there within the past fifteen years (that is, since the beginning of the Second World War). Most of them were still relatively young in 1955, 40 per cent being between twenty-five and thirty-five.

In the case of the women, the exceptionally low proportion of unmarried emigrants in other rural areas was related to the lack of rural employment opportunities for women in 1955. Only three women from Kōtare, all unmarried, were in paid employment, two as nurses and one as a Junior Assistant in a Maori school. The other unmarried women were engaged in unpaid domestic duties. Work of the kind which had been undertaken by women emigrants in earlier times—as assistants in family gum-digging enterprises and as domestic helpers in Pakeha homes—was no longer plentiful; it was, moreover, much less attractive to the present generation of Maori women, in view of the better paid and more interesting jobs available in the city.

Male emigrants found it much easier than the women not only to make a living, but to find really congenial jobs in other rural areas. Few had established themselves on the land. Only six were farming, one on land inherited from his father, three on farms belonging to their wife's family, and two on land purchased with a Returned Serviceman's Rehabilitation Loan. Instead they favoured occupations connected with primary extractive industries and high wages, such as bush-work, quarrying and mining.

Study of the personal histories of emigrants to other rural areas revealed some interesting facts. In the first place, most were unmarried when they first left Kōtare. Only a small proportion migrated immediately at marriage to live with a spouse in the latter's community. Most left Kōtare initially because of shortage of land and work at home, rumours of attractive jobs available elsewhere, and a desire to "see the world". Marriage was more often the result of emigration than the cause, especially in the case of those who travelled beyond the Far North. Moreover, this had been the case for at least two generations, that is, for upwards of fifty years. The oldest emigrants had sought and found work outside Kōtare, on the kauri-gum reserves of the Far North and in all sorts of work associated with the development of what was at that stage a pioneer region. Even the women had participated in rural migration throughout this period, working on the gum-fields or in Pakeha homes. Nor was emigration beyond the limits of the Far North a new development. Kōtare men had been working on the farms, in the dairy factories and in the mines of the Waikato, the King Country and the Central Plateau since the First World War. Bush-work, a favourite occupation for Northern men, had been diminishing in Northland for the last twenty-five years, and a trickle of emigrants had moved steadily southward in pursuit of it. Whatever their age, Kōtare emigrants to other rural areas had one thing in common: they had usually lived in several places after leaving Kōtare. The older ones had moved around quite extensively in rural areas, while many of those who had settled down more recently were men with records of war service and couples who had met while working in town or city.

Finally, although many emigrants settled permanently in the district from which their spouses derived, neolocal residence was just as common. Out of thirty-six married or widowed women from Kōtare living in other rural areas in 1955, only twenty were living in their husband's community, while only fifteen of the thirty-four men who were married or widowed were living in their wife's community. A certain amount of mobility, connected primarily with the search for work and experience and not confined to a self-compensating exchange of spouses, would seem to have been general between rural areas for most of the present century.

Emigration to Country Towns

About 13 per cent of the Kōtare emigrants were living in country towns in 1955, nearly half of them in the closest, Raumati, a Borough with a population of 1,800 in 1951. The other towns of Northland did not attract. Even Whāngārei, by far the largest (11,851 in 1951), had only three Kōtare emigrants in 1955. The rest were distributed among the towns of the central areas of the North Island, regional centres for rural areas which had also attracted emigrants from Kōtare.

Raumati was the only country town with more than two or three Kōtare emigrants. It did not, however, attract many as permanent settlers. Only four had lived there more than two years: three were married and had homes there; the fourth, a matron at the hospital, was an anomalous case because she maintained a house in Kōtare and occasionally spent off-duty hours there. The rest of the Kōtare emigrants in Raumati were only temporarily settled there, living with siblings or affines (4), "living in" at the hospital (7) or, in one case, a patient there; they spent most of their leisure time with their families in Kōtare. Young people who had formerly held similar positions in Raumati had nearly all migrated further afield, especially to the city.

It is difficult to generalise about emigrants to the other country towns because of the small numbers involved. Those in the larger towns were mostly married and seemed well established, but those in the smaller towns were single and moved about a good deal.

Emigration to country towns, even to Raumati, was haphazard and irregular. It was closely associated with migration to rural areas, those concerned finding similar jobs, in mines and timber mills, or in dairy factories and as domestics. In many cases residence within the limits of Borough or Town District was fortuitous, depending on the availability of accommodation.

EMIGRATION TO URBAN AREAS

Migration from Kōtare to industrialised cities was almost exclusively directed towards Auckland, which was the nearest city and the chief industrial centre and port of New Zealand. Only ten Kōtare emigrants were to be found in other Urban Areas, six in the metropolitan areas of Wellington and Christchurch, and four in Hamilton, Palmerston North and Invercargill. To Kōtare Maoris contemplating emigration, Auckland was the obvious destination. There were already so many Kōtare people living there that a prospective emigrant had no worries about accommodation or loneliness on arrival.

At the end of June, 1955, there were 115 'active' emigrants from Kōtare living in Auckland, 54 men and 61 women. This ratio between the sexes was an important feature of urban migration from Kōtare; urbanisation did not affect the men to a greater degree than the women, but rather less. In both cases, the proportion of those who migrated independently was high: 42 (77 per cent) of the men were unmarried at emigration, one widowed and four separated from their wives, while 48 (78 per cent) of the women were unmarried, one widowed and two separated from their husbands. About 15 per cent were married at the time of emigration, and these were accompanied by their spouses and children (if any). Most of the emigrants living in Auckland in 1955 belonged to the younger age groups, 44 per cent being under twenty-five years of age. Auckland drew off most of the young and unmarried persons who left Kōtare.

Auckland had much to offer in the way of educational and vocational training, but only a small proportion of the Kōtare emigrants were taking advantage of these opportunities. The majority were unskilled or semi-skilled workers, mainly domestics, labourers and factory hands. There were only four skilled tradesmen (all foremen), three apprentices and one nurse-in-training. Only one woman, a dietician with a University degree, held a professional position; two others were attending University and Teachers' Training Colleges respectively.

Migration to Urban Areas—the really large centres of population of over 20,000—as distinct from small, non-industrial country towns, began in earnest in the early years of the Second World War. Some emigrants from Kōtare reached Auckland before the war: twelve were there still in 1955, having raised families and acquired permanent homes there, except for one man whose earnings were financing a home in Kōtare. But most of those who took part in the influx to Auckland during the war, and most of the Kōtare men who spent some months or even years there after demobilisation from the Armed Forces, had left the city. Almost 75 per cent of the Kōtare emigrants in Auckland had been living there for less than ten years, that is, since the end of the war, and almost 50 per cent —56 out of 115—had arrived within the last five years, a few, admittedly, for the second time. Twenty-six had been in Auckland only a year or less. Whereas in the early stages of the trend most of the emigrants had already lived outside Kōtare and in many cases migrated to the city from other places, recent emigrants tended to go direct from Kōtare to the city. Eighteen of the thirty-seven who had arrived in Auckland within the previous two years had come straight from Kōtare.

Migration to Urban Areas was increasing in importance and increasing at the expense of migration to other destinations. Nevertheless, emigration from Kōtare was still far from being exclusively directed towards industrialised Urban Areas, even if those taken away from Kōtare by the normal processes of marriage and adoption are left out of account. (On the other hand, it was in some cases just these "normal processes" of marriage and adoption which took some Kōtare folk to the city, for neolocal residence, even in rural areas, was more frequent than virilocal and uxorilocal marriage put together, and the city was a favourite place for setting up house at marriage, or as soon as a couple began to want a place of their own.) Urban migration is set in its true perspective when it is remembered that, in 1955, 34 per cent of the 'active' Kōtare emigrants were living in other rural areas, another 14 per cent in small country towns, which were urban but not industrialised, while Urban Areas accounted for just over half.

IMMIGRATION INTO KŌTARE

Kōtare was not affected only by emigration. Nearly one-third of its Maori residents did not "belong" there in the Maori sense of the word, and a considerable proportion of the remainder were either not born in Kōtare or had passed some part of their lives in other places.

An important part of this immigration was what may be called socially normal, the inflow of Maoris from other communities as spouses, adopted and foster children to Kōtare residents. Fourteen men and thirty-two women of 'immigrant' status and one *tangata whenua* woman brought up elsewhere had come into the community as a result of marriage. All but four of the women married *tāngata whenua*. Another seventeen immigrants had come to Kōtare initially for other reasons but remained after marrying local residents, both *tāngata whenua* (13) and 'immigrant' settlers (3). Seven (some of whom came to Kōtare on marrying *tāngata whenua*, some as 'immigrant' settlers) remained there after the death of their spouses and two in the absence of their husbands in the city. Finally, four children from other districts were being brought up by foster parents in Kōtare, three had been legally adopted and four had come as stepchildren to their mother's second husband.

Most of the forty-six adults who settled in Kōtare as a direct result of marriage came from other parts of the Far North. Sixteen came originally from other Rarawa communities, four were Aupouri, four Ngāti Kahu, and eight Ngāpuhi from Hokianga and the Bay of Islands. The others (apart from two whose origin I did not discover) came from widely scattered places: three from Northern Wairoa (Ngāti Whātua) and three from Whāngārei county (Ngāpuhi) in Northland; a 'native' Ngāti Whātua and a city-born Ngāpuhi from Auckland; two from Taranaki; and one each from Rotorua and Ōtaki (near Wellington). Now the astonishing thing about these marriages was that only five spouses came from adjacent communities. Not merely the figures but nearly every case-history showed that intra- and extra-regional mobility had more effect on the choice of spouses than ordinary social relations between neighbouring districts. Ten matches had their beginning in Auckland, one in Hamilton, six in towns as far separated as Raumati and Pātea (in Taranaki), and one as the result of a season's hop-picking in Nelson. Many returning emigrants had brought home spouses met on the Northland gum-fields and in other rural districts.

Not all the outside spouses living in Kōtare in 1955 had come into the community immediately at marriage. Thirty-one had arrived some time later, in many cases after the birth of children.

There were also a few temporary residents in Kōtare, immigrants whose reasons for being in Kōtare would keep them there at most a few years. Under this heading came eight children boarded in local homes by the Child Welfare Department, three young teachers with limited terms of service (a Junior and two Probationary Assistants), and a student attending secondary school in Raumati.

Thirdly, there was in Kōtare in 1955 an important minority of persons who were not *tāngata whenua* nor married to *tāngata whenua*, and who are best described as 'immigrant' settlers (see Table 4). Sixteen men and fifteen women had settled in Kōtare as adults. Of these, twenty-one were already married when they arrived, four came as a result of marrying local 'immigrants' or Pakehas, three had married other 'immigrants' after arrival, and only three were still single. They had brought with them a total of fifteen children and another thirty-one had been born in Kōtare (or more accurately born in the Raumati hospital while their parents were living in Kōtare). The latter shared the 'immigrant' status of their parents. Thus only 60 per cent of the 'immigrant' settlers were immigrants in the literal sense of the word.

The adults in the group had come to Kōtare expressly to establish homes there, attracted by the accessibility of Raumati, the proximity of the sea and the availability of cheap freehold sections. Most had arrived within the last fifteen years, since the beginning of the Second World War. Nearly all those gainfully employed worked in Raumati; indeed most were established in jobs there before they decided to settle in Kōtare. The only ones working in Kōtare itself were two school teachers, a mechanic at the bus depot and a man farming land in which his first wife had had rights. Kōtare did not attract young, unmarried immigrants. There were only three there in 1955, all boarding with kinsfolk and working outside Kōtare. Unless they married in Kōtare, they were unlikely to remain for long.

Almost all the 'immigrant' settlers came from other rural communities

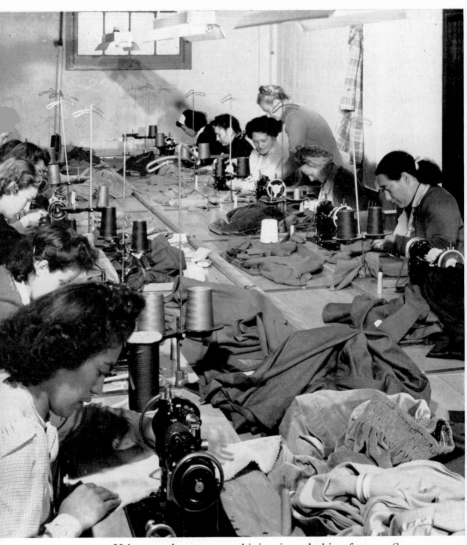

PLATE 7. Urban employment: machinists in a clothing factory. See pp. 135–6.

PLATE 8. (*a*) Country school-children practising an action-song, and (*b*) Auckland Maoris take part in the city's welcome to Royal visitors, December 1953. See p. 227.

in the Far North, and the majority from communities for which, like Kōtare itself, Raumati was the regional centre. Many did not lack entirely for kinship links with other members of the community, since they came from communities with whom spouses had been exchanged in the past, but in no case were such links strong enough to be the determining factor in the decision to settle in Kōtare. Usually these kinship relations were so tenuous that in other circumstances, when plenty of other kin were at hand, they would have been disregarded. In some cases, the absence of close kin ties with the local people was considered a positive advantage. One 'immigrant' settled in Kōtare because he "wanted to get away from my relations". He had refused the occupancy of a "family farm" because he "preferred to have my own place". On the whole, the 'immigrants' felt no need to attach themselves to any of the Kōtare 'families', although they frequently "lent a hand" at gatherings sponsored by any in which they had kin or friends.

Most of those who had come into Kōtare as 'active immigrants' hoped to remain there permanently. They were now well over thirty, they had built their own homes in Kōtare, and the wage-earners were established in steady jobs. Their older offspring, however, were as susceptible to the attractions of other places as the rest of the young and unmarried in Kōtare.

Fourthly, a substantial number of *tāngata whenua* had immigrated into Kōtare in a literal sense. First, there were 26 adults and 39 children born outside Kōtare to emigrant members of Kōtare 'families'. Secondly, there were those who had spent all or part of their childhood above the age of three (when they were old enough to remember the change) outside Kōtare. This group overlapped with the first, since 21 adults and 11 children fell into both categories, but it also included 14 other adults born in Kōtare (or in the Raumati hospital but brought home to Kōtare within a matter of weeks). In both groups, roughly half were connected to Kōtare 'families' through their fathers, so that the offspring of Kōtare males showed no greater tendency to return to Kōtare than those of women who "married out". Half the adults born outside Kōtare were born on the gum-fields and in the bush-camps of the Far North. Half of those born outside Kōtare in the last fifteen years on the other hand, were born in the city, a reflection of changes in the pattern of migration. Most in both groups came to Kōtare before they were fifteen, either with their parents or through adoption, but nine first came to live in Kōtare as adults.

The third and largest group consisted of those who, having spent at least part of their childhood in Kōtare, had emigrated as adults on their own initiative and then decided to return to Kōtare. There were more men (39) than women (26) in this group. Seven out of ten had worked in other rural districts, most at some stage outside the Far North. Very few had worked in country towns but half had lived in Auckland. One in three had had experience of the city and of other rural areas as well.

COUNTER-EMIGRATION

A considerable proportion of the immigration into Kōtare represented as it were a back-wash from the predominant trend of emigration. Most of the emigrants who returned to Kōtare were members of local 'families', but two 'immigrants' had also come back after a spell in the city and elsewhere. The most interesting feature of this counter movement was that those involved were still comparatively young. Over two-thirds of the Kōtare Maoris who had lived in towns or cities were, in 1955, still under thirty-five years of age; a quarter were even under twenty-five. Similarly, most of those who returned to Kōtare from another rural district did so before they were thirty-five. Old age was not the reason which brought most emigrants home.

The reason they themselves most often gave was "home-sickness"—a desire to be with their kinsfolk rather than an abstract attachment to the land. Many had come home in the first place to be with a parent, grandparent or sibling who was ill or dying, and remained to settle. Some said they returned because they disliked city life—but every one of them had spent many years in the city before returning. Positive attractions were the chance of occupying a family farm or house and the opening up of new types of employment in the district and its vicinity. The development of seaweed-picking and the building boom after the war both drew absentees home.

In the past, a number of returned emigrants had left Kōtare for a second time. Fifteen of the emigrants from Kōtare living in Auckland were in their second term there, after a spell home in Kōtare. But only four or five had returned home twice.

THE PATTERN OF MIGRATION: HISTORY, CAUSES AND EFFECTS

Kōtare was involved in a complex pattern of migratory movement and had been for a long period, though the details of the pattern had changed considerably over time.

Prior to the Second World War, most of the movement involving Maoris from Kōtare was confined to rural areas, and rather more than half of it to the Far North. A large proportion of the community was involved, for ways of earning a cash income in Kōtare itself were very restricted and emigrating workers normally took their families with them. Emigrants typically "travelled" (as they put it) widely in other rural areas, even after marriage. The men were engaged mainly in developmental work on a casual or contractual basis: felling bush, draining and fencing new farms, building roads and bridges. Many of the girls went to work at thirteen or fourteen in Pakeha homes in quite distant areas, marrying within three or four years. At the same time, the kauri-gum fields of Northland provided an opportunity for the elementary-family to work again as a productive unit. A gum-field was opened up in Kōtare itself, bringing a large influx of diggers. But it did relatively little to check the mobility of Kōtare workers and their families, for circulation from field to field seems to have been common. Many Kōtare gum-diggers spent most of their working life on other fields, coming home only to retire.

By 1930, however, the bottom had dropped out of the kauri-gum market, and a world-wide depression had set in, with serious repercussions on rural (and other) employment. Some Kōtare Maoris returned home to try and subsist on their land. Many more obtained "relief work" from the Government, living outside Kōtare in Public Works camps for considerable periods, planting marram grass on the west coast sand-hills, draining swampland and working on the roads. At the same time, the Government began to develop Maori land in Kōtare (under the 1929 Native Land Development Act), giving employment to many shareholders. By 1935 the developmental phase was over and the need for labourers diminished. Instead some twenty farmers and their families were established on farms just coming into production.

The Second World War absorbed most of the young men into the Armed Forces and opened up opportunities for employment in the towns and cities, resulting in a marked re-orientation of migration towards the city. Urban migration continued unabated after the war was over. In the 1950's between twenty and twenty-five emigrants left Kōtare for the city each year. The post-war period also saw an expansion of commerce and industry (particularly in the construction trades) in Raumati, opening up an important market for labour within travelling distance of Kōtare itself. Transport facilities were improved and a pattern of commuting from Kōtare to Raumati established. This development did much to check emigration on the part of older workers, and brought back many released from the Forces and from war work in the city. Forty-four of the men engaged in commuting to work from Kōtare in 1955 had settled in Kōtare since the end of the war, sixteen being 'immigrant' settlers, eight men married to *tāngata whenua*, and twenty returned emigrants. Many had acquired skills during their absence, often as part of Army or Rehabilitation training. Within the last five years, the development of seaweed-picking in the remoter bays had attracted a few Maoris to Kōtare, most of Kōtare stock. Throughout all these changes in the pattern of migration, individuals also moved in response to personal and family circumstances, sometimes even at variance with the dominant trend of the moment.

The net result of this complex pattern of migration was a considerable annual loss of population, which was not, however, sufficient to deplete the Kōtare Maori community to a point where its economic or social balance was seriously disturbed. On the contrary, there was no place in the economic life of Kōtare for those who had left it. The community was imbalanced by a phenomenally high rate of natural increase, which had the effect of weighting it heavily in the younger age groups. In spite of the emigration of so many young and able-bodied workers, 149 between the

ages of fifteen and thirty-four still remained in Kōtare, where they formed
55 per cent of the adult population and outnumbered all older inhabitants
by 3 to 2. Only 8 of the 72 wage-earners in this group were able to make a
livelihood within Kōtare itself; the rest commuted daily to work outside
it. Emigration had not caused a shortage of manpower in Kōtare, but was
itself largely the product of over-population in relation to resources. There
was irony in this situation, because the natural resources of the district
were not fully utilised.

Emigration from Kōtare would have been considerably greater if it had
not been for the availability of employment for wages and on contract in
adjacent areas, especially in Raumati. In 1955, the labour market within
reach of Kōtare was exceptionally favourable for men compared with
pre-war times, because of the prosperity of the country as a whole and the
current boom in building trades and public works. But even so, competition
for employment was keen. Much of the unskilled work was seasonal in
nature, and labourers were often laid off for several months in the winter.
The jobs available for women were restricted in range and number.
Though some of the men's jobs (such as quarrying) demanded workers
who were young and fit, most were equally suited to older workers.
Employers in general preferred to employ older married men because they
had known them longer and because they were more resistant to the lure
of the city.

The effects of over-population in relation to local resources, the restricted range of employment and the imminent saturation of the labour
market in the vicinity, were reinforced by the attitude of the people
themselves to emigration, a factor which is often overlooked and certainly
underrated. Some Kōtare residents looked on emigration as a regrettable
necessity, but they were mostly the elderly who had learnt from their own
experience that "there is no place like home". The prevailing mood was
one of curiosity about other places and eagerness to see them personally.
The average young Maori in Kōtare was attracted by the idea of emigration. He was "sick of the same old faces", he found country life "too dry"
or "too slow", and he wanted to "see new places and new people" instead
of "the same old thing all the time". A craving for new experiences, for
excitement and adventure, was typical of the young generation in Kōtare,
in spite of the fact that it was often found side by side with shyness and
lack of self-confidence (frequently disguised by assertiveness), especially
in contact with Pakehas. In most cases it was strong enough to overcome
all feelings of diffidence and to carry the individual off into an outside
world that was dominated by Pakehas.

Eager interest in the outside world was in part a legacy from the past.
In fact, though it was not overtly recognised, Kōtare had a tradition of
mobility. As we have seen, most of the older generations had themselves
lived outside Kōtare at some stage, and many of the elderly prided themselves on having been "great travellers" in their day. Many of the men

had been overseas in one of the two World Wars. The young people had no stay-at-home tradition to combat.

There was remarkably little opposition even from the older generations. Parents accepted it as part of a normal pattern that their offspring should leave them when they were old enough to support themselves, and seek work and experience elsewhere. They did not try to persuade them against migrating, but actively assisted them. Some arranged to send their son or daughter to a job in another district as soon as they left school. Several parents argued that it was good for young people to go away, because "they learn to stand on their own feet and to manage their own money": as long as they were at home they relied on parents to help them out of financial and other scrapes. Others admitted that they were glad when their older children emigrated because it eased the strain on their finances and accommodation.

It was generally accepted that the city offered the best prospects of a good life outside Kōtare, better than other rural areas or country towns. It had many positive attractions: a wide range of occupations, high wages and a social life of variety and glamour. Some parents and most *kaumātua* mistrusted the city, fearing that those who settled there might lose their "Maori ways" and "become Pakeha" in their attitudes to money and social obligations, or "get into trouble with the police". But this mistrust was not general and it was outweighed by other considerations. Parents who had known hard times on the kauri-gum fields and during the depression or had struggled to turn a small farm into a reasonable livelihood, were pleased that their children should have better economic prospects than they had had. They also argued that "there is nothing here for them and they only get up to mischief". Work was not easy to find for the young, and organised recreation was limited. Paradoxically, dances and socials run in Kōtare usually failed for lack of patronage. The young people preferred the glamour of the same type of entertainment in Raumati or less organised (and less restrained) parties in their own homes or out-of-doors. Gatherings in the community attended by "the same old faces" and following the "same old" pattern frankly bored them, and they looked around for more exciting ways of entertaining themselves. It was no wonder, then, that parents sometimes concluded that the "temptations of country life" were as great if not greater than those of the city, or that they saw the latter as the best place to absorb the surplus high spirits of their young people. They were in fact often relieved "to get them off our hands".

The frequent changes in personnel which had characterised Kōtare for a long time required constant adjustments within the community. Migratory movements had helped to break down cultural isolation and to modify traditionalism, for both immigrants and returning emigrants introduced new ideas and interests.

Partly because they were in the majority, returned emigrants did not constitute a discontented or disturbing element in the Maori community, not even those from the city. They had returned of their own free will and preference. Happy to be home, they settled into the life of the community with comparative ease, untroubled by regrets for the diversions and high wages of the city or by zeal for modernising or reforming it except in minor ways.

CONCLUSION

Emigration to the city was the most important single trend in the complex pattern of migration which characterised Kōtare, but emigration to other destinations was still significant, and emigration in general was offset to a certain extent by immigration, which included returning emigrants, many of them from the city. While urban migration dated only from the beginning of the Second World War, a tradition of mobility and interest in distant places and people had been established during the pre-war decades of pioneer development in the Far North.

Emigration in general was closely associated with the increasing inadequacy of natural resources to support even a fraction of the population at the levels of living to which they aspired. It was modified to a certain extent by the recent development of commuting to employment in neighbouring areas. On the other hand, experience of employment of this type frequently encouraged the younger workers to emigrate to the city.

The relatively long history of emigration from Kōtare and the eventual return of many emigrants had combined to modify the social isolation and conservatism of the community, producing a population in which not a small élite but an actual majority of adults had first-hand experience of the outside world. Paradoxically, the result of this situation was to minimise the disruptive influence of returned emigrants, particularly those from the city. In general, the effect of emigration was beneficial and necessary, for it drained off the surplus population and the discontented and most high-spirited elements in the community.

PART TWO

The City

6

The Demographic Background

IN 1951, 28 per cent of the urban Maori population was to be found in the city of Auckland. It had attained this importance as a result of rapid immigration over the previous twelve years. The 1936 Census recorded 1,766 Maoris in Auckland, an increase of barely 600 in ten years. By 25 September 1945 (at the end of the Second World War) there were 4,903, an increase of 177·6 per cent in nine and a half years, or 18·7 per cent per annum. Subsequently the annual rate of increase dropped to 10·8 per cent between the Censuses of 1945 and 1951 (taken on 17 April) when 7,621 Maoris were recorded for Auckland. If a rate of approximately 10·5 per cent had been maintained since 1951—and there seems no reason to doubt that it had—there would have been over 10,000 Maoris in Auckland by 31 August 1954, the date I have chosen as a baseline for my own Auckland material. It must be remembered, however, that in spite of rapid increase in the number of Maoris in Auckland, they were still only a small minority in the total population—2·3 per cent in 1951.

The purpose of this chapter is to discover the characteristics of the Auckland Maori population as a demographic unit and the extent to which it differed from the total Maori and non-Maori populations. The Census closest to the period of my own research in Auckland is that taken in 1951. The Maori Census for 1951 (Vol. 6 of the New Zealand Census) was not published until 1955 and did not contain separate statistics for Auckland under certain headings relevant to this work (marital status, dependent children, etc.). The Census and Statistics Department kindly permitted me access to their provisional unpublished returns relating to both the total and Auckland populations, and it is these that I have used in this chapter. As a result there are a few slight discrepancies from the published figures. The 1951 Census was taken three years and five months before the baseline for my own material. However, there is nothing to suggest that any major changes had occurred in the constitution of the Auckland Maori population during the interval, though it had increased in size.

The city of Auckland consisted, in 1951, of a large number of local governing bodies. That known as Auckland City comprised only the central city and eastern suburbs. I have adopted the Auckland Urban Area as defined by the Census and Statistics Department as the best available definition of the city's limits. This included: Auckland City,

Eden County and eight Boroughs occupying the Tāmaki isthmus, eleven satellite towns (nine Boroughs and two Town Districts), and parts of the adjacent Counties of Waitemata, Manukau and Franklin (see Fig. 7 inset and Table 11).

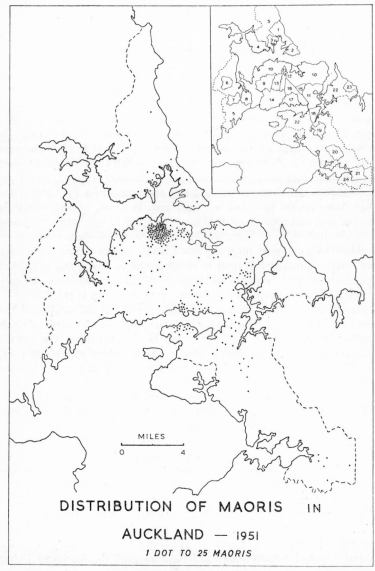

DISTRIBUTION OF MAORIS IN

AUCKLAND — 1951

1 DOT TO 25 MAORIS

MILES

0   4

FIG. 7. Distribution of Maoris in Auckland, 1951
For key to figure inset see Table 11, p. 277

Local Distribution

In 1951 the distribution of the Maori population in the Auckland Urban Area was extremely uneven and bore little relation to that of the non-Maori population (see Fig. 7). In all parts of the city, however, even those in which they were most numerous, Maoris lived scattered among Pakehas, by whom they were greatly outnumbered. There was only one exclusively Maori settlement in the city, one of *tāngata whenua* in Ōrākei in the eastern suburbs (thirty households).

Thirty-two per cent of the 7,621 Maoris in Auckland lived in the central-city area and 9 per cent in the western-central suburbs, the oldest parts of the city, where the predominantly wooden houses were beginning to deteriorate with age. Nearly 11 per cent were located in the area bordering the Tāmaki River estuary, which in 1951 was in transition from market gardens, which had supported a fair number of Maoris, to an extensive suburb of "State houses",[1] a proportion of which was reserved for Maoris. Two other sectors of the city accounted for a substantial part of the Maori population: 9·5 per cent in the south-eastern suburbs, about equally divided between State houses and the older parts of Onehunga; and 12·5 per cent in the Manukau area, half on the market gardens and half in the Boroughs of Ōtāhuhu, Papatoetoe and Papakura. The remaining 26 per cent were scattered widely over the city with minor concentrations at Avondale in the west and Ōrākei in the east.

After the Census date, the details of this pattern were modified by the movements of many families from sub-standard housing in the central city and Onehunga to new houses in the outer suburbs. Between 1 April 1951 and 30 September 1954, over 150 State houses were allocated to Maoris and 120 more were erected for Maori owners by means of housing loans advanced by the Department of Maori Affairs.[2] This affected between 800 and 1,300 Maoris. The movement to State houses was directed chiefly to the eastern suburbs of Tāmaki and Glen Innes, where 113 houses

---

[1] Houses built and administered by the State through the State Advances Corporation under a scheme introduced in 1936. In Auckland in 1953–4, the State Advances set aside a share of the houses available in each year (reckoned on the basis of the proportion of Maoris to non-Maoris among urgent applications) as a Maori pool. Applications from Maoris were handled by the Department of Maori Affairs and the houses allocated by an independent Maori Housing Allocation Committee operating under its supervision. In most other areas Maoris were allocated State houses on the same basis as other applicants. See *Report of the Department of Maori Affairs*, G–9, 1956, p. 18.

[2] Under the Maori Housing Act 1935, the Department of Maori Affairs advanced loans of up to £2,000 to Maoris wishing to build their own homes and arranged the building of the houses, in most cases on contract. The Department also helped Maori families to save the amount needed to bridge the gap between the cost of house and section and the loan maximum by acting as their saving agency. Maoris could also obtain loans from the State Advances Corporation on the same terms as non-Maoris, and this the Department encouraged those in a good financial situation to do. No figures concerning the numbers who had followed this course are available. *Ibid*, pp. 16–20.

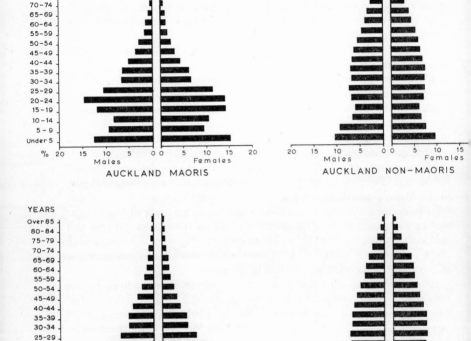

FIG. 8. Maori and Non-Maori: Age Distribution, 1951

accommodated between 550 and 750 Maoris at the end of September 1954. (There were 139 Maoris in this area in 1951.) The largest numbers of State houses allocated to Maoris during this period in other suburbs were in Ōrākei (25), Onehunga (23), Mt. Roskill (18) and Avondale (18). Houses built with D.M.A. loans were widely scattered.[1]

Sex and Age

Instead of the excess of males which has characterised the early stages of urbanisation in many countries, the sexes were almost equal in the Auckland

[1] Figures given in this paragraph were supplied by the Department of Maori Affairs in January 1955.

Maori population in 1951: 3,793 males to 3,858 females. The age structure of the group, however, was seriously imbalanced, being heavily weighted in the younger adult age-groups. Forty-five per cent of the Auckland Maoris were between fifteen and thirty-five, compared with 32 per cent of the total Maori population and 28 per cent of the Auckland and total non-Maori populations (see Fig. 8 and Table 12). On the other hand, the Auckland Maoris had a much lower percentage under fifteen than the total Maori group, though children were still relatively more numerous than among Auckland non-Maoris. (The latter group also had a smaller proportion of children than the corresponding total population, but the difference was much less, and it was balanced by an increase in the proportion of older persons and not, as in the Auckland Maori group, by an increased percentage of young adults.) In contrast to the non-Maori populations, the Maoris both in Auckland and in the total population diminished rapidly above the age of thirty-five. The low proportion of elders over fifty-five was particularly marked in Auckland.

Marital Status and Family Size

Largely because of its high proportion of young adults, the Maori population as a whole was characterised by a high percentage of adults who had never been married (30 per cent of those over sixteen in 1951). This feature was even more pronounced among Maoris in Auckland, where 40 per cent fell into the never-married category (compared with 25 per cent of the Auckland non-Maoris) (see Table 13). Furthermore, this percentage was 3 to 10 per cent higher in every age-group than in the total Maori population, while the percentage in the married category was 6 to 10 per cent below. The higher proportion of never-married Maoris in Auckland was compensated by a decrease in the percentage of married persons, and not (as in the non-Maori group) by an increase in that of the formerly-married (widowed, legally separated and divorced). Within this last category there were rather fewer widowed and more separated and divorced Maoris in Auckland than in the total Maori population, but the differences were so slight that they could not be taken as evidence of an increase in marital instability. Besides, the statistics did not indicate that the separations and divorces involved had taken place in the city: some may have occurred before migration. Nor did they take account of the incidence of so-called "Maori marriages" (unlegalised unions usually involving persons party to other, undissolved legal unions)[1] or of separation without legal settlement.

In Auckland in 1951 there were proportionately fewer Maori couples with large families than in the total Maori population, and more with few or no dependent children (see Table 14). The same was true of the widowed and separated. In the total Maori population, 14·8 per cent of the married men had more than five dependent children and 26·8 per cent

[1] Metge, 1957, p. 167.

between three and five, but in Auckland the corresponding percentages were only 8·4 per cent and 23 per cent. These were, however, well above those for the Auckland non-Maori population (0·9 per cent and 13·4 per cent). Part of the decrease in the size of Maori families in Auckland could be attributed to the high proportion of adults in the twenties and thirties; proportionately more urban Maori families were still incomplete.

Degrees of Maori Blood

Statistics relating to the degrees of Maori blood are most difficult to collect and assess. My own experience indicated that few Maoris worked out their proportion of Maori to non-Maori forebears in any detail: whether they declared themselves as full-, half- or quarter-Maori depended largely on subjective criteria. (One told me: "Both my grandfathers were Pakehas, but I always put myself down as full-Maori, because I feel Maori.") This should be borne in mind when noting that the relative importance of the degrees of Maori blood differed markedly between the Auckland and total populations in 1951 (see Table 15). The percentage of full and three-quarter Maoris was 15 per cent lower in Auckland than for the total population, while that of half-Maoris was higher by 2 per cent and of quarter-Maoris by 11 per cent. Whereas half-Maoris outnumbered quarter-Maoris in the total population, in Auckland the situation was reversed. Offspring of marriages between Maoris and other-than-Europeans were three times as numerous in Auckland, where they were mainly of Maori-Chinese parentage; but the figures were very small.

The higher proportion of persons with some non-Maori admixture in Auckland might be due to several causes, the relative importance of which cannot be determined from the statistics. There might be more intermarriage in the city. But this would not wholly explain the situation, because so many Auckland Maoris were immigrants from rural areas. Those living in the city where they were outnumbered by Pakehas might be expected to understate their degree of Maori blood. In my experience, overstatement was more common, at least among those with half-Maori blood or more. Finally, part-Maoris might tend to leave their home communities more readily than full-Maoris. Probably all these factors played their part.

Occupational Status

Unfortunately detailed information about the occupations of Maoris in Auckland was not compiled separately in 1951. In the broad terms of occupational status, considerably fewer Maoris in Auckland were in the dependent category than in the total Maori population and almost twice the proportion were working for wages (see Table 16). But the number employing labour was very low in Auckland (0·2 per cent compared with 0·8 per cent of the total Maori population), and so was the number of those working on their own account. (Higher proportions in the total Maori population were due to the number of farmers in rural areas.) The proportion of unemployed in Auckland was higher than for the Maori population as a whole or for the non-Maori population in Auckland; but as it amounted to only 1·2 per cent, unemployment was hardly a serious problem. Fewer Auckland Maoris were working without payment for kinsfolk and there were few retired persons with independent means. The differences between the patterns of occupational status of the Auckland Maoris and the total Maori population were more marked than between the two non-Maori populations.

Religious Profession

The religious professions of the Auckland Maoris in 1951 followed closely those of the Maori population as a whole. The largest number of adherents belonged to the Anglican, Ratana, Roman Catholic and Methodist churches, in that order, and the proportion of those who objected to stating their religious profession was larger than for the non-Maori population (see Table 17). In Auckland and in New Zealand as a whole Maoris differed from the non-Maoris in the number who belonged to the Ratana church, a Maori denomination, and to the Church of Latter Day Saints. Only 51 per cent of the Auckland Maoris (53 per cent of the total Maori population) belonged to the four largest denominations in New Zealand—Church of England, Presbyterian, Roman Catholic and Methodist—compared with 82 per cent of the non-Maori population.

SUMMARY

The Maori population of the Auckland Urban Area comprised a significant section of the Maori urban population and was far the largest group of Maori urban residents in New Zealand. It differed in certain significant ways from the Maori population as a whole: it was heavily weighted in the younger adult age-groups; it had an abnormally high proportion of unmarried adults; families tended to be small by rural Maori standards, though still large by Pakeha ones; more Maoris claimed a share of non-Maori blood; the proportion of dependent persons was much lower but the importance of the self-employed and employers was also diminished. In none of these respects, however, was the Auckland Maori population severely imbalanced. In at least two ways, the Auckland Maoris did not conform to the common stereotype of a recently urbanised population: there were equal numbers of men and women in the city, and the statistics did not reveal any significant tendency towards increased marital instability, though the latter might have been masked by the fact that few broken Maori marriages were dissolved legally.

The outstanding characteristics of the Auckland Maori population were: the predominance of young unmarried adults and the high proportion engaged in employment for wages.

7

The Local People

WHEN Captain Hobson chose the Tāmaki isthmus as the site of the capital of New Zealand in 1840, it was only thinly populated by Maoris, in spite of its strategic position, its rich volcanic soils and its abundant sea resources. It had once been the most densely settled area in Maori New Zealand.

In the seventeenth and eighteenth centuries warring tribes had struggled endlessly for its possession, so that it became known as Tāmaki-makau-rau, Tāmaki contended for by a hundred lovers. By 1800 the Ngāti Whātua tribe had established their ascendancy over most of the isthmus, temporarily driving out the Ngāti Paoa; they also defeated the remnants of the Waiohua occupying Māngere on the southern shore of the Manukau Harbour and settled there themselves. But the fighting had taken its toll, and two epidemics (the second in 1810) also depleted their numbers. They had to abandon many of the large hill fortresses because they no longer had the manpower to defend them. The Ngāti Paoa returned to their villages along the shores of the Tāmaki River, building two large *pa* (forts) called Mokoia and Mau-inaina. A few years later, in the face of threatened attack by the Ngāpuhi under their chief Hongi Hika, the Ngāti Whātua withdrew from Tāmaki entirely to consolidate their forces in the Kaipara area. In 1821 Hongi Hika invaded Tāmaki with his musket-armed war-parties and took Mokoia and Mau-inaina with great slaughter. The Ngāti Paoa retreated to Waiheke Island and the Hauraki hinterland. After ravaging much of the North Island Hongi defeated the Ngāti Whātua decisively when he captured their strongest pa, Te Ika-a-Ranganui on the Kaipara Harbour, near Kaiwaka, in 1825. For many years Tāmaki was virtually deserted. Remnants of Ngāti Whātua eventually returned about 1835, re-establishing their headquarters at the village of Okāhu on the eastern Waitemata Harbour, under their chief Apihai Te Kawau. They also had a village in Māngere, shared at their invitation by certain prominent members of the Waikato tribes.

Te Kawau, together with Te Tinana, Rēweti Tāmaki and other Ngāti Whātua *rangatira*, sold the original site of the city, some three thousand acres, to Governor Hobson acting for the Queen. (The deed of sale was dated 29 July 1841.) Later the Ngāti Whātua disposed of most of the isthmus by sale to the Crown and to private individuals, and by generous gifts to the city. The Ngāti Whātua remained on good terms with the settlers and refused to join their old enemies the Ngāpuhi in Hone Heke's War in the North (1844–5) or the Waikato tribes in the so-called Maori Wars (1856–65). Ultimately, after the completion of the Tāmaki Waterfront Drive in 1932, their settlement at Ōkahu was engulfed by the spreading city. Its inhabitants became urban residents by accident as it were, though those who wished avoided that fate by retreat to other parts of their tribal territory.

In 1849 Governor Grey, perturbed about the defence of the infant capital, arranged with Te Wherowhero, paramount chief of the federated Waikato tribes (and afterwards the first Maori King), to send eighty picked fighting men with their families to settle in Māngere opposite the Fencibles pensioner settlement at Onehunga. They were given inalienable grants of Crown land, one acre for a dwelling and five acres for cultivation per family; in return they were obliged to parade for twelve days a year and to serve if required, without payment except for days in excess of the specified twelve. These settlers were Ngāti Mahuta, their leader Tāmati Ngāpora, Te Wherowhero's brother. In 1863 they quietly departed to join their kinsmen fighting in the Waikato and their land was confiscated. Some, however, returned after the war and their title to the land was renewed under the Landless Maoris Act 1867.[1]

There were probably fewer than 500 tāngata whenua living in Auckland in 1953–4, even if the term is interpreted in its broadest sense to include descendants of the last Maori owners and not merely present landowners. They were not reckoned as a separate category in the 1951 Census, so that even this figure is only an informed guess. At any event, they were greatly outnumbered by 'immigrants'. The largest number in one locality were living in an all-Maori settlement, Ōkahu, in the suburb of Ōrākei, where (according to my count) there were 148 tāngata whenua at 31 August 1953.[2] A hundred or so were dispersed over the Mangere district, and the rest were scattered throughout the urban area.

Most of the Auckland tāngata whenua belonged to certain hapū of the Ngāti Whātua tribe. The rest were Ngāti Mahuta of the Waikato tribal federation. However, considerable intermarriage had taken place between the two groups within the last four or five generations, so that many could claim membership in both.

There was little Maori land left within the limits of the urban area. Most of it lay in Mangere: forty acres in small, scattered lots, which had become Maori land under the terms of the original Crown grants. Another acre was gazetted as a marae reserve, but it had no buildings. Most of the Maori land in Mangere was leased to market-gardeners, who provided work not only for the owners still living in Mangere but also for many 'immigrants'. Practically no Maori land remained in Ōrākei. By 1950 the

[1] Barr, 1922, pp. 1–32 (by George Graham), and p. 43; Wright, 1959, pp. 93–6; and information supplied by Mr G. Mitchell of Onehunga.   [2] See pp. 12, 16.

Ōkāhu people had sold or given away all their land except the traditional village site, a few acres on the seaward side of a small bay-head flat lying below sea-level. In that year, this remnant was appropriated by the Crown on the grounds that it could not be adequately drained for permanent settlement. Compensation was paid for the land and those with rights in it were offered State (rental) houses, the major shareholders on the hill above the flat, the rest in other parts of the city. The people of Ōkāhu had lost both the land and their continuity of possession. In 1953 (when I first knew them) only the churchyard remained to them. They had lost their *marae* with the village site. (The meeting-house, which had fallen into disrepair, was demolished by the Ministry of Works after the land was taken.) They were being offered an alternative *marae* site on Crown land near the new settlement, but the Ngāti Whātua maintained that nothing could replace the old site, which had special significance as one of the places where the Tainui canoe had rested. They were supported in this stand by the Waikato people under the leadership of Te Puea Herangi, who hoped that the Ōkāhu *marae* would become a centre for all the Maoris in Auckland.

Finally, there were the Auckland and Onehunga Endowment Lands held by the Maori Trustee for the benefit of Maoris of all tribes. These consisted, in the first place, of two blocks in Parnell and one in Onehunga, a total of just over four acres, set aside by Crown grant in 1850 as an endowment for the provision of hostel accommodation for Maoris in Auckland. In 1953–4, a hostelry providing temporary accommodation for Maori visitors occupied part of one of the Parnell blocks. It was managed by a caretaker responsible to the Maori Trustee. Income from the leasing of the rest of the three blocks had been used to buy (secondly) a half-acre section in Parnell as site for a new hostelry and (thirdly) three hostels for young Maoris, which were managed under lease by church organisations.[1]

Of all the *tāngata whenua* living in Auckland, only those living at Ōkāhu Bay occupied a separate settlement. The rest were scattered among Pakehas and Maori 'immigrants' throughout the city. Because they were more easily identified as a separate group, and also because of the historical importance of the Ōkāhu village, the Ōkāhu people occupied a special position in Auckland Maori society. For this reason I had planned to conclude this chapter with a brief account of the Ōkāhu community in 1953, but representatives of the people asked me to omit it. Even changed names could not have protected their anonymity because the settlement was unique in the city. However, a few brief observations are essential as background to the study of Maori 'immigrants' in the city.

Ōkāhu was characterised by its comparative isolation within the city area and by the predominance of *tāngata whenua*. The settlement proper consisted of twenty-seven State houses located along a single street on

[1] Information concerning Maori lands in Auckland was supplied by the Department of Maori Affairs and the Maori Trustee.

the side of the hill, overlooking the old village site on the flat. Surrounded by a large, undeveloped public reserve, the settlement was ten minutes' walk from other housing in any direction. On the other side of the flat, on the fringe of other housing, was an outlying group of three State houses occupied by *tāngata whenua* families who had lived in the old village and still formed an integral part of the Ōkāhu community, in spite of their physical separation. As well as being isolated in the suburb of Ōrākei, the people of Ōkāhu were removed from those parts of the city most favoured by Maori 'immigrants', other Maoris in the eastern suburbs being few and scattered. Out of 223 Maoris living in Ōkāhu in 31 August 1953, 148 were *tāngata whenua*, all of whom shared descent from a Ngāti Whātua chief who lived there in the eighteenth century. In community affairs, the *tāngata whenua* divided into five distinct 'families' stemming from certain of this *tupuna*'s descendants, but to the outside world they represented themselves as "all one big family". The State houses had been allocated only to those who had had rights in the old village site, so that the house-holders were all *tāngata whenua*: there were no 'immigrant' settlers as in Kōtare or other parts of Auckland. However, in addition to spouses and foster children from outside the group, there were 42 "guests" (mostly close affines) staying with *tāngata whenua* householders.

The Ōkāhu Maoris lived in an urban world. They could not make a living without entering into urban employment because they owned no land in the city. The children attended the Ōrākei Primary School and secondary schools in the central city. But socially the community was self-contained and community feeling strongly developed, in spite of the lack of a *marae*. Their closest contacts were with kinsfolk both in the city and in rural parts of the tribal territory, notably the Kaipara area. As a group, the people of Ōkāhu were represented in their relations with other Aucklanders by some five *kaumātua* and three formal organisations, the Ōrākei Tribal Committee, the Ōrākei Maori Women's Welfare League and the Ōrākei Concert Party. The first two of the latter were in theory representative of the Maoris of the eastern suburbs, but in 1953 their members were drawn entirely from Ōkāhu.

Strong community feeling, common descent, physical separateness and a history of disagreement with the Pakeha authorities over their village site had combined to preserve the Ōkāhu community as an enclave in the urban world, slowing down the effects of urbanisation on its members. In many ways, they were closer to the rural way of life than most' immigrants'.[1]

---

[1] The people of Ōkāhu have since accepted the offer of just over an acre of Crown Land on the hill near the settlement to serve as a *marae* for all Maoris in Auckland. In April 1959, the new *marae* was vested in a Board of Trustees "to hold and administer for the use and benefit of Maoris". The Board was to consist of four members elected by the Maoris of Ōkāhu, four from the Waitemata Tribal Executive, one each representing the Department of Maori Affairs, the Ōkāhu Bay Progressive Association and the Auckland Rotary Club, and the four Maori Members of Parliament *ex officio*, representing the Maoris of New Zealand.

8

Immigrants and City-born

IN 1954, the overwhelming majority of Maoris in Auckland did not possess traditional land rights in the urban area nor were they descendants of those who once possessed the land. From the Maori point of view, they were 'immigrants', people who really "belonged" elsewhere. Most had come, or been born to parents who had come, to the city during or since the war; but there seems always to have been a small group of 'immigrants' in Auckland. In the 'sets' of Auckland Maoris whom I knew intimately,[1] there were twenty-nine men and twenty-eight women (15 per cent) who were living in Auckland before the war. Of these, eighteen were there before 1930, and sixteen (including two women in their fifties) were actually born in Auckland.

Some two-thirds of the Auckland Maoris, exclusive of *tāngata whenua*, were immigrants in the literal sense of the word, while the rest had been born and spent most if not all of their childhood there (see Table 18). Out of the 369 Maoris in the 'sets', 159 were 'active' immigrants, who had come to the city as adults, after considerable experience of life in the country, and 76 were 'passive' immigrants, brought to Auckland by immigrating parents or (in the case of six) sent to stay at boarding schools or with relatives. Some of the 'active' immigrants were "man-powered" during the war, directed to work in the city by the Department of Labour and Employment, but most came independently. Only four of the workers in the 'sets' were directed to Auckland.

Many of the unusual demographic features of the Auckland Maori population described in Chapter 6 could be traced to migration into the city from other places. Even the growth of the city-born population was the result of immigration at only one remove, for most of the city-born were the offspring of immigrant parents. The few families which had been established in the city for two or more generations continually inter-married with immigrants. Directly and indirectly, immigration was responsible for the extraordinary proportion of young adults in the city and for the low proportion of older persons. Most city-born and indeed most 'passive' immigrants were still under fifteen in 1954 and the rest were nearly all under thirty-five. In other ways also the city-born and the 'passive' immigrant sections of the urban population reflected the character

[1] pp. 8, 269.

of the immigrant section—in the predominance of members of the "Northern" tribes,[1] for instance, and even in occupational and behaviour patterns. For this reason, we shall examine the immigrant section of the population in closest detail: What sort of people were they in respect of age, sex, marital status, economic skills and aspirations, and tribal membership? Where did they come from? Why did they come? And finally, how did they organise the move and what were its results?

THE 'ACTIVE' IMMIGRANTS

Who and what they were

As in the Auckland Maori population as a whole, men and women were fairly evenly matched in numbers among the 'active' immigrants in the 'sets'. Moreover, as many women as men in the group were unmarried and under twenty-one when they arrived. The women who immigrated after marriage were less independent in their choice, but usually the decision to migrate to the city was a joint one; sometimes the wife was the prime mover.

'Active' Maori immigrants were predominantly young at the time of their immigration (see Table 19). Roughly 36 per cent of all adult immigrants in the 'sets' were between fifteen and twenty when they came to the city and another 18 per cent between twenty and twenty-five. Older Maoris did move to the city, but not in sufficient numbers to restore the population to its proper balance: 24 per cent of the immigrants in the 'sets' were above thirty-five when they settled in the city. The elderly rarely immigrated. Those in the 'sets' who were over sixty in 1954 had all been living in the city for fifteen years or more. A very few had come to the city when in their fifties, but their cases were all unusual, like that of a couple who came to the city in the wake of a large family who had left them alone in a remote island home.

More than half were still unmarried when they came to the city, but the immigration of married couples and family groups was also relatively common (see Table 20). Of the 146 'active' immigrants in the 'sets' whose exact marital status at immigration was known, 81 had been unmarried, 57 married, 3 widowed and 5 separated from their spouses. Married men did not leave their wives and families in the country except in special circumstances. (The odd number of married persons was due to the fact that some were married to non-Maoris.) Only five of those in the 'sets' had done so, in every case as a result of marital discord. I suspect that several of those whose exact marital status at immigration was not discoverable were also fleeing from an unhappy marriage.

Those couples who had dependent children brought them with them. All but eleven of those immigrants in the 'sets' who were married when they left the country brought children with them; the rest were either childless or their children were all grown up and married. Several left

---

[1] i.e. Aupouri, Rarawa, Ngāti Kahu, and Ngāpuhi (see Fig. 9).

adult children behind and youngsters already in the care of relatives. Those who were separated from their spouses or widowed, most often migrated alone; the latter, in particular, usually belonged to the older age-groups, and their children were grown up.

The economic status of the immigrants in the 'sets' was typically fluid when they arrived in the city. They had some preferences in the field of employment, but few possessed special qualifications, training or experience. The greater proportion were completely unskilled. The most common skill was the ability to drive motor vehicles. A few—not more than one in thirty—had been trained in rural Rehabilitation Centres for returned servicemen, mostly as carpenters. Many immigrants had been marginal to rural employment, emigrating from the country because they could not compete successfully for a limited number of jobs.

The majority of 'active' immigrants had left school at fifteen years of age. Some had spent one or two years at secondary school, but most had barely finished a primary school course. In the 'sets' only one girl had completed three years' secondary school education in the country; she was the only one who came to the city to obtain a clerical post commensurate with her education. The proportion of immigrants with good education was probably a little higher in Auckland as a whole than the 'sets' suggested, for they usually sought accommodation in a church hostel and were thus not well represented in the 'sets'. But it was still low.

'Active' immigrants were thus distinguished at immigration into two main groups—those without skills or advanced education, and a very small minority with exceptional qualifications in each. There were few immigrants of intermediate status. Both groups had one thing in common: they came to Auckland to make their fortunes, and they had little cash or capital at their disposal when they arrived in the city.

Where did the 'active' immigrants come from? Geographically speaking, their origins were extremely diverse. The 'active' immigrants in the 'sets' named sixty-four separate rural localities as their 'home communities'; these were distributed throughout most of the major regions of the North Island (see Fig. 1, p. 7). But a very large proportion of immigrants came from one region, the Far North. No other region played a comparable role as a source of Auckland immigrants and there was little to choose between the several others which competed for second place. 109 out of the 159 'active' immigrants in the 'sets' were born and had spent most if not all their childhood in the Far North, 4 out of 5 coming from the west coast areas of Hokianga and Mangonui.

For most immigrants their 'home community' lay in the territory of the tribe to which they affiliated themselves, because they were born and brought up where one or both of their parents had Maori land and where their ancestors had lived. But a few had been born or spent their childhood outside either parent's 'home community', sometimes even outside their tribal territory. Usually they thought of the community where they had

TRIBAL AREAS
in the
NORTH ISLAND
of
NEW ZEALAND

Aupōuri

Ngāti Kahu!

Rarawa

NORTHERN TRIBES

Ngāpuhi

Ngāti Whātua

Ngāti Tamaterā

Ngāti Tai

Ngāti Whanaunga

Ngāti Paoa

Ngāti Maru

Waikato

Ngaiterangi &
Ngāti Rangawui

Whānau-ā-Apanui

Ngāti Porou

TAINUI
TRIBES

Arawa

Ngāti Awa

EAST
COAST
TRIBES

Whakatōhea

Ngāti Maniapoto

ARAWA
TRIBES

MATĀTUA
TRIBES

Tūhoe

Rongowhakaata

Te Aitanga-
ā-Mahaki

Ngāti Tama

Ngāti Awa

TARANAKI
TRIBES

Ngāti Tūwharetoa

Taranaki

Ngāti Ruanui

Ngārauru

Ngāti Hau

Ngāti
Raukawa

Ngāti Apa

Muaupoko

Rangitāne

NGĀTI KAHUNGUNU

N

Ngāti
Awa

Ngāti
Toa

Ngāti
Awa

0   MILES   100

FIG. 9.

spent most of their childhood as "home" but a person might name the community of one of his parents as "my real home", particularly if he had lived in several for short periods and developed personal attachment for none. The correlation between the location of the 'home community' and tribal membership, though very close, was not invariable.

In spite of this slight discrepancy, the predominance of immigrants from the Far North was matched by the overwhelming numerical superiority of members of the tribes whose territories lay in that region, Aupouri, Rarawa, Ngāti Kahu and Ngāpuhi (see Fig. 9). Together they accounted for 70 per cent of the 'active' immigrants in the 'sets'. Ngāpuhi tribal territory actually extends over a large area outside the Far North, but most of the Ngāpuhi immigrants came from its northern reaches. Maoris in Auckland commonly identified members of these four tribes, together with the Ngāti Whātua who occupied southern Northland, as "North-erners", as distinct from "Southerners", who came from tribal territories to the south of Auckland. This distinction had its roots in Maori history, particularly in the era between the arrival of the first Europeans and the Treaty of Waitangi, when the Ngāpuhi under Hongi Hika ravaged much of the North Island in a series of conquering campaigns.[1] The Ngāti Whātua occupied a special position as the tribe to which belonged the *tāngata whenua* of the Tāmaki (Auckland) isthmus and the main victims of Ngāpuhi aggression.

It is significant that only a small proportion of 'active' immigrants were of mixed tribal or ethnic parentage. In the 'sets', nine derived from parents who belonged to different tribes and one from a Maori–Pakeha union (a total of 6 per cent). Of the former, four were the offspring of parents who belonged to tribes in the same Tribal Group and five of parents whose tribes were not closely related.[2]

---

[1] Wright, 1959, pp. 93–6.

[2] In pre-European times (it is reported) tribes whose ancestors arrived in New Zealand, according to traditonal accounts, in the same canoe, grouped themselves into loose confederations known as *waka* (canoe). Firth, 1959, pp. 115–6; Best, 1924, vol. i, pp. 340–1; Winiata, 1956, pp. 212–4.

In 1953–5, the term *waka* was not widely used in this sense. The tribes did group themselves together, forming what may be called Tribal Groups, but only three of the latter (those associated with the Arawa, Tainui and Matātua canoes) stressed derivation from the occupants of the same canoe as their main link. The other Tribal Groups were mainly regional groupings, though also linked by descent from common ancestors or by marriage between their chiefly familes: e.g. the Northern tribes, the East Coast tribes, *etc.* (see Fig. 9). (Ngaiterangi, included with the Tainui tribes on this map, had close ties with the Matātua tribes but had associated more closely with the former since joining the King Movement.)

Arawa and Waikato, popularly referred to as tribes, were really post-European federations of tribes which had formerly been autonomous. Each commonly acted and was treated by other tribes as a single unit. Each comprised only some of the tribes deriving from its ancestral canoe (Arawa and Tainui respectively).

Reasons for Immigration

The reasons which caused Auckland Maoris to leave rural communities were not necessarily the reasons which brought them to the city. By no means all moved directly from one to the other.

Let us look first at the reasons given by informants in the 'sets' for leaving their home communities. Unfavourable economic circumstances were almost invariably cited first. It was a familiar refrain: "There are no jobs to be had . . . no money . . . no land . . . no future, back home." The importance of economic factors was perhaps overstressed at times, for immigrants who had been rebuked by Maori and Pakeha leaders for departing from the traditional rural pattern had found that the plea of "economic necessity" was most readily accepted. Nevertheless, economic difficulties were clearly primary among the causes of emigration from the country.

In the rural communities from which the immigrants came—so many of them in the Far North—the amount of land available for farming was limited and so were opportunities for wage labour or trade enterprises; the general level of wages was not high and much of the work offering was casual or seasonal in nature. Most of those in the 'sets' retained land interests in the country, but derived little or no income from them, because they were contained in a corporately owned block which was unutilised or which as a farm could support only one of the co-owners and his family. (The incorporated farm-station producing annual dividends for those with shares in the land was unknown in Northland.) A few, however, had given up the occupancy of a farm of economic size to come to the city, either because of ill health, because they did not like farm life, or in order to enter some branch of social welfare. The single-family dairy farm predominated in the home areas of most immigrants, so that there was little demand there for permanent farm employees, and seasonal and casual farm work was less common and less well paid than in sheep-farming areas. The more fortunate districts offered one or two men jobs maintaining the roads or working in the few small areas of bush, but for the women there were often no openings at all unless there was a local store or hotel. The employment situation typical of rural districts from which immigrants came has already been discussed in some detail for Kōtare.[1]

Economic circumstances, however bad, do not *force* people to emigrate unless they have certain aspirations in the economic field. The Maoris in the 'sets' came to the city because they refused to accept a lowered standard of living as the alternative to emigration. Their attachment to the land and community of their forefathers was not enough to hold them there on those terms. Some left home, even though their standard of living was not threatened, because they wished to share in higher standards available elsewhere.

Economic motives were always reinforced or brought into prominence

[1] pp. 32–8.

by other factors. In the majority of cases the decisive move was "sparked off" by an event or a circumstance which was not economic at all. One of the most frequent immediate causes of emigration was family quarrels. Often they were connected with the economic situation, resulting, for instance, from an attempt at joint occupancy of 'family land' or 'family house', from a difference of opinion over the division of proceeds of a family enterprise, or from resentment over the choice of occupant for a 'family farm'.[1] But they also arose at times from temperamental differences or in the course of a struggle for power within the family or in the community at large. Some emigrants left home because of social misdemeanours which had "made the place too hot for them", a few eloped with lovers, and others left because of a spouse who did not feel at home "among strangers", to forget sorrow at the death of parents, or to escape from an unhappy marriage, the nagging of relatives or the rural housing problem.[2]

In the case of the younger immigrants the real motive for leaving home could generally be traced to a longing for adventure and independence. Few of my young informants placed a positive value upon a settled, predictable life passed among scenes and faces known from childhood. Instead they evinced a consuming interest in the wider world; they wanted to "try their wings" outside the familiar home community and to shake off the hampering authority and conventions of their elders. They also had a passion for anything "modern", especially in technology, and they regarded the country as "backward".[3]

These social and personal causes of emigration were sometimes powerful enough to drive a man to leave his home community even when his economic position was satisfactory. But they were undoubtedly most effective when he was having a struggle to make ends meet.

Having decided to leave their home community, why did so many rural Maoris choose Auckland as their destination? They could seek work in other rural areas, in small rural towns or in other cities. Some in fact did.

One Auckland Maori of long standing summed up the reasons why Maoris came to the city under five heads: work, money, pleasure, which he called "the Big Three", medical service and education. The first two emphasised the primary importance of economic factors. Auckland, the largest city in New Zealand, had greater advantages in this field than any other city, besides being closer to the main areas of emigration. It was the range and variety of occupations and the general high level of wages in Auckland which attracted informants in the 'sets' and deflected them from the smaller towns and from the other cities of northern New Zealand.

[1] 'Family land' *etc.*: property registered in the name of a deceased or elderly owner and not yet divided among his heirs by the Maori Land Court.

[2] The Department of Maori Affairs advanced loans to build houses in rural areas only where there was permanent employment for the householder.

[3] pp. 106–7.

Auckland offered them not merely certain employment and a regular income, but higher rewards for work, not merely economic security but economic abundance. It offered a wide choice in the type of economic tasks to be performed, and the possibility of upward occupational mobility. Not only was it possible for the worker in Auckland to find a similar job with ease if he disliked the "boss" or fell out with his workmates, but there was opportunity to choose work that was congenial and satisfying, and to acquire skills which increased his value as an employee and even made possible a business of his own. These latter considerations, it is true, weighed only with a very small minority at the time of immigration.

The older people, remembering hard days of digging kauri-gum and draining swamps or the monotony and hopelessness of the struggle to make a living on a small, rough holding, asserted that work was "much easier" in the city—"forty hours a week and no responsibility". But a large number of younger immigrants was employed in occupations which demanded heavy and continuous physical labour.

To summarise the social aspects of the city's attractions under the heading of pleasure was to see only part of the truth. The advantage most appreciated was undoubtedly the variety which the city offered of legal (and illegal) ways of spending leisure and money. Its cinemas, dance-halls, hotels, sports clubs and shops were not only more numerous than any-where else, they were more varied and available most of the time. But in addition to offering a wide choice of things to do, the city presented an equally exciting range of possible companions to do them with. Sociologists have stressed the impersonality and lack of warmth in social relations in the city. Yet from the behaviour and conversation of my informants, especially the younger and unmarried ones, it seemed that they actively enjoyed the innumerable daily contacts with strangers which were an unavoidable condition of urban life. The young city dweller was always saying how he loved to "see new faces and make new friends". What he liked most was the power to choose his own associates out of this wide range, to choose his own social milieu and his own pattern of social activity without the restraints which he believed to operate in a rural community. For the size of urban society enabled him to escape from contact with those who disapproved of his conduct. At the same time he knew that his kinsfolk in the city would always receive and succour him if his self-chosen friends deserted him in time of trouble. In the city he could—he believed—have his cake and eat it too.

Auckland also had the very positive advantage of being to all intents and purposes tribally neutral ground. There was a half-defined feeling that, the city being "a Pakeha invention", all Maoris were on the same footing within its bounds. The embarrassment and defensiveness which haunts a Maori on tribal territory not his own was largely lacking in Auckland. Immigrant status was no circumstance to be ashamed of, but a bond which all (or nearly all) had in common.

Few immigrants were explicitly aware of the possibilities of acquiring social status through residence in the city, though it was generally agreed that urban experience was a desirable thing to have. It was problematic whether it did in fact increase status in rural society, and as immigration to the city became more common its value diminished. There was, however, a handful of ambitious folk who had realised the opportunity represented by the city for acquiring in Maori society social status or positions of leadership from which they had found themselves barred in rural communities by insistence upon "good blood" (senior descent), age, or expert knowledge of Maori traditions. The establishment of a self-made élite was easier in the city, where continuity with the Maori past had been broken, and where the heterogeneity of the Maori population meant that a man's social status depended partly upon his own valuation and partly upon his performance. Ambition to win a place in the Pakeha world on Pakeha terms was not common among immigrants and was at most only a minor motive among many more important ones. Interest in modern technology and desire to be up-to-date and "modern" in matters such as dress was typical but not associated with any wish to enter the Pakeha *social* world.

A few Maoris, significant because they were highly gifted and usually well educated, came to the city to enter the social services (as nurses, teachers, welfare officers or staff members of the Department of Maori Affairs) or in order to play for top-grade sports clubs.

Desire for medical services and education affected only a very small minority of 'active' immigrants. Most of those who came to the city to further their schooling came before they were fifteen. In the 'sets' one married couple had immigrated primarily in order to give their children a good education, while five immigrants came to the city specifically to obtain medical treatment, for themselves or in one case for a spouse now dead. Three brought their families with them, a total of eleven other persons. Two women immigrants remained in Auckland because of bad health, although they came for other reasons and would have preferred to return to the country. The total number affected by these motives was not more than 15 per cent.

While economic motivation played the major role in the immigration of Auckland Maoris, it should be seen as part of a wider search for a fuller, "modern", exciting life, symbolised by the conspicuous enjoyment of the goods, material and immaterial, of modern "urban" civilisation. The modern Maori saw the city (as the sociologist does) as the centre, the focus, the source even, of civilisation. To some this civilisation was to be distrusted and feared, but to most the city stood for two things which they valued highly, excitement and freedom: the excitement of new experiences, new faces and new places, and of holding the future in their own hands untrammelled by the past; and freedom not only from poverty, insecurity and economic hardship, but also from the authority of parents and elders, freedom from traditional ways of doing things, freedom from boredom, in short, freedom for self-determination. These were the things that the city was believed to offer more than any other place. Whether they were actually to be found there was, of course, another matter. The city was more than an escape from a difficult situation, it was the entrance to a new world. But, as we shall see, having exercised their right of choice, the majority continued to seek participation in gatherings with a Maori tone, even to the extent of paying frequent visits to the country.

Patterns of Movement

The movement of Maoris from their home community to the city was not characteristically simple and direct. Full details were obtained for only 118 of the 'active' immigrants in the 'sets', but from the histories of these 118 three distinctive patterns emerged.

Roughly about half (60 out of 118) moved directly to the city from their home community. In this group, there were 32 young people still in their teens. Some had come straight from school, but most had first worked in the country or in country towns for a year or two. The rest, with only three exceptions, were much older persons accompanied by spouses and children. This direct pattern of movement was thus peculiar to the very young and to those with family responsibilities.

Contrasted with this uncomplicated pattern was that of approximately one-third, who reached the city after moving from one rural area to another. Three distinct types of immigrants followed this pattern. First, there were those who in their youth and early married life had travelled widely in search of work. Most of them were now in their fifties. The men had been engaged in pioneer activities such as scrub-cutting, ditching, draining swamps, fencing, road-making, kaurigum-digging and, in the depression years, "relief" work planting marram grass or pine seedlings, and breaking in new land on Maori Land Development Schemes. The women had travelled no less widely, but were more restricted in the types of work they could obtain; the only alternative to domestic service in Pakeha homes or waitressing in hotels was work as a farm hand or part of a family gum-digging team. Secondly, there were those of a much younger generation who had followed the same pattern during and after the Second World War, the men in the Armed Forces or working as farm labourers, bushmen, road and railway workers, dairy factory hands and drivers of cream trucks and country buses; the women as domestics or waitresses in hotels and hospitals, telephone operators and junior assistants in Maori schools. On the whole they had had fewer jobs and fewer moves than the older "travellers". Thirdly, there were young people still only in their late teens and early twenties who had spent their childhood accompanying parents from one bush or road camp, gum-field, dairy farm or sheep station to another; or who, orphaned at an early age, had stayed with relatives living in many different localities. In all these cases it was plain that once an individual or a family group started "wandering" they rarely confined themselves to their own tribal area. Thus the "travelled" immigrant usually had a wide experience of living in communities to which he did not "belong".

It is worth noting that none of the immigrants in the 'sets' had been sheep-shearers. Shearing was not an occupation which supplied many immigrants to the city. It was a highly skilled occupation and, though seasonal, gangs had more or less permanent year-to-year arrangements with farmers. The earnings were high and all members of the family could be useful in the team as sorters, floor-clearers, etc. Moreover, most shearers were drawn from the ranks of small holders who spent the off-season farming their own land.

The third pattern of immigration led to the city via smaller towns and cities. Not very many immigrants followed this pattern: only seven in the 'sets', including two who had been overseas since the war, in Korea and the U.S.A. respectively.

The majority of the Maori immigrants living in Auckland had not left Auckland for any significant length of time since their arrival. Not quite ten per cent of those in the 'sets' had immigrated more than once. Six had returned to settle permanently in Auckland after a spell in the country. Another seven, all of them over thirty, had left the city on several occasions.

Examination of the past histories of Maoris settled in Auckland does not, of course, indicate the extent to which immigrants moved out of the city. That a considerable number did leave, we have seen in tracing the movements of Kōtare emigrants and also in the number who returned to Kōtare to live.[1] Most of the adults in the 'sets' had at least one close kinsman, sibling, parent or child, who had emigrated from Auckland, either to return to the home community, or to seek work in the country, in the Public Works town of Mangakino, in the timber camps of the Central Plateau, or in cities further south.

While the young unmarried adult predominated among the 'active' immigrants, he was rarely completely independent in his move to Auckland. At least a third of, and probably nearly half, such immigrants delayed the change until they had found a companion for the journey or for their early days in the city. About one in four was affected by his parents' immigration, either accompanying them to the city or coming to join them later. Roughly the same proportion came in pairs, travelling with siblings, friends, or cousins of anything from the first to the nth degree. Paired immigrants were usually of the same age and occupational status. This method of migration was practised most by the younger girls, who lacked the confidence to set out alone. A frequent variation occurred when an Aucklander home on a visit fired one of his young kinsmen with the desire to see the city and brought him back under his protection.

[1] p. 103.

The elementary family was second in importance to the lone immigrant as a unit of movement, more important, that is, than pairs of age-mates. Unmarried adults who were living with their parents when the latter decided to migrate usually accompanied them. Married sons and daughters acted separately from their parents, but often joined them in the same house in the city. The denuded family (which had lost one parent through death or desertion) was not a common unit of movement. The widowed rarely immigrated as long as they had dependent children, while separated persons as a rule left their children with kin or the deserted spouse and migrated alone.

Planning and lengthy preparations were not typical features of the movement of Maoris into Auckland. Once the final decision was made, it was almost invariably acted upon with dispatch—within a matter of days. The move took longest when a family was involved, but planning was still kept to a minimum. Furniture was left behind in the country: city auction rooms and stores were relied upon to supply future needs.

Very few immigrants arranged even temporary accommodation before arrival. Most went to stay with kinsfolk. A few resorted to the Maori Hostelry in Parnell which provided cheap temporary lodging.[1] Sometimes a father went ahead to obtain accommodation and a job, but it was only a matter of days or at most weeks before he sent for his family. Far the most common procedure, whatever the unit of movement, was to arrive in Auckland with personal luggage and no immediate prospects beyond the address of relatives. Sometimes the receiving family had extended an invitation: frequently they were not consulted or received a telegram announcing the arrival of guests only a few days before. Maori immigrants had complete confidence in their welcome. They were rarely disappointed.

As with accommodation, so with occupations. Few immigrants had jobs waiting for them when they arrived. Only four men and three women in the 'sets' had had certain employment arranged before they left home. The rest had wanted to "look around" for themselves or were relying on kinsfolk to get them jobs where they worked.

The light-hearted way in which most immigrants undertook a new way of life was due, in the first place, to the fact that they were willing to accept a fairly low standard of accommodation, at least temporarily. Secondly, they knew that if the worst came to the worst they could always go home. Thirdly, even in the city they were sure to have some kin who would help them out. Above all, the myth that the city was a place where living was easy and jobs to be had for the asking encouraged people to take steps which they might not otherwise have done.

The Post-Immigration Period of Experimentation

Lack of planning greatly increased the difficulties of adjustment to urban life for Maori immigrants to Auckland. As a result, nearly all went through

[1] p. 120.

an unsettled period during which they experimented with employment, residence and leisure activities. Sometimes this period lasted only a few months, in other cases for as much as two years. Its length was correlated, as might be expected, with age, sex, marital status and number of dependents.

Coming to the city under the impetus of a spur-of-the-moment decision, immigrants were often too much in need of ready money to be able to take their time over finding a job. Ignorant of how to seek expert advice, they took the first one discovered by the efforts of friends or kin. It rarely came up to their expectations, and they began to try out various kinds of work and various employers, in short, to "shop around". The ease with which work could be obtained encouraged them in this mobility and they felt that it was part of the process of getting urban experience.

Changes of residence were also frequent in the early months in Auckland, especially on the part of the unattached. Again, they tended to rely on personal contacts in finding accommodation. Ignorance, diffidence and fear of colour discrimination prevented most Maoris from making use of accommodation bureaus and newspaper columns. Families usually moved only two or three times, but the young and unmarried circulated freely and rapidly from one place of residence to another. Those who accompanied parents to the city soon left them to stay with as many as three or four sets of relatives in turn, and then in "rooms" in apartment houses.

Socially speaking, the first few months in the city were usually hectic for immigrants, except for mothers of large or young families. Most had "something doing" every night in the week, with the accent on variety and the unexpected. Apart from sampling the more conventional delights, they experimented with a wide range of unfamiliar activities—indoor sports, *haka* (action-song) teams, Youth Clubs, long-distance cycling, talent quests, girls' marching teams. Their interest in these activities never lasted long; they were continually switching to something new. This was reflected in the short-lived character of many Auckland Maori clubs.

In all these fields most of the mobility was of a horizontal kind—a circulation from one job, residence or social activity to another of similar type. It was not until the "post-immigration fever" had abated that immigrants showed any tendency to vertical mobility or any interest in seeking a better job, better living conditions and a stable social life.

The extreme restlessness that was typical of the immigrant of less than a year's standing was, however, a phase from which most emerged. Eventually the rate of change in employment and residence and the pace of social activity slowed down. In the case of the young and unattached, this final "settling-down" usually did not occur until marriage, though occasionally growing responsibility at work was the cause. The acquisition of family responsibilities reduced not only the ability to be mobile but the desire for it. Marriage usually came within two or three years of immigration if not before: seventeen of the twenty-seven in the 'sets' who married after immigration married while still under twenty-one. Those who survived unmarried into their twenties carried over the "good-time" pattern in a modified form. Their main reason for not marrying was that they did not want to sacrifice their freedom. But many even of these were settled in one place of residence and had kept their jobs for comparatively long periods. There were, however, enough 'active' immigrants passing through this phase of restlessness at any one time to establish mobility of a horizontal kind as a dominant pattern of behaviour among the Maori "young set" in Auckland.

Economic Differentiation after Immigration

'Active' immigrants were as a group mainly young and poorly equipped with skills and capital; they came from areas where opportunities for employment, for acquiring skills, and for entertainment were restricted, and they looked to the city for full employment, good wages and a satisfying social life. They went through a difficult period of adjustment and finally, in their own phrase, "settled down" in the city. To what extent were they successful in their final adjustment to city life? Later chapters will be devoted to an examination of the social patterns and organisation established by Maoris in Auckland as a whole, that is, including 'passive' immigrants and the city-born. In the economic sphere, it is perhaps easier to discuss separately what happened to the 'active' immigrants.

As we have seen, apart from the small group of highly educated or highly trained persons, 'active' immigrants were relatively homogeneous in economic status at immigration. They subsequently became differentiated to a considerable degree, but tended to be concentrated in certain fields of employment—notably in freezing works, on road maintenance, in transport and the building trades and certain types of factories—and in the unskilled and semi-skilled categories (see Table 22). This concentration was partly a reflection of the continuing supply of immigrants from rural areas. There was at all times a large pool of unskilled Maori labour in Auckland, but the personnel involved changed over time as new immigrants poured into it and most of the older ones moved out. Most immigrants fresh from the country were attracted immediately into unskilled work, particularly into certain types of manual labouring, because their rural experience had been in similar work, because it was well paid and abundant, and because it provided opportunity to work in gangs in which Maoris predominated (see Frontispiece). But a large proportion of the immigrants who at immigration possessed no skills acquired some in the city and those with limited skills extended them. Most moved into the semi-skilled class, either as manual workers, as, for instance, slaughterers at the freezing works and wool-classers in the wool-stores, or as machine operators. A significant though relatively small number became fully skilled, particularly in the trades. Only the most shiftless, the unenterprising and those too old to learn new skills remained permanently in the

unskilled category. The average immigrant, after a period of experimentation, settled into a relatively skilled job with one employer. Most of the
family men in the 'sets' had been in the same job for at least five years.

Two-thirds of the Maori women employees in the 'sets' were semi-
skilled factory workers. By far the most popular occupation among women
was that of machinist, stitching garments as varied as shirts, nylon stock-
ings and fur coats (see Plate 7, facing p. 102). There was much greater
variety and specialisation among male factory workers: those in the 'sets'
were engaged in work as diverse as salting hides, curing fish, making tents,
tending oxygen tanks and working glass.

Few immigrants entered the clerical and professional class after immigration. These categories were not well represented in the 'sets', nor were
service occupations. Those engaged in the former lived mainly in hostels[1]
or scattered in the suburbs, while those in domestic service "lived in" at
the hospitals or hotels where they worked. Clerical and professional
workers were not very numerous in the city as a whole: even in hostels,
they rarely formed more than a tenth of the residents. Service occupations,
on the other hand, accounted for roughly a quarter of the women in paid
employment even in the 'sets', though such work could not compete with
factory work in popularity.

Most Maori immigrants remained employees. Out of ninety-one men
gainfully employed in the 'sets' in 1954, only five had their own businesses:
a motor mechanic, a plasterer (in partnership with a Pakeha), a paper-
hanger, a carrier and a tar-sealing contractor. Two men held positions as
foremen, one in charge of a tiling gang, the other of a gang laying electric
cables. One young woman was a forewoman in a pottery works.

The incomes earned by immigrants working in Auckland varied considerably. The highest were earned by those in the semi-skilled class
(mostly on the wharves and in the freezing works) as a result of abundant
overtime, but were for that very reason subject to marked fluctuation. As
in Kōtare, I failed to obtain comprehensive or specific information about
incomes from my informants. This proved to be a very difficult area of
inquiry. But even from the patchy information I did assemble it was plain
that patterns of free spending and emphasis upon generosity to Maoris
and to Maori causes eliminated much of the objective differences in
income between Maoris in the 'sets'.

THE CITY-BORN AND THE 'PASSIVE' IMMIGRANTS

The city-born and the 'passive' immigrants, though outnumbered by
'active' immigrants in the adult population, were an extremely significant
element in Auckland Maori society because they had grown or were
growing to maturity within the environment of the city. To most of them,
the city was "home" at least in a physical sense. In this they differed
markedly from the 'active' immigrants, although even among the latter

[1] p. 143.

there were a few who had been brought up away from the rural communities where their parents "belonged". Were the city-born conscious of having any special relationship with a rural community? And were there any other points in which they differed fom the 'active' immigrants, or from each other?

The City-Born

As we have already remarked, most of the city-born were in 1953–4 still under fifteen years of age (84·5 per cent of those in the 'sets'). But a small number of adults had spent all or most of their life there, most of them the offspring of Pakeha–Maori marriages, while those born in the city in the early days of the urban influx (about a tenth of those in the 'sets') had just reached school-leaving age.

One of the most striking facts about the city-born, and the way in which they differed most from the 'active' immigrants, was the high proportion who belonged to two tribes. In the 'sets', only thirty-seven of those born in Auckland—less than 30 per cent—had parents who belonged to the same tribe, although eight others had a clearly primary claim on one tribe through three out of their four grandparents. The prevalence of double (and of even more involved) tribal membership among the city-born was due to intertribal mixing as a result of migration, especially to Auckland itself. Four out of five of those with double tribal membership were the offspring of parents who had met and spent most if not all of their married life in the city. Moreover, most of their parents belonged to tribes in different Tribal Groups (see Table 21). The proportion of those with one non-Maori parent was also higher than among 'active' immigrants, though still well below ten per cent.

Not only were so many of the city-born the product of intertribal and interracial unions, but the relatively few who had reached marriageable age showed a tendency to contract similar marriages. Of the eight in the 'sets' who had married, all but one was married to someone from a tribe outside his own Tribal Group, and that exception had married a Pakeha.

The Northern tribes were well represented among the city-born, but in proportion to the total they were of far less account than in the group of 'active' immigrants because of the much higher proportion with double tribal membership. Only a third (43) of the city-born in the 'sets' identified themselves wholly as Ngāpuhi, Aupouri, Rarawa or Ngāti Kahu, sixteen belonging to at least two of these tribes. (Compare this with 73 per cent of the 'active' immigrants who were "Northerners".) Twenty-two others, it is true, were "half Ngāpuhi", but they were linked through their other parent with "Southern" tribes as diverse as Ngāti Paoa, Maniapoto and Arawa.

Another interesting feature about the city-born was the number who derived from a parent who was also city-born: nearly a fifth of the city-born in the 'sets' (27). Eleven could even claim a grandparent born in the city. But there was only one family in which both parents were city-born, and all those who were the second generation born in the city belonged to two grand-families which maintained close relations with at least one rural community.

Born and brought up in the city where any land they owned could never be Maori land, the city-born occupied an equivocal position in Maori society. They were usually brought up to regard the rural community (or communities) from which their parents derived as 'home' in a special, highly abstract sense. Many parents told their city-born offspring that they could walk into any house in their home district without knocking because they were related to the people by descent from the same ancestors. Most knew that they had land interests there, though they were often extremely hazy as to their nature and value, and such holdings rarely yielded any income. Because of the difficulties of travelling with small children, most were adolescent or adult when they began to visit this home community and their visits were as a rule relatively short, for holidays or *hui*; but some had lived there for months or even a year or two with grandparents or other relatives.

Many had not merely one but two home communities, because their parents came from different places. Either they became sentimentally attached only to one, or their vacations and their affections were divided between them. Only a few did not maintain contact with any, in every case those with one non-Maori parent. The city-born were, then, aware of having origins outside the city, in specific rural communities, though their links with those communities in terms both of subjective feelings and of personal relations with kin living there were less strong than those of 'active' immigrants.

The number of the city-born who had attained school-leaving age and potential independence was too small to warrant a separate examination of their occupational, residential and leisure patterns and I shall leave these aspects to be considered in conjunction with those of the 'passive' immigrants.

The 'Passive' Immigrants

The 'passive' immigrants were in every sense intermediate or transitional between the 'active' immigrants and the city-born. A greater proportion than of the latter had passed school-leaving age (48 out of 76 in the 'sets'), but nine out of ten were under twenty-five and none over thirty-five. The proportions of persons of mixed tribal and racial parentage were also intermediate between those of the two other groups (Table 21). Not quite two-thirds were of "Northern" extraction; four had a non-Maori parent. Like the city-born and those 'active' immigrants who married in the city, they showed a tendency to marry into other tribes. Their attachment to a rural community was weaker than that of most 'active' immigrants and stronger than that of those born in Auckland, but its strength depended to a great extent upon the age at which they left it and whether their parents had been "travellers" or not. Once settled in the city, they visited the country about as often as the city-born. It is important to note, however, that both city-born and 'passive' immigrants usually continued to visit their parents' home community after they became independent adults and could make their own decision in the matter.

The City-Born and 'Passive' Immigrants as Adults

To the city-born adults, who were all city-bred, the city was a familiar world, though not necessarily a well-known one. To a lesser extent this was also true of 'passive' immigrants, especially since over two-thirds were less than ten years old when they came to the city. Neither group had to make adjustments to urban life in quite the same way as the 'active' immigrants, because they were less acquainted with a rural way of life.

In the matter of residence neither group exhibited the high mobility evinced by young unmarried 'active' immigrants. Few took the opportunity to set up separate residence from their parents when they became economically independent. The "lone wolf", living his own life in "rooms" or with easy-going relatives who let him do as he liked, was a rare phenomenon, especially among the city-born. In the 'sets' there were only four (all 'passive' immigrants) who were living apart from their parents in any real sense. (Three others occupied rooms in dwellings adjacent to those of their parents because the latter did not have the room to accommodate them, but they formed part of the same domestic unit.) Most indeed remained with their parents even after marriage.

In other spheres, although they showed in general greater stability than 'active' immigrants, they shared to some extent their restlessness, their craving for novelty and experimentation, and their preference for jobs with high wages rather than long-term prospects. While a slightly higher percentage of the city-born and 'passive' immigrants went into apprenticeships and clerical work when they left school, most preferred to leave at the earliest opportunity to take unskilled jobs as labourers and factory hands. Subsequently, they exhibited much of the horizontal mobility characteristic of 'active' immigrants in the early stages of settling in the city, followed by the same pattern of restricted vertical mobility and "settling down". This was associated in part at least with the nature of the occupations they entered, but they were also undoubtedly affected by close contact with 'active' immigrants. In leisure activities also, they followed the same "good time" pattern followed by a "settling down" at marriage, but, with less experience of the restricted social opportunities of other places and more firmly attached to a family unit, they showed far less tendency to go to extremes and were ready to settle down in a shorter time.

Thus the adult city-born and 'passive' immigrants were in many ways dominated by the 'active' immigrants who far outnumbered them. Their behaviour was governed not only by the objective urban world in which they were reared, but also by what they learnt consciously and unconsciously from parents, one or both of whom had been brought up in the country, and by constant association with young 'active' immigrants. For, though the distinctions made in this chapter between 'active' and 'passive' immigrants and the city-born are valid for the purpose of a preliminary analysis of Maori society in Auckland, they were social categories and not social groups. Any particular social grouping of Maoris in the city, whether it persisted through time like a kin-group or a domestic unit, or was assembled on an *ad hoc* basis, like that at the Maori Community Centre on any Sunday evening, invariably included persons belonging to all three categories. The city-born were in no way distinguished either by themselves or by others as a separate group, nor were they likely to emerge as such, for few married each other. Even when a grand-family came to be described in common parlance as a "city family" because it had been resident in the city for two or more generations, its members allied themselves at every generation with immigrants in marriage. In fact, in the typical elementary-family, one or both parents were 'active' immigrants, the older children 'passive' immigrants and the younger ones city-born. The existence within the same family of these three categories and constant interaction between them in every social situation tended to mute the differences and facilitated the diffusion of common values and behaviour patterns. The city-born and the city-bred on the whole had less effect upon the immigrants than vice versa, for the latter were in the majority and quickly made themselves familiar with the superficial details of urban life. There was usually little that the city-born could teach the immigrant of even a few weeks. It was possible that eventually, as increasing numbers of them grew to adulthood, the city-born would prove a stabilising factor in Auckland Maori society. As long as immigrants continued to come into the city, however, the city-born and the city-bred would never be cut off from the traditions of Maori rural society.

9

Housing and Domestic Organisation

HAVING no interest in particular land areas of the city as owners on Maori title, the Maoris of Auckland were in theory themselves responsible for the location and type of residence which they occupied and for the form of domestic organisation which they established. That their choice of the former was circumscribed or directed in some way was, however, evident from their marked concentration in certain parts of the city, in particular in the central city and other poor residential areas, in the market-garden fringe and in State houses in the suburbs.[1]

FACTORS INVOLVED IN THE DISTRIBUTION
OF MAORIS IN AUCKLAND

The Maoris of Auckland, not being as a whole a wealthy class, could not afford to build houses for themselves but had to take whatever accommodation was available to them. One of the major factors in limiting their range of choice was an acute housing shortage, which had been typical of Auckland since at least the early years of the Second World War. Even in 1953 and 1954 sole tenancies or houses with vacant possession were difficult to obtain. Many Maoris were inclined to blame colour discrimination for their failure to find accommodation except in the poorer residential areas. It was certainly true that Maori tenants were rejected by many landlords. But discrimination against Maoris was not solely a matter of *colour* prejudice. Much of it was based on experience or on popular and newspaper reports of unsatisfactory Maori tenants. In particular, Maoris had a reputation for over-crowding and for failing to treat houses with care. Thus accommodation was most readily available to Maoris in areas of sub-standard housing where landlords, anticipating demolition orders on their property, were willing to let rooms separately or to allow tenants to sub-let.

External pressure alone, however, did not account for the concentration of Maoris in areas like the central city. For certain reasons accommodation in these areas was actually preferred. Accustomed to living on their own land in the country, most immigrants were appalled by the rents demanded in other parts of the city. Also, much central city housing, though poor by city standards, was not so very much below that which they had

[1] pp. 112–14.

known in the country: they felt more "at home" there than in houses which required a lot of time and money to maintain. Once established, the concentration in such areas became self-perpetuating. For new immigrants came to stay with kinsfolk there and settled in their neighbourhood, partly because of reliance on personal methods of obtaining accommodation, but mainly because they wanted to live near kin and in a neighbourhood where Maoris were numerous. They preferred to accept lower standards of accommodation rather than to be isolated in a Pakeha world.

The central city was, moreover, highly valued for its centrality. It was within walking distance of the Maori Community Centre and all the most popular places of entertainment. Many young people left suburban homes to take "rooms" in the central city in order to be "close to things". In one case in the 'sets' when parents bought a house in the suburbs, their adult offspring stayed on in their old central-city house as boarders.

Finally, Maori belief in the prevalence of colour prejudice on the part of landlords and neighbours was itself a powerful factor in directing Maoris to areas where they could obtain accommodation with relative ease and where there were already many other Maoris. Sensitive to all sorts of real and fancied rebuffs, they rarely made full use of accommodation agencies or newspaper advertisements and were quickly discouraged in the search for good accommodation. Many resigned themselves to the slums from the beginning.

Thus not all the factors which directed Maoris into the central city were purely of urban origin. Some of the most powerful arose from their own habits, desires and fears.

Those who lived in the suburbs had nearly all passed through the central city or one of the other slum areas, but only a very small proportion had graduated out of them by their own efforts. A few had moved from the worst streets of the central city into neighbouring suburbs, where houses were still old, though in better condition, and available at rents or prices which Maori tenants or (more rarely) buyers considered reasonable. Buying a house of this type had the disadvantage that the money had to be found in cash: banks and insurance companies would not finance their purchase because of their age. The main route of escape from the central city and areas like it was into State houses, which were allocated only to those living under bad housing conditions. State houses were popular because they were new, modern, and available at a cheaper rental than comparable privately owned houses, because they could be bought on favourable terms, and because there was usually a high proportion of Maoris in State house areas compared to other suburbs. Houses built under the Department of Maori Affairs Housing Loan Scheme were beginning to rival State houses in popularity as a way out of poor housing conditions.[1] These were much more widely scattered and located mainly

[1] p. 113n.

in the outer suburbs. As yet few had actually moved into the new houses, but many living in the central city were paying instalments off loans under the scheme.

Thus the almost exclusive predominance of Maori tenants in the city was being broken down through the agency of Government departments. A few Maoris were also beginning to take advantage of the normal means of financing building, obtaining loans from the State Advances Corporation, banks and insurance companies. But for every family re-housed in the suburbs, a new one from the country moved into the central city, which also retained its hold as a favourite residential area among the young and unattached.

In addition to accommodation owned or rented by independent adults and families, there were nine hostels in Auckland catering entirely for Maoris in 1953 and 1954. Seven were managed by church bodies, one by the Department of Labour and Employment and one by the Christian Women's Temperance Union. They had a total capacity of 280. The three boys' hostels were usually filled to capacity and so were certain of the girls', but several in the suburbs, rather removed from centres of employment and entertainment, were rarely full. At any one time, the rate of vacancies was in the vicinity of 10 per cent. Other hostels, in which Maoris were in the minority, accounted for less than 100 young Maoris.

In view of obvious differences in housing standards and the way in which the central city attracted new immigrants and the more mobile sections of the Maori population, it might be profitable to examine the housing and domestic organisation of the central city and suburban areas separately. First, however, it is necessary to consider the matter of terminology.

Many houses in the central city in 1953–4 were in various stages of sub-division, occupied by several independent families sharing at least some conveniences. I have found it necessary to distinguish between the *dwelling* and the *domestic unit*. The former is a *given, physical entity*, a self-contained building with its own entrance to the street, its own yard, and one complete set of cooking and toilet conveniences. The domestic unit is a *group of persons* who co-operate consistently with each other in daily domestic arrangements, paying household expenses, cooking and eating together.

I have avoided the term *household*, because it implies not only a group of persons acting as a unit for domestic purposes but also all the occupants of a given house. There was no problem in the country, where the Maoris occupying each dwelling almost invariably formed a single domestic unit,[1] but, in Auckland, an actual majority of domestic units shared a dwelling with other domestic units.

[1] p. 43.

HOUSING AND DOMESTIC ORGANISATION
IN THE CENTRAL CITY

Dwellings occupied by Maoris were not clustered together but were scattered fairly evenly through the central-city area. The distances between them were not very great, because settlement was intensive in this area, with houses close to the street and to each other. This intensive settlement was beginning to be modified in 1953–4 by slum clearance and the erection of factories in the place of the houses demolished. In spite of the density of settlement, Maori residents and houses with Maori occupants made up only a small proportion of the total. In one of the chief streets in the area, sixteen houses with Maori occupants were scattered over a distance of a third of a mile among a hundred other houses.

Maoris in the central city were nearly all tenants. Out of the forty-five dwellings occupied by the Maoris in the 'sets', only two were owned by Maori occupants. Leases on two others were held by Maori women who let them out in "apartments". Two other families had bought houses in an adjacent suburb and were waiting for the tenants to vacate (i.e. at the end of August 1954).

The Importance of Multiple Dwellings

One of the most striking facts about Maori housing in the central city was the way in which several domestic units shared one dwelling. The 284 Maoris in the central city 'sets' (A and B) occupied 34 houses, in 17 of which there were two or more domestic units (see Table 23). Or, to put it another way, 60 per cent were living in *multiple dwellings*. There was, moreover, a marked tendency for Maoris to congregate in houses where the other domestic units were also composed of Maoris. Only 6 of the 34 houses occupied by Maoris in the central city 'sets' housed any completely non-Maori domestic units. Pakehas were, however, sometimes included in Maori domestic units, as spouses, affines, or very rarely, boarders. This happened in seven units in the 'sets'.

The multiple dwellings found in the central city could be divided into three main types. The *apartment house* was run by a "landlady" who was usually a lessee. She occupied two or three rooms in the house and let the others furnished. Herself responsible for maintenance and the cleaning of shared conveniences, she made house rules, chose and dismissed tenants and collected their rent. Sometimes tenants had cooking facilities in their own rooms; sometimes they shared a common kitchen. Occasionally, a "landlady" provided breakfast for the single ones. The *house with multiple tenancies* was occupied by a number of tenants who rented a room or set of rooms directly from the owner (or his representative). The rooms were mostly let unfurnished and provided with separate cooking facilities. Sometimes an owner appointed one of the tenants as his agent, to clean corridors, bathroom, toilet and wash-house and to collect rents from the others in return for a reduction in his own. Most often, however, no-one in particular was responsible for the common rooms, with the result that they were poorly kept, except in a few cases where one or two women cleaned them without payment for their own comfort. In the *sub-let house*, the legal tenant rented rooms to other domestic units. The occupants usually shared a common kitchen, though occasionally they had gas-rings in their rooms. In all three types, tenants shared washing and toilet conveniences, of which there was usually only one set, except in the larger apartment houses. Yards were small, mostly concrete or bare earth, and even small garden plots were rare.

As might be expected, multiple dwellings were distinguished by a large number of occupants per unit. The seventeen in the 'sets' had an average of ten occupants. Four had more than twenty. Considering the limited space and facilities secured and the dilapidation of most of the buildings, rents were high. In the 'sets' they varied from fifteen shillings to two pounds a week for one or two rooms, in many cases as high as those paid by central-city families occupying their own unit.

Of the three types, houses with multiple tenancies were the most common and had the most occupants. They were occupied mainly by family groups, who were relatively permanent tenants. Since the owners had no interest in securing tenants who would get on together, the latter belonged, more often than not, to a variety of tribes. One such house in the 'sets' accommodated the following domestic units: (a) a Rarawa, his Ngāpuhi wife, and their daughter; (b) a Rarawa widow distantly related to the first mentioned and two of her grandchildren; (c) an Arawa widower, his son and his wife (a Pakeha), and their son; (d) a grand-family consisting of a Waikato married to a Ngāti Maru, their six unmarried children, and their eldest son and his Ngāpuhi wife. Tenants in houses of this kind also varied widely in their manner of living, which was reflected in what they did with their rooms. Some worked hard to make them pleasant with fresh paint and wallpaper and print curtains. Others quickly let them slip into squalor. In the house just mentioned, the extremes of care and neglect existed side by side.

Sub-let houses were occupied mainly by kinsfolk. But the relationships were usually less than close. In the 'sets', Mrs Parani Tīpene, a widow whose children lived elsewhere, sub-let rooms in her house to the following kin: (a) a nephew (her half-sister's son), his wife (who was also her fifth cousin) and their two children; (b) the son and grandson of a "Maori cousin" (her father's father's brother's son's wife's sister's daughter); (c) another of this cousin's sons and his wife (daughter to another of Mrs Tīpene's half-sisters); and (d) a second cousin, also a widow, who kept house for three sons, her daughter's daughter and her father, a "nephew" (son of a second cousin) and a classificatory grand-niece. Occupants of a sub-let house always claimed to be "just one big family", and evidence of sub-letting was hard to obtain. But though at times they ate together at the same table, food was bought and budgeted separately most of the time, and fixed amounts of rent were paid for the rooms used. The latter were lower than in other multiple dwellings, but taken together were enough to pay the rent for the whole place several times over. This naturally led to friction. Most sub-letters had difficulty actually collecting their rents. The semi-commercial relationship between tenant and sub-tenants emerged clearly during quarrels. Ordinarily her sub-tenants referred to Mrs Tīpene as "our *kuia*" or "*tupuna*" (grandmother), but after a quarrel she was always "the landlady".

Sub-let houses were among the most overcrowded and dilapidated in the central city. The seventeen persons listed above lived in a tumble-down cottage with a frontage of barely sixteen feet. Mrs Tīpene occupied one room, the sub-tenants respectively rented two tiny upstairs bedrooms, an attic, and a basement (which had an earth floor and a ventilation hole as its only window), and they shared the kitchen. Overcrowding inevitably hastened the deterioration of such houses. Sub-tenants did not treat them as carefully as they might have had they been directly responsible to the owner, while the tenants either did not care or were powerless to do anything about it, since their sub-letting was not legally valid, and "Maori *aroha*" constrained them from "being hard on kinsfolk".

Apartment houses usually had a high proportion of unattached tenants, who were distinguished by a rapid turnover rate. Some indeed catered exclusively for the single: two out of the six in the 'sets' took only single women. But most had a mixture of individuals, couples and families. Rents were particularly high, as the rooms were mostly furnished. One of my informants paid 25s a week to share a bedroom and the use of a row of gas-rings installed on a landing. When the "landladies" were Pakeha (as were two in the 'sets'), tenants usually belonged to many different tribes, but Maori "landladies" tended to favour kin or fellow tribesmen. Also, those already living in a house often secured vacancies for *their* kin. Unlike sub-let houses, however, apartment houses were rarely occupied entirely by kinsfolk. In a typical case in the 'sets', the domestic units fell into three distinct groups: (1a) the lessee (who was Ngāti Paoa) and her husband (Ngāpuhi); (1b) the former's sister and her husband (Ngāti Raukawa) and one of their sons; (1c) another son and his wife (Ngāti Raukawa) and their two children; (2a) a Ngāpuhi couple and their granddaughter, who were remotely related to the lessee's husband; (2b) their daughter and her husband (also Ngāpuhi) and family; and (3) another Ngāpuhi couple who were no traceable connection of the other Ngāpuhis in the house.

Apartment houses were usually far superior to the other types of multiple units in their standard of appointments and cleanliness. Usually fairly large to begin with, they had been converted for the purpose by, or with the approval of, the owner. The "landlady" had an interest in preventing depreciation, for she was either the owner or a lessee responsible for all damage, and she relied upon it for all or part of her income.

Domestic Units and their Organisation

Domestic units operated as separate and autonomous units in the management of domestic finance and the handling of domestic tasks, even when sharing a multiple dwelling with others. They were of six main types (see Table 24). The first, consisting of a *single individual*, was found only within the framework of the multiple dwelling. The other five types were found both in multiple dwellings and occupying houses on their own. Far the most common was the domestic unit consisting of the *elementary-family*. Next in importance, but much less common, was the *grand-family* domestic unit. Both the elementary-family and the grand-family were sometimes augmented by boarders. Then there were certain domestic units which were not formed on the basis of kinship at all. Hostels, of which there were five for Maoris only in the central-city area, form a special category which need not concern us here.

About the *single individual*, there is relatively little to be said. Most lived in apartment houses; sometimes they even shared a bedroom with a stranger. Each paid his rent himself, looked after his room or part of a room or paid the "landlady" to do so, and made his own arrangements about meals, either cooking at home if facilities permitted, eating with relatives, or buying meals in public eating-places. Anomalies were common. Two sisters in the 'sets' occupied different rooms in the same house, paid their rent separately but often ate together, while two young men who had rooms of their own took their meals with parents in adjacent houses. Most Maoris in this category were young and unmarried, but about one in five was above twenty-five, a confirmed bachelor (or spinster) or a *quasi* bachelor separated from his wife.

The *elementary family* was the dominant type of domestic unit. The income which supported this unit was usually earned and administered by the husband-father, while the care of house and meals was in the hands of the housewife-mother, but there were wide variations in detail from one family to another, according to circumstances and personalities. In some families the older children were at work (19 belonging to 10 of the 43 elementary family units in the 'sets'); in many the mother was a wage-earner (14 in full-time jobs in the 'sets') or derived income from her activities as a "landlady" (3); even the younger children often earned money after school or at weekends delivering newspapers or working as errand boys for local shops. There was a wide range in the extent to which earnings were pooled. Some husbands handed over their pay-packets unopened to their wives, who gave them "spending money" back, some gave a fixed sum each week, others a proportion of the income earned (which might vary considerably if they did much overtime work), others again "what they felt like". When the wife was also working it was most usual for her to retain control of the money she earned and to spend it for the benefit of herself and the children, on such things as clothes and on small luxuries rather than on the ordinary running expenses of the home.

When the older children in the family began to earn, they retained control over their earnings as their own private property. They usually made some contribution to household expenses, which was described as "paying board", but the amount varied from family to family and over time within one family; it did not usually cover more than the cost of food, and was rarely paid in full or regularly. Most parents "felt sorry" for their offspring, particularly if their wages were low, and waived the payment altogether or took only a nominal sum. Some prided themselves on taking nothing, as "that is not our Maori way, for parents to be hard on their children". Occasionally a young worker "felt sorry" for a mother struggling to make ends meet and made her a present of a pound or two. In spite of the payment of board and individual control over wages, the domestic economy remained fairly simple. Careful accounting between members of the family was regarded as reprehensible ("very Pakeha") and spontaneous gifts of money were frequent.

The allocation of household tasks was more uniform—most, if not all, were carried out by the mother or by a daughter kept at home for the purpose. Young adults did not do much in the house. Occasionally they helped with the chores and errands, but on the whole they received far more help from their parents than they gave. Sometimes they gave personal gifts of value to their parents but more often they bought themselves some luxury such as a radio, radiogram or ukelele, which was generally used by the family as long as they lived at home.

In general, the domestic equipment of most families in these poorer residential areas was fairly scanty. The furniture was second-hand and decrepit, or of a makeshift character; kitchen utensils, crockery and cutlery were minimal (several families managed their meals with only two or three knives); household linen was replaced as much as possible by newspaper or plastic. Nevertheless there were considerable differences in standards of household comfort even within this narrow range. These differences were correlated not with the total amount earned by wage-earners in the units nor with the amount of income per head, but with housing conditions and to an even greater extent with the outlook and aspirations of the parents. Those who occupied houses or flats of their own spent a greater proportion of their income on domestic needs and especially on capital household goods, while those who shared a house with other domestic units devoted their domestic budget almost entirely to perishable goods, that is, to food and drink, constrained from the accumulation of furniture, crockery and household linen, by lack of space, defective washing facilities and the threat of borer-infection and theft. A small minority were genuinely more comfortable in surroundings which did not have to be "looked after", but the majority, whether in a unit of their own or not, agreed in aspiring to something better in the future. Many families were "just making do" while waiting for this "something better"—usually a State house.

Certain modern articles were to be found even in the most dilapidated dwellings. Almost every family had a radio, and ukeleles were almost as common. An occasional "spruce up" occurred in all but the most ill-kept units: for a short while a few rolls of cheap wallpaper and a pot or two of paint literally brightened up the most dismal room, for the amateur painters favoured pillarbox red and royal blue.

There were a few domestic units in multiple dwellings which, though composed of kinsfolk, were difficult to classify because the relationships between those involved were idiosyncratic. Most can best be described as *quasi-elementary-families*, for they involved persons of different generations who had "adopted" each other; e.g. one widow in the 'sets' kept house for a grandson and granddaughter and another looked after her sister's granddaughter, sent to the city for secondary school education. Groups of unmarried siblings living together as a domestic unit without their parents were rare. (There were none in the 'sets'.)

The single individual and elementary- (and *quasi*-elementary-) family domestic units can be grouped together as *simple* domestic units. Together they accounted for 80 per cent of the domestic units in the 'sets'. The remaining four types of domestic unit found in the central city included members of more than one elementary family, justifying description as *compound* domestic units.

Compound domestic units, especially those which included more than one elementary-family, displayed even greater variation in their details of internal organisation than the elementary-family domestic unit. But they differed from it in scale rather than in kind, for most had an elementary family as their nucleus and their organisation was modelled on that of the simple family, with the emphasis upon co-operation and mutual accommodation rather than on strict commercial accounting.

In the *grand-family* unit (in which one or more married sons or daughters lived with a senior couple) the several elementary-families within the unit retained their separate identities in certain respects: they occupied, for instance, bedrooms of their own, for whose cleaning and furnishing they were usually responsible, and they managed their own financial affairs. But the constituent families also had a large area of common life. They shared a common living room and a common kitchen (besides other conveniences) and usually cooked and ate together. The allocation of domestic tasks varied from one household to another and even within one household over the course of time. Occasionally each wife cooked separately for her husband and family; sometimes the women took it in turns to provide meals for the whole household; sometimes one organised all the catering and cooking while the others were busy with young children or at work. The financial side of domestic organisation was also handled in a variety of ways. Sometimes the grandparents paid the rent, running expenses and food bills, receiving from the young couples a fixed weekly payment that was an extension of the "board" paid by unmarried workers. Sometimes all expenses were divided when the bills came in. Adjustments were usually made if a daughter or son's wife helped with the housework. Whatever the details, the arrangement was always flexible. Many grandparents refused assistance with the rent if or when they could afford to. They were lavish with gifts to their grandchildren, keeping them supplied with sweets, biscuits, "picture-money" (the price of a cinema seat) and even clothes. In some households the grandmother minded the children while the mothers went to work.

Family affection as well as the difficulty of finding accommodation played a part in the formation of grand-family units. Most of the young people married without the resources to set up their own establishment immediately or the experience to run it. (The average age of those in the 'sets' who married during 1953 and 1954 was under twenty.) As might be expected, daughters remained in their parents' homes after marriage more often than sons. (There were six such cases in the central-city 'sets' compared with two of married sons.) However, most young couples did not stay with their parents for more than five or six years. By that time they usually had two or three children. The parental home became cramped, the grandparents grew impatient when the children were always underfoot or else spoiled them outrageously, and the young couple developed a desire for independence. Grand-family units also broke up when one or more of the families was allocated a State house.

Other compound domestic units were formed when elementary-families and grand-families took in boarders. Boarders were provided with a bed or bedroom and with meals according to arrangement, in return for a fixed amount of "board" per week. In the central-city 'sets', four elementary-families and three grand-families had boarders. While glad of the chance to "make a little extra", they did not make a business of taking boarders. None had more than two at once. In many cases, they took them only as a duty or favour to kinsfolk. Most boarders were related to their hosts: one in the 'sets' was the wife's sister's son, another the husband's foster brother, and so on. If not kin, they were usually friends of family members or friends of friends and kin. Treated very much as part of the family, they both gave and received many unpaid services: baby-sitting, chopping wood and collecting shopping on the one side, mending, ironing and entertaining friends on the other.

The fourth type of compound domestic unit, the *non-kin unit*, consisted of two or more individuals not related by membership or *quasi* membership in the same elementary- or grand-family. It was comparatively rare. The only example in the 'sets' was a bachelor-girl establishment consisting of eight young women between eighteen and twenty-five years of age. All were earning good wages, four in factories, one in a shop, one in a laundry and one in the Public Service. Two of them had originally rented "rooms" from a Pakeha landlady, who was sufficiently impressed to offer them the sole tenancy of their present house. Roomy and well-appointed, this was far superior to most in the area. This household had been in existence for a year, in which time four girls had left and been replaced. One of the original occupants had been from the Waikato, but in 1954 all eight were Northerners. Only three were related in any way. They lived as a family, sharing expenses, cooking and housework equally. It was their pride to provide meals for anyone who dropped in, and they often put up friends and parents and relatives from the country by doubling up two in a bed. This establishment seemed to be unusual even of its type. As far as I could find out, other units of this kind were mostly limited to two or three persons, and occupied "rooms" rather than a house. They usually involved persons of the same age, and women more often than men.

A feeling of impermanency was characteristic of compound domestic units. Grand-family units rarely survived unchanged for more than five years. Boarders and members of non-kin units came and went, often within a matter of months. The longest record of a boarder in the 'sets' was a Pakeha who had stayed with one family for four years, outlasting at least four who were kin to their hosts. Because of the likelihood of change, compound units did not accumulate common property. Pieces of furniture, utensils, crockery and so forth were used in common but in the final analysis were owned by individuals or one of the couples. In the grand-family, most of the articles in common use belonged to the senior couple. Many young couples owned their bedroom suite but not usually much else. Sometimes they supplied a deficiency in the household equipment from their wedding presents or by purchase, but usually they used what the grandparents provided and stored their own possessions away for a place of their own.

It is significant that compound domestic units were in the majority among those domestic units which occupied a dwelling by themselves. When Maori families obtained a sole tenancy they frequently expanded into a compound unit by accommodating married sons and daughters and young kinsfolk. But they were not numerous in multiple dwelling units. The latter were occupied mainly by single individuals and elementary-families. There were only three compound units in the multiple dwellings in the 'sets', two being grand-families which had lost one grandparent. Under the crowded conditions of the multiple dwelling the grand-family tended to break down into two or more simple units independent in their domestic organisation. There were two instances, in the 'sets', of parents and their married children forming distinct domestic units though living in the same house.

Thus the effect of the crowding of Maoris in the central city into multiple dwellings was to reduce domestic organisation to the small unit. In sub-let houses and in certain apartment houses the distinctions between domestic units were sometimes blurred to the observer as a result of the sharing of a common kitchen. Most Maoris disliked eating in front of others because it seemed inhospitable. Therefore, if they did not remove the food to their rooms to eat, they invited others present to share what they had. But this was hospitality, and not joint domestic organisation.

HOUSING AND DOMESTIC ORGANISATION IN THE SUBURBS

In Auckland, the typical suburban house stands in its own plot of land, completely self-contained, provided with all conveniences, and physically isolated from other units. (Occasional "double units" consist of two flats under the same roof but they are in every other respect independent.) In the suburban 'set' (C)[1] all domestic units occupied a dwelling of their own, with the exception of the family of a Maori woman employed as housekeeper by a Pakeha widower. Only one family owned its house, but another was having a new one built under a loan from the Maori Affairs Department, while the housekeeper just mentioned and her husband were building another with a loan from the State Advances Corporation. Seven of the rest were tenants in State houses, while one family occupied a house which they had rented from Pakeha owners for twenty-five years. In six out of the eleven cases, the domestic unit consisted of an elementary family. However, two of these households frequently had boarders, and it was largely fortuitous that none happened to be in residence at the end of August, 1954. Thus compound domestic units, including boarders as well as married offspring, were well represented in the suburbs. But, as in the central city, they had only a limited life. Only one had lasted more than ten years without a change in the junior couple. (In this case a married daughter who had remained in the parental home had assumed effective control of the household when her parents became elderly and frail.) Usually there was no continuity between one grand-family domestic unit and another in the next generation.

Suburban houses were typically larger, roomier, newer and better appointed than those in the central city. Many of them were State houses whose conditions of tenancy prevented sub-letting or the taking in of boarders on a commercial scale. Another factor which helped prevent suburban houses from developing into multiple dwellings was pride in the new house and genuine relief at escape from the cramped and unpleasant dwellings of the central city. This was, however, at variance with Maori traditions of hospitality. Few Maoris even in the suburbs were willing to turn away relatives. They did in fact accommodate homeless kinsfolk from time to time, but usually on a temporary and short-term basis. Perhaps of key importance in protecting them from the importunities of the less desirable type of relatives—those who quickly reduced any house they lived in to the level of a slum—was the distance of the suburbs from the central city and the most popular centres of entertainment.

The move into a suburban house usually made a considerable change in the domestic life of Maori families. Most increased immediately the proportion of their income spent on household equipment. The usual

[1] p. 8.

reaction to a new house was to furnish it thoroughly on hire purchase. Relatively few had saved either money or goods before the move. Even fewer were content to buy only the essential items at the beginning and to continue to stock the house out of income. Invariably furniture was bought first and cupboards remained scantily stocked until the furniture was paid off. Members of the family spent more time at home and expended more labour in its management, especially in the garden. Washing machines, refrigerators and gardening tools were gradually acquired. Only a small minority remained unchanged in their attitude to a house as merely a base for social activity and gradually let their new quarters assume the same aspect as their old. Most of these eventually found their way back to the central city either voluntarily or after eviction.

The single individual and the non-kin unit were comparatively rare in the suburbs. Neither was represented in the 'sets'. The suburban house was typically a family home and flats and "rooms" were difficult to obtain there, while the young or unattached, of whom such units were composed, preferred a central location. Most did not intend to settle permanently in the central city, but, looking forward to marriage or travel, wanted to spend their days of youth and single freedom "near the heart of things".

SUMMARY

In Auckland, whatever the conditions of housing, the type of domestic unit preferred by Maoris was a small one consisting of an elementary family. This showed a tendency to expand as time passed by the addition of married sons and daughters and their families and of boarders, most of whom were kinsfolk. But such compound units usually broke up again within a period of about five years, or else the personnel involved changed. Larger domestic units of kin appeared to be entirely absent.

In the central city, however, some domestic units were forced into close physical association by joint occupation of dwellings. Some of these domestic units appeared to coalesce into one large one, but this was not really so. Multiple dwellings were in part the result of the housing shortage, in part the peculiar product of slum areas and in part created by the inertia of the tenants themselves, who were either content to remain where they were because it was cheap and central, or did not know how to move out on their own, or hesitated to venture among Pakehas with higher standards of living.

The central city was also characterised by a much higher proportion of unmarried (or separated) adults living alone in "rooms" or combining in non-kin domestic units.

10

Kinship and Descent

MAORI 'immigrants' living in Auckland varied widely in the number of kinsmen they could call on in the city: some had only one or two, others as many as, if not more than, in any single rural community. One thing they had in common: they were widely separated, rarely by less than a hundred miles, from many of their closest kin. They had left siblings, parents and grandparents in home communities in the country, while those of their home kin who had also emigrated were scattered over the length and breadth of New Zealand. Auckland itself was not a single community but a large area of intensive urban settlement with a Maori population half as large as that of the whole Far North. Kinsfolk living in certain parts of it were no more accessible than those in neighbouring districts in the country, and sometimes considerably less so. A large number of tribes were represented and intertribal marriage was common. Though a majority belonged to one tribe (Ngāpuhi), its dominance was not as marked as in country areas and its members were as much "outsiders" from a Maori point of view as the rest. Under such conditions, it might be expected that kinship and descent would be much less important than in the country.

THE KINDRED IN THE CITY

Auckland Maoris professed exactly the same kinship ideals as those in Kōtare. In actual fact, I first heard them stated in detail in much the form in which I have described them in Chapter 3,[1] during my fieldwork in Auckland, long before I went to Kōtare. Even the young people were able to formulate them clearly, though (as in Kōtare) they placed the emphasis on mutual friendliness and assistance rather than on obligations connected with *hui*, which were so important to the older generations.

But most of my Auckland informants agreed that kinship practice in the city fell short of rural standards. Most still kept open house for relatives; for those living in the central city scarcely a week went by without some kinsman staying the night, having just arrived from the country or missed the last bus to the suburbs. However, they had learnt to lock their house or rooms when going out for any length of time, because of the risk of theft, and to knock before walking in on kin who shared accom-

[1] pp. 48-50.

modation with others. Visiting was affected by where kin lived in relation to each other. Though the city was well served by public transport, it could take a couple of hours to get from one side of it to the other, and fares mounted up. Kin who lived in different suburbs often forgathered in the homes of kin in the central city or at the Maori Community Centre. Most Auckland Maoris attended *hui* involving kin when they were held in Auckland, but many women complained to me that they gave far less practical help than they did in the country, and many "never give a penny piece". "It gets left to the same old few." The obligation to attend a *tangi* was still strongly felt, but because *tangi* almost invariably took place in the country (even when the deceased had been living in Auckland), they attended only those involving fairly close kin. Too much time off for *tangi* could mean the loss of a good job. Most liked to go home for other *hui*, too, but only the unattached or the retired managed it more than once or twice a year.

Fairly and unfairly, in general terms and in relation to particular cases, my informants blamed the city itself for the alleged increase in "selfishness" and a decrease in co-operation between Maoris living there. The lack of a *marae* or any other really suitable venue for *hui*, the necessity of sharing accommodation with strangers, transport costs and distances, Pakeha disapproval or curiosity, too many counter-attractions: all these were variously cited as causes or excuses for lapses from the ideal pattern. One informant asserted that "Maoris in the city have got used to having everything done for them". One relevant factor which they overlooked was the fact that a higher proportion of those who attended Maori gatherings in Auckland were non-kin, while fewer close kin were usually available than in the country.

There were undoubtedly more and worse cases of abuse of kinship privilege in Auckland than in Kōtare. The most common offender was the chronic borrower of small sums, who accused kin who expected repayment of being unreasonable and un-Maori. Others stayed indefinitely with kin without contributing to household expenses, or made a practice of using other people's homes for their beer parties. Everything favoured the offender in the city. Public disapproval was not an effective sanction in a large and scattered population with little sense of community. He could easily find other kinsmen who would put up with him for a while if his victims finally rebelled. The latter were usually beset by feelings of guilt if they refused hospitality even in these circumstances. They were also restrained by the knowledge that their "hard-heartedness" would be reported to the "folk back home", and on their next visit they would receive a cold welcome and a lecture about "holding on to their Maori ways".

Practically every Maori in Auckland had some effective kin in the city and some outside, not only in their home community (or communities), but in many other places as well. At least some of their closest kin—

grandparents and their descendants—did not live in Auckland. Two examples will show just how extensive was the scattering even of siblings. They have been chosen as typical. (1) Grace Pritchard was the eldest of nine living siblings. Her parents lived at home in an isolated community in the Far North, together with a married daughter and her family. Grace's three other sisters were also married, living respectively in Hokianga, Auckland and Australia. Two brothers lived in Te Awamutu (in the Waikato), one in Rotorua and two in Gisborne. (2) Wairau Tātana was the third son in a family of eleven. His parents were both dead. One brother (farming the family land) and three married sisters lived at home in the Hokianga area. Another brother was farming in Northern Wairoa (also in Northland), one was a shearer in Taihape and two worked in Auckland. His remaining two sisters, both married, lived in Kaikohe and Pukekohe respectively.

Contact with kin outside Auckland was inevitably affected by this physical separation. In the case of close kin it was restricted to letters, telephone calls, second-hand messages and occasional presents for much of the time, but was periodically resumed at a fairly intensive level when they exchanged holiday visits or attended *hui* involving each other. Contact with more remote kin lapsed entirely during periods of separation; and they usually met again in public, in particular at *hui*. (Relations between Auckland and country Maoris will be dealt with more fully in a later chapter.) Kinsfolk living in Auckland played a much larger part in the daily lives of Auckland Maoris than kinsfolk living elsewhere, and though not necessarily more important in general, tended to be more important than those of corresponding degrees outside Auckland.

About one-sixth of my informants had less than five kinsmen in Auckland itself, exclusive of affines. They were mostly atypical in some way. Either they had had a non-Maori parent; or they or their parents had belonged to small families, had quarrelled with their home kin or had spent most of their life "travelling" in search of work; or they had come from areas remote from Auckland or oriented towards other centres. (Many remote areas were, however, well represented in Auckland, particularly those in the Far North, such as Mitimiti, Te Kao and Te Hāpua, between 220 and 280 miles away.)

Most of those who came from the areas most affected by emigration had no difficulty in finding kinsmen in Auckland, kinsmen who had come from other communities as well as their own. About half the Maoris in the 'sets' could name between five and twenty effective kin in Auckland, while the remaining third were in continual contact with more. Their relations with some of these were extremely casual: they often lost touch for weeks or months, renewing contact only after a casual encounter or at a *tangi* or wedding. But such marginal kin were also typical of the kindreds of country Maoris.

Whatever their size, the urban kindreds of most Auckland Maoris had two features in common: really intimate kin were restricted in number by rural standards, and they were relatively less numerous in proportion to other kin. Also, relations between Auckland kinsfolk varied over time even more than in the country. Effective relations were established or disrupted, intimacy increased or diminished, as kin moved in and out of the city or its accessible parts. The young and unmarried who moved from one set of kin to another as boarders were very intimate with those with whom they were living at the time, but often saw comparatively little of them once they had moved on. When a family moved from the central city to a State house in the suburbs, they almost invariably lost some of their effective kinsmen, for those who "practically lived at our place in town" were "*hoha*" (couldn't-be-bothered) about the longer and more expensive journey into the suburbs.

Who was effective kin to whom at any given time, and even the degree of their intimacy, were thus limited in the first place by purely mechanical and idiosyncratic factors: what kinsmen were available, where they lived in relation to each other, whether their freedom of movement was curtailed in any way by illness, lack of money or the responsibility of small children. Within these limits, personal preference was the deciding factor, as it was in the country. Occasionally, kinsfolk continued to maintain fairly close relations though not particularly fond of each other, because the association was a habit of long standing, reinforced by distrust of an alien, city world. This was particularly the case with the elderly. Common membership in a corporate group, especially a family club or a particular church congregation, also usually increased intimacy between kin.

My Auckland informants did not seem particularly interested in tracing kin relationships in detail. The term "Maori cousin" was heard even more frequently than in Kōtare and seemed to be used to refer to anyone whose relationship was more complicated than third cousin. Within this limit, English terms were applied as in Kōtare, so that each included those to whom its Maori equivalent was extended. Thus one woman referred to her sister's daughter's daughter as "my granddaughter" and another to her father's second cousin as "my aunt". The city-born acquired this habit from their parents and Maori friends and relatives, even when they spoke no Maori.

DESCENT AND DESCENT-GROUPS

Interest in *whakapapa*[1] was not strong in Auckland. Only a small proportion of those qualified by age as *kaumātua* were at all well versed in it, and few of them played a prominent part in public affairs. Most of my informants knew very little about their ancestry. As far as I knew, none possessed *whakapapa* books. Some might have kept them, but most seemed to be left with elders in the home community. Most of the immigrants had come to the city at an age when they were uninterested in the

---

[1] Genealogies, see pp. 52–4.

"things of the past" and had not bothered to learn the more intricate details of their derivation. Apart from the indifference typical of the young, the city-born were thus handicapped by their parents' ignorance. However, even in the country Maori parents gave little overt instruction in *whakapapa* and allied matters, leaving those who wished to pick it up for themselves from the elders' discussions at *hui*. Once they passed forty, most Auckland Maoris began (like those in Kōtare) to show more interest in this field of knowledge and to go more often to *hui*; but their opportunities for learning were more curtailed and they had even more leeway to make up than their country cousins. Often they had to call upon older kinsmen in the country for help. One group of kinsmen in Auckland regularly sent for one of their home *kaumātua* to come and act for them on such occasions as *tomo* and weddings.

The recital of *whakapapa* at a public gathering in Auckland was rare enough to be something of an event. In the country, they were most often heard, along with the old-time chants, during the all-night discussions at *tangi* and 'unveilings', but these did not occur in Auckland, partly because there was no meeting-house or hall where people could assemble in that way, partly because the dead were nearly always buried in the country. In Auckland, therefore, *whakapapa* were heard publicly only at welcomes to parties of visitors and at weddings, when perhaps two or three of the speakers might justify their right to speak in the traditional way, by demonstrating their relationship to bride or groom. Otherwise *whakapapa* were aired only in the semi-privacy of 'family' gatherings in the home: at *tomo* or a welcome to visiting *kaumātua* from the country.

Apart from the lack of a suitable meeting-place, many Maoris felt that the leisurely pace and preoccupation with tribal and family history characteristic of country *hui* were not suited to a city environment. Time was at a premium in the city, especially for workers. And because public gatherings were attended by members of many different tribes, speakers usually cut short the discussion of purely tribal matters, either because they did not wish to bore others, or because they regarded the material itself as confidential.

Rank

Questions of rank also seemed to be little discussed. When directly challenged, most informants said that they never thought about it, or that "that's all past and gone". In particular, they felt that there was "no room" for it in the city, where "things are done the Pakeha way". Most preferred it this way, particularly the young people. Some of the elders who had claims to high rank themselves regretted the situation, but recognised that the current of public opinion was against them. One couple, proud of their descent, told me how, before they settled in Auckland, they had arranged for their eldest son to marry a girl of comparable rank in a related *hapū* so that "their children can't be bettered for descent in our tribe";

but their second daughter (to their chagrin) insisted on marrying a "nobody" met in the city. A member of the Tribal Executive once suggested that they should select a number of young people for grooming as leaders on the basis of their *hapū* and *whakapapa*: the plan was politely noted but never acted upon.

Candidates for election to Auckland Maori executive committees, in particular the Tribal Committees, did stress their rank on occasion, but neither they nor anyone else suggested that it was a primary or sufficient qualification for public leadership. Experience, education, ability, personality and popularity were all more important. Those holding office were usually adept at knowing when to play up their rank (in dealing with rural Maoris, "old-timers", and those of inferior descent) and when to emphasise their other qualities. The Secretary of a Tribal Committee, challenged over the efficiency of her administration, countered with a devastating attack on her critic's genealogy in comparison with her own, but she stressed her past record of service in appealing to those present for support, for several were of higher rank than she was.

Formal marks of respect were accorded a small handful of elders reputed to be of *rangatira* rank in their respective tribes whenever they appeared in Maori gatherings: places of honour were reserved for them, they took precedence among the speakers (which often meant the honour of speaking *last*) and were listened to in respectful silence. But the same marks of respect were given to those who qualified as "high-class" for other reasons: clergymen, teachers and other professional men, Members of Parliament, senior officials of the Department of Maori Affairs, and officers of the Maori Women's Welfare League and Auckland Tribal Committees.

High rank no longer carried economic advantages, low rank no economic disabilities. Over the last fifty years or more, so many marriages had been contracted without reference to rank that distinctions based on descent had become hopelessly blurred. The young people had enthusiastically adopted Pakeha ideals of equality and leadership based on ability and achievement. These factors had already undermined the Maori rank system in the country. Moreover, its operation depended on general familiarity with the various lines of descent and agreement on their interrelationships, conditions which were conspicuously lacking in a population as large and tribally heterogeneous as that in Auckland. Maori rank was almost entirely relative *within* the tribe. Except at the highest level (at which intermarriage took place in early times to cement alliances), intertribal comparison was impossible. In Auckland not even the experts knew enough to assess the precise rank of members of other tribes or to determine the relative status of would-be leaders. A man's rank had to be accepted largely at his own valuation.

The Iwi

All Auckland Maoris claimed membership in at least one tribe. There were none who had not got a tribe. The individual was more or less left to assert his tribal membership for himself, for he had moved outside his tribal territory. False claims were by no means unknown: a person working with members of a tribe traditionally hostile to his own sometimes claimed to belong to another, neutral tribe to avoid friction, while those who "got into trouble" (i.e. with the police) were deliberately vague about their tribal membership. The conditions of city life also gave rise to a lack of precision. Many members of the smaller Northern tribes, Rarawa, Ngāti Kahu and Aupouri, found it simpler to describe themselves as Ngāpuhi to non-Northerners, to whom the whole of Northland is Ngāpuhi territory. This was only partly a misnomer, for the tribes in question probably evolved from powerful Ngāpuhi sub-tribes.

It frequently happened in the city that a person's parents belonged to different tribes. A few of those so placed chose to belong to one tribe exclusively; these were mostly persons in the middle or older generations who, brought up in the community of one parent, had lost contact with that of the other. About half claimed to belong to both. It was common to hear an Auckland Maori describe himself as "half Ngāti A and half Ngāti P", or "both Ngāti A and Ngāti P". Nearly as many ordinarily described themselves as belonging to one but laid claim to membership in another when it was to their advantage. Many of those who claimed to belong to two tribes were the offspring of parents who had done the same. Some ignored their claims on a third or fourth tribe, but most recalled them from time to time.

The preferences expressed followed not one but several patterns and seemed to be governed mainly by personal factors. Some in identical circumstances made different decisions. Tahu Paki's daughter Ann[1] told me that she and her siblings always counted themselves as "half Ngāpuhi and half Arawa", while her sister Eliza told me that "we all go under Ngāpuhi, our mother's tribe". Those who had lived in the home community of only one parent or were more closely associated with his or her kin, were usually biased in favour of his or her tribe. Some adhered to a patrilineal rule regardless of other considerations: the Peters siblings claimed membership in their father's tribe on all normal occasions, although they were born and brought up in their mother's community and only one had ever visited their father's people. Yet others were governed by no process of conscious reasoning but "followed" the parent with whom they identified themselves psychologically. Eliza Young gave her tribe as that of her mother, although she had never visited her home community, whereas she had not only visited but worked in her father's community. Challenged to explain her choice, she was at a loss, shrugged

[1] See below, p. 172.

her shoulders and said: "That is what I was told; I didn't ask why because tribes don't bother me."

In theory, those whose parents belonged to different tribes could also have abandoned both claims. Phyllis and Selwyn Davis[1] who came from hostile tribes had discontinued attempts to instruct their children in tribal history, etiquette or the Maori language because they led to quarrels. Phyllis commented that the children were, as a result, "neither one thing nor the other" but "just plain Maori". This was, however, the reaction of a woman to whom tribal membership implied some knowledge of tribal tradition. Children in this position invariably claimed membership in their parents' tribes when they grew up and found that every other Maori belonged to one tribe or another.

The complexity of the problem facing many Maoris as a result of a series of intertribal marriages and the variety of ways in which they handled it were well illustrated by the case of Mr and Mrs Patrick Healey and their families. In an early interview Mrs Healey (Rīria) told me that she was Ngāti Paoa and that she derived this membership from her father, who took it from his mother (his father being a Pakeha). Later, when she knew me better, she explained that her father's mother was "really half Ngāti Paoa and half Waikato, that is, her father was Waikato and her mother was from Hauraki" (Ngāti Paoa territory). Moreover, her own mother had been "both Ngāti Maru and Ngāti Paoa, and it depended on where she was living at the time what she said she was". Thus Rīria had the right to claim membership in Ngāti Paoa, Ngāti Maru and Waikato, though she regarded herself as belonging primarily to the first. Her first husband had been a half-caste Waikato, but he had lived in Rīria's home community during their marriage and her children by him described themselves as Ngāti Paoa. Patrick Healey, who was Rīria's second husband, usually said he was Ngāti Maru, but on appropriate occasions he recalled links with Ngāti Paoa through his mother's mother. The Healeys' only son, Maurice, who had been born in the city, "followed" his father and called himself Ngāti Maru, though he had never visited his father's home community. He had married a girl from the Maniapoto tribe. Rīria, Patrick and Maurice had all evaded the issue of tribal membership posed on Maori electoral forms by registering on the non-Maori electoral roll.[2]

As in the country, the advantages of tribal membership were mostly intangible. Belonging to a tribe gave Maoris a certain psychological security through identification with a large and reputable group with a definite territorial base and a history of its own; they shared the public honours and prestige it commanded, both in general and on particular occasions; and they were able to establish immediately friendly relations with strangers who belonged to the same tribe, because "we must be related somehow". Those who belonged to tribes with trust funds could obtain small grants for special purposes, such as education and in a few

[1] See below, p. 171.   [2] p. 16.

cases *tangi* expenses. As far as I could find out, none of my informants in Auckland had ever applied for such assistance. These benefits were not dependent on exclusive membership but were actually increased by belonging to more than one tribe. This was particularly important in the city, where a Maori met so many strangers.

Membership in the home tribes (Ngāti Whātua and Ngāti Mahuta) offered fewer advantages than in Kōtare, for they had no special funds and not even a functioning *marae* in the city, and their precedence was only perfunctorily acknowledged. Being an "outsider" mattered less when almost every one else was one too.

Members of each tribe acquired from their parents and kin certain stereotypes and expectations about other tribes which governed their attitudes to their members, at least while they were mere acquaintances. These stereotypes were usually very general ones: members of this tribe were dishonest, members of that tribe were aggressive, members of a third were dashing lovers, and so on. They were firmly based in tribal history, reflecting past hostilities and alliances, but those who held them were rarely able to describe their historical relations except in general terms. Among the young people, jealousy in the courtship situation often reinforced tribal antagonisms. One young Ngāti Porou who "could not stand the Ngāpuhi" explained his dislike not by reference to the defeat Ngāpuhi inflicted on the people of Te Araroa, but on the grounds that "they have funny ways, they are sneaking and not to be trusted", and revealed in another context that he resented their success with the girls of his own tribe, including several cousins.

The vague feeling of kinship which existed between members of the same tribe was not strong enough to provide a basis for consistent common action. Attempts had been made to establish formal tribal associations in Auckland but they had all ended in failure. One couple who had failed in an attempt to form a tribal club, commented: "We wanted to get them together to make money to put into a fund to pay death expenses, but it fizzled out because they would not pull together." There was no precedent in rural society for a club on so extensive a basis. In any given tribe, members were too widely scattered over the city, too numerous or too heterogeneous in other ways to co-operate satisfactorily for any length of time. None of them recognised a single chief or even elder among their number, who could have served as a rallying point. Moreover, they lacked any territorial base in the city. Only Ngāti Whātua and Ngāti Mahuta had *marae*, neither furnished with a meeting-house. Halls could be hired only for short periods.

Tribal differences in dialect and customs were marked enough to give rise to comment and some friction. Most Maoris were quick to resent aspersions on their tribal honour. Whatever the issue, members of different tribes took offence more readily and bore grudges longer. According to one *kaumātua*, "People take offence at things said by people of other tribes that they would ignore from their own people". Phyllis Davis told me that whenever she and her husband (Maniapoto and Rarawa respectively) became involved in discussing their tribes with a Ngāti Porou neighbour, they all became so heated that they were not on speaking terms for several days. However, they always made it up in the end. Those in charge of hostels reported much good-natured chaffing between members of different tribes, occasional minor tiffs but remarkably few serious quarrels arising out of tribal differences. This seemed to be true for most situations. When Maoris fell out, they almost invariably brought up their tribal differences, but the latter were hardly ever the major cause of a quarrel. The older Maoris felt that they ought to support members of their tribe in public affairs as well as in private, but other considerations always weakened the support they actually gave. Members of different tribes showed no tendency to separate at social gatherings. Friendship regularly cut across tribal boundaries, and intertribal marriage was the rule rather than the exception.

The Hapū

Since size was a major factor in the lack of unity among members of the same tribe in Auckland, it might have been expected that the *hapū*, being smaller, would have a greater degree of cohesion and social significance. But membership in a *hapū* was much less meaningful for Auckland Maoris than tribal membership. Most were almost entirely uninformed on the subject. Except for a handful of elderly immigrants, relatively few in the 'sets' were able to name their *hapū* accurately and without prompting; those who could, for the most part repeated parrot-fashion what they had been told by their parents and knew nothing, for instance, about the links through which their membership was traced or the relationship of their *hapū* to the others of the tribe.

The young people in general were confused over the difference between *hapū* and *iwi*. The average Auckland Maori under twenty-five, if asked to name his *hapū*, gave the name of his tribe in reply. In filling in forms, such as those for electoral registration or wedding certificates, many wrote the name of their tribe in the space allotted to *hapū*. This confusion might have arisen from a modern tendency to use the English term *tribe* instead of the Maori *iwi*; many of my young informants honestly believed that *hapū* was Maori for *tribe*. Even some of the middle-aged were by no means certain of the distinction. One woman in her forties, who was better informed than most about her descent, knew that she belonged to Whanau Pani and to Ngāti-Uru, but she was not quite sure of the relationship between these two descent groups, for in one interview she described herself as "Whānau Pani of Ngati-Uru", thus making the former part of the latter (sub-tribe of a tribe), and in another as "part Whānau Pani and part Ngāti-Uru", which accorded them equal status as *hapū*.

In some cases, the confusion between *iwi* and *hapū* arose, not from ignorance but from the segmentary nature of Maori descent groups. It has never been clear at what point a large *hapū* achieved the status of a tribe in pre-European society, though it is plain that some tribes were formed in that way. As far as we know, the transition was never formally acknowledged but was a matter of usage. Probably one of the most common ways in which a *hapū* asserted its independence and forced recognition as a tribe in its own right was by fighting. When the Maori became part of the New Zealand state in 1840 this method was outlawed. The accepted list of tribes has remained unchanged since that date. As a result there are many anomalies in the present tribal system. Ngāti-Kahu was, for instance, described as a tribe by informants who belonged to it, but was usually treated as a branch of Ngāpuhi by others. The subtleties of this problem were, however, far beyond most of my informants.

The names of *hapū* were not often heard in Auckland, either in public or in ordinary conversation. The only times I heard them publicly proclaimed was during the "flower ceremony"[1] at weddings, a custom peculiar to the Northern tribes. Because so many tribes were represented at city weddings, and also because the elder calling the *hapū* was not usually familiar with the smaller *hapū* of other tribes, the list was normally restricted to the major *hapū* of each tribe.

Hapū in Auckland had no corporate life.[2] Like the tribe, they had neither permanent base nor meeting-place in the city. Except in the case of a few *tāngata whenua hapū*, the territory and *marae* with which they were associated by tradition lay outside its limits. As far as I knew, no-one had even attempted to set up a club on a *hapū* basis. When the planners mentioned earlier failed to establish a tribal club, they did not consider forming one on a sub-tribal basis, but turned to close kin who belonged to several different *hapū* and set up a "family club" instead.

In the city, the *hapū* had become a complete abstraction, a name without social function. The Auckland Maori looked to his tribe to give him a place in Maori society. His *hapū* was meaningless in that respect, because only a fraction of those he met had even heard of it. Moral and other kinds of support he sought from his kinsfolk. The *hapū* was too large and scattered for the purpose, besides lacking the necessary organisation. And so the *hapū* had dropped out from between the small kin-group and the large as a factor in Maori social organisation in Auckland.

The 'Family' and Family Clubs

What of descent-groups at the 'family'[3] level in Auckland? Most Auckland Maoris were conscious of belonging to a 'family' associated primarily with a rural community, though it included members living scattered through-

---

[1] p. 60.
[2] The *hapū* was not much more important in Kōtare in 1955, but subsequent experience in other tribal areas has convinced me that Kōtare and the Rarawa were atypical in this respect.   [3] pp. 61–71.

out New Zealand. They also applied the term to groups of kinsmen living in Auckland who had some degree of corporate identity, temporary or permanent, at the time of speaking. In most cases this corporateness amounted to nothing more formal than frequent association, a special feeling of kinship, and the habit of supporting each other on occasions such as weddings and funerals; but in some it was strong enough to find expression in what they called "family clubs", consciously patterned on rural models.

In Kōtare, in addition to its normal use for elementary- and grand-family, the word 'family' was applied consistently to groups which were in fact descent-groups and were recognised as such by the people themselves. In Auckland it was applied much more loosely. Some of the groups described as 'families' were basically descent-groups, consisting, for instance, of the Auckland members of a rural 'family' or of a senior couple and their descendants, together with spouses. But many included a high proportion of persons who were neither descended from nor married to persons descended from a common recent forebear. In Kōtare most adults had at least a sketchy knowledge of how members of 'families' other than their own were related to each other, and though individuals might make mistakes, there was a general consensus of opinion as to who belonged to each. Also, while spouses and foster children acted as part of the group and a few other kin were accepted as subscribers to 'family' clubs, it was never forgotten that they were not "real" members. But in Auckland, where neighbours, even those living in the same house, came from other communities and other tribes, few knew much about any kin-group but their own. Non-members described as "one family" any group of kinsmen who "stuck together" often or long enough for the fact to be noticed, but rarely knew how those in the group were interrelated. They were content with vague explanations such as "my aunt", "my nephew", or "just a Maori cousin", and did not check to see whether these terms concealed affinal or foster relationships. Different persons grouped the same people in slightly different ways or identified the same group by different names. Kinsmen sometimes proclaimed themselves as "all one family" even when they were not, because "sticking together" was to their advantage. Beset by a feeling of insecurity and isolation in the city and the added worries and cost of taking their dead back to the country for burial, they were prepared to co-operate with kin who derived from the same or neighbouring rural areas if there were not enough members of their own rural 'family' in Auckland. In many Auckland 'families', the distinction between "real" and attached members was less meaningful than in the country because so many fell into the second category.

Most Auckland Maoris did not belong to any group with enough corporate identity to be recognised as a 'family' except for short periods associated with gatherings such as weddings. Even on such occasions, groups of Auckland kin were weakly organised. The lion's share of the work and cost was borne by the close kin of the persons honoured (almost invariably including some from outside who had come to Auckland for the occasion), and the rest lent a hand only in the final stages. In Kōtare most people were aware of the distinction between members of the sponsoring 'families' and other kin, but at Auckland *hui* it was generally blurred.

However, an important minority, feeling the need of some more stable form of kin organisation, set up 'family' *komiti* or clubs based entirely in Auckland. In August 1954, 48 of the 229 adults in the 'sets' (21 per cent) were subscribing members of six such *komiti*, while another 9 (4 per cent) had belonged to one which had broken down within the last year. Analysis of the membership of the six clubs in which my informants were involved revealed two distinct structural types. As far as I could check, this distinction was typical of Auckland 'family' clubs in general.

Two of the *komiti* just mentioned (involving 19 persons from the 'sets') consisted of a married couple and most or all of their descendants living in the city, together with the latter's spouses and foster children: what I would describe as a *bilateral extended-family* (see Fig. 10). (Anthropologists differ considerably in their definition of the term *extended-family*. Some would reserve it for groups based on unilateral affiliation, others for a single domestic or economic unit. These limitations, I feel, unnecessarily restrict the usefulness of the term. I have chosen to define *extended-family* as a socially recognised group of kin descended from or married to persons descended from a living senior couple or widowed person, living close enough to each other to be able to act together for certain purposes and in fact consistently doing so on an organised basis.) The extended-family as it existed in Auckland differed from the wider 'family' in that (1) it stemmed from living progenitor(s); (2) it was comparatively localised, i.e. within the limits of the urban area; and (3) it was formally organised as a club. In structure it was comparable to the 'branch' of the rural 'family'.

Four other clubs (involving 29 adults from the 'sets') lacked consistent structure, corresponding to no known variation of descent-group, though descent still played a part of some importance in their formation. In these four cases, the nucleus of the group was formed of the descendants not of one progenitor but of two or three who were linked by kinship but not always by common descent (see Fig. 11). These progenitors were invariably deceased, so that the group was of greater genealogical depth than the extended-family. Apart from spouses and foster children, the group also included a considerable number of kinsmen attached to these nuclear lines only by affinal and foster ties established in past as well as present generations. I propose to call these groups *kin-clusters*.

Extended-family and kin-cluster resembled each other in some aspects of their composition and organisation, and performed identical functions for their members, but they also differed in certain significant ways.

Both were bilateral groups in the sense that neither patrilateral nor matrilateral affiliation was the rule; male and female descendants were equally eligible for membership. Both admitted spouses and foster children to full membership and even to executive office. Neither included all the known descendants of the progenitor (or progenitors) of the group, but only those who wished to participate and could conveniently do so. With a few rare exceptions, their members were all resident in Auckland. Both were large groups involving up to forty adults and their dependent children, distributed among a number of autonomous domestic units scattered over the city. Finally, both were composed mainly of Auckland residents of long standing. Of the forty-eight who belonged to 'family' clubs in the 'sets', only six had been in Auckland less than ten years.

These 'family' clubs were never legally registered or incorporated. Sometimes they were given a descriptive name, which was not widely known outside the group, but more often they were associated with the surname of the most prominent members, or with the name of the rural community from which they derived. As in Kōtare, adult members paid regular subscriptions into a central fund at formal meetings, which were supposed to be held regularly but postponed when there was no other business. A Chairman, Secretary and Treasurer elected by subscribing members handled the details of organisation, but most matters were discussed in plenary meetings. Maori ceremonial forms were observed at meetings, including *mihimihi* (exchange of greetings) and a set pattern and order of speeches. They took place in the homes of members, sometimes in rotation, more often in that of one of the officers. Minutes and accounts were usually kept and the money held in a Post Office Savings Account, although in at least one case it was kept under the floorboards, in order to be immediately available if a death occurred during the weekend. Subscriptions varied from club to club and from time to time, the most usual rate being five shillings per month per adult. The sums handled were often extremely large. One group had £100 in hand; another had collected £500, and was aiming at £1,000, with plans of investing it and using only the interest for payment of death expenses. A few clubs attempted or promised to give aid in sickness as well as after a death, but this was commonly felt to place too great a strain on club finances.

Auckland 'family' clubs, like rural ones, were primarily *tangi* clubs. Maoris living in Auckland insisted on taking their dead back to the home community for burial. The ceremonial observance of the *tangi* required the co-operation of a large body of kinsfolk even in the country. In the city, the costs and difficulties of organisation were greatly increased by distance from the home community and by the fact that fewer kin were usually available. Moreover, it was necessary for the initial arrangements and the journey home to be completed as quickly as possible in order that the body should lie in state on the home *marae* for two or three days before burial while still complying with the health regulations. The club type of organisation was favoured because it enabled financial resources and members to be mobilised with the minimum delay.

In addition to *tangi*, Auckland 'family' clubs usually organised the celebration of other social crises in the lives of members. They did not use club funds for such occasions but made special collections. Some clubs also promoted card evenings in order to obtain funds for some worthy cause affecting members, such as a trip to a rural gathering or a new meeting-house in their home community. Occasionally they sponsored sports teams, but the latter usually became independent in the course of time. They also helped to solve the problem of transport to *hui* outside Auckland by putting it upon a group basis and hiring a bus.

Personal association was close between members of most 'family' clubs, particularly in the extended family. Children as well as adults moved fairly freely from one residence to another within the group for meals and to sleep. The mothers assisted each other with household chores and shopping, and minded each other's children. Members spent most of their leisure in one another's company. Groups of both types provided most of their members with most of their effective kin in Auckland.

The main differences in the organisation of the extended-family and the kin-cluster were connected with their structural differences. The extended-family was formed and maintained primarily by the influence of the senior couple, whereas in the kin-cluster the motive of co-operation for mutual benefit was of primary importance, usually reinforced by attachment to the same rural community. Neither appeared to be particularly stable over time.

The extended-family group was built around a senior couple, who were usually in their sixties or older, and whose home was the rendezvous for the group. Usually some of their children (including married sons and daughters) still lived with them. The basis of the group was strong personal affection between members, which was focused especially on the senior couple. The relationship between the senior couple was one of equal partnership, and although they exerted considerable influence over the other members, their power was strictly limited. There was, in short, no sign of patriarchal tendency. Executive functions were usually in the hands of the middle generations.

The extended-family group did not usually survive the death of the senior couple on which it was centred. There was no instance in the 'sets' (or in the city as far as I was aware) of a set of siblings and their descendants holding together as a single group. Nor did it seem certain in any existing group that even one of the sons or daughters would establish a comparable group after the death of the present senior couple. For by no means all those who had achieved the status of grandparent or great-grandparent possessed the qualities needed to hold such a group together.

At times the extended-family existed in the city without maintaining a live relationship with a rural community, its members returning to their community of origin only to bury their dead. In the cases which I knew personally, the senior couple had been resident in the city for many years and most of their descendants had immigrated to the city in childhood or as young adults, or were city-born. It would seem that when attachment to home community and *marae* was strong and frequent trips were made to visit them, those involved either remained effective members of a rural 'family' or set up a city club based on a kin-cluster rather than an extended-family. The centre of gravity for the extended-family was the home of the senior couple, rather than their home *marae*.

The kin-cluster on the other hand was not centred round any one person, couple or line of descent. Its members were held together by an awareness of their vulnerability in the city as Maoris, particularly with respect to the problems contingent upon death, and by the benefits derived from co-operation. In the absence of enough kinsmen of common descent to form an effective 'family' club they had turned to kinsfolk whom they had known well in the past, usually in the same rural community. The unity derived from common origin was maintained by the organisation of frequent "trips" to the home community on a group basis, to attend gatherings associated with social crises in the lives not only of members of the Auckland group, but also of kin still resident there. The centre of gravity for the kin-cluster was the home *marae*. The importance of common origin in the composition of the kin-cluster was reflected in the fact that they were often identified in the city by the name of the rural community from which they derived: e.g. "the crowd from Waikeri", or even "the Waikeri crowd". A kin-cluster might have one acknowledged head, but more often it had several *kaumātua* of more or less equal status. One of these elders was usually elected Chairman, but the Secretary and Treasurer were in their thirties and forties, as in the extended-family.

The unity of the kin-cluster was usually further reinforced by common church membership. Of the four kin-clusters to which informants in the 'sets' belonged, one was associated with a small nativistic cult, another was composed almost entirely of Ratana adherents, and the others were Anglican and Roman Catholic respectively. On the other hand, religious differences caused some eligible for membership to stand aloof. Immigrants from a certain community in the Far North formed two distinct kin-clusters, the members of one belonging to the Ratana church and those of the other to the Methodist.

Members of the same kin-cluster usually lived fairly close to each other. Those who moved beyond adjacent suburbs were usually lost to the club.

'Family' clubs associated with kin-clusters were notoriously short-lived. Members fell behind with subscriptions, so that funds were not adequate when the need arose; or a non-financial member died and members were divided into two camps, for and against assisting his family with the expenses; or the entire fund was exhausted to pay for one funeral leaving nothing for the next; or the money was "borrowed" by those holding it and lost at the gaming table or racecourse totalisator. All these contingencies led to quarrels and the collapse of the club. There were, how-

ever, a few notable exceptions. One highly efficient club had been in operation for over ten years without intermission.

The failure of the 'family' club sometimes meant the dispersal of the
kin-cluster, but more often attempt after attempt was made to establish
a successful club. Thus while many kin-clusters lasted only a year or two,
a few had survived for five to ten, though rarely without drastic changes
in personnel. Persistence over time was directly correlated with the
strength of attachment to the home community and the frequency of
contact with it. Because the emphasis was on common local origin rather
than on the nature of kinship links, elementary-families and individuals
within the group could change without affecting its stability as a whole.
While some members were lost because of migration or quarrels, new
recruits were always available.

KINSHIP PATTERNS IN AUCKLAND: EXAMPLES

This account of kinship patterns among Maoris living in Auckland is an
abstraction based on personal knowledge of three arbitrarily selected 'sets'
of residents. It might be useful to illustrate the most important patterns
and trends with actual cases, chosen more or less at random from those
available.

EXAMPLE A.   A single individual living in "rooms", with a small circle of
effective urban kin and little contact with kin in the country.

Eighteen-year old Hoki King shared a room and kitchenette in an apartment house with a (Maori) girl who was a stranger to her when she moved in.
She worked as a waitress in a café. She had two married sisters in Auckland,
both living in the same suburb, and a brother who stayed with the elder.
Hoki spent the weekends when she did not have to work on Saturday with
one or other of her sisters. One sister did all her dressmaking.

The only other kin Hoki knew in Auckland were two unmarried male
cousins of her own age whom she saw frequently at the dance halls and
cinemas she attended. She knew no aunts or uncles. Her father had died
when she was small and her mother left the Hokianga area, where they
belonged, and settled in Northern Wairoa after a second marriage. "Mother
never talked about any family. She never told us who's who, and we did not
ask." Hoki knew that she was Ngāpuhi, but not which *hapū*.

Hoki's mother died when she was fifteen and she came to Auckland to
stay with her brother and his wife. She later went back to Hokianga with
her brother but returned to Auckland after working there for several months
because she "did not like it". Since then, she had visited two married
sisters living in different parts of Northland; but she had never seen the
homes of two others living in Taumarunui and Invercargill respectively.

Hoki's main companions when she was not visiting her sisters were one
of the girls from the apartment house (an Aupouri and no relation) and her
current boy-friend, who as often as not belonged to a different tribe. They
moved within a circle of young people known vaguely as "the Community
Centre crowd".

EXAMPLE B. An elementary-family domestic unit with a limited number of effective kin.

Selwyn and Phyllis Davis and their four sons occupied a flat in the central city, sharing a backyard and wash-house with the occupants of two other flats. Both just thirty, they had married young during the war. Selwyn, a Rarawa, came from Kōtare in the Far North; Phyllis was a Ngāti Maniapoto from the King Country. Selwyn was making a success of running his own business in partnership with a Pakeha.

Selwyn had only one sibling in the city, a brother whom he and Phyllis visited about once a year. He saw very little of anyone from Kōtare, of whom there were many in Auckland. He was only sixteen when he left Kōtare; his family had "died right out there" and its few members were scattered all over New Zealand. His mother's brother, who was living some fifty miles south of Auckland, came to Auckland in 1954 and spent several months working there. He stayed with Selwyn and Phyllis, joined for part of the time by his Arawa wife and two small sons.

Selwyn's main associates were not kinsmen, but his partner, two Pakeha friends met through the latter, and some half dozen young Maoris of his own age and interests from a variety of different tribes. According to Phyllis, "he won't recognise any relatives further out than first cousin. He is very Pakeha in this way".

Phyllis's family had been broken up and scattered when both parents died when Phyllis was very young. She had spent her childhood with several different relatives and her adolescence in boarding school and domestic service in Hamilton, before coming to Auckland at the age of seventeen. In 1953–4 she saw comparatively little of the siblings and other kin she had in Auckland; on her own avowal she was "very independent". When she was in hospital for several weeks in 1954 her visitors were all friends and neighbours. One brother, living less than half a mile away, she had not seen for four years, and it was two years since she visited an older sister in the suburbs. She had lost touch with several siblings as a result of their separation in childhood, and on one occasion learnt from outside sources that a younger brother was not only living in Auckland but was shortly to marry a city girl. Phyllis saw most of her favourite brother and his wife, who also lived in the central city, but the initiative was all on their side, and their visits had been much curtailed since the birth of their first child. (Phyllis herself was tied to the house with four children, two of whom were under school age.) Selwyn had struck up a friendship with this brother, who was skilled in a trade complementary to his own, and they often co-operated on a job.

Selwyn and Phyllis and the boys were all very fond of Phyllis's first cousin and her husband, who were old enough to stand *in loco parentis*. Phyllis lived with them before her marriage and they had sponsored her wedding. But they lived on the fringe of the city and meetings were not particularly frequent or regular. Phyllis and Selwyn and the boys spent two or three weekends staying with them every year.

Phyllis maintained effective relations with two other kinsfolk in the city, son and daughter of two of her mother's brothers. The latter lived in a neighbouring street and sometimes called in as she passed on her way to the shops. The friendship was a casual one; meetings were unplanned and often weeks or even months apart. When the cousin was rushed into hospital in 1954, Phyllis knew nothing of it until she came home. When they quarrelled once, Phyllis commented that "it is a pity, because we are the only women of the family in the city and ought to stick together". (The older cousin referred to above was related to Phyllis on her father's side.) Phyllis's other cousin was studying at the university. He was not a frequent caller, but he had given Selwyn some assistance with his business accounts.

Selwyn visited Kōtare in 1954 for the first time since he left, fourteen years earlier. He took the family north during the Christmas vacation, spending four days with his sister in Taheke, five camping at Kōtare, and a week with a brother in Awanui (near Kaitaia). Phyllis had visited her parents' home community in the King Country three times since her marriage, staying a fortnight after the birth of her second and third sons and a weekend in May 1954, when she went to collect the eldest two who had spent the school holidays with her sister on the farm. The latter and her family stayed with the Davises at the time of Phyllis's brother's wedding early in 1954.

EXAMPLE C.   A grand-family domestic unit, with few effective urban kin but close ties with the grandfather's home community.

Tahu Paki, an Arawa, had lived thirty years in the central city with his city-born, Ngāpuhi wife. They had three daughters living with them: Ann, her husband Sam and two children, Eliza, a divorcée, and her two children, and Ellen, who was still at school. Another married daughter Olga lived in the suburbs, but she and her husband often stayed in the household for several days. The four girls and their mother were in every sense each other's best friends. Before they married, the girls had always gone out to dances and films together; they still did so when their husbands were not available. Mrs Paki worked in the central city and Ann and Eliza shared the housekeeping, taking turns to go to work. They minded the children and did the family's washing and sewing, with occasional help from their mother and young sister. The girls and their parents always spent Christmas together, mostly at home, but one year in Olga's new home. It was to each other that they turned in times of sickness and trouble.

Relations with other urban kin were weakly developed. A son of the family lived in a State house in the suburbs, but the members of the Paki household were very infrequent visitors there, and in two years I never met him or his wife visiting his parents. Neither Tahu nor his wife appeared to have any other kin in the city. The girls' marriages had not resulted in the establishment of any close ties between the Paki family as a whole and their affines. In Eliza's case the marriage had ended in divorce. Ann maintained amiable but not intimate relations with her husband's parents and siblings, who were not in the habit of visiting the house. They usually spent an annual holiday staying in a house belonging to one of Sam's brothers. Chief visitors to the house were non-kin friends.

Under stress of new conditions, however, kinship ties were re-discovered. When Ann and her family eventually moved into a State house in 1954 she discovered a "cousin" who had formerly lived in the central city now in the same street. How close a "cousin" she was, however, leaves room for doubt, for Ann commented that "anyone from Dad's home area is a relative". They were thrilled to find each other among so many strangers and immediately began to "live in each other's kitchens". Much the same relationship was, however, established at the same time with the other Maori family in the street, who were no relation at all, but had once been close friends when they lived in the central city.

The Pakis had lost touch completely with kin living in Mrs Paki's home community, but most of them visited Rotorua at least once a year. In 1953–4, they stayed most often on such visits with a son who had been brought up there by kin to Tahu and who had married a Rotorua girl and established his own home there. Ann and Eliza had both worked there while still single, staying with relations.

EXAMPLE D.   A denuded grand-family, with a large circle of effective kin.

Anaru Pera was a middle-aged widower with a large family, living in a State house in New Lynn. His eldest daughter Kathleen and her husband, Hepa Williamson, lived in a State house in an eastern suburb, while his second daughter Hine and her husband of a few months alternated between Anaru's home and Kathleen's. (Another married daughter lived in Mangakino.) His two unmarried daughters took turns in running his house and "looking after the little ones". There was a continual traffic between the households. When there was someone ill in her father's household Kathleen would stay there with her own four children for as long as three weeks; her father frequently kept her eldest child with him for months at a time; and her teenage siblings were often called upon—or volunteered—to act as baby-sitters to her children. On special occasions the two households amalgamated: at Christmas 1953 they spent a week at one house and a week at the other; in January 1954 they combined to hire a taxi to take them to Mangakino to visit Anaru's third daughter. When Hine was married Kathleen and Hepa alone of all his kin supported Anaru at the *tomo* and helped him bear the expenses which were not covered by the bride and groom's own savings, contributions from the groom's side and *awhina* from guests.

Anaru had formerly had several siblings in the city, but they had all migrated to Mangakino, with the exception of one sister living in an outer suburb. He also had several first cousins, offspring of his mother's sister, whose children had been brought up in the central city when Anaru had also been living there, and had attended school with Anaru's children. In 1953–4 Anaru and his family maintained casual relations with these cousins, occasionally accompanying them to the cinema or to the Maori Community Centre, along with other old acquaintances from the central city. They attended each other's parties and weddings: two of these cousins asked Hine and Meriana Pera to be bridesmaids at their weddings. But when Hine was married she chose her bridesmaids from her sisters. While they met quite often in the social life of the central city, these cousins were not frequent visitors to each other's homes. Two young and flighty girl cousins had stayed for some months in Anaru's house, but their behaviour became so outrageous that he turned them out. Anaru himself had little to do with his cousins except on formal occasions. His preferred companions were his sons-in-law and five friends of his own age, two no relation, and the other three with extremely tenuous claims to be kin. His two closest "pals" were, respectively, half-brother to his father's brother's son, and brother of his dead wife's mother's sister's daughter's daughter's husband. Anaru was, however, a kindly uncle, and his house was a refuge for a succession of nieces and nephews, children of the brothers and sisters he had left behind in his home district.

Anaru's wife had been born in the city of *tangata whenua* stock and she had a large number of relatives there. When she was alive her father had lived with her and the house was always full of her kin, but after her death her father went to stay with his son, his visits grew less frequent, mainly because he was elderly and ailing, and ceased entirely when Kathleen and Anaru both left the accessible central city. The rest of the late Mrs Pera's kin had likewise lost touch with her family, with the exception of Will and Puni Shannon and their descendants, who were bound to them by two affinal links, for Mrs Pera's mother was sister to Puni Shannon's mother, and Anaru's younger brother had married one of Will Shannon's daughters. The two families were on friendly but far from intimate terms, attending each other's 'family' gatherings only after they had been invited.

Anaru was Ngāti Maru and his children "go under Father's tribe"; none of them knew what his *hapū* was. According to Kathleen, they used to go "home" to Anaru's birthplace near Coromandel every Christmas, but their last visit was for Easter 1952. It was too expensive a trip with a large family. But Anaru took some of the children to Paeroa two or three times a year to stay with his brother and his family, and they visited his daughter in Mangakino *en masse* twice in 1954.

EXAMPLE E.   An extended-family with a 'family' club and highly developed corporate life. (See Fig. 10).

"The Shannons" were a devoted 'family' group; in common parlance, they "stuck together". Will and Puni Shannon lived in a State house in the Tāmaki area with their four youngest children and two sons, who, with their wives and children, were hopefully waiting for State houses of their own. They had four other offspring scattered over the city: their oldest daughter, Rere, who had married her father's sister's son, in the central city, the second daughter, Pauline, in a State house, and another daughter and a son in homes of their own, in other suburbs. Despite this scattering of elementary-family units the visiting of each household was largely confined to the 'family' circle, the daughters in particular finding their closest friends among their sisters and sisters-in-law. Pauline, for instance, tied to her home by five children under six, visited only her parents, Rere, and her brother on her rare outings. Rere, who was more mobile, was a weekly visitor in her parents' house. Even the youngest unmarried sisters stated that "we visit only family, that is, Rere, Pauline and brother Tom, and we go to the pictures with our young brother and sister".

The family solidarity was expressed in a "family club", which was managed by the women. Pauline was treasurer and every month thirteen women paid her a monthly subscription of 10s each, which she banked for use in time of death or illness. The thirteen involved were Puni, six of her adult daughters, four daughters-in-law and two daughter's daughters. This included four living outside the city and two unmarried women.

Yet even within this devoted extended-family each constituent family was an independent unit which did not always act in concert with or with the approval of the rest of the group. The tendency towards independence became more marked as each generation grew older. It was facilitated by dispersed residence and encouraged by marriage with persons from other tribes. When Pauline's husband's parents or siblings came to stay with them, Pauline's parents and siblings stopped visiting her until they left, for "they knew I had strangers in the house". Any authority Will and Puni had over the 'family' group stemmed from the affection in which they were held and not from any rights imputed to them. Neither Rere nor Pauline tolerated any interference from their parents or their siblings in the way they brought up their children, and all but one of Will and Puni's own

THE SHANNON EXTENDED – FAMILY

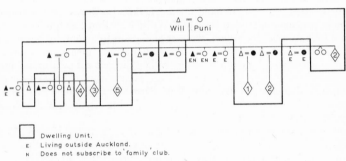

E	Dwelling Unit.
N	Living outside Auckland.
	Does not subscribe to 'family' club.

FIG. 10. For explanation of symbols, see Fig. 5, p. 62

children had married "strangers" in the face of strenuous parental opposition. 'Family' solidarity was continually undergoing modification as a result of the independent actions and decisions of individual members or married couples.

This was well illustrated by the fate of the 'family' sports club. At the beginning of the 1953 football season, the Shannon men formed themselves into a football team and affiliated the new club to a suburban football association. The club had twenty-six members, five of whom came from outside the extended-family. The twenty-one other members were: the senior couple, three of their sons and three daughters-in-law, six daughters and four sons-in-law, a grandson, and a granddaughter and her husband. It was interesting that all important executive posts were held by husbands of women of the 'family'. The 'family' members attended the matches together, usually gathering before and afterwards at Pauline's house, which was close to the home sports ground. Most of them also turned up there for the fortnightly mid-week club meeting. Pauline catered for the meals they ate and was paid the cost of the food from club funds. She was also paid for washing the club jerseys.

These arrangements lasted only a few months. Pauline resented the extra work and being left to mind all the children during matches. She complained, and meetings were transferred to a newly completed club shed at the home sports ground, where they were attended only by players and officers. Later, however, when some unsuccessful trips depleted club funds, the 'family' rallied round to put it back on its feet. At the beginning of the second season, several 'family' members (including the Secretary) migrated to Mangakino and non-'family' members were elected as officers in their place. Although most of these were kinsmen, the women complained that the club had been "taken over by strangers".

William Shannon had two siblings in the city. Rīria, the eldest, lived in the central city with her second husband, their only son, his wife and three children. Three of her five children by her first marriage were also in the city, one married to Will's eldest daughter. Rīria's descendants also formed an extended-family but it was less tightly knit than Will's. The third sibling, Ike, died in 1954, leaving a daughter his only descendant in the city.

Will, Rīria and Ike and their descendants remained effective kin, visiting each other occasionally, but coming together on occasions of social crisis. When Ike died, they all attended the *tangi*. Ike's body was taken to his home *marae* in a hearse, attended by Rīria, Will's wife Puni, and Ike's intended second wife as chief mourners, the rest of the kin following by bus and car. Pauline's husband assumed charge of catering arrangements at the meeting-house. But even in the context of death they did not act as a group but as an aggregation of individuals. Ike had set aside a sum of money for *tangi* expenses: the deficit was shared by Will, Rīria and their uncle (who lived in the home community), the deceased's closest living relatives, with voluntary contributions from younger kinsfolk.

Will and Puni Shannon were both Ngāti Paoa from the Hauraki Plains. Neither they nor their offspring were in the habit of visiting their home communities. The only time they went home in 1953–4 was to Ike's *tangi*.

EXAMPLE F.   A kin-cluster with a 'family' club and close relations with the community of origin (see Fig. 11).

A certain house in the central city was occupied by a number of individuals and families from one rural community which we shall call Waikeri, and it was the base for social activity for more immigrants from the same community, who lived in two houses in the same street a few minutes' walk away. All the immigrants from Waikeri who lived in these three houses claimed to be related, and they formed a group with a fair degree of corporate unity. It took me the best part of two years, however, to construct a table showing exactly how the participants were related to each other. No one individual saw all the relationships clearly: to every member of the group there were others who were "relations' relations". There were four main sub-groups. Members of each could detail their relationship to one or more of the others, but were content to accept the others on the basis that they were related to one of the sub-groups to which they themselves could actually trace their relationship.

This group of Waikeri immigrants consisted, as far as I could ascertain, of the descendants of three progenitors, two men standing in the relation-

ship of father's brother's son to each other and a woman who was wife's
sister to one of these cousins. In other words, there was a basic division in
the group into two 'lines' of descent joined by an affinal link. "The Tīpenes"
and "the Isaiahs" shared descent from a single ancestor, but the relationship
was usually described as that of descent from two first cousins. "The Kingis"
and "the Tātanas" were derived from two daughters of the *kuia* (old woman)
through whom they were related to "the Tīpenes" and "the Isaiahs".
Descendants of this *kuia's* son, "the Mangakāhias", lived in the city but did
not normally belong to the group. The main links in the chains of descent
and of affinal connection were women. The very surnames in common use
among them to distinguish the four main "lines" were those of men who
had married into the group. (None of these men were living in the city:

THE WAIKERI KIN – CLUSTER

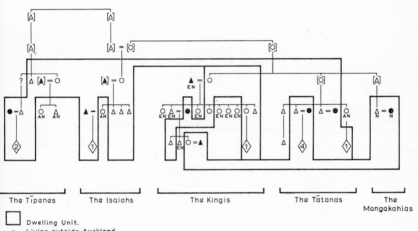

The Tīpenes   The Isaiahs   The Kingis   The Tātanas   The Mangakahias

☐ Dwelling Unit.
E Living outside Auckland.
A Living elsewhere in Auckland.
N Does not subscribe to family club.

FIG. 11. For explanation of symbols, see Fig. 5, p. 62

three were dead and the fourth, separated from his wife, dwelt in the country.)
The group was an aggregation of kin consisting of some (but not all) members of four bilateral descent-groups of shallow depth, each linked in some
cases by the common descent of their recognised progenitors and in some
cases by affinal ties.

The members of this group referred to themselves and were referred to
by others as "the Waikeri crowd". Their closest social contacts were among
themselves. Hoana Tātana told me that the only places she ever visited
were the houses occupied by "the Tīpenes" and "the Isaiahs" and by "the
Kingis", an assertion substantiated by my own observation during two
years. In everyday social activity members of the group were in constant
contact, running in and out of each others' houses several times a week and
in many cases several times a day. Whenever I visited one of the three houses

I was bound to meet someone from the others there. The children played in each other's yards and rooms. The adults formed the nucleus of a gambling circle which held periodic card parties in one or other of the three houses. They often attended card evenings in another house in the street, run by a group of remote kinsfolk, who returned the compliment. Members of the kin-cluster also shared adherence to a small religious cult which had gained a hold in their home area. Mrs Tīpene's home was the urban centre for this cult, and the Waikeri crowd gathered there for weekly services.

The unity of the group was expressed in and also defined by membership in the 'family' club. All the adults paid—or were expected to pay—a regular sum each month; the actual sum varied from time to time (and also from informant to informant!) from 2s 6d to 10s. The money was entrusted to one of the younger Kingi men who kept it in a cashbox stored under the floorboards of his room. It was the younger men who made the arrangements with transport firms for the hire of buses and rental cars, but Mrs Tīpene represented the club in its transactions with funeral companies, because she had been in the city for thirty odd years and was known to them. In short, there was no single organiser of club affairs, and those who did the work on behalf of the club were chosen for personal qualities—trustworthiness, literacy, competence in financial matters and acquaintance with specific city firms. Money was collected at club meetings on Sunday afternoon at Mrs Tīpene's place.

The members of the group made eight trips together by hired bus within two years, four to attend cult rallies, two to weddings and two to *tangi*. Strictly speaking, the club organised and paid for transport only on the occasion of a death, for the coffin and the chief mourners; but in fact the club organisers handled arrangements for other excursions as well. They paid the deposit on the bus from funds in hand, but collected enough from those travelling in the bus to cover expenses and "*marae* money". Sometimes a card party was specifically organised to raise funds for the trip. Members of the Waikeri kin-cluster also "clubbed together" periodically to buy mussels or sea-eggs in bulk, dividing them among the various families in proportion to their contribution.

Most members had some other relatives in Auckland but saw comparatively little of them. Mrs Hoana Tātana saw far less of her own brother than she did of her husband's kin in the Waikeri group. Parani Tīpene had a full brother in the suburbs who was an active member of his wife's kin-cluster, but she visited him only once in the two and half years I knew them, and he never came to her house. The activities of the Waikeri kin-cluster were also open to and attracted a number of non-members—the kin, friends and acquaintances of members. Most hovered on the fringe of the group for a few weeks and disappeared. A few became almost assimilated to the group by close identification with one of the constituent families. Harry Parata, for instance, who boarded with Keita Isaiah and was the father of her granddaughter, tagged along on the trips and took a hand at cards.

Membership in the larger group was unconsciously conceived in terms of membership of constituent "lines". The common formulation was that "We are all Tīpenes, Tātanas, Isaiahs or Kingis", or "The club consists of the Tīpenes, the Tātanas, the Isaiahs and the Kingis"; I found it impossible to get a list of individual members. Individual Kingis and Tātanas etc. opted out, either temporarily or permanently, without shaking the existence of the group in the least.

Not all the Auckland descendants of the three progenitors of the group belonged to the club. Ken Mangakāhia lived in one of the three houses occupied by members of the Waikeri crowd, but he did not pay subscriptions to the club and went on only one "trip" in two years. It took me two years to discover how closely he was related to the Tātanas. Parani Tīpene's son and daughter, who had both belonged to the club when they lived at the main house with their mother, lost contact with it when they moved into the suburbs.

URBANISATION AND MAORI KINSHIP PATTERNS

Urbanisation and the conditions of urban life had clearly brought about changes in Maori kinship patterns. On the average, Auckland Maoris maintained effective relations with fewer kinsfolk and had fewer intimate kin than was typical in the country; but kindreds were still fairly large, and extensive ones far from uncommon. Auckland Maoris were if anything more conscious of their tribal membership, for in most social contexts they were brought into association with members of a large number of different tribes, and tribal differences were a common topic of discussion and teasing. However, tribal solidarity remained completely abstract and unformalised. The *hapū* was almost entirely disregarded. Less attention was paid to descent as a qualification for leadership or a matter for study. It was also less important as a basis for corporate kin action. At least half the groups who claimed to be and were recognised by others as 'families' were not formed wholly or even mainly on the basis of common descent. Fewer Maoris belonged to 'family' clubs in Auckland —20–25 per cent of those over fifteen in the 'sets' as compared with about 33 per cent in Kōtare.[1] But those who did often derived more from their membership. Most members of urban 'family' clubs found both their most intimate kin and most of their effective urban kin within the club: for some of the elderly and conservative it comprised their whole urban world. The Auckland clubs had extended their functions to cope with the special problems of urban life: they organised transport for trips to the home community, sponsored card parties and sports teams, and even bought Maori *kai* in quantity for sharing among their members. Those who did not belong to 'family' clubs joined forces temporarily on the same occasions of social crisis as in the country, providing both finance and labour. Most Auckland Maoris maintained contact with rural 'families' to which they belonged by right of descent, and were re-absorbed into their activities during their visits home.

Personal acquaintance with Auckland Maoris and with their histories established one significant point: long residence in the city was not consistently correlated with contraction of the effective kindred or waning

[1] p. 67.

interest in 'family' clubs. On the contrary, those of my informants who had been there longest usually had large kindreds in the city and were the backbone of 'family' clubs. For the number of kinsmen available to them in the city usually increased with time as a result of immigration, they themselves were able to move about more freely as their children grew up, and, like their country relations, they became more conscious of their responsibilities with regard to death, and of the problems involved, as they grew older. They turned to 'family' clubs as the best and most familiar method of handling the situation.

Many factors were involved in these changes in kinship patterns. The size of the urban area, the numerical dominance of non-Maoris and non-kin, the distances separating Maori kinsmen (even in the same quarter of the city), transport difficulties, the distribution of Maoris among many different occupations and employers, the wide range of recreational possibilities: all these worked together to reduce the kindred and the frequency of kin relations. Because they migrated more readily than most, Auckland had a high proportion of Maoris who had been deprived of normal opportunities for acquiring a large circle of effective kin—persons who, for instance, were born into families that were small or widely scattered, or had spent most of their lives moving from one place to another. A large percentage were young and unmarried when they arrived in the city, they came from many different tribes, and they mixed freely. Inter-tribal marriage was common. As a result, descent diminished greatly in importance; also, those who married into another tribe often failed to establish effective relations with more than a few of their affines because they were *whakamā* (shy) of them. The lack of a *marae* in the city presented special problems: the dead had to be taken home to the country and most of the preparations before a *hui* handled by smaller groups of kin.

Paradoxically, the very difficulties posed by the conditions of urban life caused many Auckland Maoris to turn to kinsfolk more than ever. They spent a considerable proportion of their free time and their income maintaining relations with country kin, and a significant number formed 'family' clubs which were in many ways more closely knit than their rural models and which frequently assumed wider functions. In short, though Maoris in Auckland had fewer effective kin, especially in the city itself, they often relied on them to a greater extent for constant moral support and companionship as a protection against isolation and loneliness.

The changes effected in Maori kinship by urbanisation were modifications in the rural pattern rather than a complete transformation. On the basis of kinship studies among the French Canadians of Montreal, Garigue has challenged the proposition (propounded by Wirth and many others) that kinship range necessarily decreases with urbanisation.[1] He suggests that diminishing kinship recognition may be a function of the cultural values of the society concerned and not of urbanisation as such.

[1] Garigue, 1956, vol. 58, pp. 1098–1100.

Certainly, in the Maori case, cultural values played an important part. Also significant, however, was the high rate of urban immigration (which meant that most Auckland Maoris had a fair range of kin in the city itself), the ease of communication between town and country, and the low-density, predominantly suburban character of Auckland. It is a great pity that as yet no study has been made of the kinship patterns of Auckland Pakehas: I would be surprised if the range of kinship recognition were not very much wider than that reported for United States cities (which have provided the models for most theories of urbanisation). Studies in London have proved that given certain conditions, such as continuity of residence in the same neighbourhoods, a wide range of kinship awareness may be typical of sections of the population of a vast metropolis.[1]

[1] Firth, 1956; Young, 1954.

II

Marriage Patterns and Ceremonial

MARRIAGE is one of the fields in which tension, social and psychological, is most immediately apparent and most disruptive. Marital instability is often interpreted as a sign of breakdown in traditional values, or of failure to adjust to changing circumstances. As we have seen, the charge of increased marital instability has been levelled against the urban Maori. But is this really true? We must ask not only whether marriages between Maoris in the city are unstable, but also whether they are more unstable than those in the country and in pre-European society. For the typical marriage pattern of a society is not necessarily one of stability.

Urban conditions could affect marriage in other ways besides increasing its instability. Underlying the statistics of marital stability there is always an ideology of marriage, a constellation of beliefs and expectations about marriage, how it should be contracted and with whom, the functions it should fulfil and the circumstances under which it may be terminated. I have already suggested elsewhere that the modern Maori ideology of marriage differs from the Pakeha one at certain points and that rural Maoris have evolved their own version of Pakeha wedding ceremonial.[1] To what extent have changes taken place in the ideology and ceremonial in Auckland?

MARITAL INSTABILITY IN AUCKLAND

All Maoris I knew, in country as well as city, accepted as valid a marriage established in accordance with the laws of New Zealand, which applied equally to Maoris and Europeans and involved legal registration before authorised persons and the payment of a fee. It was with regard to the termination of marriage and the establishment of subsequent unions that Maori custom still came into conflict with the law, which required all marriages to be dissolved in the Divorce Courts before another could be contracted. The Maori as a whole had a low divorce rate, but intimate knowledge of most Maori rural communities revealed a high incidence of what were popularly described as "Maori marriages". This term was also used by the law, when according limited recognition to unions "contracted according to Maori custom" before April 1951 (when the latest Marriage Act relating to Maoris was passed); but the legal definition of a

[1] Metge, 1957, pp. 166–70.

"Maori marriage" involved only mutual consent between persons not legally married to others. Marriages of this sort were fairly rare, at least in the Far North and Auckland. Most of the unions popularly described as "Maori marriages" involved spouses who were parties to an undissolved legal marriage; they were, in short, legally invalid.

Divorce was neither popular nor common among Maoris in the city. In the Census returns the divorce rate was only slightly higher for the Auckland Maoris than in the total Maori population, while in the 'sets' there were two divorcés, compared with one in Kōtare (see Table 25). The proportion of separated persons showed a rather greater increase in the city, both in the Census returns, and in the 'sets' compared with Kōtare. But "Maori marriages" (which were not recorded by the Census) were no more numerous, relatively speaking, in the 'sets' than in Kōtare. Admittedly, the 'sets' cannot be regarded as entirely representative of the Auckland Maoris, since they omit both the professional class and the "floating population". "Maori marriages" were likely to be more common among the latter group but less in the former.

"Maori marriages" were usually well known to other Maoris in the neighbourhood and thus were easily identified; but it was difficult to obtain details, for those involved were generally sensitive about their status. I obtained the whole story at first hand from only one of the six couples in the 'sets'. What evidence I could assemble showed that half those involved had set up their present unions after their legal unions had broken down in the country. Much has been said, by Maori and Pakeha, about the higher rate of marital failure among Maoris in the city, but so far, I feel, a verdict of non-proven must be returned.

While urban conditions were not entirely responsible for such marital instability as existed in Auckland, they did place new strains upon marriage, in particular as a result of poor housing conditions and the great variety of leisure time activities, which tempted both men and women to neglect their families and over-spend their income. A real problem was also raised by the attraction of married women into paid employment. (Twenty-five of the married women in the 'sets' had full-time jobs.) The usual practice was for working wives to retain control over their earnings, which they mostly spent on extras for the house and children; but a few spent them entirely on luxuries for themselves, to their husbands' resentment. Finally, a great deal of intertribal marriage increased the possibilities of friction between husband and wife over different tribal practices.

Like the people of Kōtare, the Auckland Maoris viewed marriage as a sensible arrangement, based on mutual affection, which ought to be terminated as soon as it ceased to function effectively. Also like the Kōtare folk, their attitude towards unlegalised unions was ambivalent: on the one hand, they accepted the marriage laws as right and proper, but on the other they were aware that without them many "Maori marriages" would be accepted as valid in Maori society. They did not discriminate against those involved in such marriages, except in cases where they disapproved for reasons other than the legal status of the union. But they were sensitive to Pakeha opinion on the matter, and several expressed disapproval of "Maori marriages" to me on the grounds that they "brought the Maori into disrepute".

KINSFOLK AND MARRIAGE IN AUCKLAND

In Auckland, as in the country, the decision to marry was taken by the couple concerned, though I heard of several abortive attempts at matchmaking initiated by elderly country kin. A *tomo*[1] usually took place, even in cases involving the city-born and bred. Of the twelve weddings which occurred among my informants in 1953–4, only two were not preceded by a *tomo*. In one case this was because the bridegroom was a Pakeha; in the other, the girl's widowed father was ill in hospital and died before the wedding.

Only parents exercised any influence over the actual choice of spouses. Their consent was necessary in the case of those under twenty-one, and, apart from the claims of affection, they could influence their children by refusing to attend the wedding, thus placing them in an awkward position, both financially and socially, in relation to their prospective in-laws. Few young people were deterred by such tactics. If they were of age, they made their own arrangements for the wedding, usually seeking assistance from other kin. If they were under age, they eloped; if the parents still held out, they frequently applied to the Magistrate's Court for permission to marry without their consent, usually on the grounds of pregnancy. Although this latter course seemed to be rare in the country (at least in Kōtare), in other respects the pattern was much the same. What was interesting in the Auckland situation was that parents nearly always gave in before the wedding, in time to insist on a *tomo*, even though their objection had not really been overcome. Several who had done so told me that they preferred not to risk an estrangement; and they added that they had no choice because "in the city parents have no authority over their children".

The city *tomo* was a small quiet affair, held in the home of the bride's parents and attended only by kin specifically invited by the parents on each side. These were mostly close, effective kin living in the city, though sometimes a *kaumātua* from the home community was invited to act for the family. The total complement was rarely above ten, the usual number about six. At a *tomo* involving one of the families in the 'sets', the bridegroom's party consisted of his father, step-mother, father's brother's son, and an elderly kinsman renowned as a speaker, and the bride's of her widowed mother and her mother's brother, in whose house it was held. At another, the prospective bridegroom was accompanied by his widowed foster-father, while the bride's parents had not invited any kin at all. I heard only two cases in which a young man asked for the girl of his

[1] p. 66.

choice without the support of parents and kin, the first because he had none in the city, the second because he knew the family too well for formality, having boarded with them for a year. In cases where the girl's parents lived in the country, however, the boy's side made a special trip to see them, especially if they belonged to another tribe or any objections were anticipated. The *tomo* party might be quite large in these circumstances. One Auckland family took a whole busload of kin to ask for a bride for one of their sons: there had been fighting between their tribes in the past and they were determined to make a good impression.

No-one outside the families concerned worried whether a particular marriage was preceded by a *tomo* or not: kin approval was no longer regarded as essential to the validity of a marriage, any more than in the country. The main functions of the *tomo* were to satisfy the general wish to do things in "proper Maori fashion" and to initiate discussion about the organisation of the wedding. The kin who attended decided when and where the wedding would take place and pledged themselves to share the cost and to provide labour, if necessary. The choice of bridal attendants, however, was sometimes left to the bride and her family, in which case their number was usually limited to two or three. But at more than half the weddings which took place among my informants' kinsfolk, there were five or six bridesmaids and groomsmen, half chosen by each 'side' from related branches of their respective family groups, as in Kōtare.

Auckland Maoris held to the rural ideal that the two sides should contribute equally to a wedding, but the pattern was more often distorted by circumstances in the city. If either bride or groom belonged to a city 'family' club, the executive of the latter usually took over the principal burden of organisation. If one had few effective kin in the city, the other's side took care of the pre-wedding arrangements, while the country party, arriving only shortly before the wedding, redressed the balance by larger contributions in cash and in kind. In particular they brought food from sea, farm and garden: *kūmara* (sweet potatoes), *pūhā* (sow thistle), shellfish, preserved peaches and pears, and cooked pork and ham. At one wedding I attended, the bridegroom's city kin booked the Maori Community Centre, ordered and paid for food from city shops, and provided nine of the dozen main workers in the kitchen on the wedding day. The bride's mother arrived from the country with two kinswomen two days before the wedding, bringing the wedding cake, several sacks of vegetables and a large sum of money. They helped with the cooking and preparation of the dining hall. The rest of the bride's kin arrived by bus just before the wedding ceremony and left in the afternoon after the wedding breakfast.

One of the most important roles at a Maori wedding was that of Master of Ceremonies. In the country it was usually filled by a close kinsman of the bride (or of the groom if the wedding was held on his *marae*). In Auckland the choice usually fell upon someone with a reputation for competence in it. When his daughter Hine was married, Anaru Pera, too shy to act himself, first sought a prominent political personality for the post; when he was not available he asked an affinal kinsman who "always does it at weddings among our relatives, because he is well educated and speaks beautiful Maori".

After the wedding, the kin who participated so fully in its organisation had no more influence over the fate of the marriage than they had over the decision to marry. They had no vested interest in its stability, for the money they gave at the time of the wedding was swallowed up by the expenses and did not constitute anything remotely resembling an exchange of payments. Their co-operation was limited to the wedding. The size of the city and the scattered and fragmentary nature of urban Maori society relieved them of any necessity for close personal association with each other afterwards. Most often the young couple maintained social relations with each side separately. Mārama Jones regularly entertained her husband's parents or his siblings to dinner on Saturdays while her own came to dinner on Sundays. This separation of the two sets of affines was particularly clear cut when they belonged to different tribes. In short, marriage in the city established a new effective relationship between a man (or a woman) and his (or her) spouse's parents and some but rarely all her (or his) effective kin, and not between two kin-groups.

In broad outline, the part played by kinsfolk in a marriage in the city differed very little from that in the country. There were, however, several significant differences in detail, notably the limitation of the number of kin involved at *tomo* and behind the scenes at the wedding, and a modification in the emphasis on kinship in the allocation of certain tasks, such as chief speaker at the *tomo*, bridesmaids and groomsmen and Master of Ceremonies at the wedding. The extent of kin participation in wedding organisation and the manner in which it was carried out still differed markedly from the Pakeha pattern.

THE CHOICE OF MARRIAGE PARTNERS

Speaking about marriage in general, Auckland Maoris of all generations agreed that to-day everyone had a right to choose his marriage partner on the basis of personal attraction; but they admitted to approving of certain matches more than others.

Elders and parents liked to see their young people marry other Maoris. Few were stongly prejudiced against Pakehas, but disapproval of marriage to Islanders and Chinese was fairly general. Some advocated "keeping the blood pure", especially when high rank was involved, but this did not seem to be the main reason for preferring marriage to Maoris. Most were afraid that those who married non-Maoris would have divided loyalties and become partially alienated from their Maori kin and "Maori ways". Joyce Green explained that "Maoris go to *huihui* several times a year and stay for days all sleeping together. The Pakeha couldn't stand that. If there is a wedding or a *hui* the Maori will take along the last bit of food in

the house, whereas the Pakeha thinks of himself first before putting anything down." Phyllis Davis held that "Maori–Pakeha marriages aren't
right: their ways of life are so different. Betty" (a Pakeha friend married
to a Maori) "has a rough time of it. She was brought up to a different way
of living by her parents. They should never have married—I can't quite
explain it, but they are two different people." Two parents, however, were
in favour of their daughters marrying Pakehas because they would have
an easier life: "Pakehas don't expect their women to do a lot of heavy
work and wait on them the way Maoris do." In general, the younger
generations also preferred to marry other Maoris. Many girls thought
that marrying a Pakeha was a step up in the social scale, but they argued
that material advantages were not worth while when they meant separation
from Maori relatives and friends. I heard of two girls who decided to marry
Pakehas after romances with members of other tribes had broken up
because they thought the latter's kin had tried to "put a hoodoo on"
(bewitch) them.

All generations expressed strong preferences for marrying within the
tribe. Most informants were hotly opposed to intermarriage with tribes
with whom they had fought in the past, the young people often being the
most outspoken. With regard to matches between descendants of a common great-grandfather (the degrees within which marriage is reported to
have been forbidden in pre-European times), opinion varied from tribe
to tribe, from *hapū* to *hapū* and even between 'families'. Some welcomed
them as "keeping the family and its land together", but others opposed
them strenuously on the grounds of Maori custom. Few had really strong
views about rank, but most of my older informants said they liked to see
their young kinsmen marry persons whose rank was at least equal to their
own; it was not good for a Maori to marry someone much "higher" than
himself because it exposed him to taunts from his affines. Some parents,
however, expressed doubts about the value of "good" descent, for, as
Joyce Green remarked, "often a man who is no good" (from the Maori
point of view) "because he hasn't good blood makes a better husband than
one who is high class". The young people in general asserted with relief
that rank "does not count any longer", especially in the city. All agreed
that wealth and social status were unimportant compared with mutual
affection. "Maoris do not marry for money or position", they said, clearly
believing that Pakehas did. All these attitudes closely matched those of
Maoris in Kōtare.

But did the Auckland Maoris follow their own expressed preferences
in their actual choices? Certainly little attention appeared to be paid to
rank, economic position or social status. The relative rank of a couple
was rarely discussed at Auckland *tomo*. Nor was a man's earning capacity
or occupation the main point of enquiry. It was often not even mentioned.
He was not expected to provide a home or even to have any savings. Young
women did not usually keep a "bottom drawer". Marriage once decided

upon at a *tomo* was not delayed for economic reasons. "Maoris never wait to get married, not even to avoid having to live with in-laws. They are always afraid of losing each other." Even when a man was notoriously unreliable as a worker parents hesitated to break up an affair in which their daughter's affections were involved. One father disapproved strongly of his daughter's lover, who never stayed in a job more than a couple of weeks and belonged to a once hostile tribe; he refused to attend a *tomo* or help pay for a wedding, but did nothing to stop the boy continuing to visit the house in his absence. Aspiration to higher social status, whether based on wealth, rank, education or white-collar occupations, was extremely rare. I only once heard this motive even imputed to a parent—a widow who had refused consent to a son's marriage. The few guilty of such un-Maori ambitions were ridiculed by the majority.

Intermarriage between Maoris and Pakehas could be expected to be relatively common in the city, because the former were such a small proportion of the total population and because so many, by force of circumstances or deliberate choice, were independent of elders and close kin. In the 'sets', there were only three women and one man married to non-Maoris met in the city, all to Pakehas. This understated the amount of intermarriage in Auckland in 1954, partly because such couples settled in the suburbs rather than in the central city, but it would still be true that most Maoris who married while living in Auckland married other Maoris (see Table 26).

They also tended to marry Maoris met in Auckland who did not belong either to their own close kindred or to the same rural community. There were four cases of marriage between first cousins in the 'sets', none between second cousins. Two were not really city matches, having begun in the country and ended in elopement and a city wedding as a result of kin disapproval. The third involved the son and daughter of two brothers brought up in mother's and father's communities respectively and meeting for the first time as adults in Auckland. As far as I could discover there had been no objections to this match. In the fourth case, a girl born and bred in the city fell in love with her father's brother's son when he came to board in the same house. The family was not unaware that they had formed an attachment, but considered marriage entirely out of the question until the girl announced that she was pregnant. Her widowed father and his brother and his wife held a hurried consultation, as a result of which the two were married quietly at a country Registry Office. There were only two cases of marriages between persons from the same district in the country. In both, romance had resulted from living near each other in the city and had been opposed by the parents because of status differences and factional disputes in the home community. Families from the same place often "knew too much about each other" to favour intermarriage.

Despite their professed preference for marriage within the tribe, Auckland Maoris married members of other tribes more often than members of their own. This was true even of the Ngāpuhi, who out-numbered the members of all other tribes put together. Intermarriage was, moreover, most common between members of tribes which did not belong to the same Tribal Group.[1] Out of the sixty-two persons in the 'sets' whose romance was essentially a city affair, only eight chose a spouse wholly from the same tribe, while another six shared the same tribal membership through one parent. In contrast, thirty-six married spouses from a tribe in another Tribal Group. The majority of such marriages involved spouses from the north and south of Auckland respectively. Beyond this, there was no detailed pattern in the intertribal marriages in the 'sets', all but four matches being idiosyncratic. The high incidence of marriages between Northerners and Southerners was remarkable in view of their traditional hostility (culminating in Hongi Hika's campaigns) and the predominance of the former in Auckland.

Most of these intertribal marriages took place in the face of opposition, covert if not overt, from parents and kin, and in contradiction to the expressed views of the young people themselves. According to Pauline Muru (née Shannon),[2] feeling against "marrying out of the tribe" was so strong in her family that her father's brother had sent his two motherless girls back to the country so that they would marry back into their mother's tribe; neither would stay, and both eventually married Ngāpuhi boys. Pauline herself gave up one Ngāpuhi suitor for her parents' sake but eventually married another. Only one out of eight siblings in the Shannon family married into the same tribe, as their parents wished.

The prejudices and tribal stereotypes which young people in the city absorbed from older kin, instead of discouraging, lent a spice to romance with someone from another tribe, especially those with a reputation for rakishness and dash. Moreover, because they were stereotypes, they were easily discarded when acquaintance proved them false.

Tension was inevitably present, at least potentially, in intertribal marriages. It was generally recognised that the in-law relationship was a particularly delicate one under these circumstances. The couple might consider traditional hostility between their tribes irrelevant to their personal relationship, but the love and trust given to each other was not so easily extended to each other's kin. Parents and kin who were against the marriage were prone to interfere when the couple fell out, widening instead of healing the breach. Also, dialect differences and divergent tribal custom often caused friction between the spouses. This was particularly true with regard to taboos, both in personal hygiene and domestic arrange-ments in everyday living, and on such important occasions as births and deaths. More than one of my informants had been shocked to hear her husband using a word which in her dialect was indecent, though entirely innocent in his. One Southerner was perturbed at what seemed to her the laxness of the observance of *tapu* at her Ngāpuhi father-in-law's

[1] p. 126 n. [2] pp. 174-5.

tangi, in particular by the fact that the crucifix was removed from the coffin and kept in the house; when she had occasion to sleep in the room in which it was kept she insisted that it be removed to another room, although her husband's siblings teased her unmercifully. The problem became acute when it involved the instruction of the children in Maori language and tradition: each spouse advocated his own brand of *Maoritanga*.

Yet in spite of these tensions intertribal marriages did not in actual fact exhibit any greater tendency to instability than other marriages. In four cases out of five, those in the 'sets' who had been party to a marriage that failed (divorcés, separated persons and those living in "Maori marriages") had been married to members from the same tribe. When intertribal marriages did break down, tribal differences were not the sole or most important cause of failure. They proved serious only if the relationship was insecure for other reasons, when they provided rich material for name-calling.

The tensions inherent in intertribal marriage were in practice fairly easily resolved. Settling permanently in the city was itself a partial solution, for it was neutral, non-tribal territory in which neither spouse felt a "stranger" or outnumbered. Mere and Robert Herewini bought a section and built a house in the city, though both had farmable land in the country, because it was "halfway between our two homes, so we can visit both". Heta Muru refused his father-in-law's invitation to take over the family farm (which his own sons did not want), because he would always be a "stranger" in his wife's community. Irritating minor differences in dialect and custom were usually ignored or discarded in family life. Phyllis and Selwyn Davis had stopped talking to each other in Maori, because "it caused too many rows". Many parents refrained from teaching their children to speak Maori because "they only learn a muddle of the two dialects". In other matters also, particularly taboos, they often did not pass on either of the conflicting usages. They themselves did not discard "Maori ways" except in the context of tension. Thus the high incidence of intertribal marriage was most important, not in the field of marital instability, but in that of the socialisation of young Maoris.

THE CEREMONIAL OF MARRIAGE

Maoris frequently complained that weddings in the city had "gone all Pakeha", that is, that they approximated more to the Pakeha ceremonial pattern than to the Maori. To a Pakeha, however, even those weddings against which this charge was levelled with most feeling were subtly different from the European version.

The *tomo*, for instance, (which was essentially part of wedding ceremonial), was peculiar to the Maori pattern of marriage. Its form in the city was on the whole simple and relatively informal, but this was also true of the rural *tomo*, at which few parents now submitted the suitor and his kin to inquisition about his family background or his personal prospects, and the old convention of putting up a show of resistance had been completely abandoned. I was never invited to attend a *tomo* in the city, a fact which emphasised the private, family nature of this meeting, but I was informed on reliable authority that traditional conventions were observed with regard to the form of speeches and the sequence of speakers. Usually the boy's father made the request for the girl on his behalf or delegated the task to a more capable speaker. Only rarely did the suitor himself play a leading role.

When both bride and groom lived in Auckland, they usually chose to hold the wedding there. Sixty-two of the one hundred and ten legally married Maoris in the 'sets' met and courted in the city and forty-seven were known definitely to have been married in Auckland also. Only four couples had gone home to the country for the wedding, in every case to the bride's community. Three of these weddings had taken place within the last few years, so there was no trend *away* from the rural wedding. It does not seem ever to have been the rule. The expense was too great and the incentive far less than in the case of taking home the dead for burial.

A Maori wedding in Auckland was a major social event. Ideally it included a church service. A Registry Office ceremony was symptomatic of opposition from parents or of religious divergence between the two sides. Even if the young people themselves wanted a quiet wedding, their parents were likely to insist on a proper Maori wedding, that is, a church ceremony and the full panoply of white bridal gown, bridal attendants, wedding feast, tiered wedding cake, speech-making, present-giving and dancing.

But Auckland Maoris were handicapped in their efforts to stage weddings on the rural model. No home could provide the space needed for a "proper" wedding breakfast, which was by Maori convention a public affair to which all comers were welcomed and to which no invitations were issued. There was no *marae* in the city which could be used for the purpose. The best halls available were church halls where liquor could not be served. The Maori Community Centre was not available for private hire on a Saturday night, which made it impossible to hold the customary wedding dance. One catering establishment particularly favoured by Auckland Maoris provided a dance hall, but this solution had the disadvantage that the number of guests had to be indicated beforehand, and a system of invitations introduced. The general result was that city weddings fell into two parts: the church or registry office ceremony and the "breakfast" in the morning or early afternoon, and an evening function, either a dance or a party held in a private home. Between the two, close kin of the bride and groom did whatever work there was to be done and other guests disappeared to the hotel, the sports field or the cinema.

Yet despite these difficulties, and the fact that a substantial proportion of the guests at Auckland weddings were Pakehas, the form of ceremonial remained typically Maori. I have heard the *karanga*, or calling of the newly married couple on to the *marae* at their return from the church, performed in the city (which had no true *marae* in use) at a church hall, the Maori Community Centre and a commercial wedding lounge. Admittedly, these ceremonies were enacted inside the buildings, away from the curious stares of passers-by, and they were curtailed by questions of space and the timing of the meal, but they were practised nonetheless. Speeches adhered largely to the traditional form, though they sometimes took place during the feast or while the guests were still at the tables, contrary to Maori custom which did not mix important subjects with food. This was partly necessitated by restriction of space to one room. The tracing of *whakapapa* was not typical of speeches at city weddings, but it could still be heard, as I heard it on two occasions. The "flower ceremony",[1] a feature of Northland wedding ceremonial, was performed in the city whenever an elder could be found to conduct it. Food was mostly in the Pakeha style: a *hangi* (earth oven) was practically impossible to manage in the city for a wedding, though many families had their own *hangi* in the backgarden at Christmas and New Year. But where kinsfolk prepared the meal themselves, as they could at a hired hall or at the Maori Community Centre, *kūmara* and *pūhā* (sow thistle), mussels and other shellfish, and boiled plum pudding (which was almost obligatory for a "real Maori wedding") usually made their appearance.

This peculiarly Maori flavour was present even at weddings involving those born and bred in the city. At Hine Pera's wedding, for instance, described to me as "just like a Pakeha one", most of the ceremonial was definitely not Pakeha. First, there were countless speeches, since most of the kinsfolk present (both close and distant ones) and many friends made speeches in Maori, wishing the couple well, and in true Maori fashion honouring the memory of the bride's mother, who had died fifteen months before. Speeches were repeated in English, usually by the speakers themselves, for the benefit of Pakeha guests. One European custom, the drinking of toasts, appeared under a new guise, for the three toasts proposed were to the bridal couple, the bride's late mother, and to the wedding cake, which seems to have become the wedding symbol *par excellence* in Maori society, both urban and rural. The bottom layer of the cake was cut at the reception for the guests, but the fate of the rest followed a distinctively Maori pattern. The top tier was given to the bride and groom, the second sent to the groom's mother for his kin, while the bride's sister took charge of the rest of the bottom layer, distributing it among the bride's kin in the city and her father's siblings and their offspring in the country. In the evening, the dance was begun, as it is in the country, with a Grand March by the bridal party.

CONCLUSION

In the field of marriage the greatest changes from the rural pattern which had taken place among the Maoris in Auckland were in the choice of

[1] p. 60.

spouses. The range of choices actually made had expanded greatly, but differentially, with the range of possibilities. Free choices were made on the basis of personal attractiveness within the urban Maori group. Inter-tribal marriages occurred more frequently than was accounted for by the comparative strength of the tribes represented. In most other respects, Auckland Maoris, city-born and city-bred as well as immigrants, continued to adhere to the contemporary rural ideology, although in the sphere of ceremonial they were inhibited from carrying it out fully. Attitudes to legal marriage, divorce, "Maori marriages" and pre-marital liaisons were far closer to—indeed almost identical with—those of rural Maoris than to Pakeha ones, and were reflected in a comparable incidence of marital instability. The details of wedding ceremonial had changed considerably in form and relative importance, but not in the direction of conformity with the Pakeha pattern, in spite of accusations to that effect. Wedding ceremonial in the city was, in fact, a good illustration of the way in which "Maori ways of doing things" developed along their own lines in response to new circumstances, assimilating rather than being assimilated by Pakeha ways, and continuing to differ in detail and in spirit.

12

Voluntary Association

AUCKLAND Maoris could choose their friends from a far wider range than those living in the country. Apart from the size and density of the urban population, the proportion of Pakehas to Maoris was very high in the city, many more tribes were represented within the Maori group, and the range in income and occupation was greater. In the country, everyone knew everyone living in the same district at least by name and sight; but urban residents came into daily contact with numerous strangers. The array of formal associations which they could join was also more varied. The choices Auckland Maoris actually made should cast light on their social organisation—on their relations with outsiders and with each other —and also on the extent to which they had departed from the rural pattern.

For the purposes of this chapter, I have defined a friend as a person chosen purposefully and repeatedly as a companion during leisure hours. Friends may work together, but association in leisure activities is the ultimate basis of their relationship. A formal association I have defined as an association with a continuing framework of organisation consciously planned and established for specific purposes.

In discussing friendship, I have been concerned mainly to examine the relative importance of the factors which influenced choices, positively or negatively. Partly because of limitations on space, but also because I did not collect sufficient detailed data (not being aware of the problem at the time), I have not dealt with variations in intimacy in any detail, distinguishing in passing only two main types, close friends and others. In making the distinction in particular cases, I was governed mainly by the subjective assessments of informants. (A detailed study would also have to take into account frequency of contact, what friends did together and what help they gave each other.) In general I found that those who regarded each other as close friends met at least once a week, except in the case of housewives, who might not see each other for weeks at a time if they lived in different parts of the city.

FRIENDSHIP

Maori and non-Maori

Maoris in Auckland had continual contacts with Pakehas at school, at work, in the course of business and in sport. 94 per cent of the Maori children of school age attended mixed schools: the only two schools with exclusively Maori rolls were church boarding schools catering mainly for country children. No city firm employed Maoris only, nor did any serve an exclusively Maori clientele. Some Maoris lived in the same apartment houses and hostels as Pakehas, though this was not typical. Sport in particular provided a meeting-ground.

But although many personal friendships developed out of such contacts, they were not as numerous as might have been expected from the relative number of Maori and Pakeha. Most of my informants spent the greater part of their free time with other Maoris. Apart from some older women whose English was limited, few did not have one or two Pakeha friends, but barely one in ten included them among their really close friends.

Most kept their Maori and Pakeha friends apart. For instance, Moana Wiki, a typist in her early twenties, went out twice a week with two Pakeha girls from the office where she worked and spent the weekends in the company of a "gang" of Maori friends. "They are interested in different things", she said. "They would never mix. I live in two separate worlds." Few Maoris asked Pakeha friends to their homes, in most cases because they were ashamed of poor living conditions. Nor did they take them to the Maori Community Centre in any numbers. Most often Maori and Pakeha friends met in public, attending films, dances and sports matches together. Some Pakehas were always present at "occasional" gatherings such as weddings and twenty-first birthday parties. They made up a third of the guests at two weddings I attended and almost half at a third wedding. Some were usually involved in drinking parties.

My informants could not agree on an exact definition of the term Pakeha. Some applied it to all of European stock, but most preferred to reserve it for the New Zealand born, making a difference between the latter and recent immigrants (including those from the United Kingdom). Talking about the immigrants, several informants expressed resentment at "outsiders taking jobs" (or houses or girls) "away from us New Zealanders", coupling themselves with the New Zealand Pakeha for once.

Living in Auckland also brought Maoris into contact with other non-Europeans, in particular Chinese, Indians and "Islanders" from the island groups of the Pacific. They mixed little with these groups, each of which maintained a closely knit social organisation of its own. In each case, intermarriage was slightly higher than elsewhere, but the numbers involved were small. Unexpectedly, relations between Maoris and Islanders were in general anything but cordial, although most of the latter were of Polynesian stock.[1] Maoris could follow none of the Polynesian dialects except Rarotongan. They claimed that the Islanders were clannish, and aggressive when they had been drinking. When discussing whom they would prefer their children to marry, they ranked Islanders after New

[1] Challis, 1953.

Zealand Pakehas. In fact, they generally classed them with other overseas immigrants as interlopers on the New Zealand scene.

Friendship between Maoris

My informants chose most of their friends and almost invariably their closest ones from the Maori group. Liking was the main reason that they gave for choosing to associate with this person rather than that. And liking was most consistently correlated with similarity in age and leisure interests. Other factors influenced choices in individual cases and for small sections of the population, but they were not so consistently important.

As we have already seen, most Auckland Maoris spent a considerable amount of their leisure with kinsfolk, not only at kin gatherings but also in ordinary social intercourse. Few of my informants did not reckon one or two kinsmen among their close friends—because they liked doing things with them, not simply because they were kin.

Tribal differences did not present a serious bar to friendship in Auckland. Most of the younger folk drew as many of their friends from other tribes as from their own, and often more. Moana Wiki, for instance, spent most of her leisure with a "gang" of friends of whom seven were also Ngāpuhi and eight belonged to four other tribes. Those in the older age-groups took longer to become friendly with members of other tribes, but I knew none who failed to do so eventually. When discussing tribal differences in the abstract, my informants all expressed distrust and suspicion of other tribes, cherishing unfavourable stereotypes of their character. But these were soon discarded in particular cases. Friends did not forbear to comment on differences in tribal customs and dialect. Sometimes discussions on the subject waxed heated, especially between the older ones. The young people usually managed to avoid real arguments by turning the whole thing into a joke. They never tired of teasing each other about their accents and about past hostilities between their tribes.

Apart from the children, who played and went to school together, Maoris living in Auckland did not readily become intimate with strangers living in their neighbourhood. Though most of my informants could tell me which houses were occupied by Maoris in their own and adjacent streets, they did not know the names and origin of non-kin living more than a few doors away. Adults normally worked outside the neighbourhood and left it in pursuit of entertainment. Public transport made it easy to keep in touch with friends living in other parts of the city. Many used the central city dance halls and the Maori Community Centre as regular rendezvous. Friendships were most likely to develop out of proximity in the case of young people thrown together in hostels and apartment houses and of housewives who were close neighbours. Several women in the 'sets' were on friendly terms with neighbours, but only two had become really close friends. In this case, however, their friendship brought their families into close association in spite of the fact that they belonged to traditionally hostile tribes, and survived the removal of one family to a State house. Eighteen months after the move the two families still spent Christmas or New Year together and exchanged children during school holidays.

Religious profession had a limiting effect on the choice of friends only in the case of staunch members of the Roman Catholic and Mormon churches. Both of these churches sponsored a full programme of social and recreational activities for their members, the former within the framework of a Maori Mission.

Though the range in income and occupational status was much greater than in the country, social differentiation was not far advanced. Differences in income were not generally correlated with significant differences in standards of living. Instead of investing in better houses, furniture, clothes and cars or spending their leisure in different ways, many of those in the higher income brackets still preferred to spend their money on the same things as their friends and in ways that could be shared: on luxuries in food and drink, on radiograms, records and musical instruments, on taxis and on entertainment. However, two small groups did diverge from the dominant pattern, both in their manner of living and in a tendency to choose their friends from a restricted circle. One of these groups comprised those in the professional and semi-professional category. Members of the other lived at a low level of material comfort out of preference.

The first group consisted of fifteen to twenty government officials, a dentist, an accountant, two Adult Education tutors, five teachers, three clergymen and some sixty-five students at the University, at theological colleges and at the Auckland Teachers' Training College. Most of the family men owned their own homes or occupied State houses, while the unmarried stayed in hostels or shared flats. They mixed more with Pakehas than most Maoris and, apart from kin, they were not usually on visiting terms with Maoris outside their own group. The "ordinary folk" envied and distrusted their success in the Pakeha world. Tahu Paki, an Aucklander of long standing, declared that "there *is* a class distinction in town between the happy-go-lucky types and those independent Maoris who are nearly as bad as the Pakeha and look down on other people". But though they were often accused of "going Pakeha", they rarely cut themselves off completely from the rest of the Maori community, nor were they ashamed of being Maori. Few did not speak Maori. Most attended important gatherings at the Maori Community Centre. Several took an interest in Tribal Committees and in the Welfare League (the Welfare Officers admittedly as part of their job). Two of the clergymen were engaged in Maori Mission work. The teachers all took a special interest in Maori children and Maori clubs in their schools. The students maintained two of the most active Maori clubs in the city. The group provided at least five recognised Maori orators and several of the best instructors in *haka, poi* and Maori language in Auckland. Most of the instruction they gave, however, was to Adult Education classes, which were patronised mainly by Pakehas and Maoris of their own group. On the few occasions on which their help was sought by Maori organisations, the classes were not very successful. According to one young informant, the teachers were too strict for the young people and talked above their heads. Not only their general education but in most cases their knowledge of things Maori was superior to that of most Auckland Maoris.

Those in the second group consisted not of those in the lowest income brackets but of persons who, whatever their income, carried the dominant pattern of free spending to extremes. Unconcerned about appearances, they lived in a squalor for which they themselves were largely responsible: broken windows stuffed with cloth, bare walls from which paper and even boards had been ripped to feed fires, drains clogged with fat, and littered yards. (Many Maori families lived in houses just as dilapidated without producing this result.) The houses they occupied were sub-let or held on multiple tenancies and overcrowded. They were notorious for heavy drinking and gambling and marital mix-ups. At least once a week they held parties which lasted two or three days.

Most Maoris disapproved of those who lived in this way, but they were not entirely ostracised. Their kinsfolk could rarely bring themselves to turn them away from their door or refuse them help in time of trouble or bereavement. (When a cousin turned up at their suburban home with two carloads of beer and friends, Mary and Ruka Hemi could not tell her to go away, but they refused to join the party and retired to the garden in protest.) Their parties and the availability of liquor at all hours attracted other Maoris as casual visitors, in some cases out of sheer curiosity.

Of all the factors governing the choice of friends from so large a field, the most consistent was a combination of age, marital status and leisure interests. Marriage and the establishment of a family (usually achieved by the middle twenties) was almost invariably correlated with a change in ways of spending leisure and the choice of leisure companions. Other changes took place as people passed through middle age, became grand-parents and qualified for the title of *kaumātua*.

The people themselves recognised that "the generations don't mix". They saw the situation, however, as a simple dichotomy between "old" and "young". To these two groups they attributed constellations of attitudes and aims that were not only different but in conflict. According to the popular stereotype, the "old" were "interested only in the past" (i.e. in tribal and family history, *whakapapa* and the proper observance of *tapu* and traditional ceremonial); always put family and community obligations before personal comfort; held that leadership was the prero-gative of the elderly and the well-descended; and were opposed to what they called "the adoption of Pakeha ways". The "young", it was believed, were interested only in the present, dismissing traditional ways as "useless"; sought only their own enjoyment; would not listen to or obey their elders; and were "always trying to imitate the Pakeha".

This popular generalisation oversimplified the situation. In the first place, the stereotype of the "young" could not be fairly applied to those over about twenty-five years of age, although they did not rank as "old" until they were fifty-five or more. In other words, there was a large body of Maoris, most of them married, who were in the middle—in transition between "young" and "old" in age, interests and outlook. There were also, of course, significant differences between the children and the young adults. Secondly, even if restricted to those under twenty-five and over fifty-five respectively, the stereotypes were still not completely true even as generalisations. Though they were certainly interested in the past (as most people of their age usually are), few of those who were elders in years were experts in Maori language or traditions, nor did they spend much time in their study. Most were reluctant to give a firm lead either in public or in private affairs. The young people were impatient of certain of the old ways but not of Maori ways in general; and though they coveted the material goods and independence of the Pakeha, they valued the company and approbation of other Maoris more highly than that of Pakehas.

The popular view actually helped to widen the breach between the generations, because it exaggerated their differences and accepted not only lack of co-operation and companionship but actual conflict as inevitable. Anticipating rebellion, the "old" were always trying to assert their authority, while the "young", anticipating restriction, insisted aggressively on their independence. The middle generations got caught between the two. The elders, classing them with the "young", resisted their attempts to modify traditional patterns to meet the peculiar problems of urban life, while the "young" rejected their leadership along with that of the kaumātua.

The following incident illustrates this last point, as well as the typical impolite and impolitic attitude of the "young" towards their elders. In 1954 a new Chairman was elected to the Waitemata Tribal Executive at the age of thirty, no mean achievement. After some battling, he secured the Executive's support for plans which included the co-ordination and extension of youth work in the city. One evening at the Maori Community Centre he asked the Chairman of the current Centre Youth Club to assemble those present so that he could talk to them. The young man (who was twenty-two) curtly refused to do so until the club was due to close down, though they had no organised programme to follow. He added: "That's the trouble with you old people, you're always talking. The young ones don't want to listen to you." The older man pointed out that he was young himself and he was trying to do something for the young people, but the other retorted: "You're not young—you must be well over forty!"

My informants' children drew their friends and playmates from their own household, their neighbourhood and their school. For primary school children, except those at church schools, school and neighbourhood overlapped almost completely. They combined and re-combined in "gangs", playing together in the streets, in school and public playgrounds and in each other's homes. As soon as they were past the toddler stage, they were left largely to their own devices by parents busy with other things.[1] Groups of children ranging from toddlers to nine and ten-year-olds were often to be seen on central-city streets playing tag and hop-scotch and acting out dramas based on comics and films well into the dusk. However, where grandparents were included in or regularly visited the household, the children (especially the younger ones) spent at least some time in their company. The children were usually better informed about the residents and happenings of the neighbourhood than their parents. Often they were friendly when their parents hardly knew each other by sight, though their choice of special friends was influenced to some extent by the friendships and hostilities (personal and tribal) of their parents.

As children grew older, their horizon expanded. By ten they were usually allowed to go to the pictures on their own and even to take the younger ones with them. They began to play Saturday sport. Those who stayed at secondary school for several years made friends from other parts of the city, including Pakehas. Given more pocket money or able to earn their own after school, they often spent as much time away from home as their older siblings.

The young unmarried adults spent by far the greatest part of their leisure with friends of their own age. At least one in five lived in hostels or "rooms" and so did not associate with older generations even in the home. My informants in this group (who included many white-collar workers but no students) were characterised by a remarkable similarity of aims and interests, a similarity which ignored differences of tribe and occupation. In their own words, their main aim was "to have a good time". They longed "to be free", by which they meant free to go where they liked and to do what they liked when they liked. They liked to act on the spur of the moment. One twenty-year-old boasted: "I never plan what I am going to do, I just let what is going to happen happen." Their main interests were sport (the majority as spectators or casual players), dancing, films, singing and listening to popular music, playing the ukelele and various dance-band instruments, and driving and tinkering with motor-cycles and old cars. They also welcomed opportunities to learn *haka*, but their interest was never sustained for long at a time. They believed in "living for the moment" and "not worrying about the future". If they saved money at all, it was usually for a short term and to buy something for leisure enjoyment—a ukelele, radio, motor cycle or old car. Saving cut a person off from the rest of the group: "You have no fun if you start

[1] cf. Beaglehole, 1946, p. 126; Ritchie, 1957, pp. 83–9.

saving. You get afraid to go out for fear you run into friends who laugh at you for being mean if you won't join them; and if you do you have to spend."

The young people were fond of saying that they were not interested in the past and the old ways: "That's all dead and gone. We belong to to-day." The old knowledge was too closely associated with the observance of *tapu*, which in turn was linked with *mākutu* (sorcery). While they were not prepared to say there was nothing in such beliefs, they wanted to be free of them: they felt that they were backward and unenlightened, as well as burdensome. (Once when a group of girls were discussing *tapu*, one of them changed the subject, saying "We shouldn't be talking about it. It isn't good. We are modern".) So they chose to avoid them, and with them the rest of "the old knowledge". Also, they were impatient with anything that required concentrated listening—they preferred to be "up and doing all the time"—and they disliked "being sent back to the schoolroom", a situation that made them feel children again instead of adults who knew their way around.

The large majority of young Maoris from all over Auckland frequented the same centres of entertainment in the central city. The Maori Community Centre in particular had its own "crowd" of consistent patrons. Many young people formed what they called "gangs", informal associations of friends who were in the habit of "going around together". (The term was a carry-over from school-days. It was not generally indicative of criminal tendencies, though some did become involved in anti-social behaviour.) Those who belonged to a "gang" had other friends outside it and special intimates within it. They did not all act together on every occasion, merely most of them on most occasions. The typical "gang" consisted of between twelve and twenty young Maoris between the ages of sixteen and twenty-five, of varied tribal background, and in most cases of both sexes. In the "gang" to which Moana Wiki (my chief informant on the subject) belonged, there were eight Ngāpuhi, three Ngāti Maru, two Ngāti Whātua, one Arawa and two Whānau-ā-Apanui. A "gang" rarely lasted more than a couple of years without radical changes in personnel. Members married, moved away, quarrelled, or became involved in other activities. New members, often younger siblings of existing or retiring members, were drawn in, until eventually the entire membership had changed.

Moana Wiki outlined as follows the usual weekend pattern ("provided nothing special turned up") for the "gang" to which she belonged in 1953 and 1954. On Friday nights, up to half a dozen members met after work, ate at a city restaurant, then went to the cinema and later to a favourite dance hall, where they found the others. When that hall closed at midnight they walked to another which remained open until 4 a.m. They dispersed by taxi, often to one or two homes. On Saturdays in the winter some of the girls played basketball and the rest watched the boys play football, going on to eat and dance at the Maori Community Centre. (In summer they played softball.) On Sundays they visited each other's homes or went to the beach in threes and fours, and all linked up again in the evening at the Community Centre for the Sunday night Talent Quest. They also went to the cinema together once or twice a week.

"Gangs" were organised quite informally. Arrangements for group enterprises such as parties or excursions were made by whoever happened to be free and able. They could act quickly when necessary. When a party from Ratana Pa arrived on their way to attend a church festival in the Far North, Moana's "gang" decided to accompany them and were on the road in two rental cars in less than twelve hours. Whenever a member of a "gang" went home to attend a *hui*, some or all of the others went with him. In May 1955, Moana's "gang" hired a bus and made a round trip of over four hundred miles to attend the twenty-first birthday of one of their girls.

There were some young Maoris living in Auckland who were not regular patrons of the central-city centres favoured by most. They usually spent most of their leisure with a few close friends rather than with a "gang". But they, too, chose their friends from their own age-group, with little regard for kinship and less for tribal background, and, except in the case of students, mostly from the Maori group. They were interested in the same *range* of leisure interests, though they usually spent less time in dancing and more in each other's homes, talking and singing, or at church youth clubs.

Marriage marked the beginning of a change in the pattern of leisure activities and the choice of friends. By the time they had two or three children and had established a separate domestic unit, a young couple had lost touch with many of their earlier friends and spent less of their time at public entertainment and more in their own home and with kinsfolk. The break was nearly complete in the case of the women: their circle of friends narrowed to two or three married friends and older kins-women. Husbands had more friends and retained more continuity with the friends of their youth, meeting them at sport and at hotels and billiard saloons after work. Some young husbands continued to belong to "gangs" for a while, more especially to male ones interested in football or motor-cycles. The amount of time which husbands spent at home nearly always increased when they moved into better accommodation.

As their children grew up, the married began to take more interest in kin-group activities (especially 'family' clubs) and in non-kin associations also. The officers of urban clubs were drawn mainly from the middle generations. As they approached their forties, most began to regret their limited knowledge of Maori history, ceremonial and language, and to spend rather more (though rarely very much) time with older persons from whom they could learn. If closer kinsmen were lacking or incom-petent, they turned to affines, who might belong to another tribe, or to an elder from their home community. Emigrants from one northern district always gathered at one of their homes whenever a leading *kaumātua* from home paid a visit to Auckland, welcoming him "in proper Maori fashion", not only in deference to his status but also "for practice", and listening to him "talking *whakapapa*" (genealogies).

Classification of a person as "old" depended as much on appearance and behaviour as on actual age. Most of those generally recognised as "old" were over sixty, though some attained this status earlier if they looked old or were well-known as experts in traditional lore. Other people usually classified a person as "old" long before he did himself. For the most part, the elderly moved mainly within a circle of kinsfolk, their chief interests their grandchildren, *hui*, playing cards, going to the races, and talking about the past. They preferred the company of kinsmen of their own age and those of the middle generations interested in the same things. Their thoughts turned more than those of other generations towards their home communities. In spite of age, infirmity and limited incomes, they usually contrived to go home on all important occasions, especially to *tangi* and 'unveilings'. At seventy-five years of age one *kuia* undertook a gruelling two hundred and twenty mile journey at short notice to reach her sister's deathbed. Many spent nearly as much time in the country on visits as they did in the city. And they kept open house for country kin.

While Auckland Maoris spent most of their leisure with friends of their own age, three particular kinds of activities periodically brought adults of all age levels into close association for several hours at a time. The chief of these, kin-gatherings, has already been discussed. While the young among the guests tended to congregate together, workers of all ages worked cheerfully side by side. *Haka* clubs also brought different age levels together, but as we shall see later in the chapter, the older folk belonged mainly "for the sake of the young ones" and friction between the generations was often a serious problem. The third activity of general appeal was playing cards. Small groups of kin and friends played cards for pleasure and small stakes in most Maori homes. At the same time, a number of confirmed addicts met regularly in certain houses to play for higher stakes, forming a series of informal gambling circles. A circle to which several of my informants belonged involved forty regular players. (They did not all attend every meeting nor play all the time, and there were always several casual players present as well.) There were at least six such circles in the central city. Each meeting was organised *ad hoc* by one of the "regulars", who arranged the rendezvous and supplied refreshments, paying for them out of the kitty (which was his perquisite if not earmarked for some special cause) or by taking up a collection. Kinsfolk formed the nucleus of most circles, but some of the relationships were very tenuous. About two-thirds of the regular participants in the circle already mentioned belonged to two distinct kin-clusters which stemmed from neighbouring rural communities but did not co-operate in any other sphere. The rest were remote kin or friends of members of these kin-clusters and in a few cases mere acquaintances who did not otherwise associate with the other players. The middle-aged and the elderly played most regularly, but the young adults took a hand at least when meetings were held in the house where they lived.

FORMAL ASSOCIATIONS

The proportion of the Maori population who were active members of formal associations seemed to be much lower than in the country, though the associations to which they did belong covered a wider range of interests. (Maoris belonged to cycling, cricket, and girls' marching teams, *haka* clubs and boxing classes as well as the usual sports clubs, church and women's groups.) Excluding kin clubs, of which, as we have seen, proportionately fewer were members, less than 50 of the 229 adults in the 'sets' belonged to any club. Even in sport, the number of Maoris belonging to registered clubs was comparatively low. Some belonged to several associations at once, but their number, too, was less significant than in the country.

Except in sport, approximately three-quarters of those who did join formal associations preferred those that were exclusively or predominantly Maori. My informants said that they "felt more at home among our own": in a non-Maori association they felt "out-of-place and afraid of doing the wrong thing". In particular, they were reluctant to be the first Maoris to join a club. Even at the University level, most Maori students belonged only to the Maori club, at least in their first year.

Yet all-Maori associations were not numerous nor were their memberships large in proportion to the size of the Maori population. Most had less than fifty members at any one time and consisted of only one branch. The largest in respect of total membership and number of branches was the Maori Women's Welfare League. But its 78 members comprised only 3 per cent of the Maori women over twenty years of age (approximately 2,500 in 1954). In Kōtare, where there were 106 women over twenty, 22 belonged to the M.W.W.L. and 10 to a Maori branch of the Countrywoman's Institute. Typically, Auckland Maori associations suffered marked fluctuations in interest and membership. Those which were not part of larger organisations (and so subject to outside supervision and stimulation), collapsed easily and frequently. Few youth or *haka* clubs lasted more than a year. Certain kinds of 'family' clubs were also very unstable.[1] The reasons were not far to seek. The city offered so many alternative ways of spending leisure. Club members did not generally know each other as well as in a country district; often they did not meet at all outside club activities. An exceptionally large section of the population was passing through a phase characterised by restlessness and mobility, coupled with dislike of "being organised" on the one hand and a reluctance to accept responsibility on the other. Differences between the generations

[1] pp. 169–70.

and between members of different tribes caused friction. The most energetic and experienced individuals were forced into official positions in several clubs at once, with the result that they were unable to give any their full attention. Finally, the very difficulties of most clubs caused members to fall away, because "we never get anywhere: it is just struggle, struggle to keep going".

Sports Clubs

According to the figures available to me,[1] it would seem that 10–15 per cent of the Maoris between fifteen and twenty-five years of age living in Auckland belonged to organised sports clubs. (This was low compared to Kōtare, where the proportion was about 70 per cent, but, in the view of one experienced sports organiser, normal for the city population as a whole.) The majority were interested in a limited range of sports: the women in outdoor and indoor basketball and softball, the men in football (both Rugby Union and League) and softball. Far more played organised sport in winter than in summer. Maoris were prominent in all of the sports they favoured. In 1954, some 450 Maori women played outdoor basketball (25 per cent of the total number of players); 28 played indoor basketball (25 per cent); and 48 played softball (19 per cent). Maoris also supplied 15–20 per cent of the men playing Rugby Union and Rugby League football (out of about 5,800 and 3,000 to 3,500 players respectively); 15 per cent of those playing softball (75 out of 490); and 80 per cent of those playing on Sundays for an association comprising only ten ungraded teams. (The seven clubs affiliated to the latter accepted many more players than they fielded at any one time; only the keenest played every week. Several played competitive Saturday football as well.) It is worth noting that in indoor and outdoor basketball, football and women's softball, the percentage of Maori players was 3–5 per cent higher in the top grade than in the others. Most Maoris played in mixed (Maori–Pakeha) teams. All-Maori teams occurred only in outdoor basketball (eight teams, four in each association), softball (one men's and two women's teams), and Sunday football (four teams). In all cases, however, less than 50 per cent of the Maori players played in all-Maori teams: 15 per cent of the women playing basketball, 12 per cent and 37 per cent respectively of the men and women playing softball, and 40 per cent of those playing Sunday football. In outdoor basketball and in Rugby League football, there were always a number

---

[1] None of the Auckland sports associations distinguish between Maoris and Pakeha in their records. I did not have time to make a detailed study of the membership of the many sports clubs; instead I have relied upon the personal knowledge of key officials in the various sports associations. I should like to acknowledge help received from Mr J. Bonham of the Auckland Y.M.C.A. (Auckland Indoor Basketball Association), Mr Warren (Auckland Rugby Football Union), Mrs A. Larsen (Auckland Basketball Association), Mr R. G. McGregor (Auckland Rugby Football League), Mr W. Te Hira, and the Rev. F. H. Terry (Auckland Catholic Basketball Association).

of teams in which Maoris made up half or more of the players, but even in these sports at least half the total of Maori players played in teams in which they were in the minority. On the other hand, Maoris were in the majority in most of the other teams playing Sunday football. A comparatively small proportion of Maoris were interested in other sports, chiefly tennis, boxing, cricket, girls' marching teams and cycling. All belonged to mixed clubs.

Belonging to the same club fostered friendly relations between Pakeha and Maori and also between Maoris of different tribes. Pakehas learnt to respect Maori clubmates, not only as players, but also as entertainers and good companions at club concerts and on long bus trips. Since merit was the primary qualification for membership, Maori clubmates invariably belonged to several different tribes, though Northerners usually predominated, as they did in Auckland as a whole.

Most sports clubs sponsored at least some social activities for their players and to raise money. The social side was particularly highly developed in the case of three Maori clubs which sponsored teams playing Sunday football. Their memberships were large: twenty to fifty players who took it in turns to play, and numerous friends and relatives who followed the club fortunes and, if not actually subscribers, contributed indirectly to its finances by patronising its social activities. Each season these clubs organised several trips to the country, arranging matches, where possible, to coincide with *hui* on country *marae*. Such trips usually involved at least two busloads of players and supporters. One of these clubs consisted of Maoris employed by a large city corporation and belonging to several different tribes. (A club officer, himself a Maori, commented: "They get used to each other when they play together.") The second had started as a kin club[1] and the third under the name of a rural county from which many Auckland Maoris derived. Both had quickly lost their exclusiveness and taken in members of several other tribes.

Religious Groups

Maoris in Auckland preferred to attend services conducted in Maori by Maori ministers and to belong to Maori branches of church organisations. Apart from members of the Mormon church, very few attended their local churches with any regularity or joined mixed church clubs. (Only one of the families in the 'sets' did so; in this case, the husband had been elected to the vestry of their parish church.)

The Anglican, Roman Catholic, Methodist and Presbyterian churches each maintained Maori Missions in the city, staffed by one or two clergymen assisted in the last two cases by deaconesses. Each Mission had an elected church committee of laymen and was attached to a church centre in the central city. In each case, Mission workers provided at least one weekly service wholly or partly in Maori in the central city and periodic

[1] pp. 175–6.

services in the suburbs. The Roman Catholic Maori Mission sponsored an Auckland branch of the Legion of Mary, and a Catholic Maori Youth Club provided a regular programme of social activities, fielded an all-Maori basketball team and supervised members' use of tennis courts at a church school. The Anglican and Methodist churches sponsored several women's groups, and two youth clubs which met once a week for instruction and recreation (table tennis and *haka*) and, in the former case, ran occasional dances.

The Ratana church, which had the second largest number of Maori adherents in the city, was the only purely Maori denomination of any significance. Its affairs were handled by a Church Committee of seventeen members, which met once a month. In 1953–4 its main activities were weekly services in two or three different parts of the city, and the staging of a large *hui* at the Maori Community Centre on 8 November, when visitors came from beyond the city limits for an important church festival. The Ratana Youth Club, which had in the past sponsored several sports teams and social activities, was in recess in 1953–4.

Maori members of the Mormon church had no separate organisation; but they dominated one of the two Auckland branches of the church by force of numbers, and took a prominent part in the numerous church clubs.

Other Maori Associations

Apart from church organisations, the only Auckland Maori associations linked with others outside Auckland in 1953–4 were the Tribal Committees and several branches of the Maori Women's Welfare League, both of which had been set up originally under the supervision of officers of the Department of Maori Affairs. The former differed from other voluntary associations in that they had a limited number of members, elected as representatives of the Maoris living in certain parts of the city. For this reason, I have decided to discuss Tribal Committees in the next chapter, under the heading of Leadership and Social Control instead of Voluntary Association.

The Maori Women's Welfare League had seven branches in Auckland, with a total of seventy-eight financial members in August 1954.[1] All were fighting dwindling membership and attendances. Only six women in the 'sets' belonged to the League, and two were young women who had never attended a meeting, their mothers having paid their subscriptions. In each branch a core of idealistic, hard-working, middle-aged women kept the League alive. Most of my informants would not join, because (they said) belonging to the League cost too much in time and money: they needed help themselves before they could give it to others. In the struggle for survival, the League's objects (which included the sponsoring of instruction in Maori crafts and dressmaking, and hospital and prison

[1] Information supplied by the Department of Maori Affairs.

visiting) were swallowed up in the constant need to raise funds. Meetings had become dull and concerned only with business. Members lost heart when they saw no return for their labours.

Though its branches were in the doldrums, the Auckland District Council of the League (made up of delegates from the branches) played a part of considerable importance in Auckland Maori affairs, partly because seven of its members also served on Auckland Tribal Committees (three of them on the Waitemata Tribal Executive as Tribal Committee delegates), and partly because it was part of a powerful national association. The District Council organised the support and service which League members gave to the Maori Community Centre (especially in the kitchen on special occasions) and initiated the building of a lounge in the Centre, the cost and use of which were later shared by the Tribal Executive. But the importance of the District Council derived not from the collective bargaining power of Auckland Maori women but from the efficiency, hard work and personality of a handful of individuals.

Maori clubs, formed to foster interest in Maori arts and crafts, history and language, had been established, under the supervision of the teachers, at several primary schools where Maori children were numerous and at two Maori church boarding schools, and also at the University and Teachers' Training Colleges, where they were run by student committees. With the exception of the second named, these clubs usually included some Pakehas. The primary school clubs were handicapped by the difficulties of getting instructors. Efforts to enlist the help of parents usually failed. Nevertheless, they played a small part in teaching city children Maori songs and dances and (more rarely) crafts, and assisted the processes of intertribal and interracial acculturation. The church school clubs had long had a reputation outside the city as a result of periodic country tours. The students' clubs were also active. With memberships of about twenty and thirty-five respectively in 1954, they provided entertainment at University and Training College functions and undertook tours in the country. The Training College club also produced an annual play or operetta on a Maori theme.

Other Maori associations were either kin clubs, youth clubs or *haka* clubs. Kin clubs have been discussed in an earlier chapter.[1] Youth clubs existed to help the young to fill in their leisure time. They were usually attached to one particular centre. They ran "evenings" at which members could talk, improvise their own music, dance and play table tennis; they organised occasional trips and special dances, and sometimes sponsored sports teams affiliated to one of the Auckland sports associations. *Haka* clubs met to practise *haka*[2] and action songs to perform at Maori gatherings and for payment at concerts and dances (see Plate 8b, facing p. 103). Members of both kinds of clubs were mostly young and single. *Haka* clubs always had a leavening of older members as well: in one which I shall call the

[1] pp. 166–70.   [2] See glossary, p. 287.

Wikitoria *Haka* Club, six out of the twenty-three staunchest members were over twenty-five. Youth clubs also usually had two or three members above that age serving on their committees. Both kinds of club accepted members from all tribes. The Wikitoria Club included Rarawa, Ngāpuhi, Waikato, Maniapoto, Whānau-ā-Apanui and Ngāti Porou. *Haka* clubs were usually started by one or two middle-aged enthusiasts to prepare *haka* for some special occasion. Youth clubs were rarely established by the young people unaided, but were formed at the instigation of older persons—members of Tribal Committees or the Tribal Executive, Maori Mission workers, or individuals who might be either genuinely concerned about the young or seeking to attract a personal following.

Youth clubs (other than those run by the churches) and *haka* clubs were well-known for their instability. With the exception of the Ōrākei Concert Party, which was well into its second year, none of those operating in Auckland in 1953–4 survived a full year. At the Maori Community Centre, for instance, five youth clubs succeeded each other within fourteen months, while the Wikitoria Club, which mustered over fifty members for its first public performance, disbanded within six months when attendances at practices dropped to six. In each case, the club was established at a formal meeting, officers and committee elected, a name chosen, a constitution drafted and plans for future activities discussed in general terms. Enthusiasm was great at the beginning and the first few club meetings and functions well attended. (One of the Maori Community Centre youth clubs attracted 120 to its first social.) But after the first month, attendance declined rapidly, members fell out over policy, the sponsor lost interest, and officers resigned because club members were too critical and "ungrateful" and their duties burdensome.

The failure of youth and *haka* clubs (which I saw at first hand in several cases) could be traced to the same causes. One of the chief problems was the attitude of the young people. Their whole philosophy was inimical to formal association. The keenest failed to attend a meeting or a practice if a more attractive prospect opened up at the last moment. They resented "being ordered around" by their elders, but they did not want the responsibility and work involved in running the clubs themselves. They either elected any older person who could be prevailed upon to stand, or else they accepted office to "show how it should be done", only to become "disillusioned" and resign. Their enthusiasms were large but ephemeral.

Another problem was lack of sustained leadership. Apart from dislike of being "tied down", potential young leaders were reluctant to step out of the ranks for fear of criticism from their age-mates. Most of the older members had only limited time to give the club because of other commitments. They admitted that they did not understand or know how to handle the young people. In the face of dwindling membership few had ideas more constructive than the enticement of a free dance or another trip. In an attempt to avoid being "bossy", they would not correct faulty *haka* technique nor insist on punctuality and concentration at practices "for fear of putting them off". Without firm control, meetings, practices and socials always started and finished late, and a great deal of time was spent sitting around waiting for someone to start something. Members of *haka* teams made slow progress, mastering few numbers thoroughly and learning only occasional new ones. After the initial spurt, individual and group performances failed to improve and often deteriorated. Bored with "the same old thing", members started to stay away.

But though youth and *haka* clubs nearly always foundered in a matter of months, others were always being formed in their place. Though unwilling to take the initiative, the young people were always interested in attempts to cater for their needs. Most were also keen to learn *haka*, because it was distinctively Maori and because they enjoyed group practices.

CONCLUSION

As in the country, Auckland Maoris chose most of their friends from their own group. At the same time, it would probably be true to say that most had more non-Maori friends than in the country, though this generalisation ignores wide variations in the Maori–Pakeha ratio and interrelations in different country areas.

Most Auckland Maoris continued to associate with kinsfolk in other than purely kinship activities. But more of their friends belonged to other tribes. Auckland Maoris had far less to do with Maoris living in their immediate neighbourhood than in the country, and they made and kept in touch with friends living all over the city, an area equivalent to several rural districts. At either end of the socio-economic scale, there was a small group whose members tended to withdraw from close association with the rest of the Maori population.

Differences in interest and outlook between the main age-groups were particularly pronounced. Many young people lived away from home in hostels and apartment houses. The occasions on which Maoris of different age levels joined in the same activities were fewer and shorter. In both informal and formal associations, "old" and "young" wasted time and energy in bickering and opposing each other.

Proportionately fewer Auckland Maoris belonged to formal associations, though those who did were distributed over a wider range. More joined all-Maori associations than non-Maori ones. Most of the former had difficulty in holding members and officers, and those which catered specially for the young and unmarried tended to break down after starting with a flourish.

13

Leadership, Social Control and Community Solidarity

THE Auckland Maori population possessed a certain arbitrary unity in relation to rural society, defined solely by the limits of the Urban Area (see Fig. 7); within the Auckland population it was readily identifiable as a separate entity by the physical characteristics and ethnic stock of its members. It derived no unity either of structure or organisation from the past, for the large majority of its members had no ancestral connection with the land and derived from many different localities and descent-groups outside the city. Had the Auckland Maoris achieved any practical unity of organisation or leadership? And did they make any attempt, formal or informal, to control the behaviour of members of the group in those spheres left untouched by the State law and official urban authorities?

LEADERSHIP

The Place of the Tāngata Whenua

From the Maori point of view, the "proper" leaders of Auckland Maori society were the *tāngata whenua*, who alone "belonged" to the Auckland urban area by right of descent from the ancient owners, and who controlled the only *marae* in Auckland. Their long experience in living in the city might also have been expected to fit them to assume the lead, even though originally their inclusion in its limits was involuntary.[1]

Immigrants and city-born alike were well aware of the rights of the *tāngata whenua* to priority. In the early days of the urban migration, immigrants were often reminded by *kaumātua* in their home communities that they were "visitors and guests" in the city and should "leave the speech-making" (and by implication the initiative and leadership) to the "real people". The city-born were explicitly taught that their *marae* lay in the country and not in Auckland.

All admitted the precedence of the *tāngata whenua kaumātua* in ceremonial procedure. Some six distinguished by age and rank and well known to the organisers were invariably accorded the right to speak as guests of honour at any gathering they attended in the city, including meetings of the Tribal Executive (though none were official delegates). They were, however, not often present, and never more than two or three

[1] pp. 118–21.

at a time. Their advice was listened to with deference but carried little weight. Four had been elected to office in either Tribal Committees or Maori Women's Welfare League branches, but only one (a man) to a Tribal Committee other than the Ōrākei one (which was really representative only of Ōkāhu).

Tāngata whenua below *kaumātua* status were not accorded differential treatment, even of a ceremonial nature. They were not elected to office in urban Maori groups simply because they were *tāngata whenua*, nor were they distinguished in any way at any gatherings they attended. Delegates from the Ōrākei T.C. to the Waitemata Tribal Executive and from the Ōrākei branch of the M.W.W.L. to its Auckland District Council received no special consideration. One of the former was elected to the Chairmanship of the Tribal Executive in 1954, but solely on merit; he was not, in any case, a *tangata whenua* but a member of another tribe who had married into Ōkāhu.

Partly because they were so few and partly because they held aloof, *tāngata whenua* were not well represented in formal Maori associations other than those connected with Ōkāhu, and even fewer held office or acted in any capacity as leaders in them.

Sir Apirana Ngata has recorded that the Auckland Maoris could be mobilised for group action at the time of the Auckland Centennial Celebrations (in 1940) only under the leadership of the *tāngata whenua*[1]; but by 1953–54 positions of even nominal leadership were not always reserved for the *tāngata whenua*, as such, in activities concerning all the Maoris in Auckland. Their leadership was in fact actively rejected during the Royal Visit at the end of 1953 and they had to fight against complete exclusion.[2] Every one of the groups which had been started under the title of "Ngāti Akarana"[3] had been completely independent of the *tāngata whenua*.

A high proportion of 'immigrants' had settled permanently in the city, buying houses and land. Their experience of urban life was in many ways fuller, their adjustment more successful than that of the Ōkāhu *tāngata whenua* in their self-imposed semi-isolation. They were beginning to feel

---

[1] Sutherland, 1940, p. 169.

[2] When plans were first made for the Auckland visit of the Queen and the Duke of Edinburgh in December 1953, no provision was made for a Maori welcome. (Maoris played a major part in receptions at Waitangi and Rotorua later in the tour.) A delegation of Auckland Maoris waited on the Mayor and it was arranged that a Maori *haka* party should be stationed outside the Town Hall. The delegation was composed entirely of 'immigrants' and so was the *haka* party. Later, there was disagreement over the selection of an Auckland *haka* party to perform at the Waitangi reception. The Ōkāhu people proposed that their concert party should form the nucleus of the Auckland group, but as a result of differences between the organisers, a group formed for the occasion at the Maori Community Centre maintained its separate right to represent Auckland. A compromise effected at the last moment allowed both teams to appear, but as two distinct groups.

[3] A pseudo-tribal name formed by the Maori transliteration of *Auckland* with the tribal prefix *Ngāti*.

"at home" in the city, and had virtually ceased to act like "visitors and guests". The Tribal Committee system provided a formal framework of organisation which did not recognise the priority of the *tāngata whenua* either as a group or as individuals. Endorsement of the traditional bases of leadership was no part of its functions even in the country; it was assumed that if the people felt strongly about the claims of the "proper" leaders they would elect them to office.

The 'immigrants' justified their supersession of the *tāngata whenua* on a number of grounds. The *tāngata whenua* (they said) had not produced any leaders strong enough to command the respect and attention of members of other tribes, who had their own loyalties. They were themselves to blame for holding aloof and taking no interest in activities outside their own settlement. Some 'immigrants' accused the *tāngata whenua* of having forgotten the old customs and ceremonial, and even their language, but this charge could not be made to stick, at least where those in their fifties and older were concerned.

Above all, the failure of the Ōkāhu people to hold their traditional *marae* site had lost them prestige.[1] For many years it was hoped that the *marae* at Ōkāhu Bay would become the central *marae* for the entire Auckland Maori population, but nothing had come of plans to build a meeting-house there. The setting up of the Maori Community Centre in the central city in 1948 symbolised the decision of the rest of the Auckland Maoris to establish a system independent of the *tāngata whenua*, or at least on equal terms with them. In 1953, when the Centre was hired out to Maori organisations in the city, the Ōkāhu people used it on the same basis as other clubs.

Most of the non-indigenous Maoris living in Auckland were highly ambivalent in their attitude to the urban area. From one angle they saw it as Tāmaki, an isthmus once owned and occupied by Ngāti Whātua *hapū* where, as long as descendants of the original owners were still to be found, other Maoris were interlopers. But from another angle it was Auckland, a city built by Pakehas on land purchased from the Maori owners, in appearance and organisation wholly Pakeha. A Maori living in Auckland had contact with far more Pakehas than *tāngata whenua*. The latter were not numerous; they were either scattered so widely that they had ceased to be a group or else they lived together in one or two localities where they "kept to themselves". It was easy—and convenient—to forget them, and to see the city as a Pakeha world in which Pakeha values and social arrangements overrode Maori ones, at least on this score.

The *tāngata whenua* often felt slighted and withdrew from projects proposed "on behalf of all the Maoris in Auckland". At other times they tried to re-assert their claim to special status by competing against other urban Maori groups. The rest of the Auckland Maori population resented both attitudes equally, but could afford to ignore them because of their

[1] pp. 120, 121 n.

own numerical superiority. They had established a Maori society in which the participation of the *tāngata whenua* was desirable but not essential.

Other Leaders

Naturally, because of the size of the Maori population, sectional and *ad hoc* leaders were extremely numerous in Auckland; but relatively few were prominent in more than one association at once or well known outside their own limited circles. One of the most serious difficulties of Auckland Maori associations, especially the non-kin ones, was the reluctance of their members to assume office; many also suffered from a rapid turnover in elected officers. The two major reasons given were other interests—"not enough time"—and the criticism and lack of support which were the lot of those who occupied any position of superordination. This latter circumstance was familiar enough in Kōtare,[1] and has also been reported for Rakau, a very different community to the south of Auckland[2]; but in the city, where most non-kin groups consisted of Maoris from divergent backgrounds who often had little or no contact outside the group, the grounds for mistrust were multiplied, while the ties holding members together were much weaker.

In Kōtare, in addition to those elected to office in sectional associations and the *ad hoc* leaders, almost everyone agreed in recognising a number of community elders, mostly *tāngata whenua*, whom they accepted as their representatives in relations with persons from outside the community. In Auckland, however, the *tāngata whenua* elders who should have occupied this position were not known to most of the population. Some dozen 'immigrants' were fairly widely known, at least by name and reputation, having made their mark by service to the Auckland Maori "community". (One had organised one of the first and most successful concert parties, several of the women had run a canteen and club for Maori servicemen during the war, four or five had been managers at the Maori Community Centre at different times, one was running public dances in a hired hall in open opposition to the M.C.C., five were elected officers in Tribal Committees and the Maori Women's Welfare League, and one a Maori Welfare Officer.) But none commanded more than a small personal following, and criticism of their character and achievements was much more general and less qualified by respect and personal loyalty than in Kōtare. They were in fact, simply the most prominent of the sectional leaders—or had been, some having temporarily retired from public life. Three who were delegates from Tribal Committees to the Tribal Executive in 1953–4 had a good claim to represent the Maori population at large, but in practice, as we shall see shortly, the people admitted neither their authority nor their right to speak or act on their behalf, though they did not publicly challenge them. Significantly, nearly all were between forty-five and fifty-five,

[1] p. 85.   [2] Ritchie, James, 1956, pp. 88–91, 155–65.

still on the verge of being recognised as *kaumātua*. Four were women.

Auckland was very short of elders, and in particular of elders who took any interest in public affairs. In 1954, there were only seventeen Maoris over fifty-five in the 'sets'; and of these only a widow prominent in the Maori Women's Welfare League held executive office in other than a kin group. The effective organisation of both kin and non-kin groups was in the hands of those below *kaumātua* status, mostly men and women in their forties.

The young people between about fifteen and twenty-five were notoriously shy of assuming responsibility, even in youth groups, and they preferred to organise their own activities on a purely *ad hoc* and spur-of-the-moment basis. The consequences of this attitude (which was characteristic of the same age-group in Kōtare) were particularly serious in the city, because they made up a much larger proportion of the Maori population. Because opportunities were so much greater, they became more readily embroiled in delinquent activities, such as car conversion, brawling and gang thefts; and the older generations had to carry the burden of organising youth activities in addition to their own interests, in order to "keep the young people out of trouble".

Not only were a larger proportion of Maori office-holders in the middle generations than in the country, but women were in general more prominent, and personal ability and willingness to stand for office were far more important than descent. Women nearly always figured on committees which in Kōtare were exclusively a male preserve—the church and Tribal Committees. Outside Ōkāhu, the *tāngata whenua* were overwhelmingly outnumbered by 'immigrants', none of the other tribes had any claim to priority except on numerical grounds, and the importance of seniority of descent in any one tribe was greatly diminished where so many members of the group belonged to others. Knowledge of Maori language, traditions and ceremonial was still valued, but a higher proportion of sectional leaders were in fact ill-equipped in this respect. The Chairman of one Tribal Committee did not speak Maori and at least one of the other delegates to the Tribal Executive was more at home in English.

Tribal Committees

The only form of organisation which comprehended the whole of the Auckland Maori population even in theory, a series of Tribal Committees was set up by the Government in Auckland in September 1945, under the guidance of the Maori Welfare Officers. As in the country, it was planned to provide leadership for the Maori group and to serve as an agency of social control in certain spheres.

The Auckland Urban Area was arbitrarily divided into six Tribal Committee Areas which, up to June 1954, all belonged to the Waitemata Tribal District and were controlled by the Waitemata Tribal Executive, to which each Committee sent two delegates. However, the Tribal Executive was unable to devote itself entirely to the problems of the urban "community" because it also included delegates from a purely rural Tribal Committee whose Area adjoined the city on the north-west. When the Tribal Committee divisions were revised in 1954, the Onehunga Tribal Committee Area was detached from the Waitemata Tribal District and included in the Manukau Tribal District lying to the south of the city, so that the Auckland Tribal Committees were not co-ordinated in a single body.

Only two of the Tribal Committees were functioning with any efficiency in 1953–4 and both were concerned mainly with the provision of recreational facilities for the young people in their districts. In other cases meetings were irregular and largely confined to discussions of finance. Each Tribal Committee had two Wardens who patrolled the hotels at busy periods, and exercised varying control over excessive drinking by Maoris. The Waitemata Tribal Executive was preoccupied with the management of the Maori Community Centre up to August 1954, when it finally delegated this task to a sub-committee. About the same time it set up several other sub-committees to investigate Maori housing conditions and education in the city and to organise prison and hospital visiting and youth work. None was in working order by the end of the year.

The large majority of Auckland Maoris were unfamiliar with the functions, powers and personnel of the Tribal Committees, and often ignorant of their very existence. I would estimate that at least half the Maoris in Auckland did not know that there was such an organisation. Several of my informants persisted in believing that I was joking. "We thought we had left all that behind us in the country," they said. The rest had only the vaguest conception of the division into Tribal Committee Areas, and I did not find even one person, outside the families of those serving on the Committees, who could name accurately the Tribal Committee Area in which he lived. A small number were able to name the Chairman of the Waitemata Tribal Executive and perhaps one or two of its members, but few even of these knew who the Chairman and members of their own Tribal Committee were.

Few Auckland Maoris showed any interest in the election of members to the Tribal Committees, or in their success or failure. Elections (held every two years) were poorly attended. At least two in 1954 had to be postponed for lack of a quorum of electors. The greatest difficulty was experienced in securing the full number of candidates. On several occasions the complement was made up at the last minute from those present at the election meeting. In view of these facts, the Tribal Committees could hardly claim to be representative of or chosen by the urban population.

Nevertheless, it might be instructive to see who were elected to these offices. In marked contrast to many rural areas,[1] women were elected as well as men. Only one of the Tribal Committees elected for the term end-

[1] cf. Kōtare, p. 88.

ing in June 1954 had no women members, and in two women out-numbered the men. Women also occupied executive status: four were Secretaries and one a Chairman. There was no minimum age for election. One member was only twenty-one. The majority were over forty-five, but younger persons increased in number on most Committees at the 1954 elections. The two liveliest Committees had a slight majority of members *under* forty-five. No marital or property qualifications were required. Not only were those elected not usually heads of kin-groups, but many were unmarried. On occasion, Committee members stressed their rank, that is, their descent in a senior line in tribe or *hapū*, but chiefly to bolster up claims made on other grounds. Some, but not all, the younger members had good educational qualifications, but the clerical and professional class was represented only by two civil servants and a typist (exclusive of Welfare Officers who were members *ex officio*). The Committees included many manual labourers but few tradesmen. Significantly, the largest economic category were the pensioners—widows, invalids, and men and women over sixty-five; they had most time to spare. Lastly, the Tribal Committee members showed considerable tribal diversity, though in most Committees there was a preponderance of Northerners. Even that associated with Ōkāhu did not achieve tribal homogeneity, for it included several who had married into the local descent-group.

Of the traditional bases of leadership, rank and age, the former was largely disregarded and, although complaints were frequently made of domination by the *kaumātua*, many younger persons were in fact elected when offering. In theory at least, the qualities considered desirable in candidates were experience, ability, honesty, forcefulness of personality, and education. But many capable persons were not available, sometimes because they were preoccupied with their own family or business affairs, but in many cases because Tribal Committees had a reputation (among those who knew anything about it) for long, boring and futile meetings, and for dissension and "backbiting". Several informants told me they would not seek office because Tribal Committee and especially Executive members were always being accused of desiring power and "feathering their own nests". They preferred to keep their friends and avoid unpleasantness.

The members of Auckland Tribal Committees blamed (alleged) lack of coercive powers and intertribal conflicts for their ineffectiveness, particularly in regard to the control of drinking, which they conceived as their primary task. A Warden could ask or advise a man to leave a hotel bar, but he could not force him to do so without calling a policeman. Should he attempt to eject him himself he would be liable to summons for assault. Wardens were reluctant to call on the police, partly because it was an admission of failure, but mainly because it was against Maori values to get another into trouble. One Tribal Committee member summed up the situation as he and most others saw it in these words:

"Many urban Maoris take advantage of the hue and cry about equality with Pakehas to practise the Pakeha principle that a man's home is his castle and he may do as he likes there. A Tribal Committee member is powerless to stop a party in a private home. We find that a threat to bring in the police is our only effective weapon. The traditional Maori respect for their elders is dead in the city."

This explanation failed to distinguish between two important but different issues: on the one hand, the technical problems of Tribal Committee government in a large and heterogeneous population, and on the other, the widespread resistence to authority other than that of the law.

The first of the technical problems was that of identification. At the lowest possible estimate, the average population of each Tribal Committee Area was 1,250, and some had a much denser Maori population than others. Most rural Tribal Committee Areas had a population not exceeding 500. The wide scattering of Maori families in each Area, among a dense non-Maori population, and the great mobility of Maoris within the city aggravated the problem. Under such circumstances it was understandable that Maoris should query the authority of someone they did not know personally, whose occupation of a role of authority they were required to accept on trust, and with whose appointment they had had nothing to do. One Committee found a partial answer to this problem when they realised that drinkers treated Wardens with respect when they wore something approaching a uniform, with badges prominently displayed.

Secondly, there was the problem of communication. The advertisement of meetings was far from adequate, reliance being placed on verbal notification and small newspaper notices. Proceedings were not published, except by word of mouth and were as a result often distorted. There was a real obstacle here, however, for many urban Maoris disliked seeing Maori affairs, however public, discussed in print. When reports of several Executive meetings found their way into a daily newspaper in 1954, my informants firmly believed that the notices had been inserted by the Chairman "for his own glory": they refused to believe that the report had been made on the initiative of the paper's reporter, or that most public bodies published their proceedings as a matter of course.

Most Tribal Committees were also handicapped by the lack of a *marae* or comparable focus for their activities. It was no coincidence that the most active committee in the city was one which was converting an old house into a small, local community centre. In the absence of a *marae*, meetings had to be held in private homes or hired halls, which emphasised the non-traditional nature of the Committees. Without a permanent focus it was difficult for community sentiment to develop. The Auckland Maori Community Centre was central for only one Tribal Committee and the Tribal Executive, though other Tribal Committees sometimes held meetings there.

These technical problems could have been overcome if recognised. A far more fundamental problem was the insistence of individual Maoris and family groups in the city upon self-determination within the limits of the law. Auckland Maoris liked the freedom of action which the city gave them and were very reluctant to surrender it. In many cases, it was the non-traditional character of the city which had attracted them to settle there. In the country, those elected to the Tribal Committee were known to the whole community and belonged to the same tribe as most other residents. But in the city, the majority of Tribal Committee members were unknown quantities, even to the few who took an interest in Tribal Committee affairs, coming from different parts of the country, belonging to many different tribes and rarely met personally. The grounds on which the claims of Tribal Committee members to leadership status could be disputed were greatly increased.

Tribal diversity was the reason most often advanced by members for lack of harmony in the Tribal Committees. The term Tribal Committee was indeed a misnomer in Auckland, where members of many different tribes lived within the limits of each Tribal Committee Area and were eligible not only as electors but as candidates. No single tribe had succeeded in capturing an entire Committee. However, I myself did not gain the impression that intertribal friction was particularly strong or disruptive. The Tribal Committee which was most enthusiastic and successful in 1954 was that with the highest degree of tribal diversity. I observed no evidence of "lobbying" or "ganging up" on the part of tribal groups at Tribal Executive meetings. Members of the same tribe were to be found on opposite sides of an argument as often as in support of each other. Admittedly, etiquette and courtesy demanded that at least the appearance of intertribal co-operation be preserved, but I never felt that under-currents of intertribal hostility seriously threatened that appearance. On the few occasions on which I heard tribal hostilities openly aired, the argument was between two or three individuals whose antagonism had other causes, and it did not result in a general alignment of tribal groups.

There was little scope for friction to develop between *tāngata whenua* and 'immigrants', because the former were represented on only two of the six committees, several on the Ōrākei and two on the Onehunga committee.

The division into tribes was cross-cut by two other lines of division, those of sex and age. There was no doubt that the men resented women in official positions. Relations between the sexes in the Tribal Committees were confused by the fact that most of the women were also members of the Maori Women's Welfare League, which had branches in each of the Tribal Committee Areas. Both men and women tended to view the Committees and the Executive as a male sphere which had been invaded by women, a conception which was never intended by the framers of the Act which set them up, but was a legacy from experience in rural communities where Tribal Committees were often all-male and balanced by a Women's *Marae* Committee (which, however, often had some male members).[1] The Tribal Executive in particular was undermined by the fact that its women members supported the League in any controversy between the two groups. Also, because the same women held office in both, they suffered from considerable duplication of labour and were too heavily burdened with duties to do justice to any of them.

Members of the Tribal Committees also saw themselves as involved in the conflict between "old" and "young". The older members were convinced that the younger ones wished to discard *all* traditional ways and values; as a result they often stood on their dignity and resisted their proposals on principle. The younger members, on their side, impatiently classified the older ones as reactionary and old-fashioned and rejected their advice with unnecessary belligerence. A focal point of dispute was the use of English at meetings. They usually began in Maori but more and more English was spoken as they proceeded. A number of the older folk, particularly the women, found their grasp on the discussion weakening when English became dominant, while the younger people preferred English as less circumlocutory, especially when time was short.

SOCIAL CONTROL

The State judiciary, Government Departments and local governing bodies were not territorially external to the Maori population as in the country, but they were still regarded by the Maoris themselves as basically non-Maori in direction. The first was also largely non-Maori in personnel; there were no Maoris in the police force in 1953–5, though one probation officer was a Maori. Maoris were employed by the municipal authorities in some numbers, but almost exclusively as labourers. Many also found employment in Government Departments, but they did not as a rule occupy executive positions, except in the Auckland branch of the Department of Maori Affairs, where over half the staff was Maori.

The relations between Auckland Maoris and the police and the Department of Maori Affairs are rather outside the scope of this work. In brief, they distrusted the police, who were reported to be "down on Maoris", and hesitated to "get another Maori into trouble with the police". When it came to the point, the victims of criminal offences usually did call them in, even when another Maori was involved, for, as they said, what else could they do? There were no other avenues of redress or protection. Appeals to the Tribal Committees they dismissed as useless, because "they have no power", even if one knew who their members were and how to get in touch with them; and Maori Welfare Officers could do little without having recourse to the police. Indignation overcame abstract group loyalty more readily when the offender belonged to another tribe or was a comparative stranger, as was likely to be the case in the city.

The Department of Maori Affairs was relied upon as the chief means

[1] p. 68.

of obtaining a good house, and to a lesser extent for assistance with employment and other welfare problems. It had established and still supervised the Tribal Committees and Maori Women's Welfare League in Auckland through the appointment of Welfare Officers *ex officio* to each committee. But in the final analysis, the Department was identified as external to Auckland Maori society, its policy and staff controlled ultimately from headquarters in Wellington. Members of its staff, particularly Welfare Officers, were always associated with their office in the minds of the people, whether acting in their official capacity or not.

The influence of the Tribal Committees was limited to the restriction of excessive drinking, while the Tribal Executive controlled activities at the Maori Community Centre, and the Onehunga T.C. ran a smaller community centre in Onehunga. As in the country, the main sanctions on social behaviour within the Maori group itself were informal ones. In general they were even less effective.

The influence of the elders did not usually extend much beyond their own circle of kin. It depended largely on their personal qualities and the affection and respect they inspired, reinforced in some instances by their position as chief tenants who could evict the recalcitrant. But neither in extended-family nor in kin-cluster was their authority accepted without effective rebellion at some point. In fact, those elders who wielded the greatest influence in their kin-group were those who had abdicated *de facto* control over it. The really elderly, in family groups, Tribal Committees, Welfare League and other urban associations were not leaders, initiators, executors, and disciplinarians, but served instead as critics and advisers. They acted as a brake on the wild-cat schemes of younger folk, imparted dignity to proceedings varying from Tribal Committee meetings to weddings, and deplored the passing of the old standards of behaviour, without taking active steps to preserve them.

Parental discipline was not a limiting factor in the behaviour of most young persons above school-leaving age. Approximately one-fifth were "out on their own", living apart from parents. Most parents did not know where or how their teenage children spent their leisure or their money, even when they still lived at home. They knew few of their friends and little about them. Young people regularly spent the night away from home or brought friends home to sleep without telling their parents beforehand. In matters of marriage, the young people invariably had their way. At most a few of the "old-timers" managed to make their wishes felt within the limits of their own homes and in their own presence. One elderly couple forbade liquor to be brought into their house. The ban was obeyed, after they had detected one or two attempts to defy it, but one son was known for his heavy drinking away from the house.

Public opinion mattered less to most Maoris than in the country. They knew only a small percentage of Aucklanders, even the Maori ones, and if they found any censorious or interfering, they simply avoided them.

Some (heavy gamblers, "sly-grog sellers" etc.) had pursued a course of action severely reprobated by other Maoris over many years, finding friends among their own kind. Approval from other Maoris was still valued, but in so large and varied a population it was usually to be found somewhere.

In the field of ceremonial, Auckland Maoris were usually concerned to win the approval of their guests for "doing things properly", but with some guests this referred as much to an adequate supply of liquor as to the observance of traditional ceremonial. The conduct of weddings and public meetings was, however, so little standardised that few escaped a charge of having some "Pakeha" elements.

COMMUNITY SOLIDARITY

The Maoris living in Auckland did not form a single community in any real sense of the word, or even a series of communities. Only those living at Ōkāhu could lay claim to that title. With 9–10,000 Maoris in the Auckland Urban Area in 1953–4, the Maori population was too large for its members to be personally acquainted with more than a small proportion of the others. The problem was accentuated by the dispersal of Maoris over the urban area, by their pronounced mobility in residence and employment, and by a fairly wide range in occupation and income, though the development of social classes was restricted.

Continuing immigration from rural areas also created special problems. There was a cleavage between the *tāngata whenua* whose ancestors had owned the urban area and the 'immigrants' who in the Maori view "belonged" elsewhere. The 'immigrants' came from many different rural areas and many different tribes. These divisions were perpetuated even among the city-born, who inherited along with interests in Maori land in the country a sentimental attachment to their parents' home communities and membership in their tribes. Auckland Maoris varied significantly in the length of time they had lived in the city. Some were recent arrivals, some had been there for ten, twenty, and even thirty years, and some (most still under twenty-five years old) had lived there all their lives. They also varied in their adjustment to urban life, which was only partially correlated with the length of their urban experience.

Several other divisions had their roots in Maori rural society—divisions based on sex, age grading, attitudes to Maori culture, leisure interests and religious affiliation. We have already seen that these were characteristic of Kōtare.[1] Clashes between sectional groupings were, however, often less intense in Auckland than in the small rural community, for those who disagreed on any issue could more easily avoid each other.

But in spite of conflict between the generations and division along a variety of other lines, in spite of different reactions to urban conditions, in spite of lack of organisational unity even in limited spheres, the Auckland

[1] pp. 79, 94–5.

Maoris were all agreed upon the primary importance of "being Maori". Remarkably few tried to "pass" as Pakehas. They showed strong preference for the company of other Maoris. They felt strongly what they called "the pull of Maori heart".

The Maoris themselves tended to assume that there had been a general "loss of Maori culture" in the city, especially among the younger generations. The "young" in the city certainly coveted much that was Pakeha in origin, but mainly in the spheres of technology and material goods; they were impatient of Maori ceremonial and non-utilitarian traditional practices, but they expressed strong preferences for Maori food and Maori company. We have already seen that the young people of Kōtare showed similar characteristics; they too were accused of "going Pakeha".[1] But, I suggested, these attitudes had been characteristic of previous generations at the same age, and they, like their predecessors, would probably outgrow much of their impatience. In Auckland, too, impatience with ceremonial forms and "old-fashioned" elders tended to diminish as individuals grew older, and rarely hardened into complete rejection. Indeed, maturity frequently brought a revival or even an awakening of interest in things Maori. Informants in the middle generations recalled how they too had brushed aside opportunities for learning Maori traditions and ceremonial when they were young. In too many cases to be merely exceptions, what knowledge they possessed had been acquired of recent years, in the city itself, and sometimes from members of other tribes. Sam Long began to learn *haka* and the arts of Maori oratory when he was over thirty and was soon organising his own *haka* group. Rere Porter, who spoke no Maori when she came to Auckland as a young married woman, began to learn it there after she became a grandmother. Others, less interested in traditional lore, had become enthusiastic about 'family' *komiti* as a means of coping with *hui*. Variations of interest in and evaluation of various aspects of Maori culture were partly a function of the age grading typical of Maori society in the country as well as the town. Complete alienation from Maori patterns of behaviour and value orientations was atypical even among the young.

Life in the city, in close contact with a large number of Pakehas, had had an obvious effect upon the more concrete of "Maori ways": on language, arts and crafts, and customary usages, especially in the field of ceremonial. Maori was used as a means of communication in a minority of Auckland Maori homes, even when the parents spoke it fluently. Most city children did not speak more than a few words, the rest a highly colloquial version. The young people chattered among themselves in "grasshopper Maori", jumping backwards and forwards between Maori and English; their club meetings, announcements at dances and so forth were all in English. Interest in Maori crafts was conspicuous by its absence. Classes in carving, *tukutuku* (reed panels) and flax weaving had been started at various times,

[1] p. 94.

but had all collapsed for lack of patronage; there were too many alternative ways of filling in leisure time. Flax mats and kits were common in urban homes, and *tāniko* belts were popular with the young people; but mostly they were supplied by country kin. On the other hand, there was marked interest in Maori songs and dances, stimulated in part by their popularity with Pakehas; familiarity with them was a valuable asset at the social gatherings sponsored by city firms and sports clubs. Though *haka* teams so often ended in failure, the impulse towards their formation was stronger than in most rural communities. The general preference was for semi-traditional and modern arrangements rather than the "real old-time stuff".

Large-scale gatherings suffered from the lack of *marae* and meeting-houses in Auckland. Their ceremonial features were curtailed by the exigencies of commercial catering and hired halls, guest lists had to be placed on an invitation basis, and visitors could not be accommodated all together in the one place for the night. The one-day gathering, with visitors dispersing to sleep in their own homes or those of friends, was the rule. Working conditions—the forty-hour week, the abundance of over-time, the insistence of employers on punctuality and the minimum of absenteeism—restricted most social activities to the weekends; this was, however, no novelty to most immigrants. Scorn, disapproval or (worst of all) amusement on the part of Pakehas caused Maoris either to discard those things which aroused these attitudes or, more often, to practise them only when Pakehas were not present. Pakeha curiosity had banished the greeting of the *hongi* (pressing of noses) from the streets and caused mourners to postpone much of the traditional wailing over the dead until they reached the rural *marae*. Only at the most superficial level, that of casual entertainment, did Pakeha influence encourage interest in the Maori heritage.

It is necessary, however, to observe that Auckland Maoris were often influenced as much by their expectations as by objective fact, sensing censure where often there was only indifference. In many cases, an *a priori* assumption that "the city is no place for Maori ways and one must live like a Pakeha" caused them to drop certain usages even before any external pressure had been applied. Parents excused their failure to instruct their children in Maori knowledge on the grounds that it was "hopeless to compete with the Pakeha influence of the city". The latter was also used as an excuse for discarding observances which had become onerous. *Tapu* restrictions were discarded in great part, and fear of *mākutu* (sorcery)[1] was generally dormant.

In most cases, the pressures of urban life had not succeeded in eliminating customary practices, but only in restricting the publicity and less often the frequency of their observance. While a few denied that "the real Maori atmosphere" was to be found anywhere in the city, most Auckland

[1] Blake Palmer, 1954.

Maoris continued to practise many distinctively Maori customs in the privacy of their own homes: the *hongi*, for instance, the stylised wailing at the first meeting after a death in the family, or the formal speeches of welcome (*mihi*) accorded important visitors or kinsfolk not seen for a long time. Although *tangi* and unveilings did not usually take place in the city, weddings, birthday parties and sectional gatherings of all kinds followed conventional Maori procedure as far as possible. Ceremonial forms had inevitably been affected by urban conditions, in particular the lack of facilities for *hui*, but instead of being weakened or discarded, they showed signs of dynamic adaptation to the difficulties of their environment. We have seen how wedding ceremonial had diverged from its rural prototype while remaining basically Maori.[1] The same was true of certain Maori forms of organisation, notably the tribe and the 'family' club.

The Maori language and Maori food habits remained focal points of Maori self-consciousness, as they were in the country. Although Maori was not much used for every-day purposes, it was still an essential element of Maori ceremonial, used on all important occasions, in public as well as private. Maoris came from all over Auckland to attend church services in Maori. Even the young liked to hear Maori spoken on occasion. Many were *hōhā* (can't-be-bothered) about speaking it themselves, but this attitude was often rooted in shame at their poor mastery. Some very young and very new arrivals denied that they spoke it at all, for fear of appearing country bumpkins, but they rarely kept up the pretence for long, and only in the presence of Pakehas.

On a more mundane level, a similar significance was attached to Maori food preferences. These had suffered almost no modification at all under urban conditions. Auckland Maoris, more especially the unmarried, expended a great deal of energy ranging the seashore and countryside accessible from Auckland at weekends and after work to satisfy their craving for shellfish, sea-eggs, fish of all kinds, pūhā (sow thistle) and watercress. This "Maori *kai*" was eaten only in the privacy of the home or at the Maori Community Centre and was hidden from sight if a Pakeha visitor called.

The more abstract aspects of "Maori ways", however, remained almost wholly unmodified. Auckland Maoris shared many values and behaviour patterns which differentiated them from urban Pakehas and linked them closely with Maori rural society. They sought Maori company in preference to that of Pakehas in part because it was "comfortable", offering an uncarping acceptance even to the erring, and standing in sharp contrast to the critical Pakeha world. But far more important was the fact that they shared the same attitudes to time, money, the future and many other things. They continued to enjoy the large Maori-style gathering; the young were as enthusiastic as the old, though for different reasons. Because such gatherings could not always be staged satisfactorily in the city, they

[1] pp. 190-2.

made frequent trips out into the country to attend them. They maintained effective relations with a large number of kinsfolk, including many living outside the city, and a significant proportion belonged to clubs formed on a kinship basis and concerned primarily with the staging of *tangi*. Maori attitudes to time and money persisted strongly in the face of Pakeha disapproval. Auckland Maoris might manage (with difficulty) to be punctual at work, but they rarely kept a clock in their homes. If the young were more interested in the present than the past, they agreed with the older generations in refusing to worry about the future and in making free use of money while they had it. Generosity was the most prized social virtue. Hospitality was, by Pakeha standards, unstinting; Maori families took inconvenience in its cause as a matter of course. Few Maori householders could bring themselves to insult guests in their home by asking them to leave when a party lasted into the early hours of the morning, even though they knew it would annoy Pakeha neighbours.

Thus the Auckland Maoris did have a cultural identity, based on Maori rural patterns but adapted and developed in response to urban conditions and to much closer and more complex relations with the Pakeha and the Pakeha way of life. Pressure to conform to Pakeha ways in at least certain minimum respects was greater than in most rural communities, not only because of the overwhelming numbers of the Pakeha and the density of urban settlement, but also because of numerous official bodies controlling health and housing. But within these limits, the city, with its characteristic acceptance of heterogeneity, its emphasis on the rights and autonomy of the individual within the limits of the law, and the impersonality and fragmentation of social relations, allowed its Maori residents plenty of scope for retaining and elaborating an individuality of their own.

As in Kōtare, the Maoris in Auckland were most conscious of themselves as a group and of their cultural unity, in relation to the Pakeha population. This group consciousness was in part imposed by instances of discrimination and colour prejudice. The effects of the latter were magnified by exaggerated sensitivity to Pakeha criticism. As one young Auckland resident said: "There are some Maoris who think and say they are as good as the Pakeha and mix easily with them, but the majority are easily knocked back. One bad Pakeha spoils the lot for them." Even those who had not themselves experienced discrimination were ready to detect it at every turn and confessed that they were ill at ease in Pakeha company. Within five minutes of telling me that "Maori culture" was dead and the Maori race dying out, one young man commented that "blood will out, no matter how little of it there is. Maori blood boils when it hears anything bad said about Maoris". His definition of what stirred "Maori blood" was both significant and typical. He did not mention a *haka* or *karanga* or even a *tangi*. It was criticism from Pakehas, or the expectation of it, which held Auckland Maoris together.

Auckland Maoris were also conscious of themselves as Aucklanders. They were ambivalent about this position. They liked to feel that they still had rights in land and *marae* in their home communities in the country, and that they could act as members of rural 'families' whenever they chose, in short, that they "belonged" there still. They resented it when country kin called them "Ngāti Akarana", implying that they had forfeited their hereditary tribal membership, or teased them about "going Pakeha". On the other hand, they liked and enjoyed city life, with its variety and opportunity, its freedom and glamour. They tended at times to look down on country residents as "backward" and "old-fashioned", and stigmatised country life as "slow". There had even been a few attempts to adopt the name "Ngāti Akarana" as a focus for community feeling, much as the Ngāti Porou had turned the derisory nickname "Nati" into a symbol of success by adopting it as the trademark for their butter.[1] But "Ngāti Akarana" had not yet won general acceptance. It suffered from the fact that it had been used by several sports clubs and *haka* groups which had come to grief. As yet, only a few cherished a vision of a unified Maori society, a new tribe, which would be based on common urban residence and *Maoritanga*, instead of hereditary affiliation and status.

Auckland Maoris tried to give concrete expression to these feelings of unity, but usually the forces of disunity were too strong. At most they achieved it for special occasions and short periods. When the Queen visited New Zealand, they banded together to obtain a place on the official programme in the city and to send a "Ngāti Akarana" *haka* party to Waitangi. Both objects were achieved, but at the cost of a breach with the *tāngata whenua* who also had a concert party, and in neither case did the organisation survive the Royal Visit.

The strength and weaknesses of Maori solidarity were exemplified by the Maori Community Centre. The Auckland Maoris played only a minor part in the establishment of the Centre, which was opened in November 1948. The building itself, a war-time bulk store, was made available on nominal lease by the Government and converted for use with the aid of large grants from Maori Land Boards and the Maori Trustee, a Government subsidy, and £2,000 which the Auckland Rotary Clubs raised by a public appeal. Auckland Maoris contributed approximately £460. Control of the Centre, which was legally incorporated as a Society, was vested in a Trust Board of fifteen members, eight nominated by the Waitemata Tribal Executive, five by the Rotary Clubs and two by the Department of Maori Affairs. At first the Centre was run by a Secretary–Manager directly responsible to the Trust Board, but in June 1951 the management was handed over to the Waitemata Tribal Executive. During its first five years, the Centre was available for hire by various Maori associations, who took it in turn to organise all weekend activities there. But this system diverted the profits to the hiring bodies instead of being

[1] Keesing, 1929, p. 46.

available for improvements, and towards the end of 1953 the Executive took over the running of weekend activities itself. In August 1954 it set up a special M.C.C. sub-committee consisting of three delegates each from the Executive and the Auckland District Council of the Maori Women's Welfare League.

In 1953 and 1954, the Maori Community Centre was patronised only by certain sections of the population, chiefly by the "young". Its location —on the edge of the residential area of the central city adjoining an area of commercial storehouses—meant that many had to travel long distances to visit it. The Centre was constantly under critical fire from Auckland Maoris. They found faults with its standards of cleanliness, catering and entertainment, with the interior decoration, and with the behaviour of those who frequented it. It was stigmatised as "non-Maori" because it was not built on a traditional *marae* site, the building itself was not Maori in appearance, and it lacked any open space. It could not be used as a traditional meeting-house, as the Fire Department had forbidden its use as sleeping quarters. Meals were provided on a commercial basis. Since 1953 the Centre could not be hired for the evening at weekends. It was available during the week and for Saturday weddings, but hirers considered the charges too high and chafed under the restrictions placed upon them. Alleged domination of the Trust Board by Pakehas was resented: "the Centre is not really ours to do with as we like". At the same time, the people were dissatisfied with those actually managing the Centre—the members of the Tribal Executive, who were, theoretically, their representatives. They constantly levelled charges of inefficiency and worse against them. Some even boycotted the Centre because (they alleged) it was "dominated" by persons they disliked or distrusted. Certainly, changes in personnel and systems of management were frequent and improvements rarely sustained. The youth clubs which had been started at the Centre had all been short-lived.

Yet the Maori Community Centre was crowded out on Sunday nights when eight hundred or more Maoris packed a hall which seated half that number, to hear a mediocre and repetitive Talent Quest. When it was open—mostly at the weekend—it was never empty. It was the most popular rendezvous for young Maoris in the city. Admittedly, it had few rivals. (The Onehunga Community Centre, run by the Onehunga T.C., was still finding its feet and catered only for a local population). The Centre was the home of all groups which were "for all Auckland Maoris", the meeting place of the central city Tribal Committees and Welfare League branches, the Waitemata Tribal Executive, and a series of *haka* groups and youth clubs. It was used for many family affairs such as weddings. And all important gatherings of Maoris in Auckland were held there, as well as some of regional and even national importance. As the centre for Auckland Maori society, it was a symbol of its emotional solidarity and organisational disunity.

PART THREE

City and Country

14

Urban-Rural Relations

ACCORDING to the conventional view of urbanisation, rural emigrants who settle in the city either lose touch with those who remain in the country or gradually become separated from their rural antecedents as a result of assimilation to urban values and patterns of behaviour. The Maoris living in Auckland were derived from rural communities either directly or at one remove: what was their relationship with those who remained in the country? Was there in fact any sign of divergence or cleavage between Maori urban society and Maori rural society?

AUCKLAND MAORIS AND THE COUNTRY

Attachment to the Home Community

Most Maoris in Auckland had a sentimental attachment to at least one particular rural community. This community was "home" to them, first because they or one or both of their parents had lived there long enough to develop real affection for it and for the people who lived there, and, secondly, because their ancestors for at least three generations (and often many more) had lived and were buried there. They held on to interests in Maori land in the district so that they could claim the *marae* as their own and the privileges of *tangata marae*[1] during their visits home. Maoris who lacked interests in local land might be conceded rights in the *marae* as long as they lived in the district, but absentees needed to have some tangible proof that they "belonged", for the passage of time reduced the number of those who remembered when they or their parents lived there and from whom they derived their rights. "If the land goes we have no right to go back", one said to me; and another added: "We are robbed of the feeling that there is something to go back to." They wanted and needed to "belong" somewhere in the special Maori sense. And they wanted to preserve their rights for their children. Mrs Joyce Green knew that her children would never be able to live in her home community— ("There is no land or living worth going back to . . . their lives are set in the city")—yet she refused to sell out her share of the family land to her brother, leasing it to him, "so that when they visit there they will not feel strangers and divided from him".

Attachment to a rural community was naturally deepest and most

[1] pp. 30–1.

personal among those who had lived longest in the home community, particularly those who had spent their childhood and youth there. Long years in Auckland did not diminish but overlaid it with a gentle nostalgia: "I shall never leave home in my heart", as Joyce Green expressed it. 'Passive' immigrants and the city-born were well aware of their country origins. Their parents talked constantly of "home" and "the home folks", taught them that it was their "home", too, where they could claim rights in the *marae* and hospitality as kinsmen from most of the residents, and took them on visits. But their feelings for the home community were more abstract and more directly correlated with how often they were able to visit it and how well they liked the kinsmen living there. Also their loyalty was more frequently divided between two communities, their father's and their mother's. Nevertheless, most would have agreed with the girl who said: "Our real home is where Dad and Mum come from."

The best index of the strength of the attachment in individual cases was the frequency of visits to the home community, but it must be remembered that this was also affected by other variables: the distance and cost involved, the age and health of the urban resident, the extent of his responsibilities to family and employer, and whether or not he had any really close kin left there. When such kin were lacking the enjoyment derived from the visit diminished in relation to its cost in time and money, and accommodation was less easy to arrange for visits that did not coincide with *hui*. In particular, 'passive' emigrants and children born after their parents left the home community were reluctant to visit it on their own unless they could count on the sponsorship of kinsmen they already knew and liked.

Because it was largely emotional and sentimental, attachment to a specific rural community could be cherished and transmitted by persons who had not lived there for a long time or, indeed, at any time, but it was weakened if contact with persons actually living there was not maintained.

Social Relations with the Home Community

Most Auckland Maoris did in fact maintain effective social relations with Maoris still living in their home community, especially kinsmen.

Letters passed to and fro, but only in a few cases with regularity and mainly to parents. Telephone calls were preferred as more personal and less trouble, but cost limited their number. Typical was the case of seventeen-year-old Frank Matthews who, in the six months after he left Kōtare to work in an Auckland hospital, wrote to his parents not more than twice, sent occasional messages in his sister's letters, and telephoned some four times when he felt home-sick. Those who could not get home themselves often relied for news on others who could, rather than on letters. One Kōtare man settled in Auckland claimed that he always visited his cousins in the city before he went home to see if any of them had messages to send, and again on his return to deliver messages from kinsfolk at home. Auckland informants from Kōtare who were sincerely attached to it as their home community were often surprisingly out of touch with its news because of this tendency to rely on personal contacts rather than letters. But really important news—that of a death—was always transmitted with remarkable speed, by telephone where possible, or else by personal call.

Visits were by far the most important means of keeping in touch with the home community, though restricted on the average to one or two a year. In most cases, a visit home was an enterprise calling for considerable organisation and finance. Very few Auckland Maoris derived from communities close enough to Auckland to be visited for the day; on the contrary, most came from at least two hundred miles away. Distance and expense were extremely important limiting factors. In 1955, to get to Kōtare by public transport cost £2 10s by service-car to Raumati (the nearest town), plus a £1 taxi fare, because the service-car arrived after the departure of the last bus to Kōtare. An air service offered an alternative means of transport to Raumati, but was more expensive. Many rural communities were considerably less accessible than Kōtare. One which supplied many immigrants to Auckland could be reached only by the successive use of train, bus, ferry and taxi, unless the traveller had private transport. The difficulties of travel were greatly increased when parents had young children.

Most Auckland adults endeavoured to go home at least once a year for a holiday, but not more than half actually did so. Sometimes the visit was made in their annual holidays, sometimes at one of the "long weekends": when Auckland's Anniversary Day fell on Monday or Friday in January, Easter, Queen's Birthday weekend in June, or Labour Day weekend in October. The annual holiday visit was, however, a habit often broken. After the first two or three years away, young urbanites began to spend some of their holiday time with friends on visits to *their* home communities and to cut down the length of time they spent in their own. Also, as the years elapsed, Auckland residents inevitably built up family and kin ties in the city.

A decrease in the frequency of holiday visits or their cessation thus showed some correlation with length of stay in the city. But it did not necessarily mean a decrease in personal contact or the weakening of ties with the home community, for holiday visits were in most cases replaced by "occasional" visits: most Auckland Maoris went home for important gatherings, especially those connected with social crises in their own lives or those of their kin.

News of illness and death took home close kin immediately. The obligation to attend a *tangi* for a kinsman was still felt by emigrants from rural districts, though the range of kin for whom the obligation was acknowledged was definitely narrower than it was for resident members of the rural community. Auckland Maoris attended *tangi* in the country mainly when the deceased was a member of their own or their parents' elementary-family or a member of an urban 'family' club. When a Maori died in Auckland his Auckland kin were among the first to know and had time to make plans to accompany the coffin home. When the death occurred in the country the news sometimes reached the city too late for urban kin to travel home in time for the burial.

Auckland Maoris showed considerable ingenuity at getting home at short notice to a *tangi*. If there were enough of them planning to go they hired a bus: certain 'families' were well-known to city bus companies, so frequently did they patronise them. Otherwise, they travelled by private cars—their own or belonging to friends whom they persuaded to go "for the trip"—by rental car, taxi or by air. When their father died in Kōtare, two young men working in Auckland arrived home (a distance of over two hundred miles) in under twenty-four hours, one in the last un-reserved seat on the 'plane, the other with friends in a rental car.

In the country it might be possible to lose no working time through attending a *tangi*, or at most only one day, but urban dwellers attending one in their home district could count on an absence of at least three days. Travelling accounted for seven or eight hours each way, and Maori etiquette did not permit them to rush away too soon after the burial. The individual was also dependent on the majority as to the time of departure, and was stranded if it should be decided to stay another day. A number of Maori workers had lost jobs in the city as a result of recognising this obligation, the most unfortunate being a boy belonging to a closely knit kin-cluster which lost three members in as many weeks.

Maoris who died in Auckland were almost invariably taken home for burial. During two years' fieldwork I knew only one case of a Maori who was not *tangata whenua* being buried in Auckland, and that was a child only a few weeks old. Auckland Maoris conceded that the expense and organisation involved in taking home the dead was burdensome. The majority still insisted on burying their dead at home and bent their atten-tion to means of lightening the financial burden. Hence the efflorescence of 'family' clubs in the city. Several had put forward the idea of a bus or truck owned and operated by a Maori company to be kept solely for the purpose of taking home the dead. This would solve the problems presented when commercial vehicles could not be obtained at short notice and when not enough ready cash was available for the deposit. No-one had translated this idea into action. The Tribal Executive would not agree to sponsor it and the cost of licensing and fitting out were considered prohi-bitive for a private venture. One man did buy a truck privately for the use of his kin-cluster, but the older members of the group disapproved of a vehicle which was used for carrying coffins being used on other business between engagements, and when the only solution was to leave it sitting idle before the owner's house when not in use they disapproved of that also. By its association with death it became too *tapu* to be anything but an embarrassment. Burial in Auckland as a solution to the problem was favoured only by a very small minority. The city-born and bred did not query the practice of taking home the dead any more than the older residents.

Weddings and the unveilings of memorial gravestones also attracted city residents back to the *marae*. These could be arranged ahead, usually on a long weekend, especially at Easter, which fell about harvest-time. For this reason attending them was not so disruptive of a working life and frequently holidays could be arranged to coincide with them.

The weddings they attended in the country were mostly those of country kin. More than half of those in the 'sets' who decided to marry after settling in the city chose to be married there. The determining factor in the location of a wedding was the residence of the parents of the young people, especially the bride. Only in one case in the 'sets' were an Auckland couple married in the country while their parents were all living in the city, and the chief reason was that five other couples were married there at the same time and the cost of catering and hospitality was shared by all the 'families' concerned. Birthday parties, especially the important twenty-first, were also held where the principal's parents were living.

Unveilings were next in importance to *tangi* as events which Auckland Maoris felt constrained to attend. These, of course, were held in the community where the person commemorated was buried. Joyce Green, who found it a struggle to keep nine children on her husband's wages and could not afford to go home either on a holiday visit or to a wedding, felt impelled to go home twice in 1954, once to a *tangi* and once to an unveiling. Since elaborate stones costing sometimes £50 or more were favoured, it was often several years after the death before they were unveiled. In most communities, families who were planning to unveil gravestones combined to stage a single *hui*. The tombstones, which might be in several different cemeteries, were unveiled in successive religious ceremonies beginning soon after dawn. In this way an unveiling brought home a much larger proportion of emigrants at once than many *tangi*. At the unveiling which Joyce Green attended in her home community in March 1954, over forty Maoris from Auckland were present, and other kin came home from as far away as Taranaki.

Only a minority of Auckland residents made both holiday and "occasional" visits home in any given year, and whenever a choice became necessary, it was the holiday which was foregone. The result was that, in many cases, the pattern of visiting was highly irregular, two or three visits to *tangi* or weddings sometimes following each other in quick succession, with a long gap until the next.

The over-all range in frequency and duration of visits was very large, but the average Auckland family or individual visited their home community once or twice a year. At one end of the scale there was a small minority, about one-tenth, who went home at every opportunity, some-

times almost every weekend, financing their visits by working overtime.
These were chiefly married couples who were childless or whose children
were all self-supporting, who derived from communities within a fifty-mile
radius of Auckland, or who possessed their own cars. At the other end of
the scale was another small group (roughly one-fifth) who had not been
home in the last five years. Many of them were parents of young families,
but also included were some who had left home under a cloud and others
whose family had died out there. The majority fell between these two
extremes. While twenty-three of the one hundred and fifteen 'active'
emigrants from Kōtare in Auckland had not been home for five years,
forty-one paid at least one visit to Kōtare during the first seven months
of 1955.

By and large those who returned to their home communities most
frequently were the young and unmarried in the first few years after
emigration, when they still chose—and could still afford—to go home both
for holidays and for special events. They had only themselves to support,
they could afford to leave a job if they were determined to get home for
any particular purpose, and the problem of accommodation during their
visit was relatively simple. Those in the middle generations were more
circumscribed, because of their family ties. The elderly, on the other
hand, were often extremely mobile, as long as their age and health permitted. A number of widows in the 'sets' paid an average of four visits
to their home community in a year, and often more. But there were very
few 'active' immigrants of whatever age who did not go home at the call
of illness or death among their kin, even after a long absence.

The city-born and 'passive' emigrants were dependent upon their
parents as long as they were not earning for the frequency with which they
visited their parents' home community (or communities). A few were sent
to the country under the guardianship of kin or left behind in the city,
but mostly they accompanied their parents on their visits. There seemed
to be a fairly even balance between those who visited the country frequently
and knew one rural community fairly well and those who had been there
rarely or not at all. One young two-year-old visited his mother's community
four times in 1954, once with his parents on their annual holiday, once
with his mother to the *tangi* of her father's first cousin and twice with his
mother's niece in her school holidays. The children of the Waikeri kin-
cluster went on most of the trips which the group made, sometimes even
in the absence of their parents. On the other hand, some parents considered the long journey too much of a nightmare with young children,
apart from the cost. When a family was large, the children often did not
visit their home community until they were over ten years old.

Even if the children did not visit the home community of one or both
parents with great regularity, they heard a great deal about life in the
country from their parents, from city kin and from visitors from the
country. Such accounts were invariably biased to some degree, sometimes

the hardships being stressed, sometimes the co-operation and community spirit. It was impressed upon the children that they had a right to go to their parents' home community, not as "strangers" but as people who "belonged" there. They were often told that they need not knock on any door at home, but should walk straight in, for every household contained kinsfolk. (In most Maori rural communities this was not strictly true.)

The duration of visits depended largely upon the purpose for which they were made. Those who went home for the holidays stayed anything from a few days to a fortnight in the case of wage-earners and their families, and longer if they were pensioners, school-children or (less often) housewives. Visits connected with "occasional" gatherings, on the other hand, were typically short, for they fell outside the holiday period of most of those who attended them. Those which could be arranged ahead were usually fitted into a weekend, preferably a long one (when Friday or Monday was a public holiday), but *tangi* often fell in mid-week. In both cases, the whole trip (including travelling time) was usually compressed into three days. Auckland residents left Auckland by hired bus, car or taxi some time after work on (for instance) Friday, travelling all or part of the night to arrive on Saturday morning, and departed again on Sunday afternoon.

The short duration of the "occasional" visit would seem to be a disadvantage compared with the longer holiday visit, but, apart from the fact that attendance at the gatherings which gave rise to them was an obligation for all good kinsfolk, they were favoured for several important reasons. In the first place, the "occasional" visit was eminently suited to organisation on a group basis; the joint hiring of transport cut costs and simplified travel problems. Many who thought twice about undertaking the journey, with all its attendant problems, on their own initiative, would join a group trip at short notice without any qualms. Those who wished to stay longer in the home community could always remain after the bus had returned to Auckland, though at the cost of finding their own way back. Secondly, annual holidays usually occurred at Christmas, socially a quiet time of year, when country folk were either preoccupied with their farms or gardens or away on holiday; Auckland residents, who found normal country life "slow", much preferred to be at home during the bustle and excitement of a *hui*, when everyone was gathered on the *marae* over a period of several days. In the course of a short, two- or three-day visit, they could see and talk with more old friends than in a fortnight of visiting them individually. And finally, attendance at a *hui* in the home community provided valued opportunities to take part in specifically Maori forms of social activity and organisation. Visits home played a significant part in maintaining the interest of urban residents in rural methods of organising large-scale gatherings.

Attending a *hui* in a rural community was regarded as a highly enjoyable experience by Auckland Maoris, including the young people, although they naturally preferred the gayer birthday parties and weddings. The journey itself, tiring as it was, was part of the excitement when it involved a busload of kinsfolk and friends, of all ages and both sexes, with a couple of guitars strumming and everyone singing all the way. Then there was the ceremonial welcome, the meeting with kin not seen for some time, the late nights filled with speeches and gossip and perhaps dancing or a talent quest, sleeping in a crowd on mattresses spread over most of the meeting-house floor, the big meals of "Maori kai", the rushed round of visits to the homes of friends and relatives for a yarn or a bath, and the exchange of news and scandal saved up over several months. For the young ones there was the added spice of meeting kin and non-kin of their own age (especially of the opposite sex), known by name and reputation but still unfamiliar enough to be interesting.

On their own witness the older urban residents "slipped right back into the old ways" on their visits home. They spoke Maori more continuously and observed *tapu* customs which they forgot about in the city. A city housewife said that "the years just roll back when I am among my own". In the city, she did not "bother with the old customs". Like most others, she had not regarded the traditional injunction against cutting the hair and fingernails of children under a year old, nor did she take care to wash her own underclothes separately from those of the men of the family.[1] But, as she said, "I go right back to it when I go home." Even the younger urbanites behaved more circumspectly on visits home than they were accustomed to in the city, explaining that "I don't believe in it but I do it at home because of the old people". If they could not accept all the practices of their rural kin, at least they refrained from criticising them openly.

Some of the young city folk liked to show off the sophistication acquired in the city by taking home an extensive fashionable wardrobe and the latest dance steps and songs, but for most of them, as for the older ones, visits to the country were regarded mainly as opportunities for indulging in things Maori, things that were denied to them in the city or which they denied themselves, feeling that they were "out of place". The chief attractions of this sort were the warm human contact and lack of stiffness typical of gatherings on the *marae*, with everyone sleeping in the meeting-house and eating at long trestle tables in dining-hall, tent or open air; "Maori" foods (especially those of the more pungent variety like dried shark, eel and custard of fermented corn); eel and flounder fishing by torchlight, diving for crayfish, horse-riding, and watching country football. These pleasures were not enough to *hold* them in the country; they had been dismissed as boring in the days before emigration. But their value was greatly increased when they could be indulged in only infrequently, in the context of a short gay visit during which the urbanite was treated almost as a guest, and when they provided such a strong contrast to every-

[1] Beaglehole, 1946, p. 234.

day life in the city. The Auckland Maori was in the happy position of being able to enjoy the high points of the rural year without having to endure the monotony of the intervals between.

It was, then, gatherings at which specifically Maori ceremonial and values were emphasised that took Auckland Maoris home most often. This greatly increased the impact of their visits on the city-born and city-bred, and tended to lessen the divergence which could easily have developed between urban and rural practice in these matters.

The attitude of Auckland Maoris to their home communities was ambivalent in many ways. They enjoyed visiting and cherished a special affection for 'home'. Above all, they valued the opportunity for participating in social gatherings on the home *marae*, gatherings which were unequivocally Maori in terms of personnel, organisation and ceremonial. But they did not usually wish to live there permanently. It was too difficult to make a good living in the country; future prospects were circumscribed and insecure. Country parents had to face the fact that sooner or later most of their children would leave home. Besides, country life, in comparison with that of the city, was "slow" and quiet, country folk "backward" and "behind the times". The majority liked living in the city, with its variety, its opportunities, its excitement and its freedom. Access to their home communities and those aspects of community life which they valued most facilitated their adjustment to urban life and helped them to achieve what was (in their view) the best of both worlds.

Visits to Other Places

Auckland Maoris did not confine their visits to their home districts. Their interest in "new places" remained unabated. Also, the fact that so many of their kinsfolk were living outside both home community and Auckland provided them with the incentive and the excuse to visit other places, both rural and urban.

Many Auckland residents visited kin, especially siblings or parents, in other places as often as they visited their home community. These visits took them far from the latter, even into tribal regions traditionally hostile to their own. So many Maoris had been attracted to the public works and mill towns of the Central Plateau that coming and going between the city and that area was particularly marked. Anaru Pera had not been home to his birthplace (on the Coromandel Peninsula) in the last three years, because none of his siblings remained there; but in 1954 he paid two visits to Paeroa where a brother and sister were settled on farms and two others to Mangakino where he had two brothers, a sister and a married daughter.

It was not always the presence of kinsfolk, however, which caused Auckland Maoris to visit a particular place. Excursions organised by non-kin bodies were extremely popular. Usually they involved competition against sports or *haka* teams from other places. Sometimes the destination was a regional centre where a large scale tournament was in progress, sometimes a rural community where one or two matches only were played. Always the business of the trip was concluded by a dance or a concert and involved intermingling with the local people. Someone in the group was sure to have kinsfolk in the district visited, but these bodies were typically composed of persons of diverse tribal background, so that to most the local people were strangers. This element of "strangeness" was perhaps the most attractive feature of such trips, for they offered an excellent opportunity to "see what places are like" and to "meet new faces".

Some places were specially favoured as foci for trips because they were centres and show-places for Maori cultural aspirations, or because they held *hui* which were renowned as feats of organisation. Most Auckland Maoris had been at least once either to Rotorua, a thermal region where Maori entertainers are one of the chief tourist attractions, to Ngāruawāhia, the seat of the Maori King,[1] to Ratana Pa, the headquarters of the Ratana Church, near Wanganui, or to Waitangi, in the Bay of Islands, where the famous treaty of 1840 was signed. Business or leisure interests, especially sport, also took urban residents far afield. One man attended cycle races with his (non-Maori) club all over the North Island, making use of the opportunity to stay with kinsfolk in places as far apart as Wellington, Rotorua, Whangarei and Palmerston North. Many young people had been on visits and working holidays to some of New Zealand's most famous tourist resorts: to National Park, the Rotorua thermal region, even to the lake and alpine areas of the South Island. One girl at twenty-three had already spent two summers hop-picking in Nelson, a third waitressing in a hotel at a popular yachting harbour and a fourth at Chateau Tongariro on the ski slopes of one of the North Island's mountains.

Many Auckland Maoris also took part in trips to gatherings sponsored by kin-groups to which they did not belong in communities to which they were "strangers", invited along by friends who did "belong" there. Thus when a cousin of a member of a "gang" of young Aucklanders was married in Rotorua, most of the "gang" went along, though none of them had even met the bride or groom before. The excitement and pleasure derived from a *hui* in a rural community attracted Auckland Maoris whether they belonged to the community or not.

The young and unattached felt that life had become dull if they could not get out of the city approximately once a month on a weekend trip. In most cases less than half of these trips were to their home community. Moana Wiki (twenty-one years of age and unmarried) left the city on trips lasting two or more days eleven times within eight months in 1953–4. Not one of these trips was to the community which she called home, where none of her close kin was living. Four took her to communities within the territory of her tribe (Ngāpuhi): she spent her annual holiday and two weekends with her father's sister's son and his wife and, with a

[1] Sutherland, 1940, pp. 89–94 and 177–81.

cousin and two unrelated girl-friends, attended the opening of a hall in another Ngāpuhi district where she had kinsfolk. The other seven trips took her to two twenty-first birthday parties within thirty miles of Auckland, one that of a member of the "gang" to which she belonged, the other that of a "cousin" (her mother's sister's son's son), to a wedding in Rotorua and an unveiling in Te Hāpua with the "gang", to Waitangi with the Ngāti Akarana *Haka* Group to perform before the Queen during the Royal Tour, to Ratana Pa for a week for the celebrations of Ratana's birthday, and by special bus with a party of Auckland Maoris to the unveiling of the monument to Sir Peter Buck at Urenui (near New Plymouth).

As with visits to home communities, it was the young and unattached who went on visits and trips to other communities and towns most often. Expense and the difficulties of travel with small children restricted the movements of those with families. However, a few families were beginning to experiment in holidays away from the home community. Selwyn Davis and his family visited several seaside resorts (including his home community) in January 1955, travelling in a covered truck with a tent, rolls of mattress and a primus stove. Sam Long bought an ancient omnibus, pensioned off from a country run, refloored and furbished it up, and at Christmas filled it with his own family, his brother's family and his wife's sister's family, twenty-one persons in all. Escorted by his sister's son on his motor-bike they set off through the Waikato, his own tribal region, and then toured most of the central area of the North Island. They slept under canvas most of the time, but spent New Year in Rotorua with kinsfolk of Sam's brother's wife.

The visits made by Auckland Maoris outside both Auckland and their home community were almost invariably concerned with other *Maori* communities, most often in rural areas. If a trip was made to a town, its participants were usually welcomed and accommodated on the *marae* or by local Maori families. Visits to kin and trips of all kinds thus gave urban residents experience of Maori communities other than their own, increased their tolerance of members of other tribes and helped to break down tribal divisions and distrust.

COUNTRY MAORIS AND THE CITY

If city Maoris liked to visit their home communities, their country relatives found the city attractive, too, and took advantage of having kinsfolk in the city to spend their holidays there. It was a standing joke in the city that the trains and buses going out of the city at public holidays were full of Auckland Maoris on their way home, while those travelling in the opposite direction were full with country folk coming into the city. The main influx into the city took place in the winter, when much of the work in which rural dwellers were engaged was brought to a standstill by the weather, and at Christmas and New Year when most wage-earners had their annual holiday.

Country visitors came to the city to see their kin and to explore the fabled delights of the city, but often some more specific circumstance supplied an excuse. A number of women came to run homes in cases of sickness or while a daughter or sister was in the maternity hospital; a few men came to earn some extra money when temporarily unemployed during the winter. Other visits arose from the need for expert medical or legal advice, a summons to a *tomo*, an invitation to a wedding or an anniversary celebration, a Maori Land Court sitting, a big race meeting or a Rugby Test Match.

Visitors to the city stayed with relatives and friends, whenever possible. Failing that, they stayed at the Maori Hostelry in Parnell, or in a few rare cases in a boarding house or a private hotel. Of the Kōtare residents who visited Auckland in 1955, one family spent a week at the Parnell hostelry, and the rest "dossed in" with kinsfolk, even though in most cases it meant sleeping on the floor of a ten-by-twelve-foot bedroom which already held three or four sleepers.

Visits to the city by rural Maoris were, however, neither so regular nor so frequent as those which took place in the opposite direction, and they were mainly confined to those who had relatives in Auckland and could afford the trip.

Country visitors most often came singly or in small elementary-family groups, particularly for holidays, but sometimes a party of thirty or more hired a bus for a weekend trip to a wedding or a sporting fixture. City weddings always attracted rural guests. When Beryl Rahira was married in Auckland, fourteen visitors came from Hokianga in two taxis, arriving on Friday night and leaving late on Sunday. They slept at her parents' home where they were accommodated by removing the mattresses from the beds in two rooms and spreading them on the floor. For Hine Pera's wedding, her father's brother and sister and several of their children came to stay with her father, two of the cousins staying on to work in the city. Country sports teams often included the city in the itinerary of a tour, and every year three or four parties of school-children were brought by teachers from the more remote rural areas to pay an educational visit to the city's industrial plants, wharves, museum and entertainment centres. These non-kin groups were usually accommodated together by arrangement at the Maori Community Centre, at the Parnell Maori Hostelry or at hostels, where they were visited by city kinsfolk. Once, however, a busload of twenty-five children on a football tour, finding the hostelry full, descended on the home of an emigrant from their home community, who accommodated them for two nights.

Northland Maoris, who had to pass through the city on their way to other destinations, whether travelling alone or in organised parties, usually contrived to spend two or three days in Auckland. Two carloads from their home community put up with Ben and Nellie Rahira on their way to and from the unveiling of the memorial to Sir Peter Buck at Urenui.

Joyce's sister and her family spent a night with the Greens on their way to a Mormon conference in Hamilton and another on their return. Every year parties of Northerners travelling to Rātana Pa for the November and January celebrations of the Rātana Church broke their journey with relatives in Auckland.

Auckland showed signs of becoming popular as a conference centre for Maori organisations. The Maori Women's Welfare League held Dominion Conferences there in 1952 and 1954, notable for the fact that arrangements were made for all the delegates and observers to stay at hotels within easy reach of the Maori Community Centre, where the business was conducted. Each November the Rātana Church sponsored a weekend gathering at the Maori Community Centre which attracted large crowds of Rātana adherents from Northland and from areas around Auckland.

MOVEMENT OF GOODS AND SERVICES

There was surprisingly little movement of goods and services from the city to country except in association with *hui*. Kōtare parents did not expect to receive benefits from the migration of their children to the city, apart from relief from pressure on their own income and living space. Some of the young people sent or brought presents home at Christmas or at birthdays, but by no means all, and few sent home even casual remittances of money. There was little need for it, since none of the Kōtare residents was destitute without such support. One Kōtare emigrant, a man in his forties earning high wages, took a refrigerator home for his father on one of his comparatively rare visits, but this was a unique gift. One man in the 'sets' was building a house in the country on his periodic visits home, paying for materials out of current income on the Auckland wharves. This also was a rare phenomenon.

Aucklanders contributed to *hui* in their home communities mainly in cash and, when they were able to attend, in person. If they travelled home in a group they pooled their individual contributions (usually by adding a levy to each person's share of the travelling expenses) and presented them (privately) in a lump sum. They usually helped in the cook-house and dining-hall, but they did not do as much as they would have done if living in the community, because they did not arrive until the *hui* had actually started and left after the last major meal. Those who could not go home for a *hui* sent money or a present only if the person honoured was a close kinsman.

Probably more assistance, both in cash and in kind, flowed in the other direction. Young apprentices could not make ends meet in the city without help from home and, together with training college students and other trainees, they relied upon their parents to pay their fares for visits home. Even those who were earning good wages often spent too freely in the city to have enough in hand for a trip home. Sacks of *kūmara* and sweet corn, bottles of preserves and boxes of fresh fruit, home-made clothes and knitted garments nearly always accompanied visitors to Kōtare and other rural communities when they returned to the city, and similar gifts were taken or sent to relatives or friends who provided accommodation in the city. When his two eldest daughters went to Auckland, Selwyn Matthews of Kōtare opened accounts for them with a large city store with a substantial credit payment. When weddings and twenty-first birthday parties were held in the city, country kinsmen brought smaller donations in cash but large quantities of garden produce, preserves, sacks of shellfish, and haunches of cooked ham and pork.

One of the reasons why so few goods came into Kōtare from the city was that Raumati catered fairly fully for the needs of Kōtare residents. Stores there were stocked with almost every type of merchandise for which there was any demand, and what they did not stock they would obtain from the city for their customers. Goods of a personal nature, especially clothes and jewellery, were sometimes bought in Auckland in the belief that the selection and fashion value was greater than that offered in Raumati, but such purchases were made personally on visits to the city and not sent home by emigrants. Household furnishings and home appliances, trade tools, farm machinery and fertilisers were all obtained in Raumati. To buy from the city involved unnecessary expense through transport costs. Raumati also provided a normally adequate range of services. Secondary education was provided as far as University Entrance level by a State College. The only children who were sent away to school were those whose parents wished them to be educated at a church school. Doctors and dentists and a large hospital in Raumati were easily accessible to Kōtare, and only specialist advice had to be sought in Auckland. The Maori Affairs Department also had an office in Raumati which served as a base for travelling Welfare Officers and Farm Supervisors and handled all the business which came under its jurisdiction.

TENSION AND OPPOSITION BETWEEN CITY AND COUNTRY

Both urban and rural Maoris resented the other group at times. From both sides was heard the complaint that the others did not appreciate the difficulties of their situation and imposed upon them, particularly with respect to visits.

My Auckland informants complained that country visitors stayed sometimes for weeks at a time without making any contribution to the household economy. According to Joyce Green, "they think you must be rich if you live in the city but they don't realise how much it costs here where everything has to be paid for", and where rents and prices of perishable foodstuffs were much higher than in the country. They expected to be shown round the city, involving their hosts in a round of expensive entertainment. Joyce Green commented that she found if impossible to save, because "just as I am getting a little in hand someone comes to stay and it all goes". Several Auckland housewives also complained that folk from the country too often arrived unannounced at awkward times, after the shops had closed, forgetting that Aucklanders rarely had their own gardens to fall back on for food or the room to carry large stores. Then country visitors were liable to prolong their visits indefinitely. Few Auckland Maoris minded living under cramped conditions for a short time: indeed they took a pride in showing that they retained their traditional sense of hospitality by sleeping on the floor to accommodate their visitors. But when the few nights stretched into weeks or months they began to lose patience, particularly when the children suffered. Grace Pritchard told me how her sister Lucy with two small children stayed with her until she protested and then spent two months with another sister Aroha and her husband, who lived with their four children in two rooms. Aroha "wouldn't say anything", so Grace (the eldest of her family) eventually sent Lucy packing, telling her that she was being unfair both to her own children and to Aroha's. Lucy had no need to impose on her sisters, for she had a fine new home of her own in the country.

Some of the worst offenders were young people who came to the city ostensibly on holiday but with the full intention of finding a job. They stayed with any relations they could claim in Auckland, sometimes quite distant ones, remained for weeks without earning and moved on as soon as they had the means to be independent. Because they usually went into rooms in an apartment house or hostel they were unable to return the hospitality, and because their status was that of visitor and not of boarder they were a financial burden on their hosts. They were also a worry, because their parents held their hosts responsible for their welfare without giving them any authority over them. Timothy Green said: "We gave many who arrived in town with nothing a start, only to find them move on after a month and forget all about us. We know their parents and we can't see them stuck on the street. Most of them had to be asked to give a hand in the house, and then they got angry and left."

Many informants felt that the exchange of hospitality was one-sided. Often "the very ones who come to stay are those you can't visit in return" —unmarried young people, "travellers", or distant relatives with whom they would not consider staying as long as they had parents or siblings at home. Also, they were often expected to work when they went home, especially the women. Marama Jones recalled that last time she and her husband went home for his annual holiday it was not long after her father's death and visitors were so numerous that she did "nothing but wash and cook and never even got down to the beach".

Country folk on their side complained that urban residents made a convenience of *them*, getting a cheap holiday at the busiest times of the rural year, Christmas and Easter. The wife of Joe Peters, occupier of a family farm in Kōtare, told me that she dreaded holiday time because Joe's brothers and sisters regularly came home without any warning; often four or more would be there with their spouses and families at the same time. They considered they had a perfect right to come and go without reference to Joe and his family because it was still a "family house", legally in their father's name. On the other hand, another Kōtare farmer's wife liked to have her family home at Christmas, to weed her gardens for her! But most Kōtare parents recognised ruefully that having their offspring and kin home for the holidays was more likely to result in a loss than a gain of labour: as Charlotte Matthews remarked when she was preserving the new season's peaches, she would have to hide the bottles when her son and daughters came home or she would find that the lot had disappeared.

Country folk were fond of accusing Auckland Maoris of forgetting the old customs of hospitality, of "measuring everything in terms of money and what it is going to cost". Country folk on visits to the city were amazed that they could not sleep in the Maori Community Centre as they would in a meeting house, that they must pay for all the meals they ate there, and that it was not available at weekends for exclusive use by a family or a club. When country functions took longer than was expected —as they invariably did—the impatience of urban visitors who had to get back to the city in time for work seemed unmannerly to country people. Not only was it "against Maori custom" but it left the clearing up entirely to the "home folks". Once a party of Auckland Maoris hired a bus at short notice to take them to a *hui* in the Far North; the only driver available was a Pakeha who warned them that he had to be back in the city at a certain hour, and would have to leave not later than 2 p.m. on the Sunday afternoon. The big ceremonial dinner, scheduled for 12, had not been served by then, and when the visitors left without having eaten, the local people made pointed remarks about the Pakeha influence of the city.

But if Auckland Maoris could not repudiate entirely the charge of "going Pakeha", they could with justification throw it back on the rural community. In Kōtare, charges were made for the use of 'family' meeting-houses, though they were often remitted for a *tangi*. "There are few genuine Maoris left even in the country", said one Aucklander. "The old-timers would never come to stay without a sack of *kūmara*, but many now come empty-handed or else bring a lot of unnecessary cakes and sweets the day they arrive when you have stocked up well and nothing afterwards when they have cleaned out the larder. . . They live for themselves at home now just as we do in the city." The majority of rural dwellers depended on wages for income, working a forty-hour week just like their city kin. They rarely took more than one day off even for a *tangi*, except in the case of the immediate kin of the deceased. Other *hui* were arranged for weekends as much for the sake of local wage-earners as for those expected from the city. By no means all had gardens to modify the necessity for being careful with their cash. Country clubs were as familiar with account books, savings banks and committee procedure as urban ones. The feeling for the autonomy of the individual and the elementary-family unit was very strong, and even kin-group co-operation was not typically unanimous nor free from dissension.

BONDS BETWEEN CITY AND COUNTRY

In spite of friction and minor divergences in their pattern of daily living, Maoris in the city and the country continually strove not only to keep in touch but also to co-operate together on as many occasions as possible.

A large proportion of the Auckland population was itself derived directly from rural society, being composed of 'active' immigrants. In every rural community, there were also some who had at one stage lived in the city. Moreover, movement between the two was continuing at a rapid pace. The number of those born and bred in the city who had reached adulthood was as yet not sufficient to balance those recruited from rural areas. Even if the intimacy of social relations between Auckland residents and their home communities diminished with the passing of time—and that was by no means always the case—new bonds came into being every time a rural emigrant came to the city.

As a result of complex and continuing migration between city and country, Maoris living in both were linked together by a network of kinship. Members of the 'families' associated with the land area of any given rural community were not only dispersed throughout New Zealand, but a substantial proportion of each was usually represented in Auckland. Take, for instance, the Samuels 'family' of Kōtare. Twenty-nine members of this 'family' had left Kōtare as adults; some of them were living as far south as Wellington, Palmerston North and Te Kuiti, and thirteen were in Auckland (see Table 10).

Members of 'families' distributed between the home community, the city and other places, continued to forgather for certain purposes concerning one or more of their number, meeting, not as several groups, but essentially as one. On such occasions the rural-urban division became irrelevant. Whether the *hui* took place in the home community or in the city, those who had come from a distance assumed the appropriate roles as kinsfolk and did not act as guests to be waited upon and entertained. At Beryl Rahira's Auckland wedding, the bride's mother's sister, within an hour of arriving from the country, had taken control of the preparation and serving of the food, and half the waitresses were the bride's cousins who had stepped straight from the bus which brought them to Auckland. At the Matthews–Tātana wedding in Kōtare, three of the groomsmen, two of the bridesmaids and nine other official workers were Kōtare emigrants returned especially for the occasion, four from the city. Joyce Green, immediately upon arriving home for an unveiling in 1954, went to work in the cook-house, because one of the stones being unveiled was that of her mother's brother.

'Family' clubs were, on the whole, localised in either rural community or city for obvious technical reasons, but occasionally they had subscribing members living in other places. One Auckland club had three subscribing members living in various parts of Northland, and one in Wellington.

When a busload of Auckland residents went home for any *hui* they presented their *"marae* money" as a group, in one sum. But it was delivered unobtrusively, whereas a group from another community presented it openly in most areas. When the bus arrived at the home *marae* its passengers were not given the full-scale welcome proper to guests from another community but "just a *pōwhiri* (chanted welcome) and handshakes, with no speeches, because we really belong there".

Most Auckland Maoris depended largely on the support of country kin in staging the *hui* with which they still liked to observe the social crises of death, marriage and coming-of-age. Without their help with expenses and their labour, they would have had to curtail their plans. If the *hui* was held on the home *marae*, kinsmen living in the home community did a lot of the early preparations, such as bespeaking and tidying the *marae*, placing orders for goods, and spreading the news; they also provided mattresses, tablecloths and other things which it was awkward to bring from Auckland. If the *hui* was held in Auckland, country kinsmen could be relied upon to provide quantities of foodstuffs which were not readily available in Auckland or only at prohibitive prices, and which would greatly enhance the success of the gathering.

Rural residents were as a rule less dependent on help from urban kin, for they usually had more kinsmen available within the limits of the same community. However, some rural 'families' were so depleted by emigration that they had to rely on kinsfolk returning for important occasions or else call upon kin in related 'families'.[1] Urban kin did not usually give as much to country *hui* either in labour or in cash as those living on the spot, because they arrived just before it started and left soon after the major business was over, and expended a good deal of time and money simply in getting there.

Often lonely and uncertain of themselves, especially during their first years in the city, Auckland Maoris relied on country kin for moral support and affection as well as practical help on special occasions. As a result, they were influenced to a considerable extent by what their relations in the country might say and do, particularly if they neglected to attend and contribute to *tangi*, or turned kin from their door. As Joyce Green explained: "They can't say no. If they do, they know that when they are in trouble the folk back home won't help them or will throw it up at them."

Maoris in the country and in the city also shared a common attachment to the land and community of their ancestors symbolised by the *marae*. As already mentioned, most Auckland Maoris clung to land interests in the country, because they wanted to "belong" somewhere in the Maori sense and to have a *marae* of their own, where they could speak "without a by-your-leave". Also, in the absence of a *marae* in Auckland, they

[1] p. 73.

needed and continued to use the country *marae* for their *tangi* and un-veilings, and sometimes for weddings and twenty-first birthday parties.

The orientation of Maori society towards rural *marae*, which was part emotional and part organisational, was offset first, by the fact that young Aucklanders preferred to hold their twenty-first birthday parties and weddings in Auckland, where their friends were, and more significantly, by the development of Auckland as a centre for activities and organisations which aimed at transcending 'family', community or tribal groupings. Auckland had long been the site of two church secondary schools for Maori boys and girls respectively; boarding establishments catering mainly for rural children, they were recognised sources of young Maori leaders. Its University and Teachers' Training College each had a significant proportion of Maori students and thriving Maori clubs, which were beginning to establish a reputation for experimentation and creativity in the field of the arts. Its Museum had a superb Maori collection from which city children, on conducted school tours, learnt a little of the material culture of their ancestors. Classes in the Maori language were available in certain secondary schools, at the University, and under the auspices of the Adult Education Centre. By and large, only a very small proportion of the Auckland Maori population came into contact with those involved in these activities, but their reputation and influence were considerable outside the city. The regional (Tai-Tokerau) headquarters of the Maori Affairs Department and the Maori Land Court were also in Auckland in 1953–4. In recent years, a number of supra-regional con-ferences had been held in Auckland, which was centrally located for the main areas of Maori population, and could also be regarded from some points of view as tribally neutral territory.

Common *Maoritanga* was another powerful bond between Maoris living in the country and in the city. The urban practice of ceremonial and organisation differed, often markedly, from the rural, but the diverg-ences were in detail rather than aim, representing a progressive develop-ment from rural prototypes, rather than a break with them. In many ways, the rural Maori were following similar lines of development. Besides, regional variations had always modified the cultural homogeneity of Maori society; unity, cultural or political, had never been characteristic of Maori society as a whole. Lastly, the social personality and philosophy of life of the urban Maori was far more closely allied to that of the rural Maori than to that of Pakehas in the city.[1]

But whatever the differences of detail, urban and rural Maoris were both proud of being Maori and strongly loyal to each other. They shared two important aspirations: the preservation of the physical and cultural identity of the Maori people and the improvement of their social and economic status individually and as a group until comparable with that of the Pakeha. These aspirations brought the women together on a national

[1] Beaglehole, *op. cit.*; Ritchie, 1956.

scale in the Maori Women's Welfare League. Above all, they were expressed in co-operation on occasions of national significance, when it was considered desirable to represent the Maori as a distinctive unit within New Zealand society. During the Royal Tour of New Zealand in 1953–4, Maoris from Auckland shared prominently in the celebrations at Waitangi, at Ngāruawāhia and at Rotorua, the three places in the Auckland Province where Maoris were responsible for a major part of the official programme. Significantly, they took part not only in the *haka* teams in the public eye, but as workers behind the scenes. Similarly, both urban and rural Maoris were to be found in force at the unveiling of the memorial to Sir Peter Buck at Urenui (1955) and of the memorial of Kupe's landing in Hokianga (1955). On such occasions there was an increasing tendency for the Auckland Maoris to participate as a group, sometimes under the name of Ngāti Akarana, in spite of a few awkward incidents when traditionalist rural elders had refused to recognise them with a formal welcome, or had made scathing comments about this "new tribe". From the technical point of view, the arrangement was a convenient one, because they usually travelled from Auckland in one or more buses. Such groups almost invariably included some persons belonging to tribes inimical to the hosts of the gathering. Kinship linked individual urban residents to individuals or at most a 'family' grouping in the country and to specific communities and *marae*, but shared pride in being Maori was the basis of unity for the whole of Maori society.

CONCLUSION

Auckland Maori society and Maori rural society were not closed and separate systems but existed in close contact and interaction with each other. Residents in both were linked by membership in the same functioning descent-groups—in 'families'—and they met periodically in both city and in rural community to co-operate in the ceremonial observance of social crises in their lives, events in which both continued to desire participation from as many kin as possible. Auckland residents retained a special attachment to specific rural communities and rural *marae*. The personnel of urban and of rural Maori society was not static, but there was a constant circulation between them, as individuals and families moved from one to the other for short or long terms. The behaviour, beliefs and aims of those in each were affected by continuing contact and exchange of personnel. Even the friction that existed at times between urban and rural Maoris arose from and expressed their feeling that they belonged together. On important occasions, of a national, regional or kin-group order, the distinctions and disagreements fell away and the fundamental unity based upon common *Maoritanga* was revealed.

15

Stability and Change in Maori Society

In outlining the problem of Maori urbanisation in Chapter 1, I posed two questions which it seemed to me required to be answered first: Were modern Maori rural communities as homogeneous and conservative as was generally assumed? From what sections of the rural population were Maori urban immigrants drawn?[1]

Kōtare, the community chosen for study in the Far North, diverged at many points from the popular stereotype. It was neither static nor intransigently conservative, but in the process of rapid social and economic change. Modern communications had broken down the barriers of time and space. Traditional nucleated settlement had been scattered over the district by economic changes and interpenetrated by Pakehas and Maoris not of local derivation. Social relations of considerable warmth and intimacy had been established with these "outsiders". Descent had been superseded by voluntary association as the main principle of social and economic organisation, but remained valid, on a voluntary basis, in certain social spheres. Leadership had become diffuse and depended at least in part on achievement and personality. The present structure of the community showed continuity with the structure and locale of that of the past, but had also developed away from it. I would venture to claim that most if not all these features were also true for Maori communities in the Far North in general, though they might vary more or less according to distance from a country town, the Maori–Pakeha ratio and the extent of Maori control over local resources.

The city attracted as immigrants a high proportion of country Maoris who were: (a) between the years of sixteen and thirty, and especially those who were unmarried, both male and female; (b) unskilled and un- or under-employed; (c) well-educated or interested in occupations for which there was little scope in the country; (d) eager for adventure and new experience; (e) social misfits or delinquent. As a result, the urban Maori group was imbalanced by a preponderance of adults in those age-groups which have the highest crime-rates in all societies and were associated in Maori society in particular with an emphasis on good-time patterns and individual autonomy. In comparison, elders were few. Most immigrants came to the city in search of higher standards of living and work that was more

[1] p. 5.

congenial or more highly paid than that offering in the country. They came of their own choice, in most cases intending to settle permanently. But they made as few plans as possible beforehand, relying mainly on kinsmen and friends already in the city for help on arrival.

The urban community that was formed in Auckland as a result of this immigration differed from contemporary Maori rural society (at least as it existed in the Far North) in a number of significant ways. The overwhelming majority of its members lacked historical association with the urban land area and controlled a negligible proportion of its land resources, either on Maori or freehold title. Auckland Maoris lived scattered among Pakehas, by whom they were heavily outnumbered. They had not grouped themselves into self-conscious communities on a territorial basis as in the country, and they did not have even one functioning *marae*. The Maori Community Centre was the main focus for the group, but it could not fulfil all the functions of a *marae* or serve so large a group adequately. Tribal heterogeneity and intertribal marriage were both marked. More than half the Maoris in Auckland belonged to domestic units which shared a house with others. There was a much wider variety of occupations than in the country and more specialisation, but the percentage of unskilled workers was still high, and differentiation into social classes was not far advanced. Auckland Maoris were too numerous, too scattered and too diverse in many ways to constitute a single community in any real sense. But common aspirations and a strong emotional solidarity in the face of the Pakeha majority had preserved their identity as a group, in spite of lack of organisation. They exhibited certain attitudes, patterns of behaviour and forms of organisation which were clearly derived from Maori rural society. These had been altered in detail, modified and adapted to urban conditions, and remained vigorous, though atypical of the "urban way of life" as normally defined.

While Maori urban society and Maori rural society differed in structure and organisation, they were variations on a basic theme, rather than fundamentally alien to each other. There was no social hiatus between them, no real divergence of aims and aspirations. Elements of opposition and competition were evident in their relationship, but these were offset by consistent co-operation and interaction. They were linked by a constant interchange of personnel, by a network of kinship obligations, and by shared *Maoritanga*. The Maori rural community was based on continuity with the land and the traditional way of life associated with the land, but was penetrated by many influences which derived ultimately from the city. The urban "community" existed in a setting that was non-traditional and alien and in which it was a relative newcomer. But it was not beleaguered in the city or cut off from its source. It was open to and affected by influences from outside the city as well as by those within it.

The changes taking place in Maori society in 1953–5 were not confined to those sections living in urban areas. The same trends, the same themes, were generally observable, usually intensified and accelerated in the city, sometimes distorted and inhibited in the country, but fundamentally the same.

Some of these trends involved departure from traditional forms of organisation: modification of the importance of local derivation and land ownership as the basis of community membership; abandonment of economic self-sufficiency at both the family and community level in favour of individual employment for wages and economic specialisation; limitation of the domestic unit to the elementary family; emergence of the individual adult as the basic social unit; proliferation of voluntary, non-kin associations for social purposes; complete or partial rejection of the authority of traditional leaders; a high degree of permissiveness towards offenders against both the State law and the norms of the community; diffusion of leadership, and insecurity of leadership status.

But in both city and country the Maori group continued to adapt certain old, specifically Maori forms of organisation and behaviour to new circumstances. Thus, descent-groups were not abandoned altogether, but were restricted to certain spheres of social action, where they acquired new functions. The custom of burying the dead in their home community retained a firm hold, in spite of the expense involved in the case of urban deaths. The *tomo* and ceremonial observances at weddings, unveilings and public gatherings remained firmly Maori in character. Food habits, value orientations towards time, money, pleasure and Maori companionship persisted strongly.

There was in the Maori situation not one dominant process but an interplay of factors promoting change *and* stability. Both urban and rural Maori society were affected by these forces, but to differing degrees and in different combinations. The process of urbanisation, which had popularly been credited with effecting drastic changes in Maori society, was the most obvious and the most dramatic. But it was only the culmination of a long history of Maori–Pakeha acculturation in behaviour, in social and economic organisation and in philosophy of life. Traditional themes of organisation had played and continued to play an active part in the evolution of post-European Maori society and culture. Finally, the strongly developed group consciousness of the Maori was itself an important stabilising force in the midst of social upheaval.

Urbanisation

Maori migration to the cities was strongly criticised by both Maori and Pakeha on the grounds that it would lead to social disorganisation, with increases in marital instability, and in crime and delinquency. Maori elders predicted that urban residents would lose their attachment to traditional values and patterns of behaviour and would become assimilated entirely to Pakeha ways.

Urban immigrants showed many signs of maladjustment and insecurity on first arriving in the city, but in most cases it was a phase from which they emerged. Such maladjustment was aggravated by the fact that so many were unmarried and between the ages of fifteen and twenty-five, an age grade characterised even in rural society by aggressive rejection of authority and irresponsibility. Marital instability was considerable, physical mobility pronounced, and informal controls weakly developed among Auckland Maoris as a group; but exactly the same terms could be used to describe Maori rural society. The incidence of crime and delinquency has been omitted from this study. At least part of the reported increase in this direction can be accounted for by the exceptionally high proportion of young people (i.e. the most crime-prone group) in the city and by the fact that the city attracted many misfits and delinquents from the country.

Neither those who had lived in the city for many years nor those who were born and bred there were in fact alienated from Maori rural society. On the contrary, they maintained effective social relations with its members, continuing to share certain climactic aspects of their social life and a philosophy of life that was fundamentally the same, they utilised forms of organisation and ceremonial based on those found in the country but adapted to suit their circumstances, and they were explicitly aware of belonging to a wider, national, Maori group.

In many ways, the Maoris in Auckland failed to conform to the "urban way of life" described by the sociologists. Kinship remained important in the organisation of everyday life and of social crises in the individual life cycle, although proportionately more individuals were not active members of corporate extra-domestic kin-groups. Social distinctions based on wealth and occupational status were poorly developed. While their social relations were largely segmentalised (i.e. they had frequent casual contacts with a great many individuals, most of whom were strangers to each other), Auckland Maoris spent most of their leisure with Maoris whom they knew relatively well. They made frequent, lengthy and expensive trips to visit Maoris living in the country, and to take part in gatherings for specifically Maori ends, on a community, regional and national scale.

It could fairly be argued that such non-"urban" characteristics as an extended kinship system and group action on a large scale persisted among Auckland Maoris only because of the relatively short history of Maori urbanisation. There were, however, indications that their elimination was not merely a matter of time. In the first place, those who were already living in the city when the urban movement began did not appear to be more "urbanised" in these respects than more recent settlers. The Ōkāhu *tāngata whenua* maintained their solidarity as a community; early 'immigrants' were often the prime movers in 'family' clubs and other urban Maori associations and kept in touch with their country kin. The young adults, who were typically impatient with tradition and "the old ways" and often vocally hostile to the authority of Maori elders, showed a pronounced preference for Maori company, were enthusiastic in attending Maori *hui* in both city and country, and continued to visit their home community and to honour kinship obligations after they had become independent of parental direction. This was as true for the offspring of urban residents of long standing as for those who had immigrated of their own volition. Interest in "things Maori" usually increased with age, just as it did in the country. Finally, those who had made the best adjustment to life in the city in terms of personal contentment and good citizenship were all proud of being Maori and interested in Maori affairs and gatherings, and they retained many attitudes and patterns of behaviour that were Maori rather than Pakeha. In many cases, keeping in touch with rural kin and community actually helped immigrants to settle down more happily in the city by counteracting nostalgia and loneliness.

Urbanisation in the Maori case had not involved a drastic or traumatic break with rural kin or the rural way of life. Why had this been so? The vitality of the Maori cultural tradition was an important factor. The Maoris who settled in Auckland placed so high a value upon Maori ideals of hospitality, generosity, and group loyalty, the Maori language and Maori forms of organisation and ceremonial, that they had not only resisted pressure to abandon them, but had adapted them to their new environment. Secondly, good wages earned in the city and the comparative ease and cheapness of modern transport facilitated intercourse between the country and the city. Thirdly, rural Maoris were as much part of the modern Western economy of New Zealand as Maoris in the city. They had already felt the influence of the city, mediated through Pakeha neighbours, through mass media, in particular the radio, newspapers and the cinema, and as a result of visits to the city and contacts with returning emigrants.

The fact that urban influence and the social and economic organisation characteristic of the "urban way of life" can extend outside the city has been recognised and conceptualised in various ways. Louis Wirth defines "urbanisation" as including changes in the direction of modes of life recognised as urban among people who have come under influences emanating from city institutions and personalities through the means of communication and transportation.[1] Robert Redfield conceives "urban society" and "folk society" as polar types, between which there exists a unilinear continuum, and describes as urbanisation all processes of change which occur as a society moves from one pole to the other.[2] Walter Goldschmidt, on the other hand, asserts that a rural society ought to be called "urbanised" only when it exhibits the features of social and economic organisation associated with cities, such as impersonality in social relations and the maintenance of social distinctions without reference to personal qualities. Urbanisation of a rural society has taken place when "industrial-

[1] Wirth, 1938, p. 5.   [2] Redfield, 1946-7.

isation has changed farming enterprise from a livelihood to a means of achieving wealth".[1] Thus the terms "urbanised" and "urbanisation" have been extended to include rural society in the hinterland of the city. In Redfield's terms Maori rural society would be identified as considerably urbanised. This conceptualisation helps to explain why the Maori experience of urbanisation was not traumatic. By Goldschmidt's standard, however, Maori rural society was not yet urbanised, for though kinship and descent had declined in importance as principles of social and economic organisation, social relations were still primarily personal and distinctions based on impersonal criteria of little importance.

This use of the terms "urbanised" and "urbanisation" to distinguish a societal type as well as the population of a geographic unit is confusing, but it does point up a truth which needs to be re-stated, namely, that cities are not separate and self-sufficient entities but are bound into one social and economic system with the population of surrounding rural areas. A strong case can be made for distinguishing between "folk societies", "peasant societies" and "urban societies". There is undoubtedly a cleavage between the first (which are by definition entirely rural), or rural sections of the second (which are characterised by urban aggregations of a pre-industrial nature) on the one hand, and cities typical of "urban societies" on the other. Migration from rural areas of the former kind to cities of the latter kind is almost invariably traumatic. But the concept of a rural–urban dichotomy is not equally valid for national societies, or for minority groups within them. In most West European states, urban and rural groups, as defined in geographic terms, are economically and socially interdependent, the latter supplying much of the personnel of the former, while the city acts as "the initiating and controlling centre of economic, political and cultural life".[2] The problem is complicated wherever a national society includes a minority with a distinctive culture. As long as its members are located in rural areas only, the cultural cleavage may be expressed in rural–urban terms; but except where legal or class or caste barriers prevent change, such a group must be progressively integrated into the total urban-centred system.[3] Whatever the terminology accepted —whether it is described as "partly urbanised" in Redfield's terms or "non-urbanised" in Goldschmidt's—country Maoris were no longer a folk society, but a self-conscious minority group within New Zealand society. Continuity of social relations between city and country Maoris was far more normal than a cleavage, given the state of contemporary Maori rural society and the legal status of the Maori as a free citizen.

The standard definitions of urbanisation and urban society are based on the study of cities in the so-called Western societies; hence urbanisation, both within city limits and in rural society, has been identified with Westernisation. Mintz has demonstrated that immigrants living in the

[1] Goldschmidt, 1947, pp. x–xi.   [2] Wirth, *op. cit.*, p. 2.
[3] Compare Garigue, 1956, p. 138.

city can retain many non-urban characteristics, by being incorporated as an enclave into the bottom class of its class-structured society.[1] The Maori experience shows that the integration of a cultural minority into city life may take place without complete assimilation to the Western–urban pattern and yet be successful in terms of individual adjustment and usefulness to the community. Members of such a group may not only retain elements and forms of organisation derived from their own cultural heritage which do not conform with those of the standard urban pattern, but may even adapt and develop them to cope with the problems of their new life. The Maori had established an "urban way of life" which was a variation on that characteristic of the Pakeha tradition, notably in the role accorded to extra-family kinship ties and the maintenance of close relations with persons and specific localities outside the city. This Maori pattern will inevitably change over time, with the ageing of the city-born and city-bred element of the Maori urban population, with probable changes in the pattern of migration and in the economic prosperity of the State; but it would be a mistake to assume that it will necessarily change in the direction of assimilation to the Pakeha pattern. As Louis Wirth himself observed, "Since the city is the product of growth rather than of instant-aneous creation, it is to be expected that the influences which it exerts upon the modes of life should not be able to wipe out completely the previously dominant modes of human association."[2] The fact that the Maori minority, once established in the city, had begun to exercise some influence over Maori rural society in purely Maori affairs, should show up the fallacy of confusing urbanisation with assimilation to the dominant culture.

It is important to remember that in New Zealand, urbanisation, like acculturation, took place within a framework of liberal ideology. By the Treaty of Waitangi (1840) the Maori were promised equal rights as citizens and although there were periods when relations between European settlers and certain sections of the Maori population were in total eclipse or marred by mistrust and chicanery (on both sides), the promises of the Treaty were ultimately fulfilled.[3] Thus Maoris were free not only to move to the city as they liked, but to choose where to live, what jobs to take, what places of entertainment to patronise, and how often and for what purposes to visit the country.

Yet even under these circumstances, urbanisation was less smooth than for non-Maoris. The high visibility of Maoris in the city, where formerly they had been rare, focused attention upon them, spotlighting instances of maladjustment, irresponsibility and anti-social behaviour. The sudden development and rapid progress of the urban trend was almost inevitably correlated with a resurgence of discrimination in the city. But acts of discrimination and prejudice, although present, were, as in rural areas,

---

[1] Mintz, 1954, p. 87.   [2] Wirth, *op. cit.*, p. 3.
[3] Sutherland, 1940, pp. 75–95.

individual and unsystematised. By 1955 the Maori Affairs Department and Vocational Guidance Officers, aided by the quality of many of the immigrants, had succeeded in breaking down much of the prejudice towards Maoris, at least in the field of employment.

Finally, progressive interaction between urban and rural groups especially when they belong to an ethnic and cultural minority, is itself an important factor of both stability and change in the development of each. Contact and co-operation with rural kin encouraged urban Maoris to carry on with the ceremonial observance of social crises and to use the Maori language, fostered the efflorescence of 'family' clubs and group trips, and maintained the emphasis on generosity and hospitality and other Maori ideals. And the Auckland Maoris, by speech and example, encouraged rural Maoris to aspire to better housing and more technical equipment, widened their social and cultural horizons, and stimulated interest in intertribal co-operation.

Acculturation

In a general sense, acculturation refers to the "purely factual effect of contact between two cultures on either of them".[1] Most often, however, it is used specifically for changes brought about in a folk or peasant culture (in Redfield's terms) as a result of contact with a more advanced group, particularly with a section of modern, industrialised world-civilisation. Urbanisation in the restricted sense—that is, that which occurs as a result of actual movement into urban areas—is really a separate process, though often confused with acculturation when it occurs as a result of the latter. It provides conditions favourable to the acceleration of acculturation, but is not the only means by which acculturation is achieved. The Maori are interesting in this regard because acculturation was already far advanced when they began to settle in cities. They had been subjected to a hundred years of close contact with Pakehas within the framework of the same state; they had long been assimilated to a money economy and into systems of political organisation, medical care, formal education, law and order on a national scale; and they were subject with the rest of New Zealand to influences from outside the country.[2] In the fifteen years since the urban trend began, changes in the structure and organisation of Maori society had been accelerated by the Second World War, the post-war boom, and rapid advances in techniques of transport and communications. Service in the Armed Forces during the war broadened the outlook and experience of a large number of Maoris, provided many with professional and trade training and established them in new jobs and new houses by means of Rehabilitation loans. Post-war prosperity brought full employment, high wages and many new avenues of employment. Individual mobility was greatly increased by improved road and air travel; the extension of mass media was associated with a

---

[1] van Baal, 1960, p. 108.   [2] Sutherland, *op. cit.*, pp. 182–306.

rise in the standard of education and increased interest in contemporary trends in dress, music and vocabulary, especially those derived from the United States of America.

In New Zealand, certain important writers (notably Ernest and Pearl Beaglehole and the authors of the Rakau Studies)[1] have described the Maori situation in terms of inevitable assimilation to the dominant Pakeha way of life. The Rakau Studies postulated an "acculturation gradient moving diagrammatically from aboriginal Maori culture at one end of the continuum to contemporary New Zealand culture at the other", through the phases Acculturated Indigenous, Median Acculturated, Advanced Acculturated and High Level Acculturated.[2] There are problems about this unilineal view of Maori acculturation. First, there is the difficulty of defining the categories. At the time of my study, increasing approximation to the Pakeha norm in fields such as economic status, levels of living, housing and education was not invariably associated with diminishing interest in the Maori language, traditions and ceremonial: in fact many of the experts in these fields were highly acculturated in other respects. Secondly, the dominant culture to which the Maoris were expected to assimilate was itself in the process of rapid change. A variant on Western culture, little was known objectively about its character. Thirdly, the Maori had played a far from purely passive role in the process of acculturation. They had not simply abandoned their customary values and institutions to replace them with Pakeha ones. They had retained certain elements of their traditional culture, adapting them to changing conditions: the tribe, the extended-family, the *marae* and the *hui* had all changed greatly in the last hundred and fifty years. At the same time, the Maoris had adapted many practices and ideas of Pakeha origin to their own ends, subtly changing them in form and function: wedding and funeral ceremonial, unveilings and coming-of-age parties, committee procedure, for instance. And they had welded both together to form patterns that were still distinctively Maori—*modern* Maori.[3]

The changes which had taken place in Maori society since the arrival of the Pakeha were not determined entirely by the influence of the latter: the Maori adapted their traditional forms and developed new ones along lines of change inherent in or at least compatible with the structure of their traditional society. Perhaps the most important legacy which the modern Maori derived from pre-European society was a tradition of flexibility and adaptability, which was at least in part a function of its type of structure. An ambilateral descent-group system, in which freedom of choice with respect to membership in local groups was possible among a limited number of alternatives, in which the aristocractic class was closely linked to the rest of the local community by common descent, and

[1] Beaglehole, 1946; Ritchie, James, 1956.
[2] Beaglehole and Ritchie, 1958, p. 150; Ritchie, Jane, 1957, pp. 32–7.
[3] Metge and Campbell, 1958, pp. 357–60.

in which leadership was preferably but not rigidly hereditary, afforded more scope for adjustment to unexpected and unfamiliar circumstances than a rigidly unilateral or ranked society. As a result, its experience of contact with another culture proved on the whole less shattering. The processes of internal change continued to operate, masked and distorted, but not obliterated, by those of acculturation and urbanisation.

For pre-European Maori society was not a static "functional" system which had exhausted the possibilities of internal change, though the early ethnographers often assumed that it was. In the four and a half hundred years that elapsed between the date at which the last wave of migration is estimated to have reached New Zealand and the early phase of contact with whalers, sealers and missionaries, the Maori had developed a society which differed in so many respects from other Polynesian systems that at one time it was thought to have a Melanesian strain.[1] In the eighteenth and early nineteenth centuries they embarked upon an era of intertribal hostility which was in the process of modifying the distribution, land ownership and relative strength of their structural units and social classes, and which might have resulted in the development of new forms of organisation if the Treaty of Waitangi had not intervened.[2] Change— rapid and sometimes violent—was an outstanding characteristic of the known history of the Maori.

In the early 1950's most Maoris rejected complete assimilation as a goal, but shared the static ideal of Maori culture on which it is based, distrusting change as "loss of Maori culture". This attitude often inhibited healthy development and helped to weaken "Maori ways" by insisting on "preserving" them. The tribal structure, for instance, had been virtually frozen as it was in 1840; yet many tribes had grown to a size at which under pre-European conditions they would have segmented, while others dwindled; new alignments, such as the King Movement, had developed; and in certain towns and cities new intertribal communities had come into existence. The traditional pattern no longer reflected reality. Resistance to change was particularly marked in the arts. The experts held up the accurate reproduction of classical Maori forms as the ideal and criticised as un-Maori those which departed from them, whether in carving, weaving, *haka* or *waiata*. It had become the fashion to decry the action songs favoured by young *haka* teams because they made use of European tunes and rhythms. This clinging to the forms of the past was directly opposed in spirit to the creativity and lack of repetition characteristic of pre-European Maori art. In discarding the chants of a hundred years ago in favour of music and sentiments closer in mood to their own times, the young people were being truer to their heritage than they knew. If the intrinsic merit of much modern Maori art was inferior to that of the past, it was partly because only the best of the latter had survived, and partly because of lack of guidance. Happily,

[1] Keesing, 1928, p. 17.   [2] Sutherland, *op. cit.*, pp. 75–6, 100–1.

there was increasing appreciation of the fact that development did not necessarily involve disloyalty to "Maori culture". Judges at *haka* competitions, notably those held annually at Ngāruawāhia, had begun to allot marks for originality of theme, words and actions. Maori clubs at the Auckland and Ardmore Teachers' Training Colleges (the latter just outside the limits of the Auckland Urban Area) pioneered in the field of drama with a series of plays based on Maori legends with interludes of *haka* and *poi*, the Auckland T.T.C. club reaching a significant level of achievement in 1954 with *War in the North*, a dramatised version of the account of Hone Heke's war recorded by Maning as a supplement to *Old New Zealand*. At the same time, Maori students at the Training Colleges and at the School of Fine Arts were experimenting in other new media.

[*Note:* This trend has become even more marked in the field of the arts since the period with which this book deals. In addition to chants in the traditional style, several anthems have been composed for important *hui* with Maori words set to music in the European tradition, notably an anthem written for a Church of England *hui tōpū* (held in Rotorua in May 1960) and a lament for Maharaia Winiata, both composed in 1960 by Arapeta Awatere. A number of young Maoris have attracted favourable notice for their painting (e.g. Mrs Kathleen Mataira, Rau Hōtere, Muru Walters and Selwyn Wilson, who is also a potter), sculpture (e.g. Arnold Wilson), poetry (Hone Tuwhare), and prose writing (Mrs Arapera Blanc, who won the prize for the best short article in the Katherine Mansfield Memorial Competition 1959). Two major contributions to knowledge of the Maori past have been made by John Te H. Grace in his tribal history, *Tūwharetoa* (1959), and Pei Te Hurinui Jones in the first full length biography of the first Maori King, *King Pōtatau* (1960). In every case, the work done by Maoris in these non-traditional media has a strong Maori flavour. At its best it has something to say to and for all New Zealanders, Pakeha as well as Maori.]

Maori Group Consciousness

Lastly, any cleavage or divergence of development between Maori urban and rural residents, any abrupt break with their antecedents, was checked by their consciousness of themselves as Maoris, a distinctive ethnic and cultural group within (but not independent of) the wider New Zealand society.

Maori society was an "open community".[1] At no stage had it been completely "closed" like the Jewish ghetto, except for a limited period after the Maori Wars in certain parts (notably the King Country). In 1953–5 it was "open" in four crucial fields: the law of the New Zealand state operated directly upon Maoris as individuals, without hindrance or

[1] Brotz, "The Outlines of Jewish Society in London", in Freedman, 1955, pp. 165–88.

addition; Maoris were free to mix with Pakehas in every sphere of economic and social life and to assimilate to the wider society; Maoris shared in representative Government; and intermarriage took place on a considerable scale.

But a minority group cannot survive unless it is also to a certain extent "closed", unless it has some conception of itself as a group. What differentiated the Maori from the rest of the New Zealand population? In the first place, the outer limits of the group were set by descent: from the Maori point of view anyone who had a Maori forebear had the right to call himself a Maori. In general, however, most of those with only a dash of Maori blood were absorbed into the Pakeha population. The Census, which numbered all those who described themselves as half Maori or more in the Maori population, probably gave a fairly accurate indication of the strength of the Maori group, for in filling in Census forms most gave a subjective, not an objective, assessment of their Maori blood. Those who were half Maori or more were distinguished by certain physical characteristics, including a brown skin. This distinctiveness was itself a strong unifying force. Maoris as well as Pakehas felt that it was of fundamental importance. They were inclined to connect it causally with social and cultural differences.

Secondly, Maoris adhered to certain common patterns of behaviour, certain forms of social organisation, and a constellation of value orientations which were not shared by and were sometimes at variance with those of the Pakeha. These were not clearly formulated or identified as Maori under all circumstances, different individuals and different sections of Maori society placing varying interpretations and emphases upon them. Nevertheless, they gave a positive content to "being Maori". Maoris were most conscious of themselves as a group in relation to Pakehas. Pressure from the latter had not resulted in large-scale defection from the Maori group, but rather heightened its solidarity. Few Maoris repudiated membership in the Maori minority. Those who as individuals had attained high status in New Zealand society as a whole were invariably proud to acknowledge their status as Maoris.

The fact that the Maori were the prior inhabitants of New Zealand and that they were not conquered but ceded their country to the British Crown voluntarily and on equal terms had a considerable bearing on their place in New Zealand society. In the former respect they differed, for instance, from the Jews in Britain, and in the latter from most other "native" peoples. Their right to be full citizens did not have to be earned, nor was it a gift from a benevolent Government; it was secured to them for all time by the Treaty of Waitangi. In their wars with the Pakeha they had commanded respect for indomitable courage, resourcefulness, and gallantry to the enemy. They had fought off apathy and disease to achieve one of the highest rates of natural increase in the world. This history was a source of deep pride to the Maori. It enhanced the value they placed on their own "way of life" and modified their admiration for Western civilisation. Far from feeling any obligation towards the Pakeha, their attitude was tempered with resentment over past injuries—especially over the alienation and confiscation of their land—and at present instances of discrimination.

Maori society in the city was in many ways more "open" than Maori rural society. There was a greater tendency to call in the police to deal with cases in which other Maoris were involved, there was more mixing with Europeans at work, in education and in leisure, greater approximation to European standards of prestige and wealth, more intermarriage, a greater tendency to reject authority from other Maoris, including the old. But in comparison with the opportunities for expansion along these lines, the "openness" of urban Maori society was still restricted. Maoris were such a small minority in Auckland that if they had chosen friends and spouses without any reference to ethnic and cultural criteria they would have associated almost exclusively with Pakehas. But in fact they associated mainly with other Maoris. Moreover, while they mixed with Pakehas and appeared in many ways to assimilate to their standards, they did so on a highly selective basis (though not always a discriminating one), and in certain circumstances only. Most preserved a certain sector of their life from which they could exclude Pakehas and in which they could practise unobserved the behaviour patterns which they believed to attract Pakeha disapproval or curiosity. Hence the great popularity of the Maori Community Centre, the concentration in houses accommodating only Maoris, the proliferation of all-Maori clubs, many of which parallelled non-Maori organisations. They reacted to the greater pressure from the Pakeha way of life not by eliminating the points of difference as quickly as possible, but by placing an increased value upon the emotional security provided by the Maori group. Paradoxically, this emotional solidarity was not expressed in organisational unity.

CONCLUSION

Urbanisation and its part in the social changes taking place in Maori society has been the central theme of this book, viewed not only from the point of view of those who have settled in the city, but from that of Maori rural society as well. The Maori experience is an interesting variant upon the theme of urbanisation. Sociologically, it presents a rather different problem from the movement of non-Maoris to the cities of New Zealand, which, though equally pronounced at the time this study was made, was no longer popularly regarded as a "problem", partly because it had begun so much earlier (about the turn of the century) and partly because it involved no physical and few obvious cultural differences. The Maori urban movement was also very different from that of many non-European peoples migrating to Western cities. It was a free movement, in no way directed by any external agency, it did not affect men and women differentially, and it did not divide the elementary family, although it scattered larger kin-groups. It was in general, a permanent movement; the relatively small proportion who returned to the country did so as a matter of preference and at a fairly young age, so that there was no problem of recalcitrant ex-emigrants or a top-heavy proportion of elderly persons in Maori rural society. It acted upon a rural people who were at least partly urbanised and who were already familiar with patterns of extra-community mobility. Finally, it involved an ethnic and cultural minority which had already been wholly incorporated into a Western-type "urbanised" nation within the framework of a liberal tradition of race relations.

The Maori experience of urbanisation suggests that while certain social changes invariably take place when rural dwellers move into the city, the extent and severity of these changes are greatly affected by certain variable factors. In the first place, the effects of urbanisation are least likely to be traumatic when both the communities from which the migrants come and the city to which they go belong to the same societal type and are contained within one national system. Secondly, even when they belong to the same social system, differences will occur according to the nature of the rural society and the extent to which it has been affected by urban influence on the one hand, and the size, heterogeneity and stage of industrialisation of the city on the other. Thirdly, immigrants who are members of an ethnic or cultural group which is either in a minority or in a depressed or restricted class or both, will differ in their adjustment to the urban way of life. They may be incorporated in the bottom class of a class-structured society, with little loss of their traditional ways; they may be completely assimilated and lost in the melting pot of the city; or they may work out their own variant of the standard pattern. The Maori experience suggests that social disorganisation and the abandonment of traditional rural social patterns and values are not necessary concomitants of urbanisation, even when a cultural and ethnic minority is involved, or at least that disorganisation does not always occur in all sectors of social life. While some aspects of traditional practice may be weakened and even destroyed, adaptation and re-organisation may also occur. Under certain circumstances it is even possible for urban residence to result in the revival or increased valuation of forms of organisation of non-urban origin, if they fit into urban life or provide an answer to some of its problems. The course of urbanisation is also affected, fourthly, by the composition of the immigrant group, the manner of migration and the reasons behind it, and fifthly by the nature of the relationship maintained between urban residents and their home communities. The establishment of effective social relations may retard adjustment to urban life, but may equally well aid it by mitigating the personal strains involved. The latter is more likely in situations where attachment to specific land areas is socially and emotionally significant for the rural society.

The Maori experience of urbanisation shows that urbanisation even for a cultural and ethnic minority need be neither traumatic nor disintegrative, though still a difficult process calling for much change and adjustment. Nor need it result in alienation and cleavage between rural and urban dwellers. Urban society, while developing its own characteristics may still retain continuity with rural society, in terms of behaviour patterns and forms of organisation of rural origin adapted to urban conditions, and by the maintenance of effective social relations. While urban dwellers may share a common "way of life" with those in other cities, the importance of the national and cultural bonds which unite them with the rural society in the hinterland of the city should not be forgotten.

Tables

Tables

TABLE 1

Distribution of Maori Population: Urban and Rural, 1951 Census

	North Island	South Island	Total
Urban proper:			
(i) Cities and Boroughs	20,294	1,288	21,582
(ii) Urban Counties	737	37	774
Semi-urban:			
(i) Town Districts	2,002	58	2,060
(ii) Parts of Counties included in Urban Areas	2,754	176	2,930
Total Urban	25,787	1,559	27,346
Rural (Counties excluding parts included in Urban Areas)	85,725	2,605	88,330
Total Maori Population	111,512	4,164	115,676

TABLE 2

The Three Auckland 'Sets': Sex and Age, August 1954

	A	B	C	Total	Percentage
Sex:					
Male	106	28	44	178	
Female	116	34	41	191	
Age:					
Under 15 years	84	18	38	140	37·6
15–24	51	22	22	95	25·7
25–34	29	8	8	45	12·3
15–34[1]	5	1	5	11	3·0
35–44	18	8	5	31	8·4
45–54	19	3	2	24	6·5
55–64	7		1	8	2·2
45–64[1]	3	2	2	7	2·1
65 and over	6		2	8	2·2
Total	222	62	85	369	100·0

[1] Ages estimated or obtained from uncertain sources

TABLE 3

Kōtare Maoris: Age, Sex, Household and Local Distribution, June 1955

Sub-District	A Te Kāinga	B Hākea	C Seashore	D Puriri	E S.W. Valley	F S.E. Valley	G Karaka	H Northern Lowland	Total
No. of Households	25	8	14	21	4	9	10	7	98
Sex:									
Males	74	20	23	55	8	19	32	19	250
Females	66	37	28	61	17	20	36	22	287
Age:									
Under 15	77	29	20	59	13	16	41	21	276
15–24	22	11	10	27	5	7	3	6	91
25–34	13	9	5	9	1	5	12	4	58
35–44	15	6	3	8	1	4	8	6	51
45–54	5	2	4	5	2	3	1	2	24
55–64	2		2	2		1	1		8
65 and over	3		3	1	3	2	2	2	16
N.S. Over 15	3		4	5		1			13
Total Population	140	57	51	116	25	39	68	41	537

TABLE 4
Kōtare Maoris: Derivation, June 1955

		Male	Female	Total
K	*Tāngata whenua*	179	205	384
KS	Spouses to *tāngata whenua*	19	36	55
KF	Persons fostered by *tāngata whenua*	5	5	10
IM	'Immigrant' settlers			
	(*a*) 'active' immigrants	16	15	31
	(*b*) 'passive' immigrants	9	5	14
	(*c*) Kōtare-born	16	15	31
T	Temporary residents	6	6	12
Total		250	287	537

TABLE 5
Kōtare Maoris: Occupations, June 1955

	Working in Kōtare						Working outside Kōtare				Other	
	On own Account		Wages or Salary		Relative assisting unpaid		On own account		Wages or Salary			
	m.	f.	m.	f.	m.	f.	m.	f.	m.	f.	m.	f.
Primary Production:												
farmer	8	1			1	3	2		1			
farm labourer	1											
fisherman	1											
seaweed-picker	1	2										
contract worker			1									
Quarrying:												
foreman									1			
labourer									8			
Manufacturing:												
worker at cement works									2			
worker at dairy factory									1			
worker at timber mill									2			
Construction:												
carpenter							6		3			
carpenter's labourer									3			
painter									1			
plasterer									1			
foreman, bridgebuilding									1			
labourer, bridgebuilding									4			
Transport:												
driver			1						4			
mechanic			1									

TABLE 5 (contd.)

	Working in Kōtare						Working outside Kōtare				Other	
	On own account		Wages or Salary		Relative assisting unpaid		On own account		Wages or Salary			
	m.	f.	m.	f.	m.	f.	m.	f.	m.	f.	m.	f.
Miscellaneous: (part time fishing and contract work)	1											
Labourers n.e.i.					2				24			
Services:												
barman									1	1		
waitress										9		
domestic										5		
laundry-worker									1	1		
office cleaner									1			
groundsman									6			
storeman												
shop assistant									1	4		
boilerman									3			
linesman												
Clerical and professional:												
welfare officer										1		
typist										2		
teacher			2	3					1			
Unemployed											2	
Women engaged in home duties												76
Pensioners											14	16
Children over 15 at school											11	12
Total adults over 15	12	3	5	3	3	3	8	0	70	23	27	104

TABLE 6

Kōtare Maoris: Domestic Units, June 1955

	Units	Occupants
A Single individual[1]	3	3
B Single individual with boarder(s)	1	2
C Elementary family[2]	69	352
D Elementary family with boarder(s)	13	87
E Grand-family[3]	3	34
F Grand-family with boarder(s)	3	30
G Two or more siblings, with spouses and children (if married)	3	21
H Other kin combinations[4]	3	8
I Non-kin units	0	0
Total Maori occupants[5]	98	537

[1] One boarding with a Pakeha family.

[2] Including (a) denuded elementary-families lacking one parent and (b) *quasi* elementary-families consisting of a married couple or widowed person with step-, adopted or foster children and/or grand-children in the absence of their parents.

[3] Including denuded grand-families lacking one grand-parent.

[4] e.g. owner and mother's mother's brother's son.

[5] In addition to Maori occupants there were 7 Pakehas in these households, all married to Maoris.

TABLE 7

Kōtare: Official Workers at the Matthews–Tātana Wedding[1], April 1955

	K	KS	E	ES	O	Total
The Tātanas (bride's paternal 'family')	5	2	6	2		15
The bride's maternal 'family'					1	1
The Morgans (related to bride's paternal 'family')	5	2	1			8
The Samuelses (groom's maternal 'family')	10	4	9	2		25
The Matthews[2] (groom's paternal 'family')	1	1	1			3
The Iraias (related to groom's maternal 'family')	2					2
The Rapatas (ditto)	1					1
Other kin	2	1			4	7
Friends	5	1				6
Total	31	11	16	5	5	68

Key: K: *tāngata whenua* living in Kōtare.

KS: spouse or foster child to K.

E: *tāngata whenua* emigrants home on visit.

ES: spouse to E.

O: visitor from outside Kōtare.

[1] Inclusive of bridal attendants.

[2] Excluding the groom's siblings and their offspring, reckoned as members of the Samuels 'family' because the reception was held on the Samuels 'family' *marae*.

TABLE 8

Kōtare: Location of 'Active' Emigrants, June 1955

Emigrants living in	Male	Female	Total
Rural areas:			
(a) in Far North	18	30	48
(b) other parts of Northland	6	6	12
(c) outside Northland	18	6	24
Total rural areas	42	42	84
Towns:			
(a) large (2,500–19,500)	8	5	13
(b) small (under 2,500)	10	11	21
Total towns	18	16	34
Urban Areas:[1]			
(a) Auckland	54	61	115
(b) Other	6	4	10
Total Urban Areas	60	65	125
Overseas or whereabouts unknown	4		4
Total 'active' emigrants	124	123	247

[1] As defined by Census and Statistics Department

TABLE 9

Kōtare: Age Distribution of 'Active' Emigrants, June 1955

	Rural Areas	Towns	Urban Areas	Other	Total
15–24 years	19	16	54	2	91
25–34	33	6	35	1	75
35–44	14	4	16	1	35
45–54	9	4	13		26
55–64	5		4		9
Over 65	1	2	1		4
Not specified	3	2	2		7
Total	84	34	125	4	247

TABLE 10

(To accompany Fig. 5)

Kōtare: Location, Sex and Marital Status of Emigrants belonging to the Samuels 'Family', June 1955

No. on Figure	Sex	Age (approx.)	Marital Status	Offspring living outside Kōtare	Location
1.	Male	60	Widower	1 child	Urban: Auckland
2.	Female	33	Married	7 children	Urban: Auckland
3.	Female	22	Unmarried		Urban: Auckland
4.	Female	19	Unmarried		Urban: Auckland
5.	Female	40	Married	Several children	Urban: Auckland
6.	Female	40	Married	1 child	Rural: Far North
7.	Male	40	Married	1 child	Urban: Te Kuiti
8.	Male	40	Married	1 child	Urban: Te Kuiti
9.	Male	40	Married	1 child	Rural: Waikato
10.	Female	40	Separated	1 child	Rural: Far North
11.	Female	54	Separated	4 adult children	Urban: Far North
12.	Male	25	Married	2 + grandchildren	Urban: Auckland
13.	Female	24	Unmarried	2 + children	Urban: Auckland
14.	Male	50	Married	7 children	Rural: Far North
15.	Male	29	Married	many grandchildren	Urban: Auckland
16.	Male	21	Unmarried	3 children	Urban: Auckland
17.	Male	18	Unmarried		Urban: Wellington
18.	Female	25	Married		Urban: Auckland
19.	Female	24	Married	Childless	Urban: Whangarei
20.	Male	20	Unmarried	Several children	Rural: Rotorua
21.	Male	45	Married	8 children	Urban: Auckland
22.	Female	24	Married	4 children	Urban: Auckland
23.	Female	19	Unmarried		Rural:Waikato
24.	Female	18	Unmarried		Urban: Auckland
25.	Male	17	Unmarried		Urban: Auckland
26.	Female	19	Unmarried		Urban: Far North
27.	Female	40	Widowed	2 children	Rural: Far North
28.	Female	36	Married	8 children	Rural: Far North
29.	Female	35	Married	8 children	Urban: Palmerston North

TABLE II

The Distribution of the Maori Population in Auckland:
By Administrative Districts, 1951 Census

		Population	Percentage
1.	Takapuna Borough	77	1·0
2.	Devonport Borough	73	1·0
3.	Northcote Borough	94	1·2
4.	Birkenhead Borough	37	·5
5.	Waitemata County (part)	123	1·6
6.	Henderson Borough	11	·1
7.	Glen Eden Town District	8	·1
8.	New Lynn Borough	95	1·3
9.	Mt. Albert Borough	156	2·1
10.	Auckland City	3,986	52·3
11.	Eden County	737	9·7
12.	Newmarket Borough	32	·4
13.	Mt. Eden Borough	185	2·4
14.	Mt. Roskill Borough	161	2·1
15.	Ellerslie Borough	31	·4
16.	One Tree Hill Borough	149	2·0
17.	Onehunga Borough	540	7·1
18.	Ōtāhuhu Borough	150	2·0
19.	Papatoetoe Borough	151	2·0
20.	Manurewa Borough	12	·1
21.	Papakura Borough	87	1·1
22.	Manukau County (part)	671	8·8
23.	Howick Town District	8	·1
24.	Franklin County (part)	47	·6
	Auckland Urban Area Maoris	7,621	100·0

TABLE 12

Maori and non-Maori: Age Distribution, in percentages, 1951 Census

	Auckland[1] Maoris	Total Maori Population	Auckland[1] non-Maoris	Total non-Maori Population
Under 15	32·9	46·4	24·8	28·4
15–24	27·5	19·5	13·1	13·6
25–34	17·7	12·7	14·6	14·7
35–44	11·1	9·5	14·3	14·0
45–54	6·1	5·8	12·1	11·1
55–64	3·0	3·4	9·9	8·6
Over 65	1·5	2·5	11·1	9·5
Not specified	·2	·2	·1	·1
Total numbers	7,621	115,676	321,502	1,823,796

[1] Urban Area

TABLE 13

Maori and non-Maori: Marital Status in percentages, 1951 Census

	Auckland Maoris	Total Maori Population	Auckland non-Maoris	Total non-Maori Population
Never Married	41·6	31·5	24·7	25·7
Married	50·2	59·7	63·5	64·6
Legally separated	2·0	1·2	1·5	1·1
Widowed	5·1	6·9	10·2	7·4
Divorced	·9	·4		1·1
Not specified	·2	·3	·1	·1
Total adults over 16	4,937	59,277	238,206	1,283,226

TABLE 14

Maori and non-Maori: Dependent Children (married men only) in percentages, 1951 Census

No. of dependent children	Auckland Maoris	Total Maori Population	Auckland non-Maoris	Total non-Maori Population
0	33·0	22·2	48·6	44·0
1	20·3	17·1	19·8	19·3
2	15·3	16·2	17·4	18·4
3	9·9	12·7	8·9	10·3
4	9·4	9·4	3·3	4·7
5	3·8	7·6	1·1	1·9
6	2·6	5·5	·4	·7
7	2·4	3·7	·2	·3
8	1·5	2·6	·06	·2
9 and more	1·0	2·6	·04	·1
Not specified	·8	·4	·2	·1
Total married men	1,177	17,170	75,254	415,921

TABLE 15

Degrees of Maori Blood, 1951 Census

	Auckland Urban Area Population		Total New Zealand Population	
	no.	%	no.	%
Numbered in Maori Population				
Full Maori	4,848	47·0	76,918	57·0
Three-quarter Maori	681	6·6	15,201	11·3
Half Maori	1,967	19·1	23,183	17·2
Maori-Polynesian	95	·9	374	·3
Not specified	30	·3		
Numbered in non-Maori Population				
Quarter Maori	2,494	24·2	18,421	13·7
Maori-Other races[1]	193	1·9	756	·5
Total	10,308	100·0	134,853	100·0

[1] i.e. those distinguished from Europeans in the Census

TABLE 16

Maori and non-Maori: Occupational Status in percentages, 1951 Census

	Auckland Maoris	Total Maori Population	Auckland non-Maoris	Total non-Maori Population
Employer	·2	·8	2·6	3·7
Own account	·4	2·5	2·7	4·2
Wages or salary	42·5	23·8	34·0	30·1
Relative assisting unpaid	·1	·4	·1	·2
Unemployed	1·2	·7	·8	·5
Retired, independent means	·3	·4	2·2	2·2
Dependent on public or private support	55·2	71·3	57·5	59·0
Not specified	·1	·1	·1	·1
Total numbers	7,621	115,676	321,502	1,823,796

TABLE 17

Maori and non-Maori: Religious Professions in percentages, 1951 Census

	Auckland Maoris	Total Maori Population	Total non-Maori Population
Church of England	29·5	32·2	37·8
Presbyterian	1·7	2·0	24·3
Roman Catholic	13·2	11·4	12·1
Catholic	3·7	3·1	1·5
Methodist	7·0	7·3	8·1
Ratana	14·5	14·3	·1
Ringatu	·4	4·2	·0
Latter Day Saints	6·3	7·0	·1
Object to state	16·1	12·7	6·2
Other	7·6	5·8	9·8
Total numbers	7,621	115,676	1,823,796

TABLE 18

Auckland: Derivation of Maoris in the 'Sets', August 1954

	A	B	C	Male	Female	Total
Tāngata whenua:	1			1		1
'Active' immigrants	98	34	27	74	85	159
'Passive' immigrants	45	18	13	40	36	76
City-born	75	9	44	61	67	128
Not specified	3	1	1	2	3	5
Total Maoris in 'sets'	222	62	85	178	191	369

NMM T

TABLE 19

Auckland: Ages at Immigration of Immigrants in the 'Sets', August 1954

	A	B	C	Total
Under 5 years	16	4	7	27
5– 9	20	7	2	29
10–14	7	7	4	18
Not specified under 15	2			2
Total 'passive' immigrants	45	18	13	76
15–19	31	13	14	58
20–24	17	5	7	29
25–29	10	6		16
30–34	3	3		6
Not specified 15–34	9	2		11
35–39	3	2	4	9
40–44	5		2	7
45–49	4	2		6
50–54	3	1		4
55–59	1			1
Over 60				0
Not specified over 35	12			12
Total 'active' immigrants	98	34	27	159

TABLE 20

Auckland: Marital and Family Status at Immigration
of 'Active' Immigrants in the 'Sets'

Status at Immigration	Accompanied by children	Children left behind	Childless	Total
Unmarried				81
Married	46	2	9	57
Widowed		1	2	3
Separated	2	2	1	5
Not specified				13
Total	48	5	12	159

TABLE 21

Auckland: Tribal Membership of Maoris in the 'Sets', August 1954

	'Active' Immigrants	'Passive' Immigrants	City-Born	Not Spec.	Total
A. Membership in one tribe[1]:					
Aupouri	8	1	0		9
Rarawa	25	5	0		30
Ngāpuhi	74	30	27	1	132
Ngāti Whātua	1	0	0		1
Ngāti Paoa	8	7	5		20
Ngāti Maru	7	0	0		7
Waikato	2	0	0		2
Maniapoto	2	0	0		2
Ngaiterangi	0	1	0		1
Arawa	7	1	2	1	11
Tuwharetoa	1	0	0		1
Whakatohea	1	0	0		1
Whānau-ā-Apanui	1	0	0		1
Ngāti Porou	3	1	0		4
Ngāti Kahungunu	2	0	0		2
Ngāti Raukawa	2	1	2		5
Ngārauru	2	5	1		8
Other	1	0	0		1
Total	147	52	37	2	238
B. Membership in two or more tribes in the same Tribal Group[2]:					
Northern Group	4	8	16		28
East Coast Group	0	7	0		7
Tainui Group	0	0	1		1
Total	4	15	17		36
C. Membership in two or more tribes not in the same Tribal Group					
Total	5	4	52	3	64
D. One parent non-Maori	1	4	14		19
E. Not specified	2	1	9		12
Grand Total	159	76	129	5	369

[1] In order of location from north to south. See Fig. 19. [2] See p. 126, footnote 2.

TABLE 22

Auckland: Occupations of Maoris in the 'Sets', August 1954

	'Active' Immigrants		'Passive' Immigrants		City-born		Total
	Male	*Female*	*Male*	*Female*	*Male*	*Female*	
Labourers	27	0	10	0	3	0	40
Factory hands	9	24	5	4	2	1	45
Workers in transport	13	0	3	0	1	0	17
Tradesmen:							
(a) Ordinary employees	8	0	3	0	1	0	12
(b) Foremen	1	0	0	0	0	0	1
(c) Contractors with own business	4	0	0	0	0	0	4
Workers in service occupations	1	8	0	0	0	0	9
Clerical workers	0	2	0	3	0	2	7
Professional persons	0	0	0	0	0	0	0
Total	63	34	21	7	7	3	135

TABLE 23

Auckland: Types of Dwellings in the 'Sets', August 1954

Type of Units	A	B	C	*Total*
Simple dwellings	13	4	11	28
Multiple dwellings				
(a) Apartment houses	3	3	0	6
(b) Houses with multiple tenancies	5	2	0	7
(c) Sub-let houses	3	1	0	4
Total dwellings	24	10	11	45

TABLE 24

Auckland: Domestic Units in the 'Sets', August 1954

	A	B	C	*Total 'Sets'*
Single individual	11	5		16
Elementary-family	32	11	6	49
Elementary-family with boarder(s)	2	2	1	5
Elementary-family house-keeping for Pakeha			1	1
Grand-family	6		1	7
Grand-family with boarder(s)	3		2	5
Non-kin units		1		1
Total domestic units	54	19	11	84

TABLE 25

Marital Status

	Kōtare, June 1955		Three Auckland 'Sets', August 1954		Auckland Urban Area Maoris, 1951 Census	
	no.	%	no.	%	no.	%
Never Married	71	28·8	84	37·2	2054	41·6
Married:						
First legal marriage	131	53·0	104	46·0		
Second legal marriage						
(a) after widowhood	6	2·4	5	2·2		
(b) after divorce			1	·4	2477	50·2
Partner to "Maori marriage"						
(a) both spouses legally free	2	·8	2	·9		
(b) one or both legally married to someone else	19	7·7	10	4·4		
Formerly married:						
Widowed	15	6·1	9	4·0	251	5·1
Separated	3	1·2	5	2·2	100	2·0
Divorced	0	0	1	·4	45	·9
Not specified	0	0	5	2·3	10	·2
Total adults over 16 years	247	100·0	226	100·0	4,937	100·0

TABLE 26

Auckland: Intertribal and Interracial Marriage
(Analysis of legal marriages contracted by Maoris
in the 'sets' while living in Auckland)

	Husband	Wife	Couples
Marriages between members of the same tribe:	Ngāpuhi	Ngāpuhi	4
	Ngāpuhi/Rarawa	Rarawa	1
	Ngāpuhi	Chinese/Ngāpuhi	1
	Ngāti Raukawa/ Ngāti Paoa	Ngāti Raukawa	1
Marriages between members of tribes in same Tribal Group:	Ngāpuhi	Rarawa	1
	Rarawa	Ngāpuhi	3
Marriages between members of tribes in different Tribal Groups:	Rarawa	Maniapoto	1
	Ngāpuhi	Ngāti Paoa	2
	Ngāpuhi	Ngāti Maru/ Ngāti Whātua	2
	Ngāpuhi	Ngaiterangi	1
	Islander/Ngāti-Whātua	Arawa/Ngāpuhi	1
	Ngāti Maru	Pakeha/Ngāpuhi	1
	Ngāti Paoa	Rarawa	1
	Ngāti Paoa	Ngāti Kahungunu	1
	Waikato	Ngāpuhi	1
	Waikato/Ngāti Maru	Ngāpuhi	1
	Waikato	Ngāti Maru	1
	Arawa	Ngāpuhi	1
	Ngāti Tuwharetoa	Pakeha/Rarawa	1
	Ngāti Awa	Ngāpuhi	1
	Ngāti Raukawa	Ngāti Paoa	1
	Ngai Tahu	Ngāpuhi	1
Marriages with non-Maoris:	Chinese/Ngāpuhi	Pakeha	1
	Pakeha	Ngāpuhi	2
	Pakeha	Rarawa	1
Total			33

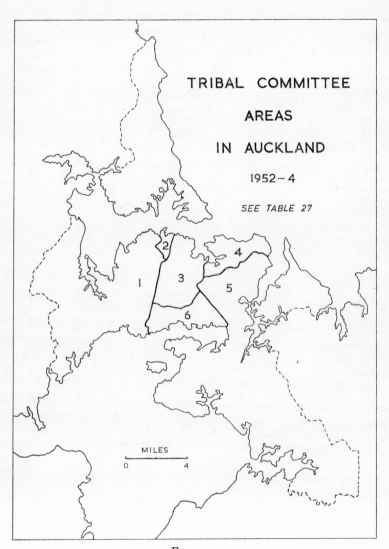

TRIBAL COMMITTEE

AREAS

IN AUCKLAND

1952–4

SEE TABLE 27

MILES

0   4

FIG. 12.

TABLE 27

Auckland: Tribal Committee Membership
(including Wardens but not Welfare Officers), 1952–4

	Tribal Committees[1]						Delegates to Tribal Executive
	1	2	3	4	5	6	
Sex:							
Male	4	8	4	10	13	9	7
Female	8	4	6	3		4	5
Age:							
15–24 years				2		1	1
25–34	1			2	4	4	3
35–44	1	2		3	1	3	1
45–54	3	1	4	2	2		4
55–64	5	1	1	2	4		3
Over 65	2		2	1	1		
Not specified		8	3	1	1	5	
Tribal Membership:							
Aupouri	1	3	1				2
Rarawa	1					1	1
Ngāpuhi	8		7	1	8	1	4
Ngāti Whatua	2	1		11		1	1
Waikato					1	4	2
Maniapoto						1	
Ngaiterangi						1	
Whakatohea					1	1	
Ngāti Porou					2		1
Ngāti Kahungunu			1			1	
Not specified		8	1	1	1	2	1
Total Members	12	12	10	13	13	13	12

[1] For Tribal Committee Areas see Fig. 12

Glossary

For guide to Maori pronunciation see note on p. 289

Aotearoa: Maori name for New Zealand
ariki: high chief
aroha: love
awhina: assistance, donation at *hui* (*"marae* money")

bach: *coll.* cottage not intended for permanent occupation

domestic unit: for definition, see p. 143
dwelling: for definition, see p. 143

elementary-family: parents and children
extended-family: for definition, see p. 166

'family': for definition see p. 55

gardens: plots up to three acres in extent, growing *kumara*, maize, potatoes, marrows, etc.; *mara*
grand-family: a three-generational family (parents, children and their spouses, and children's children)

haka: Best (*The Maori*, vol. ii, pp. 102–11) describes *haka* as a posture dance accompanied by a song and lists several different kinds. To-day the term is popularly used for the men's war-dance. The repertoire of *haka* teams also includes *poi* dances and action songs, a comparatively recent development, which adapt European melodies
hāngi: earth oven
hapū: sub-tribe (see pp. 55–7, 70)
hōhā: (adj.), tired and short-tempered; not interested, "can't-be-bothered"; (noun), nuisance
hongi: to press noses, the traditional Maori greeting

NMM U

hui: assembly or gathering, from the verb *huihui*, to assemble; specifically used to refer to a Maori gathering on a *marae*

iwi: tribe

kānga pirau: literally rotten corn; a custard made from fermented corn, a favourite Maori dish
kai: food
kai-: one who—, e.g. *kai-awhina* (helper), *kai-karanga* ("caller"), *kai-kōrero* (orator), *kai-mahi* (worker), *kai-whakahaere-o-te-hui* (one who runs the *hui*)
kāinga: an unfortified, nucleated settlement; also a single house ("home")
karanga: vb., to call; noun, a chant of invitation and welcome
kaumātua: elder, especially a 'family' or community leader (p. 69)
kina: sea-egg (*Evechinus chloriticus*)
kin-cluster: for definition, see p. 166
kindred: an ego-oriented circle of kin
komiti: club; Maori version of a committee (pp. 67–8)
kōrero: (verb), to tell or speak; popularly used as a noun to refer to a public discussion
kuia: old lady; a term of respect
kūmara: sweet potato (*Ipomoea batatas*)

mākutu: sorcery
mana: inherent power and prestige
mānuka: tea-tree scrub (*Leptospermum ericoides*)
Maoritanga: Maorihood (pp. 94–5)
mara: cultivations, "gardens"
marae: community assembly ground (p. 25 n.)
matua: father; father's sibling or cousin; elder (pp. 50–1)

mihi: formal exchange of greetings

mokopuna: grandchild (p. 50)

muru: pre-European custom of legalised plunder for offences within the tribe

pā: fortified village; often erroneously applied to any Maori village

Pakeha: Maori word in common use by both races for New Zealanders of European stock

papakāinga: residential area adjoining *marae*

papatupu: land held on Maori title (p. 16)

pāua: a univalve shellfish (*Haliotis iris*)

pipi: bivalve shellfish in general

piupiu: a skirt made of dried flax cylinders

poi: action song performed by women with flax balls

pōwhiri: to welcome; a formal chant of welcome

pūhā: sow-thistle (*Sonchus oleraceus*)

rangatira: head of *hapu*; wellborn, noble

taiaha: a long club with a blade for striking and a proximal point carved as a head for stabbing

tāki: ceremonial challenge to visitors to a *marae*

tama: son, nephew (p. 50)

tamahine: daughter, niece (p. 50)

tamaiti, pl. *tamariki*: child (pp. 50–1)

tāne: man, husband

tangata, pl. *tāngata*: man, person

tangata haere mai: person without rights in local Maori land, "immigrant"

tangata whenua: person owning local Maori land, "native inhabitant"

tangi: to weep, wail; lamentation, dirge

tangihanga: funeral wake, commonly referred to as *tangi*

tāniko: ornamental border for flax cloak, finger-woven in geometric designs; nowadays used for belts

tapu: sacred, prohibited or defiled according to context; under religious restriction

teina (also *taina*): younger brother of a male, younger sister of a female, cousin of the same sex in a junior line

tomo: betrothal (p. 66, 66 n.)

tuahine: sister or female cousin of a male

tuakana: elder brother of a male, elder sister of a female, cousin of the same sex in a senior line

tuatua: a bivalve shellfish (*Amphidesma subtriangulatum*)

tukutuku: ornamental latticework used for interior walls in meeting-houses

tungāne: brother or male cousin of a female

tūpāpaku: corpse

tupuna (also *tipuna*): ancestor, grand-parent

wahine: woman, wife

waiata: song

waka: canoe; sometimes used for a group of tribes whose founding ancestors migrated to New Zealand in the same canoe (p. 126 n.)

whaea: mother, mother's sibling or cousin (pp. 50–1)

whakamā: shy, ashamed

whakapapa: genealogy (pp. 52–4)

whānau: pre-European patriarchal extended-family

whanaunga: kinsman

whanaungatanga: kinship

whare: a single roomed house or hut

NOTE ON MAORI PRONUNCIATION

In Maori, every syllable ends in a vowel.

Each vowel has the one sound but may vary in length, the long vowel being a simple prolongation of the short, not a diphthong:

a as *u* in "cut"; ā as in "father";
e as in "pet"; ē as in "pleasure";
i as in "tin"; ī as in "teen";
o as in "or"; ō as in "orb";
u as in "put"; ū as in "rule".

When two vowels occur together, each has its own correct sound, but there is no break as one glides into the other.

As a general rule, the first syllable is slightly accentuated; but in words beginning with the prefix *whaka-* accentuate the third.

The Maori digraph *wh* was formerly pronounced like the "wh" in "where" but in modern Maori often has an "f" sound; *ng* is pronounced as "ng" in "singer".

Bibliography

VAN BAAL, J.: 'Erring Acculturation', *American Anthropologist*, vol. 62, No. 1, 1960, pp. 108-121.

BARR, JOHN: *The City of Auckland New Zealand 1840-1920*, Auckland, 1922.

BEAGLEHOLE, ERNEST and PEARL: 'Contemporary Maori Death Customs', *Journal of the Polynesian Society*, vol. 54, 1945, pp. 91-116.

— : *Some Modern Maoris*, New Zealand Council for Educational Research, Educational Research Series No. 25, Wellington, 1946.

BEAGLEHOLE, ERNEST and RITCHIE, JAMES: 'The Rakau Maori Studies', *Journal of the Polynesian Society*, vol. 67, 1958, pp. 132–154.

BEALS, RALPH L.: 'Urbanism, Urbanization and Acculturation', *American Anthropologist*, vol. 53, No. 1, 1951, pp. 1–10.

BEST, ELSDON: *The Maori*, 2 vols., Wellington, 1924.

— : *Tuhoe, Children of the Mist*, 2 vols., New Plymouth, 1925.

BLAKE PALMER, G.: 'Tohungaism and Makutu', *Journal of the Polynesian Society*, vol. 63, 1954, pp. 147–163.

BUCK, SIR PETER HENRY: *The Coming of the Maori*, Wellington, 1949.

CHALLIS, R. L.: *Social Problems of Non-Maori Polynesians in New Zealand*, South Pacific Commission Technical Papers, No. 41, 1953.

Department of Census and Statistics (New Zealand): *Population Census 1951*, vol. 1, 'Increase and Distribution of Population'; vol. 6, 'Maori Census'.

Department of Maori Affairs: Annual Reports, *Appendices to the Journal of the House of Representatives* (New Zealand), Wellington.

— : *Te Ao Hou* (The New World), monthly magazine.

FIRTH, RAYMOND: *The Kauri–Gum Industry: Some Economic Aspects*, Wellington, 1924.

— : *Economics of the New Zealand Maori*, Wellington, 1959 (Second Edition).

— : (Ed.) *Two Studies of Kinship in London*, London, 1956.

— : 'A Note on Descent Groups in Polynesia', *Man*, vol. lvii, 1957, No. 2, p. 4.

FREEDMAN, MAURICE: (Ed.) *A Minority in Britain*, London, 1955.

GARIGUE, PHILIP: 'St. Justin: A Case-Study in Rural French–Canadian Social Organisation', *Canadian Journal of Economics and Political Science*, vol. 22, 1956.

— : 'French Canadian Kinship and Urban Life', *American Anthropologist*, vol. 58, No. 6, 1956, pp. 1090–1101.

GOLDSCHMIDT, WALTER: *As You Sow*, New York, 1947.

GORST, J. E.: *The Maori King*, London and Cambridge, 1864.

HAWTHORN, H. B.: *The Maori: A Study in Acculturation*, American Anthropological Association Memoir 46, 1944.

HOLST, HALVOR: 'The Maori Schools in Rural Education', *Education* (New Zealand Department of Education), vol. 7, No. 1, 1958, p. 53.

KEESING, FELIX: *The Changing Maori*, New Plymouth (New Zealand), 1928.

— : 'Maori Progress on the East Coast', *Te Wananga*, (Board of Maori Ethnological Research), vol. 1, Nos. 1 and 2, 1929.

MANING, F. E.: *Old New Zealand*, first published 1863.

METGE, A. JOAN: *The Distribution and Geographic Character of the Maori Population of the Auckland Province of New Zealand*, unpublished M.A. thesis, Auckland University College 1951.

— : 'The Maori Population of Northern New Zealand', *New Zealand Geographer*, vol. 8, 1952, pp. 104–124.

— : 'Marriage in Modern Maori Society', *Man*, vol. lvii, 1957, No. 212, pp. 166–170.

METGE, A. JOAN and CAMPBELL, DUGAL: 'The Rakau Maori Studies: A Review Article', *Journal of the Polynesian Society*, vol. 67, 1958, pp. 352–386.

MINER, HORACE: 'The Folk–Urban Continuum', *American Sociological Review*, vol. 17, No. 5, 1952, pp. 529–537.

MINTZ, SIDNEY W.: 'On Redfield and Foster', *American Anthropologist*, vol. 56, No. 1, 1954, pp. 87–92.

— : 'The Folk–Urban Continuum and the Rural Proletarian Community', *American Journal of Sociology*, vol. lix, No. 2, 1953–4, pp. 136–143.

NGATA, A. T.: 'Native Land Development', *Appendices to the Journal of the House of Representatives* (New Zealand), 1931, G–10.

PHILLIPPS, W. J.: 'European Influences on *Tapu* and *Tangi*', *Journal of the Polynesian Society*, vol. 63, 1954, pp. 175–198.

REDFIELD, ROBERT: 'The Folk Society and Culture', *American Journal of Sociology*, vol. xlv, No. 5, 1939–40, pp. 731–742.

— : 'The Folk Society', *American Journal of Sociology*, vol. lii, No. 4, 1946–7, pp. 293–308.

RITCHIE, JAMES: *Basic Personality in Rakau*, Victoria University College Publications in Psychology, No. 8, Wellington, 1956.

RITCHIE, JANE: *Childhood in Rakau*, Victoria University College Publications in Psychology, No. 10, Wellington, 1957.

SCHAPERA, I.: *Migrant Labour and Tribal Life*, Oxford, 1947.

SINCLAIR, KEITH: *A History of New Zealand* (Pelican), London, 1959.

SMITH, NORMAN: *Maori Land Law*, Wellington, 1960.

The Social Science Research Council Summer Seminar on Acculturation, 1953: 'Acculturation: An Exploratory Formulation', *American Anthropologist*, vol. 56, No. 6, Part 1, 1954, pp. 973–1002.

SUTHERLAND, I. L. G.: (Ed.) *The Maori People Today*, Wellington, 1940.

WILSON, GODFREY: *Essay on the Economics of Detribalisation*, Rhodes–Livingstone Institute, Livingstone, 1941.

WINIATA, MAHARAIA: 'Leadership in Pre-European Maori Society', *Journal of the Polynesian Society*, vol. 65, 1956, pp. 212–231.

WIRTH, LOUIS: 'Urbanism as a Way of Life', *American Journal of Sociology*, vol. xliv, No. 1, 1938, pp. 1–24.

— : 'The Urban Society and Civilization', *American Journal of Sociology*, vol. xlv, No. 5, 1939–40, pp. 743–755.

WRIGHT, HARRISON M.: *New Zealand, 1769–1840 : Early Years of Western Contact*, Harvard University Press, 1959.

YOUNG, MICHAEL: 'Family and Kinship in East London', *Man*, vol. liv, 1954, No. 210, pp. 137–139.

Index

LONDON SCHOOL OF ECONOMICS
MONOGRAPHS ON SOCIAL ANTHROPOLOGY

Titles marked with an asterisk are now out of print.